Street by Street

MANCHESTER

2nd edition August 2003

© Automobile Association
Developments Limited 2003

Original edition printed
May 2001

Ordnance Survey This product
includes map
data licensed from Ordnance
Survey® with the permission of
the Controller of Her Majesty's
Stationery Office.
© Crown copyright 2003.
All rights reserved.
Licence No: 399221.

Published by AA Publishing
(a trading name of
Automobile Association
Developments Limited,
whose registered office is
Millstream, Maidenhead Road,
Windsor, Berkshire SL4 5GD.
Registered number 1878835).

Mapping produced by the
Cartography Department of The
Automobile Association. A1709

Key to map pages	ii-iii
Key to map symbols	iv-1
Enlarged map pages	2-9
Main map pages	10-133
Index – towns & villages	134
Index – streets	137-224
Index – featured places	224-230
Acknowledgements	230

A CIP Catalogue record for this book is available from the British Library.

Printed by G. Canale & C. S.P.A., Torino, Italy

The contents of this atlas are believed to be correct at the time of the latest revision. However,
the publishers cannot be held responsible for loss occasioned to any person acting or refraining
from action as a result of any material in this atlas, nor for any errors, omissions or changes in
such material. This does not affect your statutory rights. The publishers would welcome
information to correct any errors or omissions and to keep this atlas up to date. Please write to
Publishing, The Automobile Association, Fanum House (FH17), Basing View, Basingstoke,
Hampshire, RG21 4EA.

Ref: MN042z

ii

National Grid references are shown on the map frame of each page.
Red figures denote the 100 km square and blue figures the 1 km square.
Example, page 3 : Manchester Victoria Station 384 399

The reference can also be written using the National Grid two-letter prefix
shown on this page, where 3 and 3 are replaced by SJ to give SJ8499.

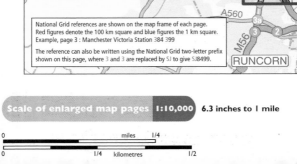

Scale of enlarged map pages 1:10,000 **6.3 inches to 1 mile**

| miles | 1/4 |
| kilometres | |

0 miles 1/4

0 1/4 kilometres 1/2

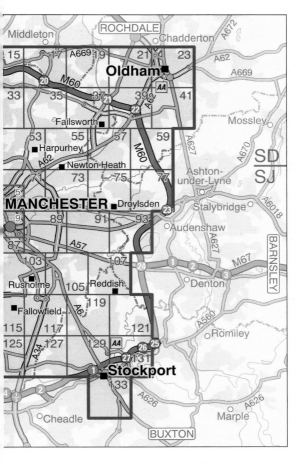

4.2 inches to 1 mile **Scale of main map pages** 1:15,000

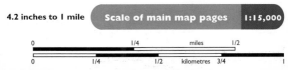

iv

Symbol	Description
Junction 9	Motorway & junction
Services	Motorway service area
	Primary road single/dual carriageway
Services	Primary road service area
	A road single/dual carriageway
	B road single/dual carriageway
	Other road single/dual carriageway
	Minor/private road, access may be restricted
← ←	One-way street
	Pedestrian area
========	Track or footpath
	Road under construction
	Road tunnel
AA	AA Service Centre
P	Parking
P+	Park & Ride
	Bus/coach station
	Railway & main railway station
	Railway & minor railway station
⊖	Underground station
⊖	Light railway station
+++++	Preserved private railway
LC	Level crossing
•—•—•	Tramway
- - - - -	Ferry route
··········	Airport runway
- · - · -	County, administrative boundary
vvvvvv	Mounds
93	Page continues 1:15,000
7	Page continues to enlarged 1:10,000
	River/canal,
	Aqueduct, lock, weir
465 Winter Hill ▲	Peak (with height in metres)
	Beach
	Woodland
	Park
	Cemetery
	Built-up area
	Featured building
ЛЛЛЛ	City wall

A&E	Hospital with 24-hour A&E department		⚔	Castle
PO	Post Office		🏛	Historic house or building
📖	Public library		Wakehurst Place NT	National Trust property
i	Tourist Information Centre		Ⓜ	Museum or art gallery
i	Seasonal Tourist Information Centre		🐎	Roman antiquity
�petrol	Petrol station, 24 hour *Major suppliers only*		⚱	Ancient site, battlefield or monument
†	Church/chapel		🏭	Industrial interest
🚻	Public toilets		✽	Garden
♿	Toilet with disabled facilities		⚙	Garden Centre *Garden Centre Association Member*
PH	Public house *AA recommended*		🌷	Garden Centre *Wyevale Garden Centre*
🍴	Restaurant *AA inspected*		🌳	Arboretum
Madeira Hotel	Hotel *AA inspected*		🛒	Farm or animal centre
🎭	Theatre or performing arts centre		🦌	Zoological or wildlife collection
🎥	Cinema		🦜	Bird collection
⚑	Golf course		🦆	Nature reserve
▲	Camping *AA inspected*		🐟	Aquarium
🚐	Caravan site *AA inspected*		**V**	Visitor or heritage centre
▲🚐	Camping & caravan site *AA inspected*		⛲	Country park
🎡	Theme park		◉	Cave
🏛	Abbey, cathedral or priory		✖	Windmill
			🛢	Distillery, brewery or vineyard

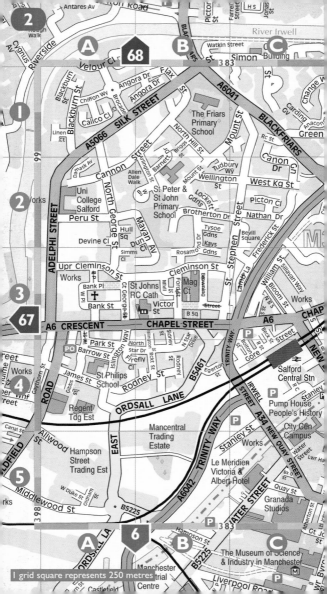

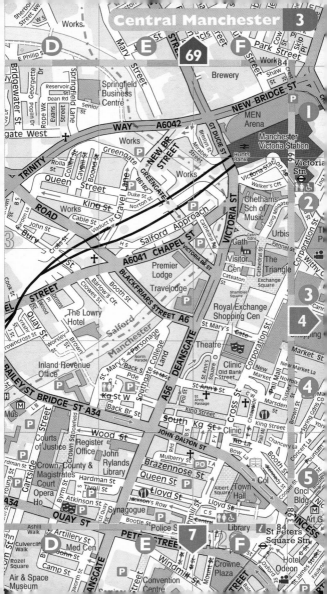

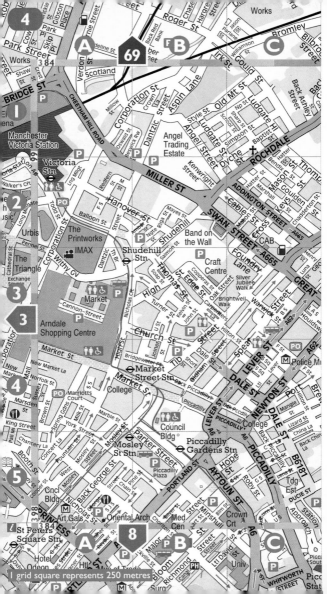

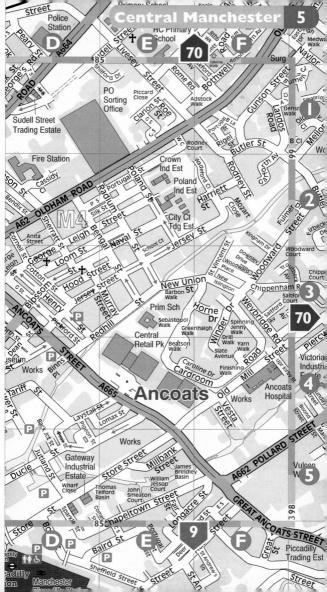

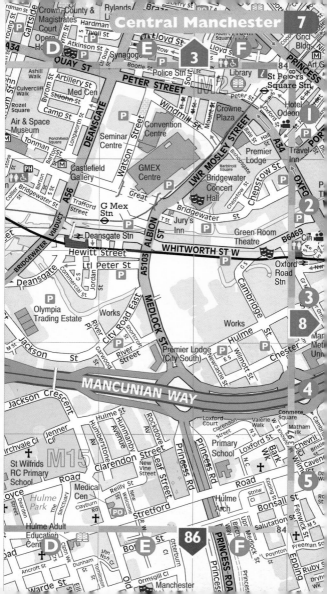

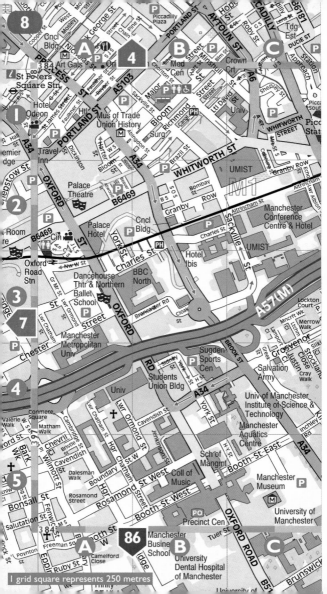

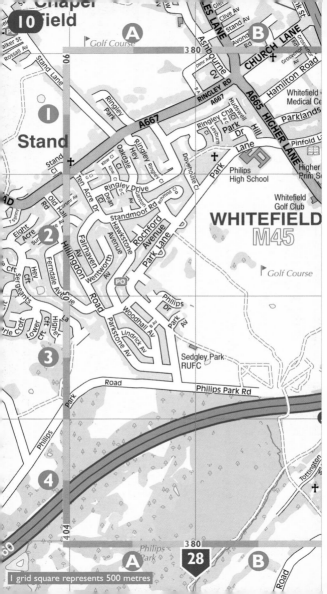

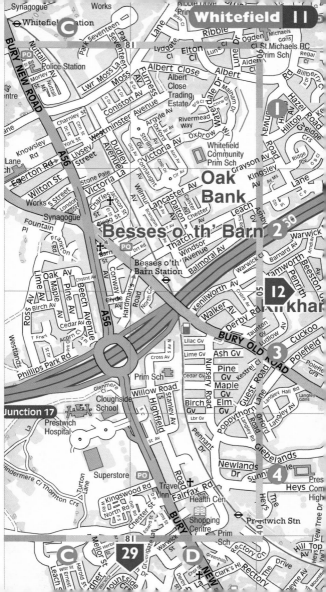

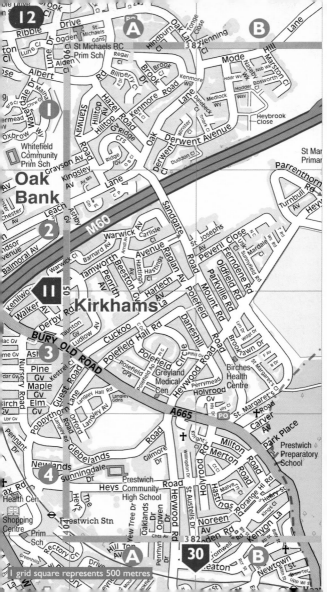

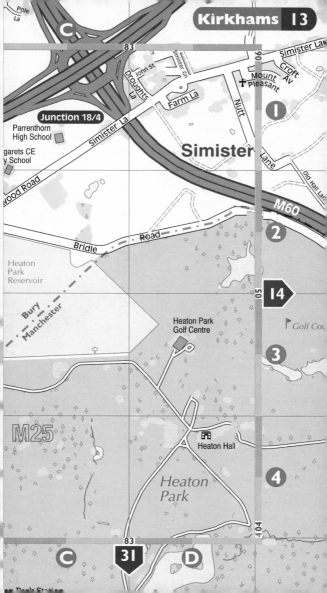

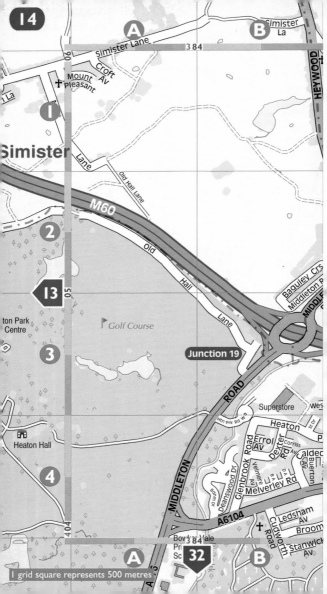

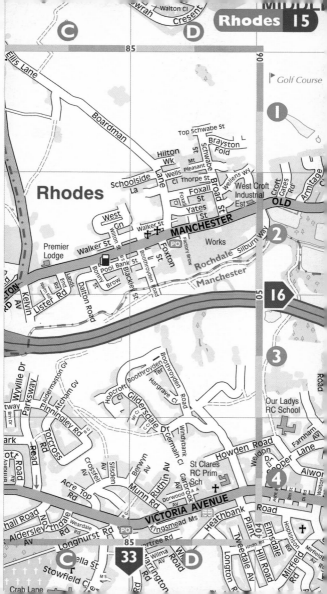

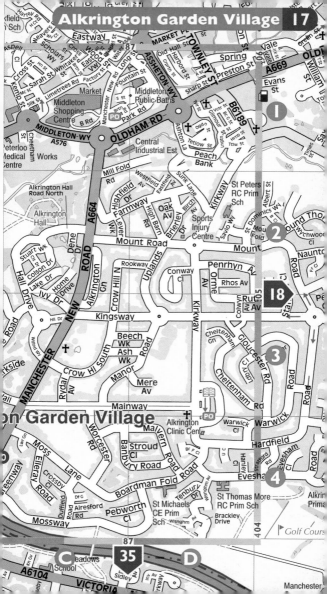

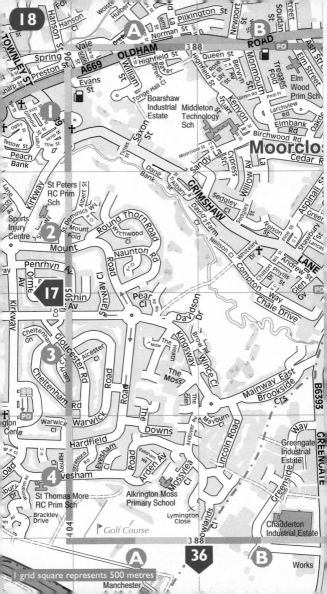

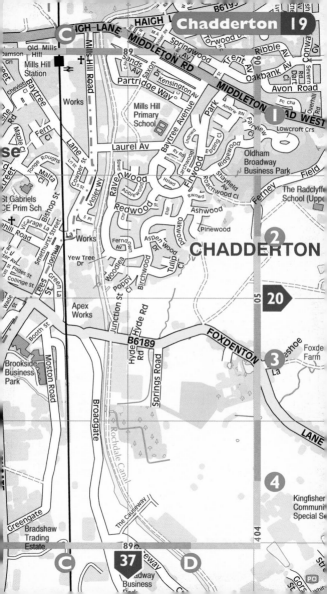

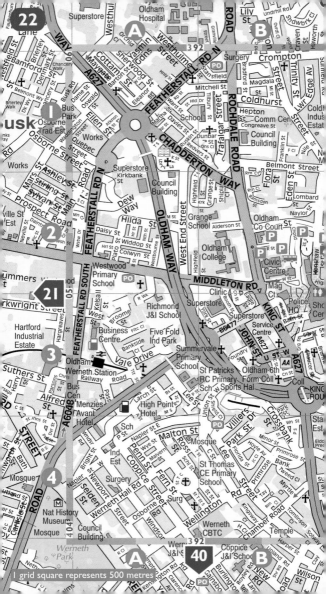

1 grid square represents 500 metres

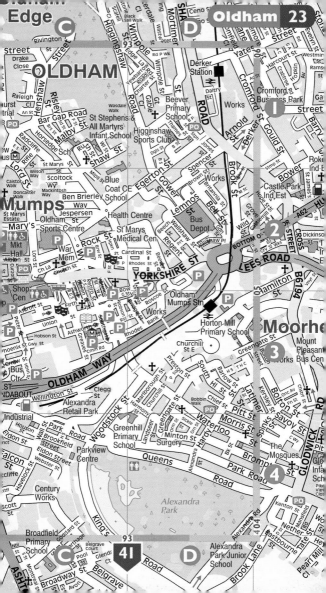

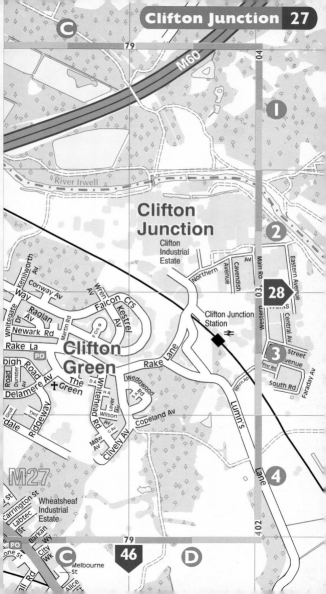

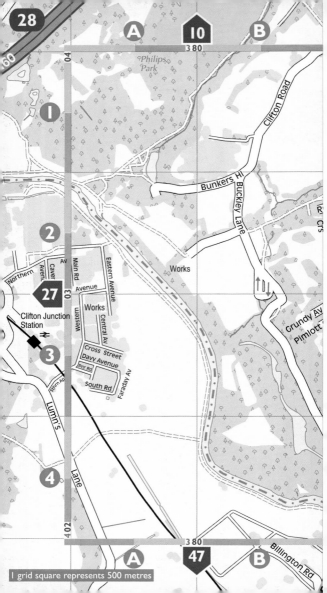

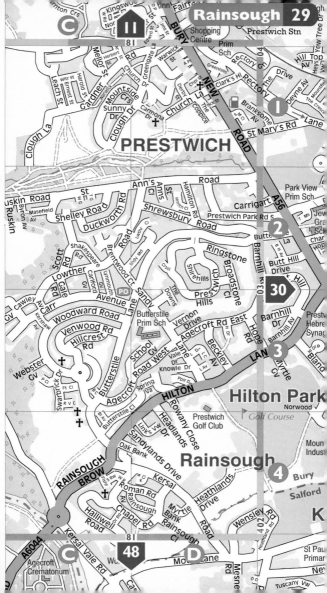

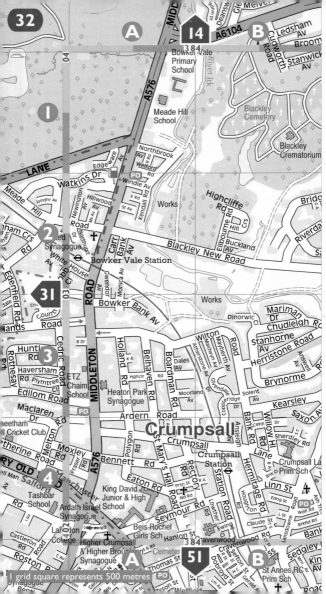

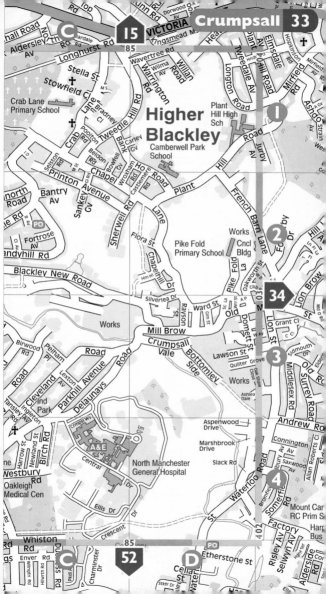

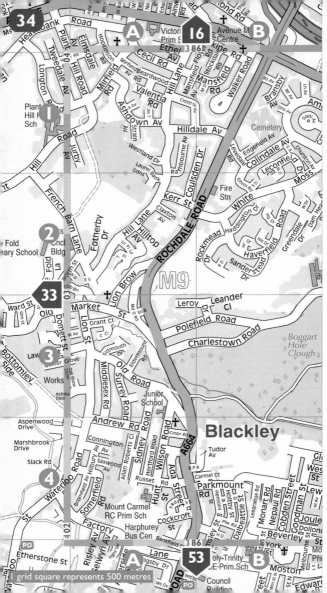

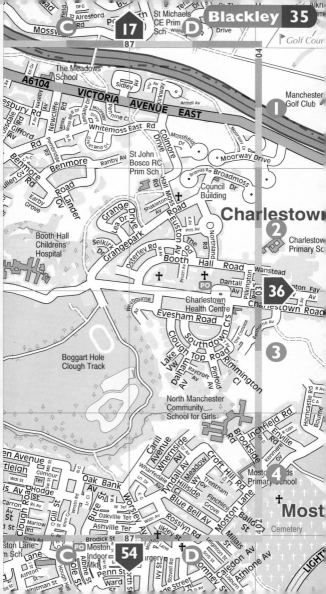

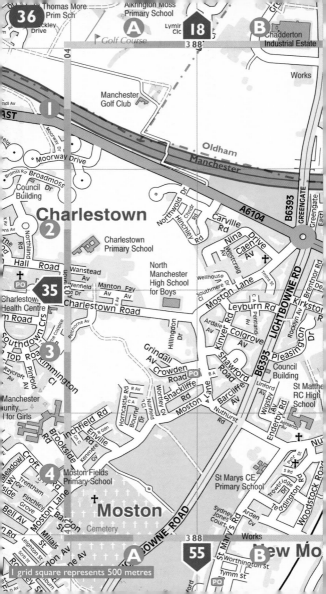

36

Thomas More Prim Sch

Beckley Drive

Alkrington Moss Primary School

Ⓐ Golf Course

Lymir Clc

18

Ⓑ Chadderton Industrial Estate

Works

04

3 88

Ⓘ EAST

Manchester Golf Club

Moorway Dr

Oldham Manchester

A6104

B6393

GREENGATE

Greengate

Moorway Drive

ndl Av

Bramss Av

Broadmoss Dr

Council Building

Northland Av

Ⓑ **Charlestown** ②

Northwold Dr

Chtar Rd

Hinchley Rd

Carville Rd

Nina Drive

Caen Av

Westcraig

Tmms Rd

Brenthor Rd

Kirkstor

The Rd

Charlestown Primary School

Hall Road

Wanstead Av

Wenfield Dr

Manton Fay Av

North Manchester High School for Boys

Wellhouse

Moston Lane

Leyburn Rd

LIGHTBOWNE RD

Rocklyn Av

Pleasington Dr

35

PO

Charlestown Health Centre

m Road

Charlestown Crs

Charlestown Road

Southmere Cl

Ardale Rd

Kinver Rd

Pentland Av

Colgrove Av

B6393

Council Building

St Matthe RC High School

Southdown

③

The Copice

Belthorne Av

Hillingdon Dr

Grindall Av

Shawford Road

Linford

Wigsby

Enderby Rd

Ashlands Rd

Nu

Top Road

Raycroft Av

Pinfold

Kimmington Cl

Crowden Road

PO

Shackliffe Rd

Barcliffe Rd

Nuthurst Rd

Moston Lane

Manchester unity l for Girls

Inchfield Rd

Brookside Rd

Croft

Horncastle Rd

Enville

Bourne

Nunfield

Wortley Gv

Trowb dge

Tedington Rd

St Matthe

Meadow

Trentham

Finchley Grove

④

Moston Fields Primary School

Kenmere Gv

St Marys CE Primary School

Sydney Jones Court

Arden Gv

Woodstock Road

Bell Av

Moston Lane

Balloon St

Millais

Moston

Cemetery

LIGHTBOWNE ROAD

3 88

St Marys Rd

Works

New Mo

St Worthington st

Tymm St

55

Ⓐ

PO

Ⓑ

Leighton St

l grid square represents 500 metres

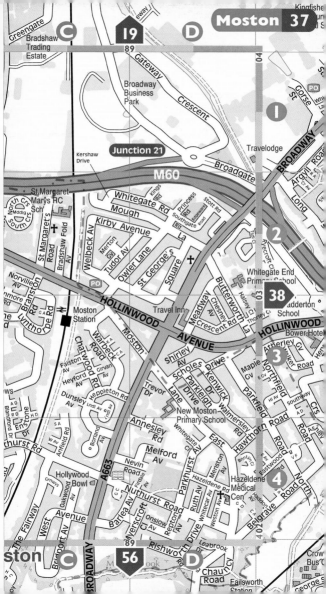

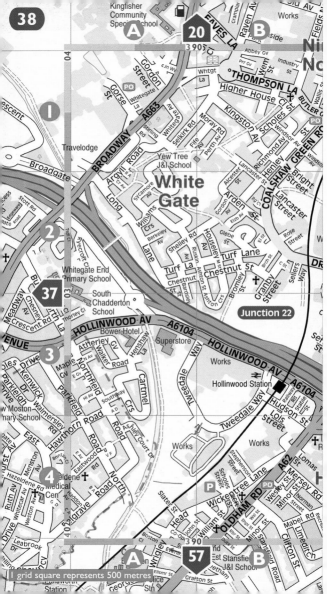

1 grid square represents 500 metres

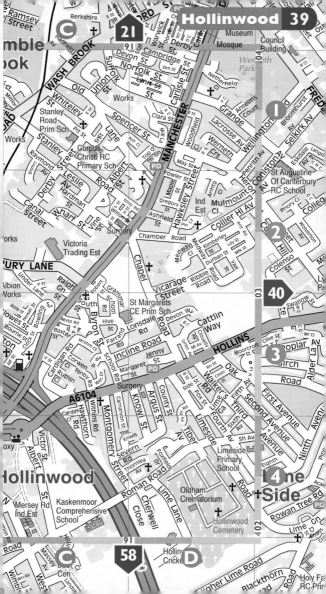

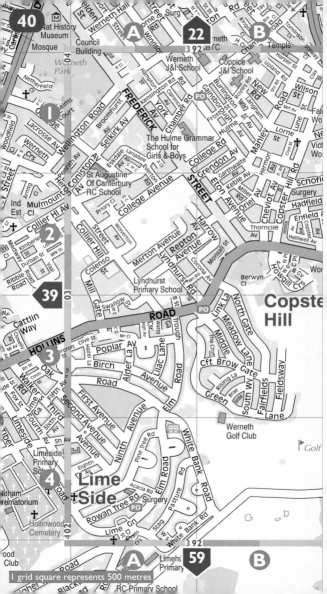

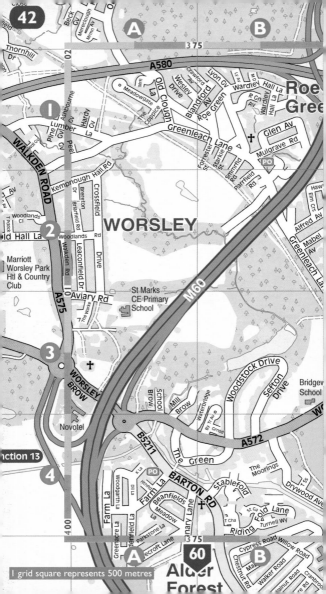

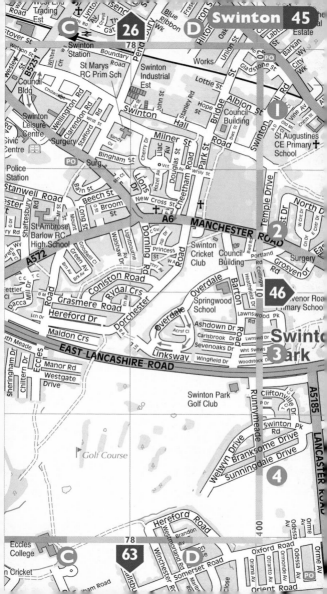

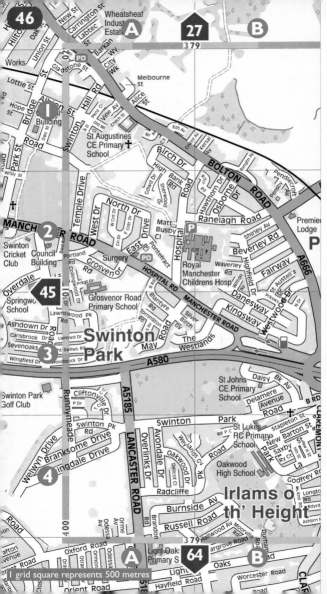

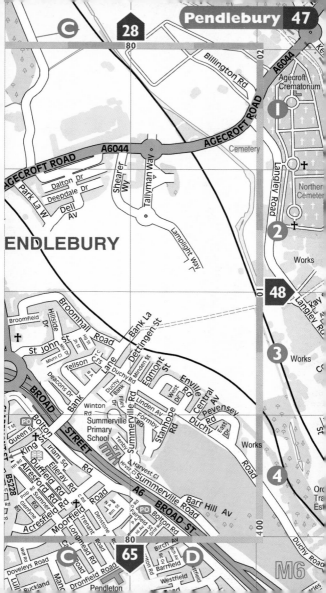

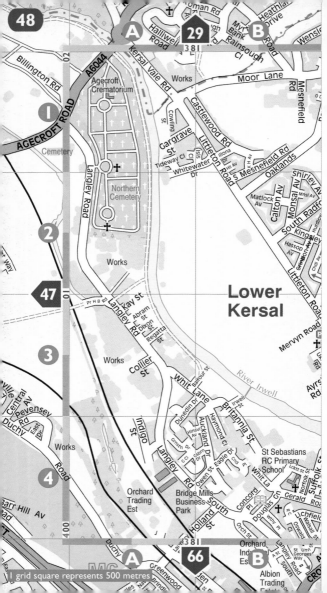

48

A Halliwell Road

29

B Heathlan Drive

Myr Bank Rainsough Cl

Wensle

Billington Rd

A6044

Kersal Vale Rd

Works

Moor Lane

Mesnefield

1

AGECROFT ROAD

Agecroft Crematorium

Cowling St

Castlewood Rd

Mesnefield Rd

Oaklands

Shirley Av

Cemetery

Cargrave St

Littleton Road

Illona Dr

S Mesnefield Rd

Matlock Av

Calton Av

Monsal St

South Radf

Mnsl Av

Tideway Cl

Whitewater Dr

Hill Av

Kingsley

Hassop Av

2

Langley Road

Northern Cemetery

Works

47

Pr H B Rd

Langley Rd

Kay St

Abram St

Dixon

Regatta St

Lower Kersal

Littleton Road

Mervyn Road

Avrs Rd

3

Works

Collier St

Whit Lane

Balfour St

River Irwell

Central Av

Pevensey

Duchy Rd

Baird Dr

Works

Indigo St

Langley Rd

Dunedin Dr

Hinsvi Av

Ginsen Dr

Auckland Dr

Haymond Cl

Irwell St

Britannia St

St Sebastians RC Primary School

4

Barr Hill Av

Orchard Trading Est

Bridge Mills Business Park

Owen St Eagle Dr Cnd

South Holland St

Concord Pl

Douglas

Gerald Road

Norfolk

Suffolk

Lichfield

A Greenwood

66

381

B

Orchard Ind Es

Albion Trading

St Georges

Langley Road

1 grid square represents 500 metres

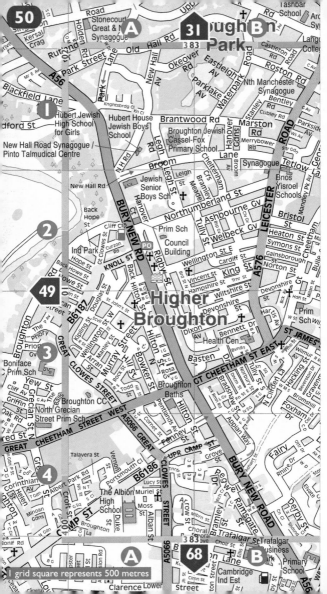

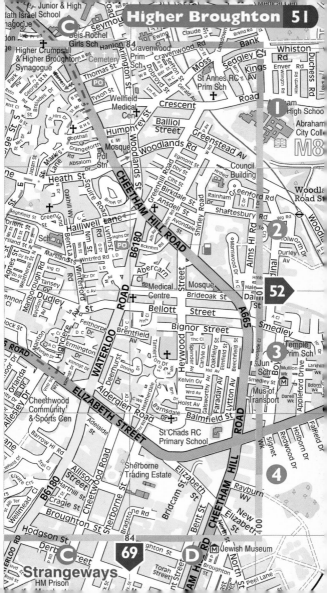

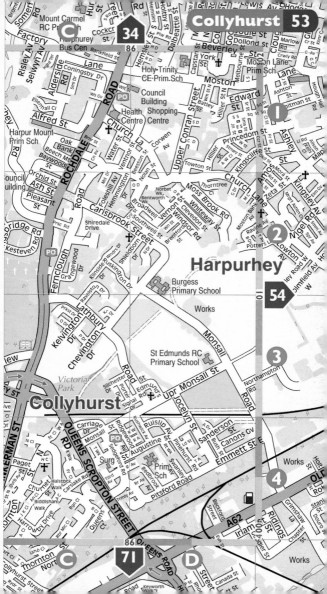

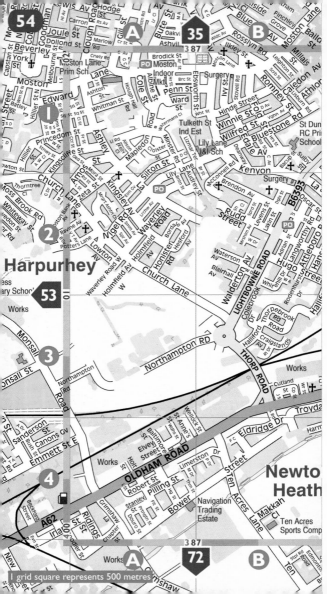

I grid square represents 500 metres

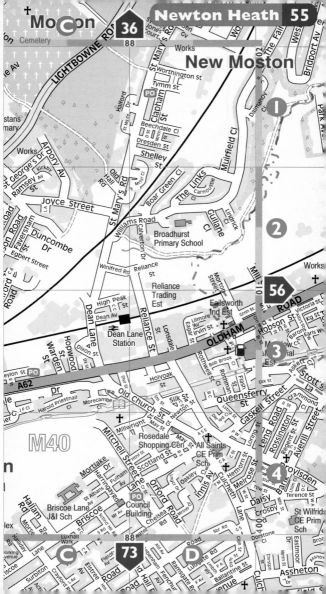

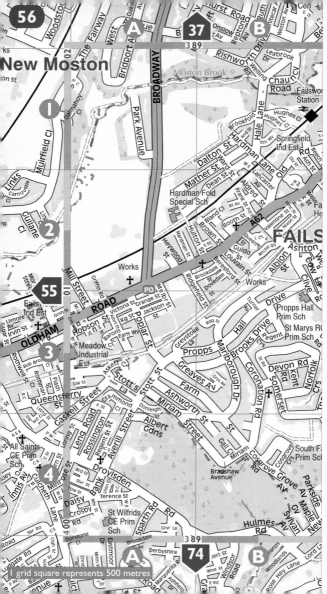

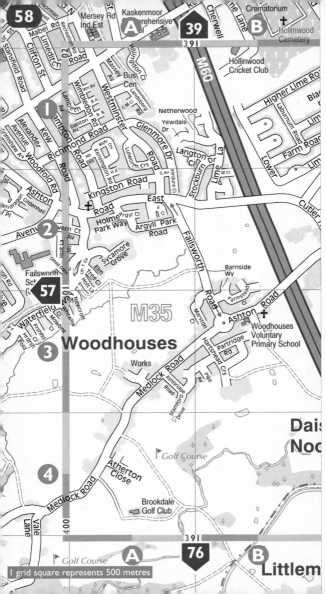

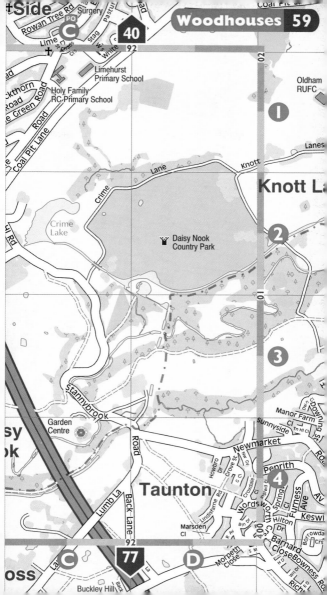

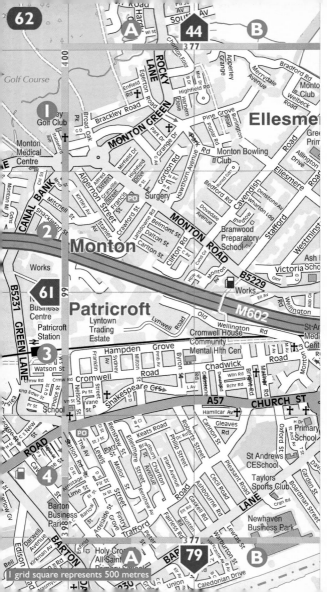

I grid square represents 500 metres

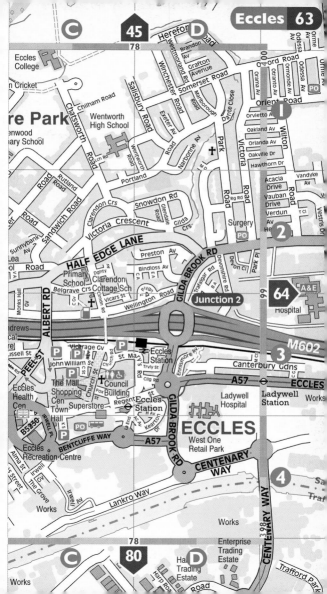

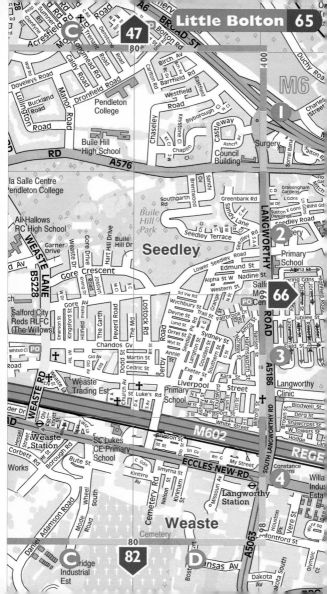

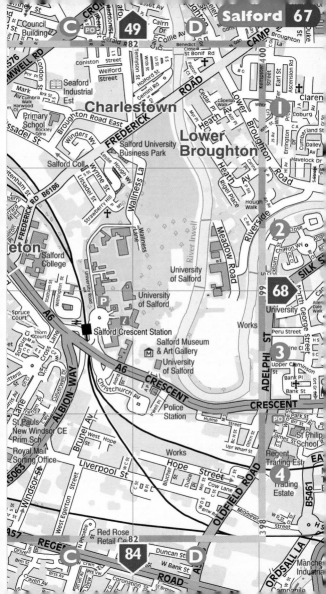

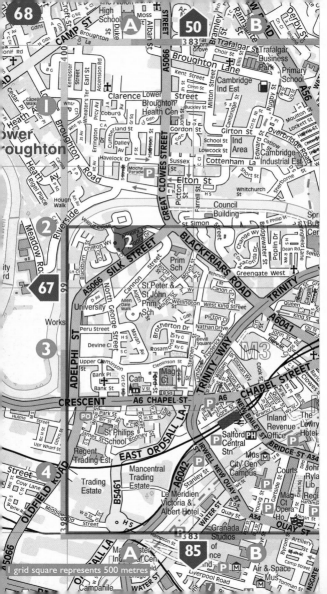

I grid square represents 500 metres

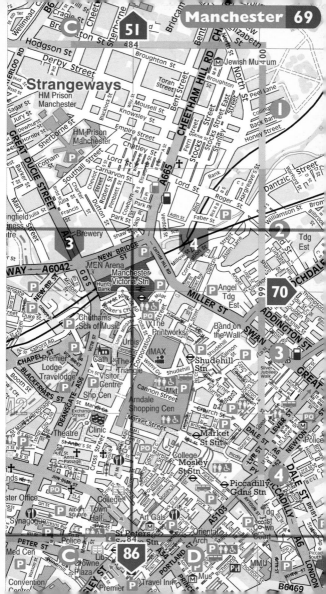

I grid square represents 500 metres

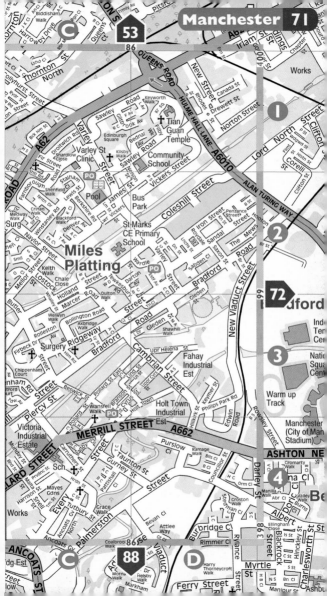

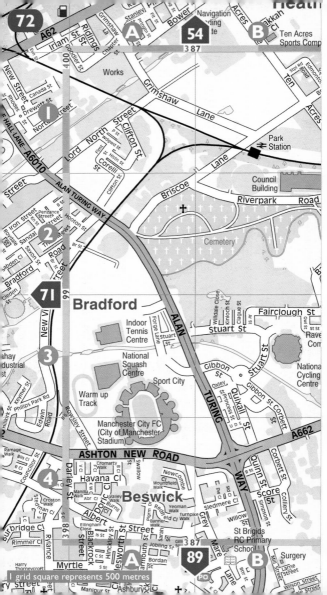

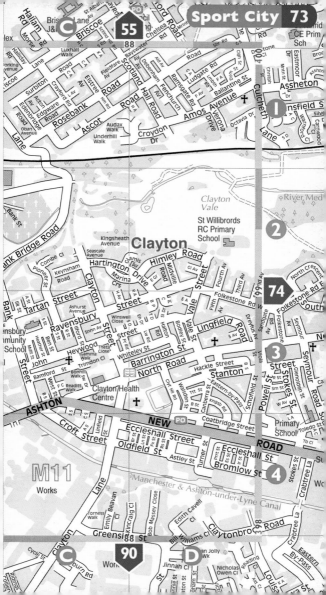

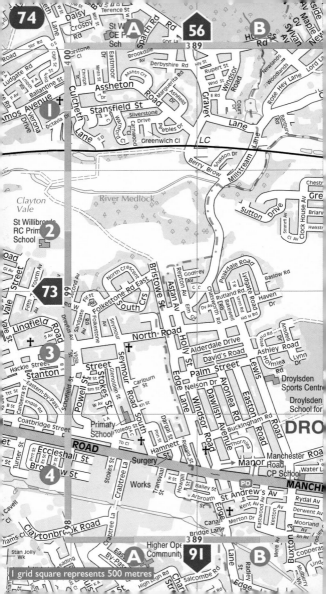

I grid square represents 500 metres

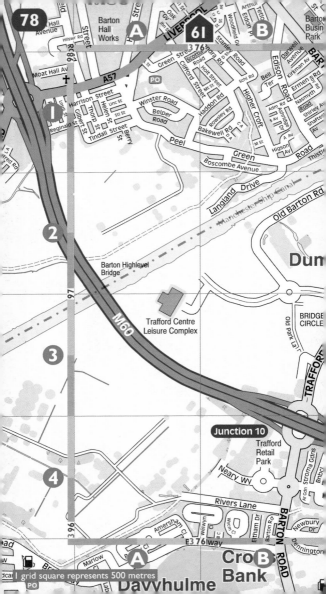

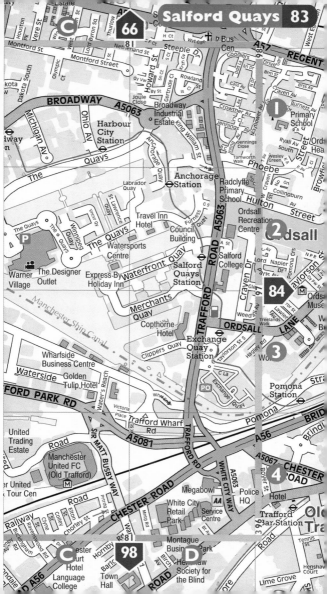

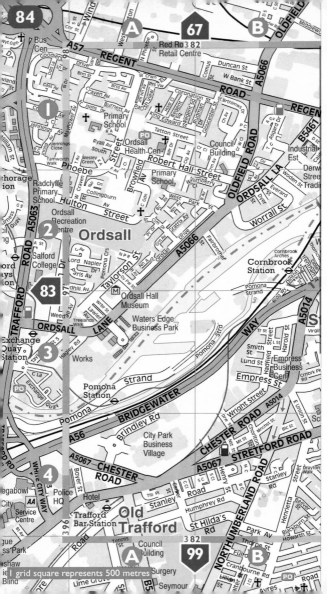

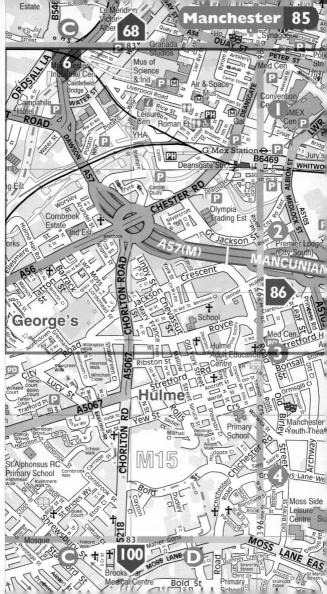

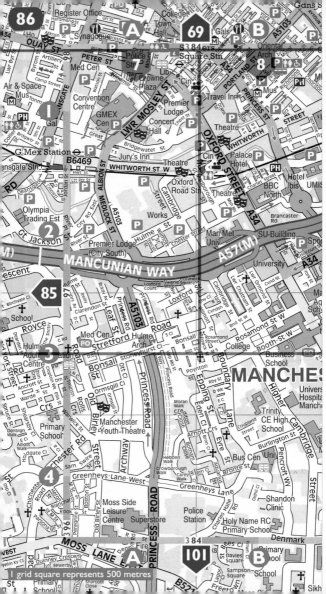

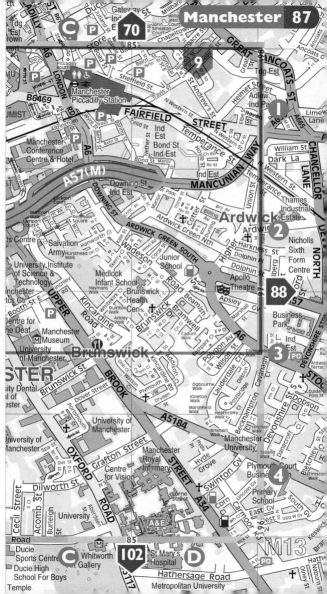

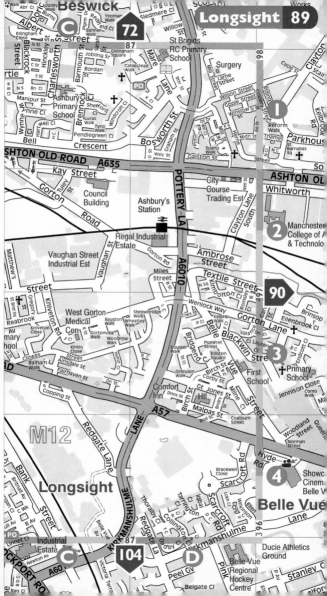

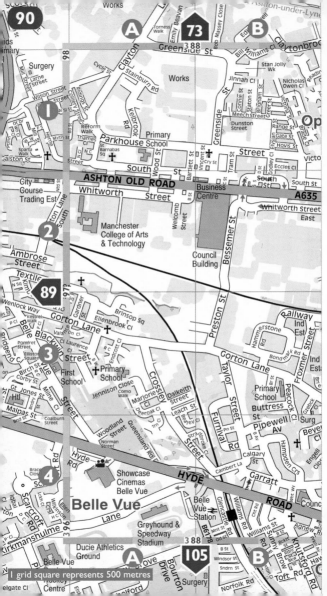

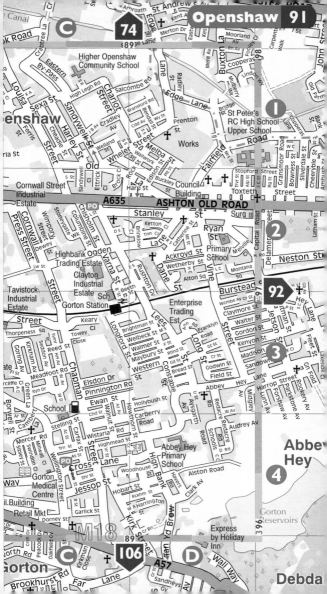

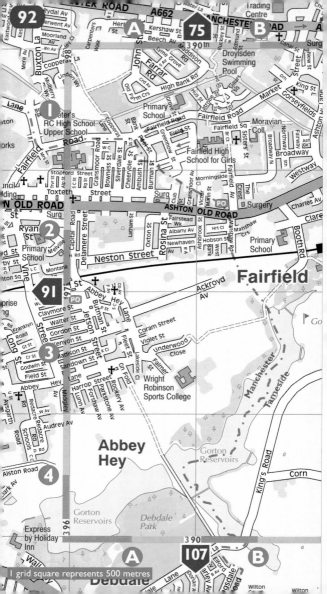

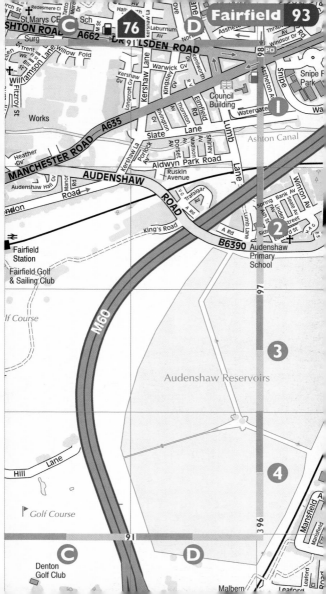

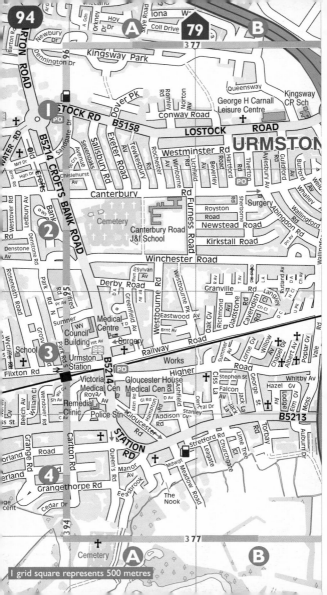

I grid square represents 500 metres

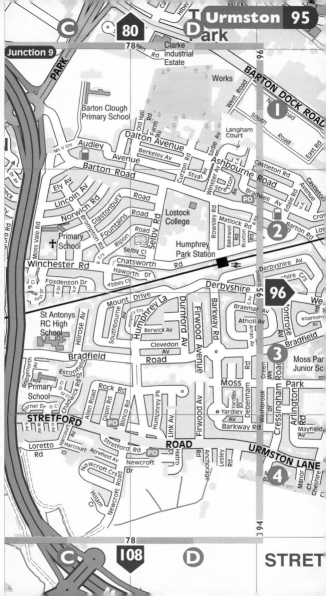

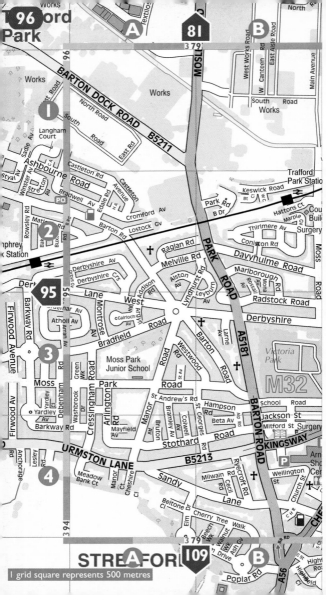

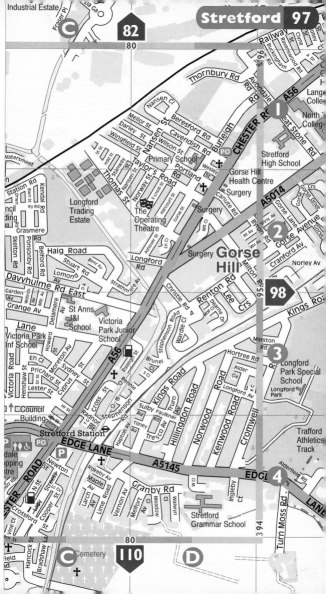

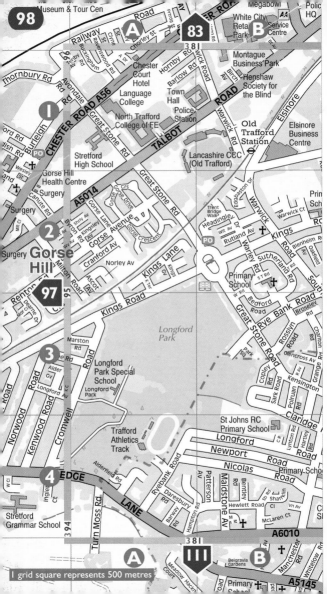

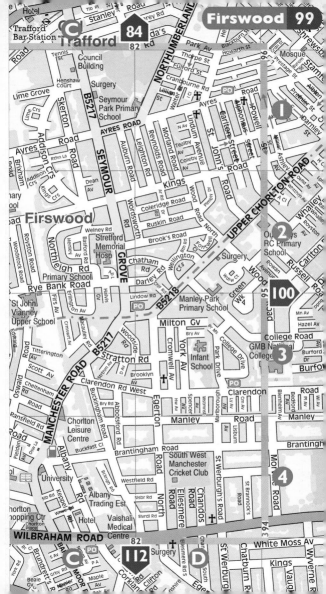

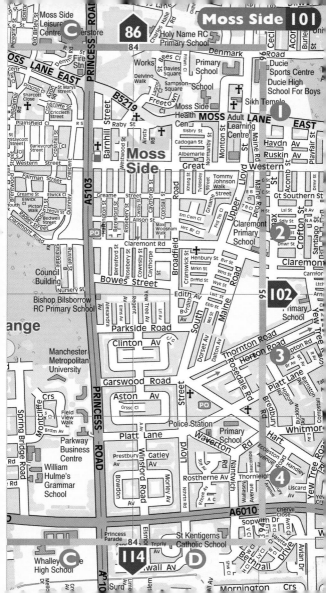

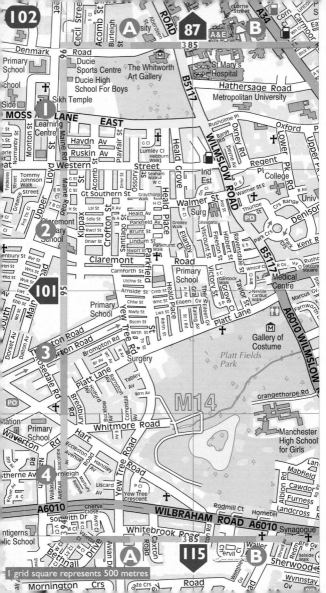

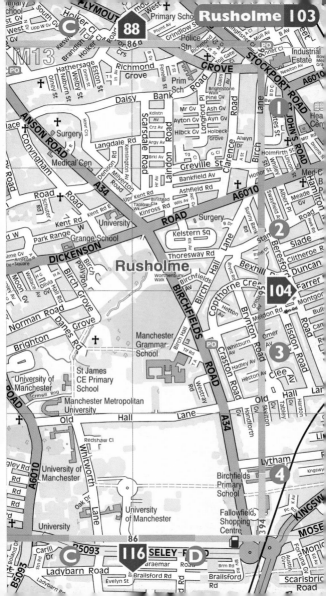

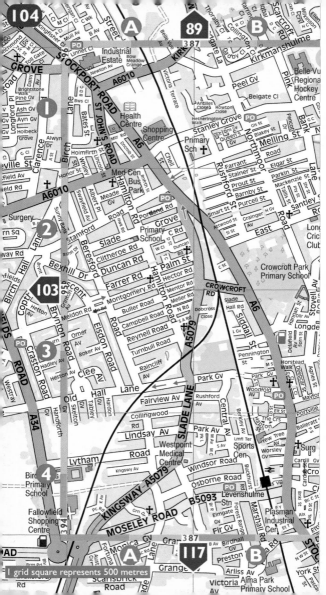

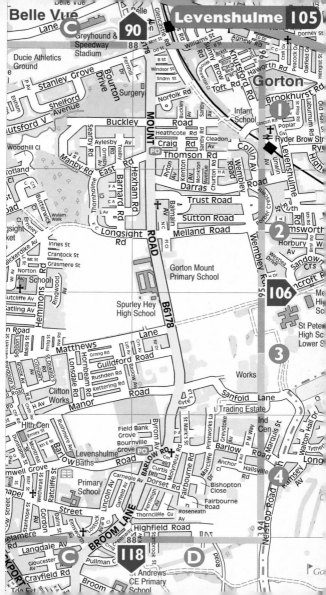

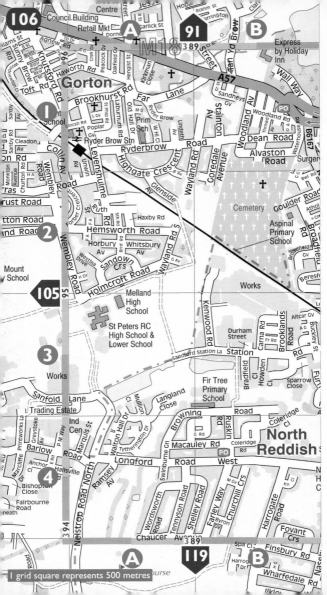

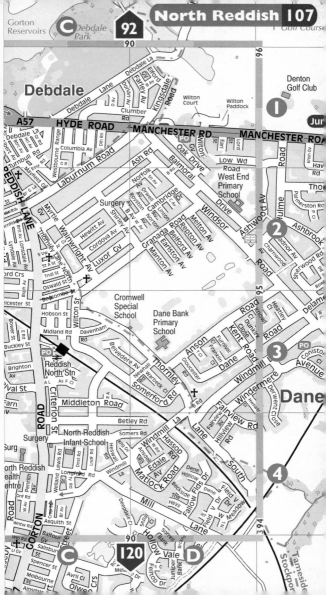

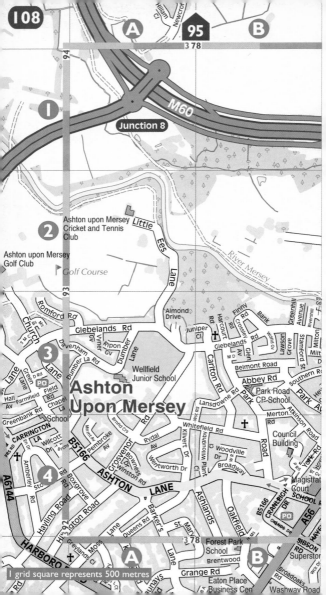

A

95
3 78

B

1

M60

Junction 8

Ashton upon Mersey
Cricket and Tennis
Club

Little Ees Lane

Ashton upon Mersey
Golf Club

Golf Course

2

River Mersey

94

93

Hillam
Cl

Newcrof

Romford Rd

Church

Lane

Greenbank Rd

CARRINGTON

Field Rd

A6144

Amberley Rd

3

4

Hall Farmfield

Davenham Rd

Glebelands Rd

Vyner

Ripon Gv

Dumber Lane

Dumber La Rd

Almond
Drive

Juniper
Cl

Harcourt

Glebelands Rd

Wellfield
Junior School

Ashton
Upon Mersey

Brentd Crs

Rydal
Av

Carlton Rd

Lansdowne Rd

Finny Crossfield
Rd

Bank

Glen
Rd

Abbey Rd

Greenhill
Avenue

Lawson Grove

Stamford Rd

Milton

Belmont Road

Park Road
CP School

Atkinson Rd

Merton Rd

Southern Rd

Park
Road

Park Av

York Rd

Whitefield Rd

Woodville
Dr

Broadway

Kilvert Dr

Wentworth Dr

Willowmoor
Plant

Ashlands

Oakfield

Council
Building

Magistrat
Court

CRANLEIGH DR

B5166

SCHOOL R

A56

PO

Pembroke
Av

Bowness
Rd

Grosvenor
Cl

Winston Gv

Wilcott
Dr

B5166
ASHTON
LANE

Boxgrove Rd

Hayling Road

Hington Road

Creylands Cl

Moss

Lane

Barker's

St Mary's

Queens Rd

HARBORO

A6144

A

3 78

B

Forest Park
School

Brentwood

Grange Rd

Eaton Place
Business Cen

SIBSON

RD
Superstor

Broadoaks

Washway Road

110 CHESTER A 97 B tford Grammar School

CHESTER ROAD A56

Highfield Road

I

Junction 7

2

Barfoot Bridge

109

Cemetery

Hawthorn Road

Trafford Water Sports Centre

Danefield Rd

3

DANE

Cranford Av

Merlyn Av

ROAD

Priory Rd

Mornington Rd

B5397

Sale Cricket Club

High Gates

Cow Lane

Arnesby Av

DANE ROAD

Ravenstone Dr

Caldbeck Av

Oulton Avenue

Stapleford Cl

Whitstanley Road

4

Pinewood

Kingston Dr

Russell Av

Clarendon Crs

Vale Av

B5397

Junior School

Charlton Dr

Road

A Ondon Road

Carlyn

Broad

B Leith Av

OLD HALL ROAD

1 grid square represents 500 metres

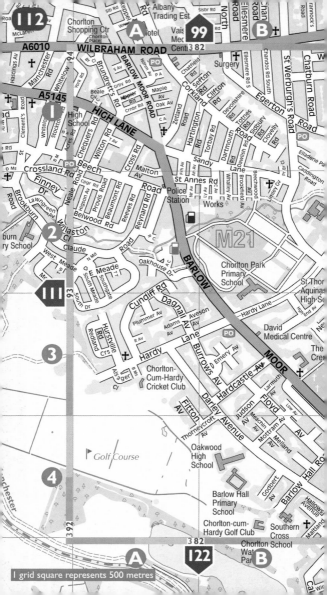

I grid square represents 500 metres

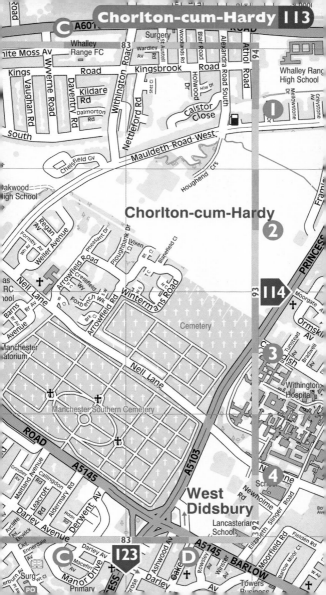

Chorlton-cum-Hardy 113

Chorlton-cum-Hardy

West Didsbury

Cemetery

Manchester Southern Cemetery

Manchester Crematorium

Withington Hospital

Whalley Range FC

Whalley Range High School

Oakwood High School

Lancasteriane School

Darley Primary

Towers Business

Neil Lane

Wintermans Road

Arrowfield Road

Mauldeth Road West

A6010 ROAD

A5145 ROAD

A5103

A5145 BARLOW

PRINCESS

Withington Road

Nettleford Rd

Athol Road

Alexandra Road South

Holwood Dr

Calstor Close

Houghend Crs

Kingsbrook

Wardley Av

St Austell

Woodlands Rd

Blair Road

Mellowstone Dr

Greystone Av

Kings Vaughan Rd South

Wwerne Road

Daventry Road

Kildare Rd

Dalmorton Rd

Chelsfield Gv

Regan

Formby Av

Weller Avenue

Phasant Dr

Ploughbank Dr

Vixen

Cressfield Wy

Foxdenton Wk

Barns Avenue

Neil Lane

Blakefield Cl

Moorgate

Ormskirk

Tunstead Av

Bradwell

Withington Hospital

Newholme Rd

Newfield Rd

Slinger Road

Elizabeth

Moorfield Rd

Fielden Rd

Barlow Moor Ct

Grindley Av

Maitland Avenue

Callington Rd

Leacroft Rd

Aldermary Rd

Darley Avenue

Derwent Av

Aycliffe Av

Bowick

Enerdale

Manor Drive

Macefin

Ashwood Av

Rowsley

Winster Av

Oake

Darley Av

1 2 3 4

114 93

C A6010 83 46 1

2

114

3

4

C 83 123 D A5145 BARLOW

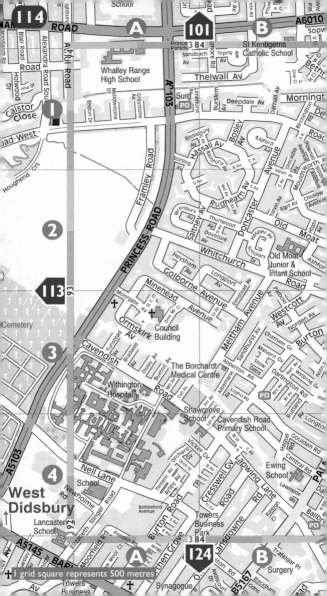

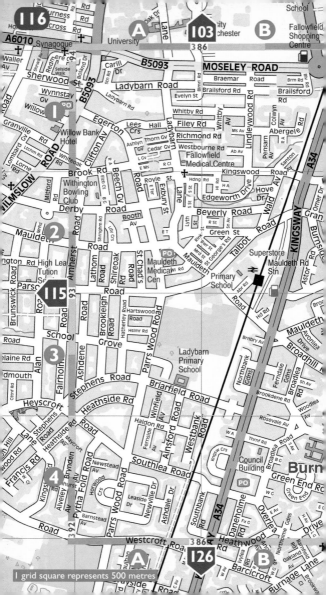

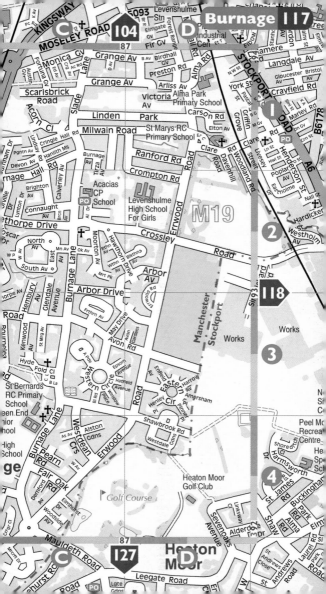

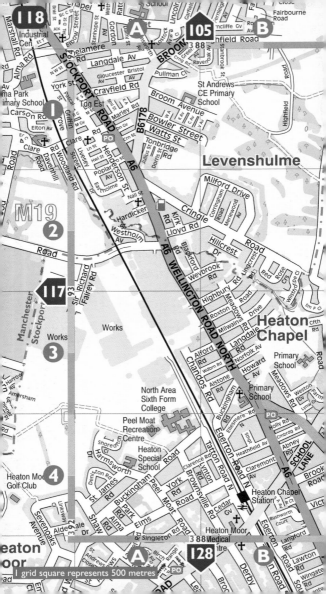

I grid square represents 500 metres

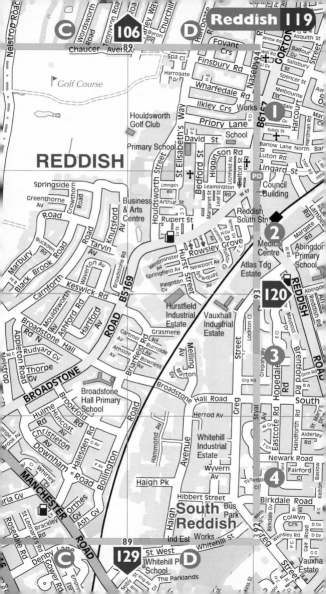

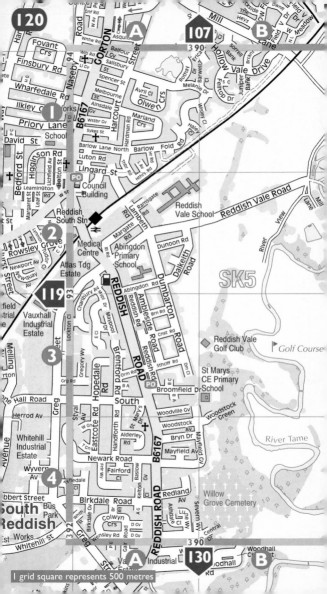

C

91

94

Ross

Lave

Tameside Stockport

M60

River Tame

I

2

Far Cromwell

93

Hollow End

Blackberry

Lane

Tame Valley Primary School

Grasscroft

The Clough

Lapwing

North

Cawood Square

Matley Gn

Castle Hill School

Cromwell Rd

3

Erith Cl

Rainham Wy

Penshurst

The Link

Lennan

Lane

Bridg

Busi

Cent

Romney

Wy

Keston Crs

Northumberland

Westmorland

Shropshire Av

Cornwall Crs

Deal Av

Darford

Eynford

Middlesex

Road

PO

Brinnington Station

Westmorland Prim Sch

Suffolk Dr

Rutland

Pembry Cl

Trent Cl

Hereford Road

Brinnington Health Centre

4

Brinnington

Falmouth

Road

Dorset Av

Bodmin Crs

Dunster

Exeter Road

Truro Av

Hampshire Road

Essex Rd

Essex

Bude Av

Foliage Crs

Mann

Road

Surrey

Worcester

Brindale Primary School

A560

C

131

D

St Bernadettes RC Primary School

Foliage Rd

Kimmel

Wiltshire Av

White Bank

92

M60

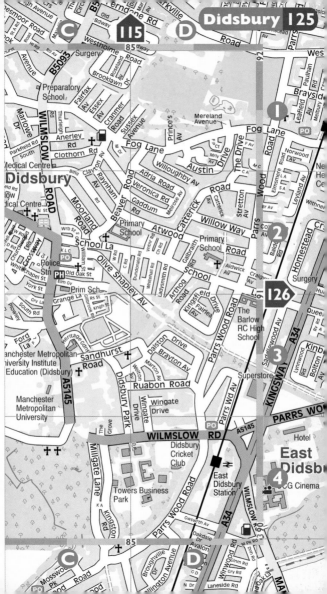

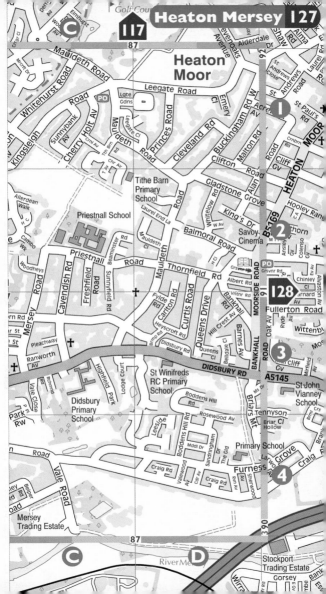

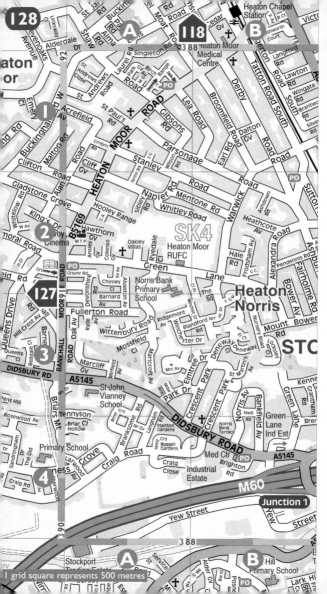

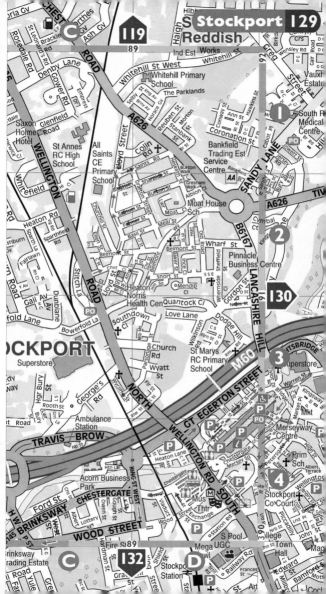

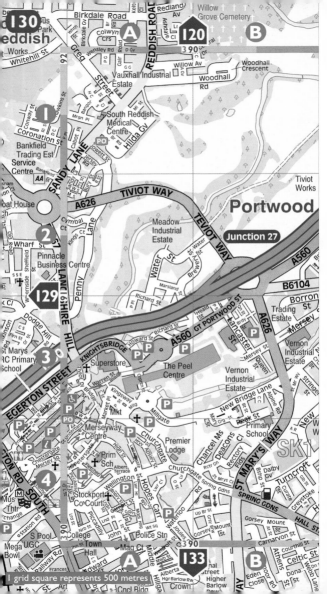

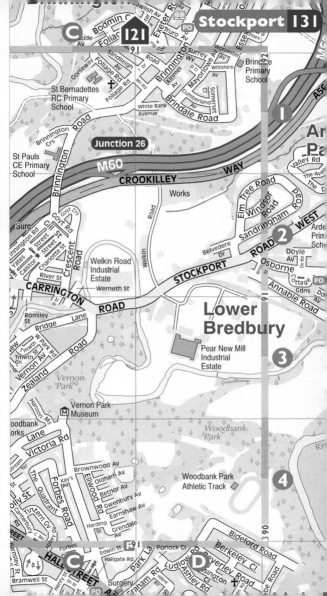

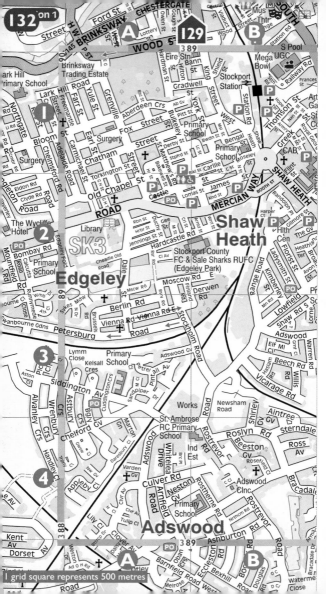

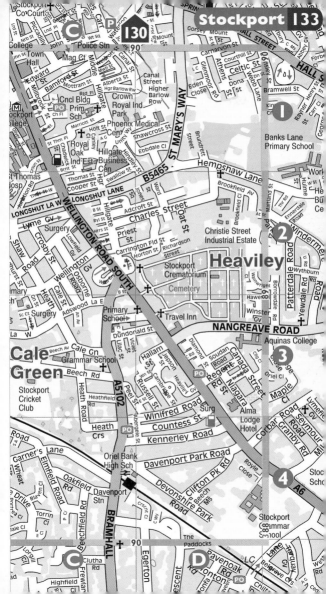

USING THE STREET INDEX

Street names are listed alphabetically. Each street name is followed by its postal town or area locality, the Postcode District, the page number, and the reference to the square in which the name is found.

Standard index entries are shown as follows:

Abberley Dr *NEWH/MOS* M40 ....**37** C3

Street names and selected addresses not shown on the map due to scale restrictions are shown in the index with an asterisk:

Abbeyfield Sq *OP/CLY* * M11..................**90** A1

GENERAL ABBREVIATIONS

ACC	ACCESS	DRY	DRIVEWAY
ALY	ALLEY	DWGS	DWELLINGS
AP	APPROACH	E	EAST
AR	ARCADE	EMB	EMBANKMENT
ASS	ASSOCIATION	EMBY	EMBASSY
AV	AVENUE	ESP	ESPLANADE
BCH	BEACH	EST	ESTATE
BLDS	BUILDINGS	EX	EXCHANGE
BND	BEND	EXPY	EXPRESSWAY
BNK	BANK	EXT	EXTENSION
BR	BRIDGE	F/O	FLYOVER
BRK	BROOK	FC	FOOTBALL CLUB
BTM	BOTTOM	FK	FORK
BUS	BUSINESS	FLD	FIELD
BVD	BOULEVARD	FLDS	FIELDS
BY	BYPASS	FLS	FALLS
CATH	CATHEDRAL	FLS	FLATS
CEM	CEMETERY	FM	FARM
CEN	CENTRE	FT	FORT
CFT	CROFT	FWY	FREEWAY
CH	CHURCH	FY	FERRY
CHA	CHASE	GA	GATE
CHYD	CHURCHYARD	GAL	GALLERY
CIR	CIRCLE	GDN	GARDEN
CIRC	CIRCUS	GDNS	GARDENS
CL	CLOSE	GLD	GLADE
CLFS	CLIFFS	GLN	GLEN
CMP	CAMP	GN	GREEN
CNR	CORNER	GND	GROUND
CO	COUNTY	GRA	GRANGE
COLL	COLLEGE	GRG	GARAGE
COM	COMMON	GT	GREAT
COMM	COMMISSION	GTWY	GATEWAY
CON	CONVENT	GV	GROVE
COT	COTTAGE	HGR	HIGHER
COTS	COTTAGES	HL	HILL
CP	CAPE	HLS	HILLS
CPS	COPSE	HO	HOUSE
CR	CREEK	HOL	HOLLOW
CREM	CREMATORIUM	HOSP	HOSPITAL
CRS	CRESCENT	HRB	HARBOUR
CSWY	CAUSEWAY	HTH	HEATH
CT	COURT	HTS	HEIGHTS
CTRL	CENTRAL	HVN	HAVEN
CTS	COURTS	HWY	HIGHWAY
CTYD	COURTYARD	IMP	IMPERIAL
CUTT	CUTTINGS	IN	INLET
CV	COVE	IND EST	INDUSTRIAL ESTATE
CYN	CANYON	INF	INFIRMARY
DEPT	DEPARTMENT	INFO	INFORMATION
DL	DALE	INT	INTERCHANGE
DM	DAM	IS	ISLAND
DR	DRIVE	JCT	JUNCTION
DRO	DROVE	JTY	JETTY

KG	KING
KNL	KNOLL
L	LAKE
LA	LANE
LDG	LODGE
LGT	LIGHT
LK	LOCK
LKS	LAKES
LNDG	LANDING
LTL	LITTLE
LWR	LOWER
MAG	MAGISTRATE
MAN	MANSIONS
MD	MEAD
MDW	MEADOWS
MEM	MEMORIAL
MKT	MARKET
MKTS	MARKETS
ML	MALL
ML	MILL
MNR	MANOR
MS	MEWS
MSN	MISSION
MT	MOUNT
MTN	MOUNTAIN
MTS	MOUNTAINS
MUS	MUSEUM
MWY	MOTORWAY
N	NORTH
NE	NORTH EAST
NW	NORTH WEST
O/P	OVERPASS
OFF	OFFICE
ORCH	ORCHARD
OV	OVAL
PAL	PALACE
PAS	PASSAGE
PAV	PAVILION
PDE	PARADE
PH	PUBLIC HOUSE
PK	PARK
PKWY	PARKWAY
PL	PLACE
PLN	PLAIN
PLNS	PLAINS
PLZ	PLAZA
POL	POLICE STATION
PR	PRINCE
PREC	PRECINCT
PREP	PREPARATORY
PRIM	PRIMARY
PROM	PROMENADE
PRS	PRINCESS
PRT	PORT
PT	POINT
PTH	PATH
PZ	PIAZZA
QD	QUADRANT
QU	QUEEN
QY	QUAY
R	RIVER
RBT	ROUNDABOUT
RD	ROAD
RDG	RIDGE
REP	REPUBLIC
RES	RESERVOIR
RFC	RUGBY FOOTBALL CLUB
RI	RISE
RP	RAMP
RW	ROW
S	SOUTH
SCH	SCHOOL
SE	SOUTH EAST
SER	SERVICE AREA
SH	SHORE
SHOP	SHOPPING
SKWY	SKYWAY
SMT	SUMMIT
SOC	SOCIETY
SP	SPUR
SPR	SPRING
SQ	SQUARE
ST	STREET
STN	STATION
STR	STREAM
STRD	STRAND
SW	SOUTH WEST
TDG	TRADING
TER	TERRACE
THWY	THROUGHWAY
TNL	TUNNEL
TOLL	TOLLWAY
TPK	TURNPIKE
TR	TRACK
TRL	TRAIL
TWR	TOWER
U/P	UNDERPASS
UNI	UNIVERSITY
UPR	UPPER
V	VALE
VA	VALLEY
VIAD	VIADUCT
VIL	VILLA
VIS	VISTA
VLG	VILLAGE
VLS	VILLAS
VW	VIEW
W	WEST
WD	WOOD
WHF	WHARF
WK	WALK
WKS	WALKS
WLS	WELLS
WY	WAY
YD	YARD
YHA	YOUTH HOSTEL

POSTCODE TOWNS AND AREA ABBREVIATIONS

ANC	Ancoats	NTHM/RTH	Northern Moor/Roundthorn
AULW	Ashton-under-Lyne west	OFTN	Offerton
BKLY	Blackley	OLD	Oldham
BNG/LEV	Burnage/Levenshulme	OLDE	Oldham east
BRO	Broughton	OLDS	Oldham south
BRUN/LGST	Brunswick/Longsight	OLDTF/WHR	Old Trafford/Whalley Range
CCHDY	Choriton-cum-Hardy	OP/CLY	Openshaw/Clayton
CHAD	Chadderton	ORD	Ordsall
CHD/CHDH	Cheadle /Cheadle Hulme	PWCH	Prestwich
CHH	Cheetham Hill	RAD	Radcliffe
CMANE	Central Manchester east	RDSH	Reddish
CMANW	Central Manchester west	RUSH/FAL	Rusholme/Fallowfield
CSLFD	Central Salford	SALE	Sale
DID/WITH	Didsbury/Withington	SALQ	Salford Quays
DROY	Droylsden	SLFD	Salford
DTN/ASHW	Denton/Audenshaw	STKP	Stockport
ECC	Eccles	STRET	Stretford
EDGY/DAV	Edgeley/Davenport	SWIN	Swinton
FAIL	Failsworth	TRPK	Trafford Park
FWTH	Farnworth	URM	Urmston
GTN	Gorton	WALK	Walkden
HTNM	Heaton Moor	WCTN/LGST	West Gorton/Longsight
HULME	Hulme	WHTF	Whitefield
MDTN	Middleton	WYTH/NTH	Wythenshawe/Northenden
MPL/ROM	Marple/Romiley		
NEWH/MOS	Newton Heath/Moston		

Abb - Add

Index - streets

A

Abberley Dr NEWH/MOS M40	**37** C3
Abberton Rd DID/WITH M20	**114** B3
Abbey Cl STRET M32	**95** C2
Abbey Dr SWIN M27	**44** B1
Abbeyfield Sq OP/CLY * M11	**90** A1
Abbey Gv CHAD OL9	**38** B3
ECC M30	**62** B3
Abbey Hey La GTN M18	**91** D5
Abbey Lawn OLDTF/WHR M16	**99** C2
Abbey Rd DROY M43	**75** C2
FAIL M35	**58** A1
SALE M33	**108** B3
Abbeyville Wk HULME * M15	**85** D4
Abbeywood Av GTN * M18	**106** B1
Abbots Cl SALE M33	**110** A4
Abbotsford Rd CCHDY M21	**99** C3
CHAD * OL9	**19** D1
Abbotside Cl OLDTF/WHR M16	**100** A2
Abercarn Cl CHH M8	**51** D2
Abercrombie Ct SALE M33	**110** A4
Aberdaron Wk BRUN/LGST M13	**9** D5
Aberdeen Crs EDGY/DAV SK3	**132** A1
Aberdeen Gv EDGY/DAV SK3	**132** A1
Aberdeen St BRUN/LGST M13	**87** C4
Abergele Rd RUSH/FAL M14	**116** B1
Abergele St OFTN SK2	**133** C1
Abemant Cl OP/CLY M11	**72** A4
Abersoch Av RUSH/FAL M14	**116** B1
Abingdon Cl CHAD * OL9	**39** C1
Abingdon Rd RDSH SK5	**120** A3
URM M41	**94** B2
Abingdon St CMANE M1	**7** F4
Abney Rd HTNM SK4	**118** B4
Abram Cl RUSH/FAL M14	**101** D4
Abram St SLFD M6	**48** A3
Absalom Dr CHH M8	**51** C1
Acacia Av SWIN M27	**44** B3
Acacia Dr SLFD M6	**64** A2
Acacia Gv RDSH SK5	**130** A1
Acacia Rd OLDS OL8	**40** A4
The Acacias URM * M41	**94** B3
Academy Wk HULME * M15	**85** D4
Ace MI CHAD * OL9	**38** A1
Acheson St GTN M18	**91** C4
Ackers St BRUN/LGST M13	**87** C4
Ackroyd Av GTN M18	**92** B3
Ackroyd St OP/CLY M11	**91** D2
Ackworth Rd SWIN M27	**25** D4
Acme Dr SWIN M27	**46** A1
Acomb St BRUN/LGST M13	**87** C4
RUSH/FAL M14	**102** A2
Acorn Cl BNG/LEV M19	**117** C3
WHTF M45	**11** C3
Acorn Wy OLD * OL1	**22** B2
Acrefield Av HTNM SK4	**127** D1
URM M41	**95** C4
Acresfield Av DTN/ASHW M34	**76** A4
Acresfield Cl SWIN M27	**45** D3
Acresfield Rd SLFD M6	**47** C4
Acres Rd CCHDY M21	**111** D1
Acre St CHAD OL9	**39** C3
Acre Top Rd BKLY M9	**15** C4
Acton Av NEWH/MOS M40	**73** C1
Acton St OLD OL1	**23** D1
Adair St CMANE M1	**9** F1
Adams Av CCHDY M21	**112** A3
Adamson Gdns DID/WITH M20	**124** A2
Adamson Rd ECC M30	**78** B1
Adamson Wk RUSH/FAL * M14	**102** A2
Adam St OLDS OL8	**41** C3
Ada St BKLY M9	**34** A4
Adcroft St STKP SK1	**133** C2
Addenbrook Rd CHH M8	**50** B4
Addington St ANC M4	**4** C2

Addison Cl *BRUN/LGST* M13 ....87 D3
Addison Crs *OLDTF/WHR* M16 ....99 C2
Addison Rd *STRET* M32 ....96 B5
   URM M41 ....94 A4
Adelaide St *CHH* M8 ....51 C4
   ECC M30 ....62 A4
   MDTN M24 ....17 D1
   SWIN M27 ....44 A2
Adeline St *ANC* M4 ....69 D2
Adelphi St *CSLFD* M3 ....2 A3
Aden Cl *WGTN/LGST* M12 ....88 A1
Adlington Dr *STRET* M32 ....98 A1
Adlington Wk *STKP* * SK1 ....129 D4
Adrian St *NEWH/MOS* M40 ....54 B2
Adria Rd *DID/WITH* M20 ....125 D2
Adscombe St *OLDTF/WHR* M16 ......100 B1
Adstone Cl *ANC* M4 ....71 C4
Adswood Cl *EDGY/DAV* SK3 ....132 A3
Adswood La East *OFTN* SK2 ....133 C3
Adswood La West *EDGY/DAV* SK3 ...132 B3
Adswood Old Rd *EDGY/DAV* SK3 ...132 A4
Adswood Rd *NEWH/MOS* M40 ....71 D3
Adswood Ter *EDGY/DAV* SK3 ....132 B3
Aegean Cl *BRO* M7 ....49 D4
Agecroft Rd *SWIN* M27 ....47 C2
Agecroft Rd East *PWCH* M25 ....29 C3
Agecroft Rd West *PWCH* M25 ....29 C3
Agnes Cl *CSLFD* OL9 ....39 D1
Agnes St *BNG/LEV* M19 ....104 B3
   BRO M7 ....51 C2
   CHAD OL9 ....21 C4
Agnew Pl *SLFD* M6 ....66 B1
Agnew Rd *GTN* M18 ....90 B4
Aigburth Gv *RDSH* SK5 ....106 B3
Ainsdale Cl *NEWH/MOS* M40 ....53 C4
Ainsdale Ct *RDSH* SK5 ....40 A1
Ainsdale Cv *RDSH* SK5 ....120 A1
Ainsdale St *WGTN/LGST* M12 ....89 C3
Ainsford Rd *DID/WITH* M20 ....116 A4
Ainsty Rd *RUSH/FAL* M14 ....101 D1
Aintree Gv *EDGY/DAV* SK3 ....132 A3
Aintree St *OP/CLY* M11 ....73 C4
Aintree Wk *CHAD* * OL9 ....21 D2
Airton Cl *NEWH/MOS* M40 ....70 B2
Aitken St *BNG/LEV* * M19 ....105 C3
Aked Cl *WGTN/LGST* M12 ....88 A1
Alan Av *FAIL* M35 ....57 C4
Alanbrooke Wk *HULME* * M15 ....85 D4
Alan Rd *DID/WITH* M20 ....115 C3
   HTNM SK4 ....127 C2
Alasdair Cl *CHAD* OL9 ....20 A1
Alba Cl *ECC* M30 ....62 A4
Alban St *BRO* M7 ....50 A4
Albany Av *OP/CLY* M11 ....92 A1
Albany Rd *CCHDY* M21 ....99 C4
   ECC M30 ....61 C2
Albany St *MDTN* M24 ....18 A2
Albany Wy *SLFD* M6 ....66 B1
Alba Wy *STRET* M32 ....80 B4
Albemarle Av *DID/WITH* M20 ....114 B3
Albemarle Rd *CCHDY* M21 ....111 D1
Albemarle St *RUSH/FAL* M14 ....101 C3
Albemarle Rd *SWIN* M27 ....44 B2
Alberta St *STKP* SK1 ....133 C1
Albert Av *GTN* M18 ....106 B1
   PWCH M25 ....30 B4
   URM M41 ....94 B3
Albert Cl *WHTF* M45 ....11 D1
Albert Gdns *NEWH/MOS* M40 ....56 A4
Albert Gv *WGTN/LGST* M12 ....104 B1
Albert Hill St *DID/WITH* * M20 ....125 C2
Albert Park Rd *BRO* M7 ....49 D4
Albert Pl *BRUN/LGST* M13 ....104 A1
Albert Rd *ECC* M30 ....63 C3
   HTNM SK4 ....127 D2

WHTF M45 ....11 D1
Albert Sq *CMANW* M2 ....3 F5
Albert St *DROY* M43 ....76 A4
   EDGY/DAV SK3 ....129 C4
   MDTN M24 ....18 A2
   OLDS OL8 ....39 C4
   OLDTF/WHR * M16 ....84 B3
   OP/CLY M11 ....72 A4
   PWCH * M25 ....12 B4
Albert St West *FAIL* M35 ....56 A3
Albine St *NEWH/MOS* M40 ....54 A1
Albion Cl *HTNM* SK4 ....129 D2
Albion Dr *DROY* M43 ....75 D3
Albion Fold *DROY* M43 ....75 D3
Albion Pl *BRO* * M7 ....49 D4
   ORD M5 ....67 D3
   PWCH M25 ....29 D1
Albion Rd *RUSH/FAL* M14 ....102 B4
Albion St *CHAD* OL9 ....20 B3
   CMANE M1 ....7 E2
   FAIL M35 ....56 B1
   OLD OL1 ....23 C2
   OLDTF/WHR M16 ....100 A1
   SWIN M27 ....45 C2
Albion Wy *ORD* M5 ....67 C4
Albury Dr *BNG/LEV* M19 ....126 A3
Albyns Av *CHH* M8 ....51 D2
Alcester Cl *MDTN* M24 ....18 A3
Alcester St *CHAD* OL9 ....38 B2
Aldborough Cl *DID/WITH* M20 ....115 C3
Aldbourne Cl *NEWH/MOS* M40 ....53 C4
Aldcroft St *GTN* * M18 ....92 A3
Alden Cl *WHTF* M45 ....11 D1
Alder Ct *CHH* * M8 ....52 A3
Alderdale Dr *DROY* M43 ....74 A3
   HTNM SK4 ....117 D4
Alder Dr *SWIN* M27 ....24 B4
Alderfield Rd *CCHDY* M21 ....98 A4
Alder Forest Av *ECC* M30 ....60 B3
Aldergiem Rd *CHH* M8 ....51 C3
Alder Gv *STRET* M32 ....97 D3
Alder La *OLDS* OL8 ....40 A3
Alderley Rd *RDSH* SK5 ....120 A4
Alderman Sq *WGTN/LGST* M12 ....88 B1
Aldermary Rd *CCHDY* M21 ....113 C4
Aldermaston Gv *BKLY* M9 ....15 C3
Aldermoor Cl *OP/CLY* M11 ....90 B1
Alder Rd *FAIL* M35 ....57 C4
Alderside Rd *BKLY* M9 ....33 C1
Aldersley Av *BKLY* M9 ....33 C1
Alderson St *CHAD* OL9 ....22 B2
   SLFD M6 ....66 B1
Alder St *ECC* M30 ....66 B1
   SLFD M6 ....66 A3
Aldford Cl *DID/WITH* * M20 ....125 C2
Aldham Av *NEWH/MOS* M40 ....73 D1
Aldred Cl *CHH* M8 ....52 A3
Aldred St *ECC* M30 ....61 D4
   FAIL M35 ....56 B2
   ORD M5 ....67 C3
Aldsworth Dr *NEWH/MOS* M40 ....53 C4
Aldwick Av *DID/WITH* M20 ....125 D2
Aldwych Av *RUSH/FAL* M14 ....102 A2
Aldwyn Park Rd *DTN/ASHW* M34 .....93 C3
Alexander Av *FAIL* M35 ....57 D1
Alexander Gdns *BRO* M7 ....68 A1
Alexander St *SLFD* M6 ....65 D3
Alexandra Av *RUSH/FAL* M14 ....101 C3
   WHTF M45 ....11 D1
Alexandra Dr *BNG/LEV* M19 ....117 C2
Alexandra Ms *OLDS* * OL8 ....23 D4
Alexandra Rd *ECC* M30 ....61 C4
   HTNM SK4 ....128 B2
   OLDS OL8 ....41 D1
   OLDTF/WHR M16 ....100 B1
Alexandra Rd South
   OLDTF/WHR M16 ....100 B2

Alexandra St BRO * M7 .... 68 A2
  OLDS OL8 .... 23 D4
Alexandra Ter BNG/LEV M19 .... 104 B4
Alford Av DID/WITH M20 .... 114 B1
Alford Rd HTNM SK4 .... 118 A3
Alford St CHAD OL9 .... 39 C3
Alfred Av WALK M28 .... 42 B2
Alfred James Cl NEWH/MOS M40 ...... 5 F1
Alfred St BKLY M9 .... 53 C1
  CHAD OL9 .... 21 D3
  ECC M30 .... 62 A2
Algernon St ECC M30 .... 62 A2
  SWIN M27 .... 44 A1
Alice St SWIN M27 .... 46 A1
Alison Kelly Cl BKLY M9 .... 54 A1
Alison St RUSH/FAL M14 .... 101 C2
Aiker Rd NEWH/MOS * M40 .... 71 C2
Alkrington Gn MDTN M24 .... 17 C3
Alkrington Hall Rd North MDTN M24 .. 17 C2
Alkrington Hall Rd South MDTN M24 .. 16 B3
Alkrington Park Rd MDTN M24 .... 16 B2
Allandale Rd BNG/LEV * M19 .... 104 A4
Allan Roberts Cl BKLY M9 .... 34 A4
Allanson Rd WYTH/NTH M22 .... 123 C4
Alldis Cl WGTN/LGST M12 .... 88 B4
Allenby Rd SWIN M27 .... 43 D3
Allen Dale Wk CSLFD M3 .... 2 A2
Allen Rd URM M41 .... 95 C4
Allen St OLDS OL8 .... 22 A3
Allerdean Wk HTNM SK4 .... 127 C4
Allerford St OLDTF/WHR M16 .... 100 B1
Allerton Wk BRUN/LGST * M13 ...... 87 C3
Allesley Dr CHH M8 .... 51 C4
Alligin Cl CHAD OL9 .... 20 B1
Allingham St BRUN/LGST M13 ...... 103 D1
Allington Dr ECC M30 .... 62 B1
Alliott Wk HULME M15 .... 85 D4
Allison Gv ECC M30 .... 61 C4
Allison St CHH M8 .... 51 C4
Allwood St ORD M5 .... 2 A5
Alma Rd BNG/LEV M19 .... 117 C1
  HTNM SK4 .... 118 A4
Alma St ECC M30 .... 63 C4
Alminstone Cl NEWH/MOS M40 ..... 74 A1
Almond Cl FAIL M35 .... 57 C3
  SLFD M6 .... 66 B3
Almond Dr SALE M33 .... 108 A3
Almond St NEWH/MOS * M40 .... 70 A1
Alms Hill Rd CHH M8 .... 51 D2
Alness Rd OLDTF/WHR M16 .... 100 B3
Alnwick Rd BKLY M9 .... 16 A4
Alpha Pl HULME * M15 .... 7 D3
Alpha Rd STRET M32 .... 96 B3
  SLFD M6 .... 66 A2
Alpha St West SLFD M6 .... 65 D3
Alphonsus St OLDTF/WHR M16 ..... 99 D1
Alpine Rd STKP SK1 .... 130 B4
Alpine St OP/CLY M11 .... 73 C3
Alport Av OLDTF/WHR * M16 .... 99 D3
Alresford Rd MDTN M24 .... 17 C4
  SLFD M6 .... 47 D1
Alsager Cl CCHDY M21 .... 112 A3
Alsop Av BRO * M7 .... 49 C2
Alston Av STRET M32 .... 96 A2
Alstone Rd HTNM SK4 .... 118 B3
Alston Gdns BNG/LEV M19 .... 117 C4
Alston Rd GTN M18 .... 91 D4
Altair Pl BRO * M7 .... 67 D1
Altcar Gv RDSH SK5 .... 106 B3
Alton Sq OP/CLY M11 .... 91 D2
Alton St OLDS OL8 .... 41 C2
Altrincham St CMANE M1 .... 8 A1
Alvan Sq OP/CLY * M11 .... 91 D2
Alvaston Av HTNM SK4 .... 128 A2

Alvaston Rd GTN M18 .... 106 B1
Alveley Av DID/WITH M20 .... 115 D4
Alverstone Rd DID/WITH M20 ...... 115 D3
Alwinton Av HTNM SK4 .... 126 B2
Alworth Rd BKLY M9 .... 16 A4
Alwyn Dr BRUN/LGST M13 .... 103 D1
Amber St ANC M4 .... 4 B2
Amberley Wk CHAD OL9 .... 21 D2
Amber St ANC M4 .... 4 B2
Amberwood CHAD OL9 .... 19 D1
Ambleside Rd RDSH SK5 .... 120 A3
Ambrose Ct DID/WITH M20 .... 123 C4
Ambrose Dr DID/WITH M20 .... 123 C1
Ambrose St WGTN/LGST M12 .... 89 D2
Ambush St OP/CLY M11 .... 92 A2
Amersham St URM M41 .... 78 A4
Amersham Pl BNG/LEV M19 .... 117 D3
Amersham St ORD M5 .... 66 A4
Amesbury Gv RDSH SK5 .... 120 A4
Amesbury Rd BKLY M9 .... 34 B1
Amherst Rd DID/WITH M20 .... 115 D2
Ammon Wrigley Cl OLD * OL1 .... 9 E2
Amory St WGTN/LGST M12 .... 9 E2
Amos Av NEWH/MOS M40 .... 73 D1
Amos St BKLY M9 .... 54 A2
  SLFD M6 .... 65 D3
Ampney Cl ECC M30 .... 61 C4
Amwell St CHH M8 .... 52 A2
Anaconda Dr CSLFD M3 .... 2 C1
Anchorage Quay SALQ M50 .... 83 D1
Anchorage Rd URM M41 .... 95 D4
Anchor Cl BNG/LEV M19 .... 105 D4
Anchor Ct CHH * M8 .... 32 A4
Anchorside Cl CCHDY M21 .... 112 A2
Anchor St OLD OL1 .... 23 C1
Ancoats Gv ANC M4 .... 71 C4
Ancoats Gv North ANC M4 .... 71 C4
Ancroft St HULME M15 .... 85 D3
Andoc Av ECC M30 .... 63 C4
Andover Av MDTN M24 .... 18 A4
Andover St ECC M30 .... 61 D4
Andre St OP/CLY * M11 .... 73 D3
Andrew Rd BKLY M9 .... 34 A4
Andrew St CHAD OL9 .... 20 B1
  DROY M43 .... 76 B1
  FAIL M35 .... 56 B1
  MDTN M24 .... 18 B2
Anerley Rd DID/WITH M20 .... 125 C1
Anfield Rd NEWH/MOS M40 .... 37 C4
  SALE M33 .... 109 D4
Angela St HULME M15 .... 6 B4
Angel St ANC M4 .... 4 B1
Anglesea Av OFTN SK2 .... 133 C3
Angleside Av BNG/LEV M19 .... 126 B1
Angora Dr CSLFD M3 .... 2 A1
Anita St ANC M4 .... 5 D2
Annable Rd DROY M43 .... 76 A4
  GTN M18 .... 91 D3
Annald Sq DROY M43 .... 92 B1
Anne Nuttall Rd HULME M15 .... 6 B4
Annesley Rd NEWH/MOS M40 ...... 37 C4
Annie St SLFD M6 .... 65 D3
Annisdale Cl ECC M30 .... 61 C3
Ann Rd RDSH SK5 .... 129 D1
Anscombe Cl NEWH/MOS M40 ..... 71 C2
Ansdell Av CCHDY M21 .... 112 A2
Ansdell Dr DROY M43 .... 74 B3
Ansdell Rd RDSH SK5 .... 107 D4
Ansdell St CHH * M8 .... 51 D2
Ansell Cl GTN M18 .... 91 C3
Anselms Ct OLDS OL8 .... 39 D1
Ansleigh Av CHH M8 .... 32 B4
Ansley Gv HTNM SK4 .... 128 A2
Anslow Cl NEWH/MOS M40 .... 53 C4
Anson Av SWIN M27 .... 44 B3
Anson Rd DTN/ASHW M34 .... 107 C3
  RUSH/FAL M14 .... 103 C1
  SWIN M27 .... 44 B3
Anson St ECC M30 .... 61 C2

Answell Av *CHH* M8 ....32 B3
Antares Av *BRO* M7 ....68 A2
Anthony Cl *WGTN/LGST* M12 ....88 B2
Antilles Cl *WGTN/LGST* M12 ....104 B1
Antrim Cl *BNG/LEV* M19 ....126 A3
Anvil Wy *OLD* * OL1 ....22 B2
Apfel La *CHAD* OL9 ....21 C3
Apperley Gra *ECC* M30 ....62 B1
Appian Wy *BRO* M7 ....50 B4
Appleby Cl *EDGY/DAV* SK3 ....132 A4
Appledore Wk *CHAD* OL9 ....21 C3
Appleford Dr *CHH* M8 ....52 A3
Appleton Rd *HTNM* SK4 ....119 C3
Apple Tree Ct *ORD* M5 ....66 B3
Apple Wy *MDTN* M24 ....18 A3
Applewood *CHAD* OL9 ....19 C2
Apsley Gv *WGTN/LGST* M12 ....9 F5
Apsley St *STKP* SK1 ....130 A4
Aquarius La *SLFD* * M6 ....67 D1
Aquarius St *HULME* M15 ....86 B4
Arbor Av *BNG/LEV* M19 ....117 D2
Arbor Dr *BNG/LEV* M19 ....117 C2
Arbor Gv *DROY* M43 ....75 C2
Arbory Av *NEWH/MOS* M40 ....55 C1
Arbour Cl *SLFD* M6 ....66 A2
Arbroath St *OP/CLY* M11 ....74 A4
Archer Pk *MDTN* M24 ....16 B1
Archer Pl *STRET* M32 ....95 C3
Archer St *OP/CLY* M11 ....72 B3
Archie St *ORD* M5 ....83 D2
Archway *HULME* M15 ....86 A4
Arcon Dr *OLDTF/WHR* M16 ....100 B2
Ardale Av *NEWH/MOS* M40 ....36 B3
Ardcombe Av *BKLY* M9 ....15 D4
Ardeen Wk *BRUN/LGST* M13 ....9 E3
Arden Av *MDTN* M24 ....18 A4
Arden Gv *NEWH/MOS* M40 ....36 B4
Ardens Cl *SWIN* M27 ....25 C3
Arden St *CHAD* OL9 ....38 B2
Ardent Wy *BRO* M7 ....30 A4
Ardern Gv *STKP* SK1 ....133 C1
Ardern Rd *CHH* M8 ....32 A4
Ardern Wk *STKP* * SK1 ....129 D4
Ardwick Gn North *WGTN/LGST* M12 ....9 E3
Ardwick Gn South *BRUN/LGST* M13 ....9 E3
Ardwick Ter *WGTN/LGST* M12 ....88 B3
Argus St *OLDS* OL8 ....39 D3
Argyle Av *RUSH/FAL* M14 ....103 C3
  WHTF M45 ....11 D1
Argyle St *DROY* M43 ....75 D4
  GTN M18 ....91 C4
  SWIN M27 ....44 B2
Argyll Av *STRET* M32 ....96 A3
Argyll Cl *FAIL* M35 ....58 A2
Argyll Park Rd *FAIL* M35 ....58 A2
Argyll Rd *CHAD* OL9 ....38 A2
Arkendale Cl *FAIL* * M35 ....58 B2
Arkle Dr *CHAD* OL9 ....20 A1
Arkley Wk *BRUN/LGST* M13 ....9 D5
Ark St *BNG/LEV* M19 ....104 B3
Arkwright St *CHAD* OL9 ....21 D3
Arley Av *DID/WITH* M20 ....114 A4
Arley Moss Wk *BRUN/LGST* * M13 ....9 D4
Arlington Av *PWCH* M25 ....30 A3
  SWIN M27 ....44 A4
Arlington Rd *STRET* M32 ....96 A4
Arlington St *CHH* M8 ....32 A4
  CSLFD M3 ....2 B1
Arliss Av *BNG/LEV* M19 ....117 C4
Armadale Av *BKLY* M9 ....35 D1
Armentieres Sq *EDGY/DAV* SK3 ....132 B1
Arne St *CHAD* * OL9 ....20 B4
Arnfield Rd *DID/WITH* M20 ....115 D3

Edgy/Dav *EDGY/DAV* SK3 ....132 A4
Arnold Dr *DROY* M43 ....132 A4
Arnold Rd *OLDTF/WHR* M16 ....100 B4
Arnold St *EDGY/DAV* SK3 ....132 B2
  OLD OL1 ....23 D1
Arnott Crs *HULME* M15 ....86 A4
Arnside Av *CHAD* OL9 ....20 B4
  HTNM SK4 * 119 C3
Arnside Dr *SLFD* M6 ....64 A2
Arnside Gv *SALE* M33 ....109 C4
Arnside St *RUSH/FAL* M14 ....102 A3
Arran Av *OLDS* OL8 ....41 C2
  STRET M32 ....95 D3
Arrandale Ct *URM* * M41 ....94 A2
Arran Gdns *URM* M41 ....79 C4
Arran St *BRO* M7 ....50 A3
  NEWH/MOS M40 ....54 A1
Arras Gv *RDSH* SK5 ....107 C2
Arreton Sq *RUSH/FAL* M14 ....103 C2
Arrowfield Rd *CCHDY* M21 ....113 C3
Arrow St *BRO* M7 ....50 A4
Arthog Rd *DID/WITH* M20 ....125 D3
Arthur Rd *OLDTF/WHR* M16 ....99 D2
Arthur St *ECC* M30 ....61 D4
  PWCH M25 ....29 D1
  RDSH SK5 ....119 D2
  SWIN M27 ....44 A2
Artillery St *CSLFD* M3 ....7 D1
Arundale Av *OLDTF/WHR* M16 ....100 B4
Arundel Av *WHTF* M45 ....12 A2
Arundel St *HULME* M15 ....6 B3
  SWIN M27 ....24 B4
Ascension Sq *BRO* M7 ....68 A4
Ashbridge *TRPK* M17 ....81 C5
Ashbridge Rd *FAIL* M35 ....58 A3
Ashbrook Farm Cl *RDSH* SK5 ....107 C3
Ashbrook La *RDSH* SK5 ....107 C3
Ashbrook St *OP/CLY* M11 ....92 B2
Ashburn Av *BNG/LEV* M19 ....117 C4
Ashburn Gv *HTNM* SK4 ....128 B2
Ashburn Rd *HTNM* SK4 ....128 B2
Ashburton Rd West *URM* M41 ....79 C2
Ashbury Pl *NEWH/MOS* * M40 ....71 D1
Ashby Av *BNG/LEV* M19 ....126 B1
Ashby Gv *WHTF* M45 ....11 D2
Ashcroft Av *SLFD* M6 ....65 D1
Ashdale Cl *RDSH* SK5 ....120 A4
Ashdale Crs *DROY* M43 ....75 C4
Ashdale Dr *DID/WITH* M20 ....116 A4
Ashdene Rd *DID/WITH* M20 ....116 A3
  HTNM SK4 ....126 A3
Ashdown Av *BKLY* M9 ....34 A1
Ashdown Dr *SWIN* M27 ....45 D3
Ashdown Gv *BKLY* M9 ....34 A1
Ashdown Rd *HTNM* SK4 ....128 B2
Ashdown Ter *BKLY* M9 ....34 A1
Ash Dr *SWIN* M27 ....24 B3
Ashfield Cl *SLFD* M6 ....65 D2
Ashfield Dr *NEWH/MOS* M40 ....74 A1
Ashfield Gv *GTN* * M18 ....107 C1
Ashfield Rd *BRUN/LGST* M13 ....103 D2
  SALE M33 ....98 B4
  URM M41 ....94 A3
Ashfield Sq *DROY* M43 ....75 C4
Ashfield St *OLDS* OL8 ....39 D2
Ashford Av *ECC* M30 ....78 B1

RDSH * SK5	107	C3
SWIN M27	43	D3
Ashford Rd DID/WITH M20	114	B2
HTNM SK4	119	C3
Ashford Wk CHAD * OL9	20	B3
Ash Gv DROY M43	92	B3
HTNM SK4	119	C4
PWCH M25	11	D3
RUSH/FAL M14	103	D1
STRET M32	109	D1
SWIN M27	44	A4
Ashill Wk CSLFD M3	7	D1
Ashkirk St GTN M18	91	C4
Ashlands SALE M33	108	B4
Ashlands Av NEWH/MOS M40	36	B4
SWIN M27	43	B4
Ashlar Dr WGTN/LGST M12	88	C3
Ashlea Dl BKLY M9	33	D3
Ashley Av OLDTF/WHR M16	100	A1
SWIN M27	44	A3
Ashley Court Dr NEWH/MOS M40	38	A4
Ashley Crs SWIN M27	44	A2
Ashley Dr SWIN M27	44	A3
Ashley La BKLY M9	54	A1
Ashley Ms WHTF M45	12	A2
Ashley Rd DROY M43	74	B3
Ashley St CTN M18	21	D1
SLFD M6	65	D3
Ashlyn Gv RUSH/FAL M14	116	A1
Ashover Av WGTN/LGST * M12	89	C3
Ashover St STRET M32	97	D2
Ashridge Dr ECC M30	78	B1
Ash Rd DROY M43	75	C3
DTN/ASHW M34	107	D3
Ash St BKLY M9	53	C2
FAIL M35	56	B1
SLFD M6	66	A3
Ashton Crs CHAD OL9	38	B2
Ashton Hill La DROY M43	92	B1
Ashton La MDTN M24	17	D1
SALE M33	108	A4
Ashton New Rd OP/CLY M11	72	B4
Ashton Old Rd OP/CLY M11	88	B1
Ashton Rd BKLY M9	16	A4
DROY M43	75	D4
FAIL M35	58	B3
OLDS OL8	41	C1
Ashton Rd East FAIL M35	57	C1
Ashton Rd West FAIL M35	56	B2
Ashton St BKLY M9	54	A1
CHAD OL9	38	A2
Ash Tree Av DROY M43	75	C3
Ash Tree Rd CHH M8	32	B4
Ashurst Av OP/CLY M11	73	C3
Ashville Ter NEWH/MOS M40	35	C4
Ash Wk CHAD * OL9	21	C1
MDTN M24	17	C3
Ashwood CHAD OL9	19	D2
Ashwood Av DID/WITH M20	123	D3
DTN/ASHW M34	107	D2
Ashworth Cl CHAD OL9	39	C1
Ashworth St CHH M8	50	B4
FAIL M35	56	A3
OLD OL1	23	C3
Askett Cl NEWH/MOS M40	56	A3
Aspell Cl MDTN M24	17	C1
Aspen Wood Dr CHAD OL9	19	D2
Aspenwood Dr CHH M8	33	D4
Aspinall St MDTN M24	18	B2
RUSH/FAL M14	102	B2
Aspin La ANC M4	4	B1
Asquith St RDSH SK5	107	C3
Assheton Av DTN/ASHW M34	76	B3
Assheton Crs NEWH/MOS M40	74	A1
Assheton Rd NEWH/MOS M40	74	A1
Assheton Wy MDTN M24	17	D1
Assisi Gdns WGTN/LGST M12	88	B3
Astan Av DROY M43	74	A2
Astbury Av DTN/ASHW M34	77	C4
Astbury Crs EDGY/DAV SK3	132	A3
Astley St HTNM SK4	129	D4
OP/CLY M11	73	D4
Aston Av RUSH/FAL M14	101	C3
Astor Rd BNG/LEV M19	116	B2
SALQ M50	64	B4
Atcham Gv BKLY M9	15	C3
Athenian Gdns BRO M7	49	D4
Athens St STKP SK1	130	B4
Atherley Gv NEWH/MOS M40	38	A3
Atherstone Av CHH M8	32	A3
Atherton Cl FAIL M35	58	A4
Atherton St CSLFD M3	6	C1
ECC M30	62	A1
EDGY/DAV * SK3	132	A1
Athlone Av NEWH/MOS M40	54	A1
Athole St ORD M5	66	A4
Atholl Av STRET M32	95	D3
Athol Rd OLDTF/WHR M16	100	B4
Athol St ECC M30	61	C4
GTN M18	106	D2
HTNM SK4	129	C2
Atkinson Rd SALE M33	108	B3
URM M41	94	A3
Atkinson St CHAD OL9	22	A1
CSLFD M3	3	D1
STKP SK1	133	D2
Attercliffe Rd CCHDY M21	111	D3
Attewell St OP/CLY * M11	89	D1
Attleboro Rd NEWH/MOS M40	54	B2
Attlee Wy WGTN/LGST M12	71	D4
Attwood St WGTN/LGST M12	104	B2
Atwood Rd DID/WITH M20	125	D2
Atwood St CMANE M1	8	A2
Aubrey Rd DID/WITH M20	116	B3
Aubrey St ORD M5	83	D2
Auburn Dr URM M41	94	B4
Auburn Rd OLDTF/WHR M16	99	C1
Auburn St CMANE M1	8	A3
Auckland Dr SLFD M6	48	B4
Auckland Rd BNG/LEV M19	117	C1
Audax Wk NEWH/MOS M40	73	C1
Auden Cl OP/CLY M11	90	A1
Audenshaw Hall Gv DTN/ASHW M34	93	C2
Audenshaw Rd DTN/ASHW M34	93	D2
Audlem Cl NEWH/MOS M40	71	C1
Audley Av STRET M32	95	C1
Audley Rd BNG/LEV * M19	105	C3
Audrey Av GTN M18	91	D4
Audrey St BKLY M9	54	A1
Augustine Webster Cl BKLY M9	53	D1
Augustus St CSLFD M3	69	D1
Augustus Wy OLDTF/WHR M16	100	A1
Austen Rd ECC M30	62	A4
Austin Dr DID/WITH M20	125	D1
Austin Gv BNG/LEV M19	117	C1
Autumn St BRUN/LGST M13	102	B1
Avebury Cl CHH M8	51	C3
The Avenue BRO M7	49	D4
ECC M30	62	A4
Avenue St STKP * SK1	130	A3
Averill St NEWH/MOS M40	56	A4
Aveson Av CCHDY M21	112	A3
Avian Dr RUSH/FAL M14	115	C1
Avonbrook Dr NEWH/MOS M40	38	A3
Avoncourt Dr DID/WITH M20	124	B1
Avondale SWIN M27	26	B3
Avondale Dr SLFD M6	46	A4
Avondale Rd STRET M32	97	D1
Avondale St CHH M8	51	D2
Avon Gdns BNG/LEV M19	117	D3
Avonlea Dr BNG/LEV M19	116	B3
Avonlea Rd DROY M43	74	B3
Avon Rd BNG/LEV M19	117	C3
CHAD OL9	20	A1
Avon St EDGY/DAV SK3	132	B2
OLDS OL8	41	C1

Avril Cl *RDSH* SK5 ....120 A1
Avro Cl *RUSH/FAL* M14 ....102 A4
Axbridge Wk *NEWH/MOS* M40 ....71 C3
Axford Cl *CHH* M8 ....51 C3
Axon Sq *OLDTF/WHR* M16 ....101 C1
Aycliffe Av *CCHDY* M21 ....113 C4
Aycliffe Gv *BRUN/LGST* M13 ....103 D2
Aylesbury Av *URM* M41 ....94 B1
Aylesbury Cl *ORD* M5 ....66 B4
Aylesby Av *GTN* M18 ....105 C1
Aylesford Rd *RUSH/FAL* M14 ....103 C1
Aylsham Ms *SWIN* M27 ....44 A4
Ayres Rd *OLDTF/WHR* M16 ....99 D1
Aysgarth Av *GTN* M18 ....91 D3
Ayton Gv *RUSH/FAL* M14 ....103 D1
Aytoun St *CMANE* M1 ....5 D1
Azalea Av *GTN* M18 ....91 D3

B

Babbacombe Gv *BKLY* M9 ....15 C4
Back Acton St *CMANE* * M1 ....8 C1
Back Adcroft St *STKP* * SK1 ....133 C2
Back Ashley St *ANC* M4 ....4 C1
Back Balloon St *ANC* * M4 ....4 A2
Back Bank St *CHH* M8 ....69 D1
Back Bridge St *CSLFD* M3 ....3 E4
Back Chapel St *BNG/LEV* M19 ....104 B4
Back China La *CMANE* M1 ....4 C5
Back College Land *CSLFD* * M3 ....3 E4
Back Duncan St *BRO* M7 ....49 D1
Back Elsworth St *CSLFD* M3 ....69 D2
Back George St *CMANE* * M1 ....4 A5
Back Gilmour St *MDTN* M24 ....17 D1
Back Greaves St *OLD* OL1 ....23 C2
Back Halliwell La *CHH* * M8 ....51 C2
Back Hamilton St *BRO* * M7 ....50 A3
Back Hampson St *NEWH/MOS* M40 ....71 C1
Back Hilton St *BRO* M7 ....50 A2
Back Hope St *BRO* M7 ....50 A2
Back Howe St *BRO* M7 ....49 D2
Back Hulme St *ORD* M5 ....67 D4
Back Junction St *CMANE* M1 ....5 D4
Back King St *OLD* OL1 ....22 B3
Back La *AULW* OL7 ....59 C4
Back Piccadilly *CMANE* M1 ....4 B4
Back Pool Fold *CMANW* * M2 ....3 F4
Back Quay St *CSLFD* M3 ....2 C1
Back Red Bank *ANC* M4 ....69 D2
Back Roman St *BRO* M7 ....50 B3
Back St George's Rd *ANC* M4 ....4 C1
Back St Mark's La *CHH* * M8 ....51 C1
Back Scott St *OLDS* * OL8 ....23 C4
Back South Pde *CSLFD* M3 ....3 E4
Back Spear St *CMANE* M1 ....4 C3
Back Thomas St *ANC* * M4 ....4 B3
Back Turner St *ANC* * M4 ....4 B3
Back Water St *STKP* * SK1 ....130 A1
Bacup St *NEWH/MOS* M40 ....54 B1
Badby Cl *ANC* M4 ....71 C2
Bagot St *OP/CLY* M11 ....73 D3
  SWIN M27 ....24 B1
Baguley Crs *EDGY/DAV* SK3 ....132 A2
  MDTN M24 ....14 B5
Baguley St *DROY* M43 ....76 A4
Baildon St *NEWH/MOS* M40 ....54 B1
Bailey Rd *TRPK* M17 ....80 B2
Bailey St *OLD* * OL1 ....23 D2
  OP/CLY M11 ....74 A4
  PWCH M25 ....12 B4
The Bails *BRO* M7 ....49 D3
Bainbridge Cl *WGTN/LGST* * M12 ....88 A3
Bain St *SWIN* M27 ....45 C2

Baird St *CMANE* M1 ....9 D1
Baker St *HTNM* SK4 ....129 D2
  MDTN M24 ....18 A1
Bakewell Dr *DROY* M43 ....74 B3
  ECC M30 ....78 A1
  STRET M32 ....95 D2
Bakewell St *EDGY/DAV* SK3 ....132 A1
  GTN M18 ....105 D1
Bala Cl *ORD* M5 ....66 B3
Baldock Rd *DID/WITH* M20 ....126 A2
Baldwin Rd *BNG/LEV* M19 ....117 C3
Bale St *CMANW* M2 ....7 F1
Balfour Gv *RDSH* SK5 ....107 C4
Balfour St *CHH* M8 ....51 D1
  SLFD M6 ....48 A3
Balham Wk *WGTN/LGST* M12 ....89 C3
Ballantine St *NEWH/MOS* M40 ....73 D1
Ballbrook Av *DID/WITH* M20 ....114 B4
Balleratt St *BNG/LEV* M19 ....104 B4
Balliol St *CHH* M8 ....51 D1
  SWIN M27 ....44 B1
Balloon St *ANC* M4 ....4 A2
Balmain Av *GTN* M18 ....105 D2
Balmfield St *CHH* M8 ....51 D4
Balmforth St *HULME* * M15 ....6 B3
Balmoral Av *STRET* M32 ....97 C2
  WHTF M45 ....11 D2
Balmoral Dr *DTN/ASHW* M34 ....107 D3
Balmoral Gra *PWCH* M25 ....31 D2
Balmoral Rd *HTNM* SK4 ....127 D2
  RUSH/FAL M14 ....116 A1
  SWIN M27 ....26 B3
Balmoral St *GTN* M18 ....105 D1
Balsam Cl *BRUN/LGST* M13 ....9 D4
Baltic St *SLFD* M6 ....65 D3
Baltimore St *NEWH/MOS* M40 ....54 A4
Bamber St *BKLY* M9 ....16 A4
Bamburgh Dr *AULW* OL7 ....59 D4
Bamford Gv *DID/WITH* M20 ....124 B2
Bamford Rd *DID/WITH* M20 ....124 B2
Bamford St *CHAD* OL9 ....21 D1
  OP/CLY M11 ....73 C3
  STKP SK1 ....133 C1
Banbury Ms *SWIN* M27 ....25 C4
Banbury Rd *FAIL* M35 ....74 B1
  MDTN M24 ....17 C4
Banbury St *STKP* SK1 ....130 A1
Bancroft Rd *SWIN* M27 ....25 D4
Banff Rd *RUSH/FAL* M14 ....102 A1
Bangor St *HULME* * M15 ....85 C4
  RDSH SK5 ....130 A1
Bank Bridge Rd *OP/CLY* M11 ....72 B2
Bankfield Av *BRUN/LGST* M13 ....103 D2
  DROY M43 ....75 D3
  HTNM SK4 ....128 B3
Bankfield St *BKLY* M9 ....34 A4
  RDSH SK5 ....129 D1
Bankhall Rd *HTNM* SK4 ....127 D3
Bankhirst Cl *CHH* M8 ....32 B4
Bank House Rd *BKLY* M9 ....33 D1
Bank La *SLFD* M6 ....47 D3
Bankley St *BNG/LEV* M19 ....104 B4
Bankmill Cl *BRUN/LGST* M13 ....9 D4
Bank Pl *CSLFD* M3 ....2 B2
Bank Rd *CHH* M8 ....32 B3
Bankside *CHAD* OL9 ....22 A3
Bankside Ct *HTNM* * SK4 ....127 D5
Bank St *BRO* M7 ....51 C1
  CSLFD M3 ....2 A5
  DROY M43 ....92 A1
  OP/CLY M11 ....72 B3
  SALE M33 ....109 D4
Bannach Dr *CHAD* OL9 ....20 B1
Bannatyne Cl *NEWH/MOS* M40 ....37 D4
Banner Dale Cl *BRUN/LGST* M13 ....104 A1
Bannerman Av *PWCH* M25 ....30 A2
Bannerman Rd *DROY* M43 ....76 A4
Banner Wk *OP/CLY* M11 ....72 A4

Bannister St *STKP* SK1 ....133 C2
Bann St *EDGY/DAV* SK3 ....132 A1
Bantry Av *BKLY* M9 ....33 C2
Baptist St *ANC* M4 ....4 C1
Barbeck Cl *NEWH/MOS* M40 ....71 C3
Barber St *OP/CLY* * M11 ....91 D2
Barbican St *DID/WITH* M20 ....115 C3
Barbirolli Sq *CMANW* M2 ....7 F2
Barbon Wk *ANC* M4 ....5 E3
Barcicroft Rd *BNG/LEV* M19 ....126 B1
Barclays Av *SLFD* M6 ....47 C3
Barcliffe Av *NEWH/MOS* M40 ....36 B3
Barcombe Cl *STRET* M32 ....95 C2
Bardsley Av *FAIL* M35 ....57 C2
Bardsley St *CHAD* OL9 ....38 A2
HTNM SK4 ....129 C2
NEWH/MOS M40 ....56 A4
Barff Rd *ORD* M5 ....64 B3
Barfoot Br *SALE* M33 ....109 D2
Bar Gap Rd *OLD* OL1 ....23 C1
Baring St *CMANE* M1 ....9 D2
Barkan Wy *SWIN* M27 ....46 A1
Barker's La *SALE* M33 ....108 A4
Barker St *CSLFD* M3 ....69 C1
Barking St *NEWH/MOS* M40 ....71 D2
Bark Wk *HULME* M15 ....7 C5
Barkway Rd *STRET* M32 ....95 C4
Barlea Av *NEWH/MOS* M40 ....37 C3
Barleycroft St *OLDTF/WHR* M16 ...101 C1
Barlow Fold Rd *RDSH* SK5 ....120 B1
Barlow Hall Rd *CCHDY* M21 ....112 B4
Barlow La *ECC* M30 ....61 D3
Barlow La North *RDSH* SK5 ....120 A1
Barlow Moor Ct *DID/WITH* M20 .....124 A1
Barlow Moor Rd *CCHDY* M21 ....112 A3
DID/WITH M20 ....123 D1
Barlow Pl *BRUN/LGST* M13 ....9 E4
Barlow Rd *BNG/LEV* M19 ....105 D4
ORD M5 ....67 D4
STRET M32 ....98 A1
Barlow's Cft *CSLFD* M3 ....3 D3
Barlow St *ECC* M30 ....62 A4
OLDE OL4 ....23 D3
Barmouth St *OP/CLY* M11 ....89 C1
Barmouth Wk *OLDS* OL8 ....39 C3
Barnard Av *HTNM* SK4 ....128 A3
WHTF M45 ....12 A1
Barnard St *GTN* M18 ....105 C2
Barnby St *WGTN/LGST* M12 ....104 B2
Barnes Av *HTNM* SK4 ....127 D3
Barneswell St *NEWH/MOS* M40 .....55 D4
Barnett Av *DID/WITH* M20 ....115 C3
Barnett Dr *CSLFD* M3 ....2 B2
Barnfield Cl *ORD* M5 ....66 A4
Barnfield Crs *SALE* M33 ....108 A4
Barnfield Rd *BNG/LEV* M19 ....126 B1
SWIN M27 ....25 C3
Barnhill Av *PWCH* M25 ....30 A3
Barnhill Dr *PWCH* M25 ....30 A3
Barnhill Rd *PWCH* M25 ....29 D2
Barnhill St *RUSH/FAL* M14 ....101 C1
Barnsdale Dr *CHH* M8 ....51 D3
Barnsfold Av *RUSH/FAL* M14 ....115 D1
Barnside Wy *FAIL* M35 ....58 B2
Barnsley St *STKP* SK1 ....133 D1
Barnstable Dr *NEWH/MOS* M40 ......52 B3
Barnstead Av *DID/WITH* M20 ....116 A4
Barnston Av *RUSH/FAL* M14 ....102 A3
Barn St *OLD* OL1 ....22 B3
WHTF M45 ....11 C2
Baroness Gv *BRO* M7 ....67 D1
Barons Ct *FAIL* M35 ....56 A3
Barrack St *HULME* M15 ....6 A4
Barra Dr *URM* M41 ....79 C4
Barrass St *OP/CLY* M11 ....91 C2
Barrfield Rd *SLFD* M6 ....65 D1
Barr Hill Av *SLFD* M6 ....47 D4
Barrhill Cl *HULME* M15 ....6 C5

Barrington Av *DROY* M43 ....75 C4
Barrington St *OP/CLY* M11 ....73 D3
Barrow Hill Rd *CHH* M8 ....51 C4
Barrow St *CSLFD* M3 ....2 A4
Barry Lawson Cl *CHH* * M8 ....51 C2
Barry Rd *NTHM/RTH* M23 ....122 A3
RDSH SK5 ....120 A4
Bartlam Pl *OLD* OL1 ....23 C2
Bartlett St *OP/CLY* M11 ....90 A2
Barton Dock Rd *STRET* M32 ....95 D1
URM M41 ....95 D1
Barton Hall Av *ECC* M30 ....60 B4
Barton Highlevel Br *ECC* M30 ....78 A2
Barton La *ECC* M30 ....63 C4
Barton Rd *ECC* M30 ....78 B1
HTNM SK4 ....126 B4
MDTN M24 ....17 C1
STRET M32 ....109 D1
SWIN M27 ....45 D2
URM M41 ....78 B4
WALK M28 ....42 A4
Barton St *CSLFD* M3 ....7 D2
OLD OL1 ....22 A1
Barway Rd *CCHDY* M21 ....98 A4
Barwell Cl *RDSH* SK5 ....120 B1
Basechurch Wk *WGTN/LGST* * M12 ..89 C3
Basford Rd *OLDTF/WHR* M16 ....99 C1
Basildon Cl *BRUN/LGST* M13 ....88 A4
Basil St *HTNM* SK4 ....129 C2
RUSH/FAL * M14 ....102 B2
Baslow Av *BNG/LEV* M19 ....105 C3
Baslow Gv *RDSH* SK5 ....120 A4
Baslow Rd *DROY* M43 ....74 B2
STRET M32 ....95 D2
Baslow St *OP/CLY* M11 ....71 D4
Basset Av *SLFD* M6 ....48 B4
Basten Dr *BRO* M7 ....50 A3
Batchelor Cl *CCHDY* M21 ....113 D2
Bateson St *STKP* SK1 ....130 B3
Bateson Wy *OLDS* * OL8 ....23 C4
Bates St *BRUN/LGST* M13 ....104 A1
Bath Crs *OLDTF/WHR* M16 ....84 B4
Bath St *CHAD* OL9 ....21 D1
Batley St *BKLY* M9 ....53 D1
Battersby St *OP/CLY* * M11 ....91 D2
Battersea Rd *HTNM* SK4 ....126 B4
Batty St *CHH* M8 ....52 B4
Baxter St *OLDS* OL8 ....39 C3
Baydon Av *CHH* M8 ....51 C3
Bayfield Gv *NEWH/MOS* * M40 ....35 D4
Bayston Wk *WGTN/LGST* M12 ....89 C3
Bay St *CHAD* OL9 ....22 A2
Bayswater Av *NEWH/MOS* M40 ......73 C1
Baytree Av *CHAD* OL9 ....19 D1
Bay Tree Av *WALK* M28 ....42 B4
Baytree La *MDTN* M24 ....19 C1
Baywood St *BKLY* M9 ....53 C1
Bazaar St *SLFD* M6 ....66 B1
Bazley Rd *WYTH/NTH* M22 ....123 C4
Beacon Rd *TRPK* M17 ....79 D2
Beaconsfield *RUSH/FAL* * M14 ......115 D2
Beadham Dr *BKLY* M9 ....34 B4
Beal Cl *HTNM* SK4 ....126 A2
Beale Gv *CCHDY* M21 ....112 A1
Bealey Cl *GTN* M18 ....90 A3
Beaminster Rd *HTNM* SK4 ....127 D4
Beaminster Wk *BRUN/LGST* * M13 ..87 D4
Beamish Cl *BRUN/LGST* M13 ....9 E5
Beanfields *WALK* M28 ....42 A4
Beard Rd *GTN* * M18 ....105 D1
Beard St *DROY* M43 ....75 C4
Beardwood Rd *BKLY* M9 ....34 A1
Beatrice Av *GTN* M18 ....107 C1
Beatrice Rd *WALK* M28 ....43 C2
Beatrice St *SWIN* M27 ....25 C4
Beatrice Wignall St *DROY* * M43 ....92 B1
Beatson Wk *ANC* M4 ....5 E4
Beattock St *HULME* M15 ....6 B4

Beattock St HULME M15	6	B4
Beaufort Av DID/WITH M20	114	B4
SWIN M27	44	A1
Beaufort St CSLFD M3	6	C2
ECC M30	61	C2
PWCH M25	30	B1
Beaumont Rd CCHDY M21	112	B4
Beaver Rd DID/WITH M20	125	C2
Beaver St CMANE M1	8	A4
Bebbington St OP/CLY * M11	73	D4
Beckenham Rd CHH M8	51	D2
Becket Av BRO M7	50	B3
Beckett St GTN M18	105	C1
Beckfoot Dr BRUN/LGST M13	103	D2
Beckford St NEWH/MOS M40	53	D4
Beckhampton CI BRUN/LGST M13	87	D4
Beckley Av PWCH M25	29	D3
Beckside RDSH SK5	107	D4
Beck St CSLFD M3	7	D2
OP/CLY * M11	91	D2
Bedford Av OLDTF/WHR M16	100	A3
SWIN M27	44	A1
Bedford Rd ECC M30	62	B2
OLDTF/WHR M16	98	B3
Bedford St PWCH M25	12	B4
RDSH SK5	119	D2
Bednal Av NEWH/MOS M40	71	C4
Bedwell St OLDTF/WHR M16	101	D1
Beech Av DROY M43	75	C4
EDGY/DAV SK3	133	C3
SLFD M6	65	D1
WHTF M45	11	C1
Beech CI PWCH M25	30	B2
Beechcroft PWCH M25	30	B3
Beechcroft CI NEWH/MOS M40	71	C4
Beechdale CI NEWH/MOS M40	55	D1
The Beeches DID/WITH M20	124	A1
Beeches Ms DID/WITH M20	124	A1
Beechey Sq OLD * OL1	23	D2
Beechcroft Rd SWIN M27	44	B4
Beechfield St CHH M8	51	D3
Beech Gv RUSH/FAL M14	116	A1
SLFD M6	65	D1
Beech Hurst CI OLDTF/WHR * M16	100	A3
Beech Ms CCHDY M21	111	D1
OFTN SK2	133	D4
Beech Mt BKLY M9	53	C1
Beech Rd CCHDY M21	112	A1
EDGY/DAV SK3	132	B3
Beech St ECC M30	61	C4
FAIL M35	56	B1
MDTN * M24	17	C1
OLD OL1	23	D2
SWIN M27	45	C2
Beech Wk MDTN M24	17	C1
STRET M32	109	D1
Beechwood Av CCHDY M21	112	B4
Beechwood Dr WALK M28	43	C3
Beechwood Gv BKLY M9	53	D2
Beechwood Rd OLDS OL8	41	C3
PWCH M25	31	C2
Beede St OP/CLY M11	90	A1
Beehive St OLDS OL8	41	C2
Beeley St SLFD M6	49	C4
Beeston Av BRO M7	49	C3
Beeston Gv EDGY/DAV SK3	132	B4
WHTF M45	12	A2
Beeston St BKLY M9	53	D2
Beeth St OP/CLY M11	91	C3
Beeton Gv BRUN/LGST M13	103	D1
Beever St OLD OL1	23	D2
OLDTF/WHR M16	84	B4
Belding Av NEWH/MOS M40	38	A4
Beldon Rd BKLY M9	33	C1
Belfield Av DID/WITH M20	125	C2
PWCH M25	31	D1
Belford Av DTN/ASHW M34	107	D2
Belford Rd STRET M32	97	C2
Belfort Dr ORD M5	84	A1
Belgate CI WGTN/LGST M12	104	B1
Belgrave Av FAIL M35	58	A4
OLDS OL8	41	D1
Belgrave Ct OLDS OL8	41	C1
Belgrave Crs ECC M30	63	C2
Belgrave Rd NEWH/MOS M40	37	D4
OLDS OL8	41	C1
Belgravia Gdns CCHDY M21	111	D1
Belhaven Rd CHH M8	32	A3
Bell Clough Rd DROY M43	76	A2
Bell Crs OP/CLY M11	89	C1
Belldale CI HTNM SK4	127	D3
Bellerby CI WHTF M45	10	B1
Belle Vue Av WGTN/LGST M12	89	C4
Belle Vue St WGTN/LGST M12	89	D3
Bellew St OP/CLY M11	88	B1
Bellfield Av OLDS OL8	41	C3
Bellhill Gdns SLFD M6	66	A2
Bellis CI WGTN/LGST M12	71	D4
Bellott St CHH M8	51	D3
Bellott Wk OLD * OL1	22	B1
Bells Croft Av NEWH/MOS * M40	55	C2
Bell St DROY M43	76	A3
OLD OL1	23	D2
Bell Ter ECC M30	78	B1
Belmont Av SLFD M6	63	D2
Belmont CI HTNM SK4	129	D2
Belmont Rd SALE M33	108	B3
Belmont St ECC M30	62	A2
HTNM SK4	129	D2
OLD OL1	22	B1
ORD M5	65	C4
Belmont Wk BRUN/LGST M13	9	E5
Belmont Wy CHAD OL9	21	D1
HTNM SK4	129	D2
Belper Rd ECC M30	78	A1
HTNM SK4	127	C4
Belroy Ct PWCH * M25	30	A2
Belsay CI AULW OL7	59	D3
Belthorne Av SLFD M6	35	D3
Beltone CI STRET M32	96	A4
Belton Wk CHAD * OL9	22	A3
Belvedere Av RDSH SK5	107	C3
Belvedere Ct PWCH * M25	29	D2
Belvedere Dr MPL/ROM SK6	131	D2
Belvedere Rd RUSH/FAL M14	116	B1
SLFD M6	66	B2
Belvedere St SLFD * M6	67	C2
Belvoir Av BNG/LEV * M19	104	B3
Belwood Rd CCHDY M21	111	D1
Bembridge CI RUSH/FAL M14	102	B2
Bemsley PI ORD * M5	83	D1
Benbecula Wy URM M41	79	C4
Benbow Av WGTN/LGST M12	89	C4
Benbow St SALE M33	109	C4
Ben Brierley Wy OLD OL1	23	C2
Bendall St OP/CLY M11	91	D1
Bendix St ANC M4	4	C1
Benedict CI BRO M7	49	D4
Benfield Av NEWH/MOS M40	36	B3
Benfleet CI WGTN/LGST * M12	89	D3
Bengal St ANC M4	5	D2
EDGY/DAV SK3	132	B1
Benmore Rd BKLY M9	35	C2
Bennett Dr BRO M7	50	B3
Bennett Rd CHH M8	32	A4
Bennett St STRET * M32	96	B4
WGTN/LGST M12	88	B3
Benny La DROY M43	77	C2
Benson CI BRO M7	50	B4
Ben St OP/CLY M11	73	C3
Bentcliffe Wy ECC M30	6	C4
Bentinck St HULME M15	6	A4
Bent La CHH M8	51	C2
PWCH M25	30	B1
Bentley Rd BRO M7	50	B1
CCHDY M21	98	B4

Bentley St *CHAD* OL9 ....21 C2
Benton St *BKLY* M9 ....54 A2
Bent St *CHH* M8 ....51 D4
Bentworth Wk *BKLY* M9 ....53 D2
Beresford Crs *RDSH* SK5 ....106 B2
Beresford Rd *BRUN/LGST* M13 ....104 A2
   STRET M32 ....97 D1
Beresford St *FAIL* M35 ....56 B2
   RUSH/FAL M14 ....101 C2
Berigan Cl *WGTN/LGST* M12 ....88 B4
Berkeley Av *CHAD* OL9 ....38 A2
   RUSH/FAL M14 ....103 D1
   STRET M32 ....95 D1
Berkley Av *BNG/LEV* M19 ....104 B3
Berkshire Cl *CHAD* OL9 ....21 C4
Berkshire Pl *CHAD* * OL9 ....21 D1
Berkshire Rd *NEWH/MOS* M40 ....71 C2
Berlin Rd *EDGY/DAV* SK3 ....132 A3
Bermondsay St *ORD* M5 ....84 A1
Bernard St *BKLY* M9 ....53 C1
Berne Cl *CHAD* OL9 ....21 D3
Bernice Av *CHAD* OL9 ....21 C3
Berriedale Cl *OLDTF/WHR* * M16 ....100 A3
Berrie Gv *BNG/LEV* M19 ....117 C1
Berry Brow *NEWH/MOS* M40 ....74 A1
Berry St *CMANE* M1 ....9 D2
   ECC M30 ....78 A1
   SWIN M27 ....26 A3
Bertha St *OP/CLY* M11 ....90 A2
Bertram St *WGTN/LGST* * M12 ....89 D3
Berwick Av *HTNM* SK4 ....126 A3
   URM M41 ....95 D3
   WHTF M45 ....11 D2
Berwyn Av *BKLY* M9 ....15 D4
   MDTN M24 ....18 B1
Berwyn Cl *OL8* OL8 ....40 B2
Bessemer St *OP/CLY* M11 ....90 B2
Bessemer Wy *OLD* * OL1 ....22 B2
Beswick Dr *FAIL* M35 ....57 D3
Beswick Rw *ANC* M4 ....4 A2
Beswick St *ANC* M4 ....71 C3
   DROY M43 ....76 A4
Beta Av *STRET* M32 ....96 A3
Bethel Av *FAIL* M35 ....56 B2
Bethesda St *OLDS* OL8 ....41 C1
Bethnall Dr *RUSH/FAL* M14 ....114 B1
Betley Rd *RDSH* SK5 ....107 C4
Betley St *CMANE* M1 ....9 E1
Betnor Av *STKP* SK1 ....131 C4
Bettwood Dr *CHH* M8 ....32 A3
Betula Gv *BRO* M7 ....50 A3
Bevan Cl *WGTN/LGST* M12 ....71 D4
Bevendon Sq *BRO* M7 ....50 B3
Beveridge St *RUSH/FAL* M14 ....101 D2
Beverley Av *URM* M41 ....94 B1
Beverley Rd *SWIN* M27 ....46 B3
Beverley St *BKLY* M9 ....54 B4
Beverley Wk *OLDS* * OL8 ....22 B4
Beverly Rd *RUSH/FAL* M14 ....116 A2
Beverston Dr *BRO* M7 ....50 B3
Bevill Sq *CSLFD* M3 ....2 C1
Bewley St *OLDS* OL8 ....40 A3
Bexhill Dr *BRUN/LGST* M13 ....103 D2
Bexhill Wk *CHAD* OL9 ....21 C3
Bexington Rd *OLDTF/WHR* M16 ....100 A2
Bexley Sq *CSLFD* M3 ....2 B3
Bexley St *CHAD* OL9 ....21 D4
Beyer Cl *GTN* M18 ....90 B4
Bibby La *BNG/LEV* M19 ....117 C3
Bickerdike Av *WGTN/LGST* M12 ....105 C3
Biddisham Wk *NEWH/MOS* M40 ....53 C4
Bideford Rd *OFTN* SK2 ....131 C2
Bignor St *CHH* M8 ....51 D3
Bilbrook St *ANC* M4 ....70 A4
Billberry Cl *WHTF* M45 ....12 A1
Billing Av *WGTN/LGST* M12 ....9 E3
Billington Rd *SWIN* M27 ....47 D1
Bill Williams Cl *OP/CLY* M11 ....90 B1

Billy La *SWIN* M27 ....26 A3
Bindloss Av *ECC* M30 ....63 D2
Bingham St *SWIN* M27 ....45 C1
Bingley Cl *OP/CLY* M11 ....89 C1
Binns Pl *CMANE* M1 ....5 D4
Binstead Cl *RUSH/FAL* M14 ....103 D2
Birchacre Gv *RUSH/FAL* M14 ....116 A2
Birch Av *FAIL* M35 ....57 C3
   HTNM SK4 ....128 A1
   MDTN M24 ....17 D2
   OLDS OL8 ....40 A3
   OLDTF/WHR M16 ....98 B1
   SLFD M6 ....66 B2
   WHTF M45 ....11 C3
Birch Dr *SWIN* M27 ....46 A1
Birchell Wy *HULME* M15 ....7 F5
Birchenall St *NEWH/MOS* M40 ....54 A1
Birchenlea St *CHAD* OL9 ....38 B2
Birchfields Av *BRUN/LGST* M13 ....103 D2
Birchfields Rd *BRUN/LGST* M13 ....103 D2
Birch Gv *PWCH* M25 ....31 D3
   RUSH/FAL M14 ....103 C2
Birch Hall La *BRUN/LGST* M13 ....103 D3
Birchington Rd *DID/WITH* M20 ....114 B1
Birchin Pl *ANC* * M4 ....4 B4
Birch La *BRUN/LGST* M13 ....103 D1
Birchleaf Gv *ORD* M5 ....64 B3
Birch Polygon *RUSH/FAL* M14 ....103 C2
Birch Rd *CHH* M8 ....44 A4
   SWIN M27 ....44 A4
Birch St *DROY* * M43 ....93 C1
   WGTN/LGST M12 ....89 D3
Birchvale Cl *HULME* M15 ....6 C5
Birchwood *CHAD* OL9 ....19 D3
Birchwood Rd *MDTN* M24 ....18 B1
Birdhall Gv *BNG/LEV* M19 ....117 D1
Birkdale Av *WHTF* M45 ....10 A3
Birkdale Gv *ECC* M30 ....63 C3
   RDSH SK5 ....120 A4
Birkdale Pl *SALE* * M33 ....108 A3
Birkdale Rd *RDSH* SK5 ....120 A4
Birkdale St *CHH* M8 ....51 D2
Birley Pk *DID/WITH* M20 ....124 A2
Birles Av *RDSH* SK5 ....107 C2
Birtley Wk *NEWH/MOS* * M40 ....5 F1
Birt St *NEWH/MOS* M40 ....71 C1
Birwood Rd *CHH* M8 ....33 C3
Biscay Cl *OP/CLY* M11 ....72 A4
Bishop Cl *OLDTF/WHR* M16 ....100 B1
Bishopgate St *CHAD* OL9 ....20 B4
Bishop Marshall Cl *NEWH/MOS* * M40 ....53 C4
Bishop Rd *SLFD* M6 ....64 A1
Bishopsgate *CMANW* M2 ....7 F1
Bishops Rd *PWCH* M25 ....30 B2
Bishop St *MDTN* M24 ....19 C2
   STKP SK1 ....130 B4
Bishopton Cl *BNG/LEV* M19 ....105 D4
Bisley St *OLDS* OL8 ....22 A3
Bismarck St *OLDS* OL8 ....23 D4
Bispham Av *RDSH* SK5 ....107 C2
Bispham Gv *BRO* M7 ....50 B2
Bittern Dr *DROY* M43 ....76 B2
Blackberry La *RDSH* SK5 ....121 C2
Black Brook Rd *HTNM* SK4 ....119 C2
Blackburn Gdns *DID/WITH* M20 ....124 B1
Blackburn Pl *ORD* M5 ....67 D4
Blackburn St *CSLFD* M3 ....2 A1
   OLDTF/WHR M16 ....84 B4
   PWCH M25 ....30 B1
Blackcroft Cl *SWIN* M27 ....44 B1
Blackdown Gv *OLDS* OL8 ....40 B2
Blackett St *CMANE* * M1 ....88 A1
Blackfield La *BRO* * M7 ....50 A1
Blackfields St *BRO* * M7 ....50 A1
Blackford Rd *BNG/LEV* M19 ....118 A2
Blackford Wk *NEWH/MOS* M40 ....71 C2
Blackfriars Rd *CSLFD* M3 ....2 C1
Blackfriars St *CSLFD* M3 ....3 E3

Blackhill Cl *BRUN/LGST* M13 ....9 D4
Blackley New Rd *BKLY* M9 ....32 A2
Blackley Park Rd *BKLY* M9 ....34 A4
Blackley St *BKLY* M24 ....15 C2
  OLDTF/WHR M16 ....84 B1
Blacklock St *CSLFD* M3 ....69 C1
Blackpool St *OP/CLY* M11 ....73 D3
Blackrock St *OP/CLY* M11 ....72 A4
Blackshaw St *EDGY/DAV* SK3 ....132 B1
Blackstock St *BRUN/LGST* M13 ....102 B1
Blackthorn Av *BNG/LEV* M19 ....117 D2
Blackthorn Rd *OLDS* OL8 ....58 B1
Blackwin St *WGTN/LGST* M12 ....89 D3
Bladon St *CMANE* M1 ....8 C1
Blairhall Av *NEWH/MOS* M40 ....54 B2
Blair Rd *OLDTF/WHR* M16 ....100 B4
Blair St *OLDTF/WHR* M16 ....85 C4
Blakedown Wk *WGTN/LGST* M12 ....88 C4
Blakemore Wk *WGTN/LGST* * M12 ....71 D4
Blakey St *WGTN/LGST* M12 ....104 B1
Blanchard St *HULME* M15 ....85 D4
Blanche Wk *OLD* * OL1 ....23 D1
Bland Cl *FAIL* M35 ....56 B2
Blandford Av *WALK* M28 ....42 A1
Blandford Dr *NEWH/MOS* M40 ....37 C3
Blandford Rd *ECC* M30 ....61 D3
  HTNM SK4 ....128 A3
  SLFD M6 ....49 C4
Bland Rd *PWCH* M25 ....30 A3
Bland St *OLDTF/WHR* * M16 ....100 B1
Blanefield Cl *CCHDY* M21 ....113 D2
Blantyre Av *ECC* M30 ....79 D1
Blantyre Rd *SWIN* M27 ....46 A3
Blantyre St *ECC* M30 ....60 B2
  HULME M15 ....6 B3
  SWIN M27 ....26 B4
Blanwood Dr *CHH* M8 ....52 A2
Blaven Cl *EDGY/DAV* SK3 ....133 C4
Bledlow Cl *ECC* M30 ....62 B2
Blenheim Av *OLDTF/WHR* M16 ....100 A3
Blenheim Rd *OLDTF/WHR* M16 ....98 B2
Bletchley Cl *BRUN/LGST* M13 ....88 A4
Bletchley Rd *HTNM* SK4 ....126 B4
Blinco Rd *URM* M41 ....95 C4
Blind La *WGTN/LGST* M12 ....88 A2
Blisworth Av *ECC* M30 ....79 D1
Blisworth Cl *ANC* M4 ....71 C4
Block La *CHAD* OL9 ....21 D4
Blodwell St *SLFD* M6 ....66 A3
Bloom St *CMANE* M1 ....8 A2
  CSLFD M3 ....2 C5
Blossoms St *OFTN* SK2 ....133 C2
Blossom St *ANC* M4 ....5 D3
  CSLFD M3 ....3 D2
Blucher St *ORD* M5 ....67 D4
  WGTN/LGST M12 ....88 B3
Blue Bell Av *NEWH/MOS* M40 ....35 D4
Blue Ribbon Wk *SWIN* M27 ....26 B4
Bluestone Dr *HTNM* SK4 ....126 B2
Bluestone Rd *DTN/ASHW* M34 ....107 D3
  NEWH/MOS M40 ....54 B1
Blunn St *OLDS* OL8 ....41 C1
Blyborough Cl *SLFD* M6 ....65 D1
Blyton St *HULME* M15 ....87 C4
Boad St *CMANE* M1 ....9 D3
Boardman Fold Cl *MDTN* M24 ....17 D4
Boardman Fold Rd *MDTN* M24 ....17 C3
Boardman La *MDTN* M24 ....15 C1
Boardman Rd *CHH* M8 ....32 A3
Boardman St *ECC* M30 ....62 B4
Boar Green Cl *NEWH/MOS* M40 ....55 D2
Boat La *WYTH/NTH* M22 ....123 D4
  OLDE OL4 ....23 D3
Bobbin Wk *ANC* * M4 ....5 D3
Bob Brook Cl *FAIL* M35 ....55 D3
Bob Massey Cl *OP/CLY* M11 ....90 A1
Boddens Hill Rd *HTNM* SK4 ....127 D3
Boddington Rd *ECC* M30 ....60 A4
Bodley St *OP/CLY* M11 ....73 D3

Bodmin Crs *RDSH* SK5 ....121 C4
Boland Dr *RUSH/FAL* M14 ....116 A1
Bolderod Pl *OLD* OL1 ....23 D1
Bold St *HULME* M15 ....85 D4
  OLDTF/WHR M16 ....100 B1
  SWIN M27 ....26 A3
Bolesworth Cl *CCHDY* M21 ....111 C1
Bolivia St *ORD* M5 ....64 B3
Bollin Ct *HULME* M15 ....85 C3
Bollington Rd *HTNM* SK4 ....119 C4
  NEWH/MOS M40 ....71 C3
Bolton Av *BNG/LEV* M19 ....126 A3
Bolton Cl *PWCH* M25 ....29 C3
Bolton Rd *SLFD* M6 ....46 B3
  SWIN M27 ....26 B4
Bolton St *CSLFD* M3 ....2 C4
  RDSH SK5 ....119 D2
Bombay St *CMANE* M1 ....8 D2
Bonchurch Wk *WGTN/LGST* M12 ....90 A3
Bondmark Rd *GTN* M18 ....90 B3
Bond Sq *BRO* * M7 ....68 B2
Bond St *WGTN/LGST* M12 ....9 E2
Bonhill Wk *OP/CLY* M11 ....73 C3
Bonny Brow St *MDTN* M24 ....15 C2
Bonsall St *HULME* M15 ....7 F5
Boond St *ANC* M4 ....71 C4
  CSLFD M3 ....3 D2
Booth Av *RUSH/FAL* M14 ....116 A2
Booth Bridge Cl *MDTN* * M24 ....15 D2
Boothby Rd *SWIN* M27 ....25 D4
Boothfield *ECC* M30 ....60 B2
Booth Hall Rd *BKLY* M9 ....35 D2
Booth Rd *DTN/ASHW* M34 ....92 B2
  OLDTF/WHR M16 ....99 D3
  SALE M33 ....109 C3
Boothroyden Rd *BKLY* M9 ....15 D3
Boothroyden Ter *BKLY* M9 ....15 D3
Booth St *CHAD* OL9 ....22 B3
  CSLFD M3 ....3 E3
  EDGY/DAV SK3 ....132 B2
  FAIL M35 ....56 B2
  MDTN M24 ....19 C3
Booth St East *BRUN/LGST* M13 ....8 C5
Booth St West *HULME* M15 ....8 B5
Bootle St *CMANW* M2 ....3 E5
Bordale Av *BKLY* M9 ....54 A2
Bordan St *OP/CLY* M11 ....89 C1
Boringdon Cl *NEWH/MOS* * M40 ....55 C3
Borland Av *NEWH/MOS* M40 ....37 C4
Borough Av *SWIN* M27 ....26 B4
Borough Rd *SALQ* M50 ....65 C4
Borron St *STKP* SK1 ....130 B3
Borrowdale Crs *DID/WITH* M20 ....123 D1
Borsden St *SWIN* M27 ....25 C4
Borwell St *GTN* M18 ....91 C3
Boscombe Av *ECC* M30 ....78 B1
Boscombe St *RDSH* SK5 ....107 C3
  RUSH/FAL M14 ....102 A3
Bosden Fold *STKP* SK1 ....133 C1
Bosley Av *DID/WITH* M20 ....114 B3
Bossall Av *BKLY* M9 ....54 B1
Bostock Wk *BRUN/LGST* M13 ....9 D4
Boston Cl *FAIL* M35 ....38 A4
Boston Ct *SALQ* M50 ....82 B1
Boston St *HULME* M15 ....86 A4
  OLDS OL8 ....41 C1
Boswell Av *DTN/ASHW* M34 ....77 C4
Bosworth Cl *WHTF* M45 ....12 B1
Bosworth St *OP/CLY* M11 ....89 C1
Botanical Av *OLDTF/WHR* M16........................83 D4
Botany Rd *ECC* M30 ....80 B1
Botham Cl *HULME* M15 ....86 B4
Bothwell Rd *NEWH/MOS* M40 ....5 F1
Bottesford Av *DID/WITH* M20 ....114 A4
Bottomley Side *BKLY* M9 ....33 D3
Bottom O' Th' Moor *OLDE* OL4 ....23 D2
Boundary Gdns *OLD* OL1 ....22 B1
The Boundary *SWIN* M27 ....25 C1

Boundary La HULME M15.............86 B3
Boundary Rd SWIN M27.............45 C1
Boundary St WGTN/LGST M12.....89 D3
Boundary St East CMANE * M1......8 B4
Boundary St West HULME M15.......8 A5
Bourdon St NEWH/MOS M40........71 C2
Bourget St BRO M7.................51 C1
Bourne Av SWIN M27................45 C2
Bourne Dr NEWH/MOS M40..........36 A4
Bournelea Av BNG/LEV M19.........117 C3
Bourne St CHAD OL9...............39 C3
  HTNM SK4......................129 D1
Bournville Av HTNM SK4...........129 D1
Bournville Gv BNG/LEV M19........105 C4
Bourton Dr GTN M18...............105 C1
Bowden Rd SWIN M27...............45 D2
Bowdon Av RUSH/FAL M14..........101 C4
Bowdon St EDGY/DAV SK3..........132 B1
Bower Av HTNM SK4................128 B2
Bowerfold La HTNM SK4............128 B3
Bowers St RUSH/FAL M14...........116 A2
Bower St BRO * M7................50 B2
  MDTN M24.....................54 A4
  RDSH SK5.....................107 C3
Bower Ter DROY M43...............76 B2
Bowes St RUSH/FAL M14............101 C4
Bowfell Gv BKLY M9...............33 C3
Bowgreen Wk HULME M15............85 C3
Bowker Bank Av CHH M8............32 A4
Bowker St BRO M7.................50 A3
Bowland Av GTN M18...............107 D1
Bow La CMANW M2...................3 F5
Bowler St BNG/LEV M19............118 A1
Bowling Rd GTN M18...............106 B2
Bowness Av CHAD OL9..............39 C1
Bowness Av HTNM SK4..............119 D3
Bowness Dr SALE M33..............108 A4
Bowness Rd OP/CLY M11............92 A2
  STRET M32....................97 C2
Bowring St BRO * M7..............49 D4
Bowscale Cl BRUN/LGST M13........104 A1
Bow St CMANW M2...................3 E5
  OLD OL1......................23 C3
Boxtree Av GTN M18...............106 A3
Boyd St WGTN/LGST M12............89 D2
Boyer St OLDTF/WHR M16...........84 A4
Boyle St CHH M8..................52 A3
Brabham Cl CCHDY M21............112 A1
Brabham Ms SWIN M27..............43 D2
Bracadale Dr EDGY/DAV SK3........132 B4
Bracewell Cl WGTN/LGST M12.......89 D4
Bracken Cl DROY M43..............76 B1
Brackenlea Pl EDGY/DAV SK3.......132 A4
Brackenside RDSH SK5.............120 B1
Brackley Av HULME M15.............6 A4
Brackley Dr MDTN M24.............17 D4
Brackley Ldg ECC * M30...........63 C2
Brackley Rd ECC M30..............62 A1
  HTNM SK4.....................119 C3
Brackley Sq OLD * OL1............23 C1
Brackley St OLD OL1..............23 C1
Bradburn Cl ECC M30.............62 A4
Bradburn St ECC M30.............62 A4
Bradburn Wk CHH M8...............52 A3
Bradden Cl ORD M5................66 B4
Braddon Av URM M41..............94 A2
Braddon St OP/CLY M11............73 D4
Brade Cl OP/CLY M11..............90 B1
Bradfield Av SLFD M6.............64 B3
Bradfield Cl RDSH SK5...........106 B3
Bradfield Rd URM M41.............95 C3
Bradford Rd ECC M30.............62 B1
  NEWH/MOS M40.................71 D2
Bradford St OLD OL1..............22 B1
Bradgreen Rd ECC M30.............61 D2
Bradley Av BRO M7................49 C2
Bradley La STRET M32............109 C2

Bradleys Count CMANE * M1.........4 C4
Bradley St CMANE M1...............4 C3
Bradney Cl BKLY M9...............33 C1
Bradshaw Av DID/WITH M20........115 C2
  NEWH/MOS M40.................36 B4
Bradshaw Fold Av NEWH/MOS M40...37 C2
Bradshaw La STRET M32...........110 A1
Bradshaw St ANC * M4..............4 A2
  BRO M7.......................50 B3
  OLD OL1......................23 C2
Bradshaw St North BRO M7........50 A2
Bradstock Rd OLDTF/WHR M16......100 B2
Bradstone Rd CHH M8..............51 C4
Bradwell Av DID/WITH M20........114 A3
  STRET M32....................95 D2
Bradwen Av CHH M8................32 B4
Brady St STKP SK1...............130 B3
Braemar Av STRET M32.............95 D3
Braemar Rd RUSH/FAL M14.........116 B1
Brae Side OLDS OL8..............40 B1
Braeside STRET * M32.............95 D4
Bragenham St GTN M18.............90 B4
Brailsford Rd RUSH/FAL M14......116 B1
Brakenhurst Dr BRO * M7..........51 C3
Braley St CMANE * M1..............9 D5
Bramble Av ORD M5................84 B2
Brambling Cl DTN/ASHW M34........76 B3
Bramfield Wk HULME * M15..........6 B4
Bramhall La EDGY/DAV SK3.........133 C4
Bramhall La South OFTN SK2......133 C3
Bramhall St GTN * M18............91 D4
Bramley Av BNG/LEV M19..........117 D1
  STRET M32....................96 A3
Bramley Cl SWIN M27..............43 D3
Bramley Crs HTNM SK4............128 A4
Bramley Meade BRO M7.............50 B2
Bramley St BRO M7................50 B4
Bramwell Dr BRUN/LGST M13........9 E5
Brancaster Rd CMANE M1............8 B3
Brandish Cl BRUN/LGST M13.......103 C1
Brandon Av DTN/ASHW M34.........107 C2
  ECC M30......................50 A4
Brandon Brow OLD * OL1...........22 B1
Brandon Rd SLFD M6...............46 A4
Brandram Rd PWCH * M25...........30 A1
Brandsby Gdns ORD * M5............5 D4
Brandwood Av CCHDY M21..........123 C1
Branksome Av PWCH M25............29 D1
Branksome Dr BKLY M9.............15 C3
  SLFD M6......................45 D4
Branksome Rd HTNM SK4...........128 A2
Brannach Dr CHAD OL9.............20 B1
Bransby Av BKLY M9...............34 B1
Bransford Rd OP/CLY M11..........91 C1
Branson St NEWH/MOS M40..........37 C3
Branston Rd NEWH/MOS M40........37 C3
Brantingham Rd CCHDY M21.........99 C4
Brantwood Rd BRO M7.............50 A1
  HTNM SK4....................128 B1
Brantwood Ter BKLY * M9..........54 A2
Brassica Cl ECC M30.............60 B1
Brassington Av ORD M5............84 A1
Brassington Rd HTNM SK4.........126 B1
Bratton Wk BRUN/LGST * M13.......88 A3
Braunston Cl ECC M30.............79 D1
Bray Av ECC M30.................61 C2
Brayside Rd DID/WITH M20........126 A1
Brayston Fold MDTN M24...........15 D1
Brayton Av DID/WITH M20.........125 D3
Brazennose St CSLFD M3............3 E5
Brazil St CMANE M1................8 B2
Bread St GTN M18................91 D3
Breck Rd ECC M30.................61 C3
Brecon Av BNG/LEV M19...........117 D1
Brecon Wk OLDS * OL8.............39 C3
Bredbury Rd RUSH/FAL M14........102 A3
Bredbury St CHAD OL9.............21 C3
Breeze Mt PWCH M25...............30 A3

Brendon Av *NEWH/MOS* M40......**54** B2
  RDSH SK5..............................**120** A3
Brendon Dr *DTN/ASHW* M34......**77** C4
Brennan Cl *HULME* M15.............**86** B4
Brennan Ct *OLDS* OL8................**39** D3
Brennock Cl *OP/CLY* M11............**89** C1
Brentbridge Rd *RUSH/FAL* M14....**115** C3
Brentfield Av *CHH* M8................**51** C3
Brentford Rd *RUSH/FAL* M14.......**120** A3
Brentford St *BKLY* M9................**53** D2
Brentnall St *STKP* SK1...............**133** C2
Brentnor Rd *NEWH/MOS* M40......**36** B3
Brent Rd *HTNM* SK4...................**128** B4
Brentwood *SLFD* M6...................**65** D2
Brentwood Av *URM* M41..............**94** A3
  WALK M28..............................**43** C3
Brentwood Cl *OLDTF/WHR* M16....**101** C2
Brentwood Ct *PWCH* M25............**29** C2
Brentwood Dr *ECC* M30...............**62** A4
Brentwood Rd *SWIN* M27.............**44** A3
Brereton Dr *WALK* M28...............**42** A2
Brereton Rd *ECC* M30.................**60** A4
Breslyn St *CSLFD* M3..................**3** F1
Brethren's Ct *DROY* M43.............**92** B1
Brettargh St *SLFD* M6.................**66** B1
Brett St *WYTH/NTH* M22.............**123** D3
Brewer St *CMANE* M1...................**4** C3
Brewery St *SLFD* M3..................**130** A2
Brewster St *BKLY* M9..................**53** C1
Brian Av *DROY* M43.....................**76** B2
Brian Redhead Ct *HULME* * M15....**6** C4
Briarfield Rd *DID/WITH* M20.......**116** A3
  HTNM SK4..............................**119** D3
  WALK M28..............................**42** A2
Briar Hill Wy *SLFD* * M6..............**66** B2
Briar Hollow *HTNM* SK4..............**128** A4
Briarlea Gdns *BNG/LEV* M19.......**116** B4
Briarmere Wk *CHAD* OL9..............**21** D3
Briars Mt *HTNM* M8...................**127** D3
Briarwood Av *DROY* M43..............**74** B2
Brickley St *CSLFD* M3..................**69** D2
Brick St *ANC* * M4........................**4** B3
Bridcam St *CHH* M8....................**51** D4
Briddon St *CSLFD* M3..................**69** C2
Brideoak St *CHH* M8...................**51** D4
Bridgefield St *STKP* SK1.............**129** D3
Bridgelea Ms *DID/WITH* M20.......**115** C3
Bridgelea Rd *DID/WITH* M20........**115** C3
Bridgend Cl *WGTN/LGST* M12......**89** D3
Bridgenorth Av *URM* M41.............**95** C3
Bridge St *CSLFD* M3.....................**7** H3
  DROY M43..............................**91** D1
  MDTN * M24............................**17** C3
  OLD OL1.................................**23** D3
  STKP SK1...............................**130** A3
  SWIN M27..............................**45** D1
Bridge St Brow *STKP* * SK1.........**130** A3
Bridgewater Cir *TRPK* M17...........**78** B3
Bridgewater Pl *ANC* M4.................**4** A4
Bridgewater Rd *SWIN* M27............**46** A2
Bridgewater St *CSLFD* M3..............**7** D2
  CSLFD M3..............................**68** D3
  ECC M30.................................**61** C3
  OLD OL1.................................**23** D1
  SALE M33..............................**109** C4
  STRET * M32..........................**97** D2
Bridgewater Viad *HULME* M15........**7** D2
Bridgewater Wy *OLDTF/WHR* M16..**84** A4
Bridgnorth Rd *BKLY* M9...............**32** B2
Bridle Cl *DROY* M43....................**76** B2
Bridle Rd *PWCH* M25..................**13** C2
Bridlington Av *SLFD* * M6............**64** B2
Bridlington Cl *NEWH/MOS* M40....**55** D3
Bridport Av *NEWH/MOS* M40........**56** A4
Bridson St *SLFD* M6....................**65** D4
Briercliffe Ct *GTN* M18................**90** B3
Brierley Av *FAIL* M35..................**57** D2
Brierley Dr *MDTN* M24................**17** D2

Brierley Rd East *SWIN* M27.........**25** D4
Brierley Rd West *SWIN* M27........**25** D4
Brierley St *CHAD* OL9.................**21** D1
  OLDS OL8..............................**41** C2
Brierley Wk *CHAD* OL9...............**21** D1
Brigade Dr *STRET* M32................**96** B2
Brigadier Cl *DID/WITH* M20.......**115** C3
Brigantine Cl *ORD* M5.................**83** D1
Briggs Rd *STRET* * M32...............**98** A1
Briggs St *CSLFD* M3......................**2** B1
Brigham St *OP/CLY* M11..............**90** B1
Brightman St *GTN* M18................**91** C3
Brighton Av *BNG/LEV* M19.........**117** C2
  BRO M7..................................**50** B3
  RDSH SK5..............................**107** C3
Brighton Gv *RUSH/FAL* M14........**103** C3
  SALE M33..............................**108** B4
Brighton Pl *BRUN/LGST* M13......**87** C3
Brighton Range *GTN* * M18.........**107** C1
Brighton Rd *HTNM* SK4..............**128** B4
Brighton St *ANC* M4....................**69** D2
Bright Rd *ECC* M30.....................**62** B3
Brightside Wk *RUSH/FAL* M14.....**103** D1
Bright St *CHAD* OL9....................**38** B2
  DROY M43..............................**76** A4
  OLDS OL8..............................**22** A4
Brightwater Cl *WHTF* M45...........**11** D1
Brightwell Wk *ANC* M4...................**4** B3
Brigstock Av *GTN* M18................**90** B4
Brimelow St *MPL/ROM* SK6.........**131** D2
Brindale Rd *RDSH* SK5...............**131** D1
Brindle Cl *SLFD* M6.....................**66** A1
Brindle Heath Rd *SLFD* M6.........**66** A1
Brindle Pl *HULME* * M15..............**86** B3
Brindley Av *BKLY* M9..................**15** C1
  SALE M33..............................**109** D3
Brindley Rd *OLDTF/WHR* M16......**84** A4
Brindley St *ECC* M30...................**61** C2
  SWIN M27..............................**26** A3
Brinklow Cl *OP/CLY* M11.............**91** D2
Brinksway *EDGY/DAV* SK3...........**129** C4
Brinnington Crs *RDSH* SK5..........**131** C1
Brinnington Rd *STKP* SK1...........**130** B2
Brinsop Sq *GTN* M18...................**90** A3
Brinsworth Dr *CHH* M8...............**51** D3
Brisbane Av *HULME* M15.............**87** C4
Briscoe La *NEWH/MOS* M40.........**55** C4
Briscoe St *OLD* OL1....................**23** C1
Bristle St *HULME* M15...................**8** A5
Bristol Av *BNG/LEV* M19............**118** A1
Bristol St *BRO* M7.......................**50** B2
Bristowe St *OP/CLY* M11.............**74** A2
Britannia Rd *SALE* M33..............**109** C4
Britannia St *OLD* OL1..................**23** D2
  SLFD M6................................**48** B3
Britnall Av *WGTN/LGST* M12.......**88** B2
Brixham Rd *OLDTF/WHR* M16......**99** C1
Brixham Wk *BRUN/LGST* M13......**87** D2
Brixton Av *DID/WITH* M20..........**114** B3
Broadbent St *SWIN* M27..............**44** A2
Broadfield Gv *RDSH* SK5.............**106** B2
Broadfield Rd *GTN* M18...............**106** B2
  RUSH/FAL M14......................**101** D2
Broadgate *CHAD* OL9..................**37** D1
  MDTN M24............................**19** C3
Broadgate Meadow *SWIN* * M27....**45** C2
Broadhill Rd *BNG/LEV* M19........**116** B3
Broadhurst Av *SWIN* M27.............**26** A2
Broadhurst St *EDGY/DAV* SK3......**132** B2
Broadlands Rd *SWIN* M27............**43** D3
Broadlea Rd *BNG/LEV* M19.........**116** B4
Broadmeadow Av *OLDTF/WHR* M16..**101** C4
Broadmoss Dr *BKLY* M9...............**35** D3
Broadmoss Rd *BKLY* M9..............**35** D2
Broadmount Ter *CHAD* * OL9.......**39** C1
Broad Oak Crs *OLDS* OL8...........**41** D3
Broad Oak Pk *ECC* M30..............**62** A1

WALK M28	43	C3
Broad Rd *SALE* M33	109	D4
Broadstone Cl *PWCH* M25	29	D2
Broadstone Hall Rd North *HTNM* SK4	119	C3
Broadstone Hall Rd South *HTNM* SK4	119	C3
Broadstone Rd *HTNM* SK4	119	C3
Broad St *MDTN* M24	15	D2
SWIN M27	47	C3
Broadway *CHAD* OL9	38	A2
DROY M43	92	B1
FAIL M35	56	A1
SALE M33	108	B4
SALQ M50	82	B1
Broadway North *DROY* M43	92	B1
Broadway St *OLDS* OL8	41	C1
Broadwell Dr *BKLY* M9	53	D2
Brocade Cl *CSLFD* M3	2	A1
Brock Cl *OP/CLY* M11	91	C2
Brockford Dr *BKLY* M9	16	B4
Brocklebank Rd *RUSH/FAL* M14	115	D1
Brocklehurst St *BKLY* M9	54	B1
Brockley Av *RUSH/FAL* M14	102	A3
Brock St *ANC* * M1	5	D4
Brodick St *NEWH/MOS* M40	54	A1
Brodie Cl *ECC* M30	61	C3
Brogan St *GTN* M18	91	C1
Bromborough Av *DID/WITH* M20	114	B3
Bromfield Av *BKLY* M9	34	A4
Bromley St *ANC* M4	70	A2
CHAD OL9	38	B3
Bromlow St *OP/CLY* M11	73	D4
Brompton Av *FAIL* M35	58	A1
Brompton Rd *HTNM* SK4	127	D3
RUSH/FAL M14	102	A3
STRET M32	95	C2
Brompton St *OLDE* OL4	23	D4
Bromsgrove Av *ECC* M30	61	C3
Bromshill Dr *BRO* M7	50	B3
Brondgate Meadow *SWIN* M27	45	C3
Bronte St *HULME* M15	86	B4
Brook Av *BNG/LEV* M19	105	C3
DROY * M43	74	B4
HTNM SK4	119	C3
SWIN M27	45	C2
Brookbank Cl *MDTN* M24	18	A2
Brookburn Rd *CCHDY* M21	111	D2
Brook Cl *WHTF* M45	12	A1
Brookdale Av *NEWH/MOS* M40	74	A1
Brookdale St *FAIL* M35	56	A1
Brookdene Rd *BNG/LEV* M19	116	B3
Brook Dr *WHTF* M45	12	A1
Brookfield *PWCH* M25	30	A1
Brookfield Av *CCHDY* M21	112	B3
SLFD M6	64	B2
STKP SK1	133	C2
Brookfield Cl *OFTN* SK2	133	D2
Brookfield Dr *SWIN* M27	25	D4
Brookfield Rd *CHH* M8	32	B4
ECC M30	61	C1
Brookfield St *OLDS* OL8	23	C4
Brookfold *FAIL* M35	56	B1
Brookfold Rd *HTNM* SK4	119	C3
Brook Green La *GTN* M18	107	C2
Brookhead Av *DID/WITH* * M20	114	A2
Brookhill St *NEWH/MOS* M40	71	D2
Brookhouse Av *ECC* M30	60	B4
Brookhurst Rd *GTN* M18	106	A1
Brooklands Av *CHAD* OL9	21	C3
DID/WITH M20	114	B3
Brooklands Cl *HTNM* SK4	119	C3
Brooklands Dr *DROY* M43	76	B2
Brooklands Rd *PWCH* M25	31	C3
RDSH SK5	106	B3
SWIN M27	44	B3
Brook La *OLDS* OL8	41	D1
Brooklawn Dr *DID/WITH* M20	125	C3
PWCH M25	12	B3
Brookleigh Rd *DID/WITH* M20	116	A3
Brooklyn Av *OLDTF/WHR* M16	99	C3
RUSH/FAL M14	115	D2
Brook Rd *HTNM* SK4	118	B4
Brooks Dr *HALE* M33	56	B3
Brookshaw St *OP/CLY* M11	72	B4
Brookside Av *DROY* M43	76	B2
Brookside Crs *MDTN* M24	18	B3
Brookside Dr *PWCH* M25	31	C4
Brookside Rd *NEWH/MOS* M40	35	D4
OLDTF/WHR M16	99	D2
Brooks St *STKP* SK1	133	C2
Brookstone Cl *CCHDY* M21	113	C3
Brook St *CHAD* OL9	21	C1
CMANE M1	8	B3
FAIL M35	56	A3
OLD OL1	23	D1
SALE M33	109	D4
SLFD M6	67	C1
SWIN M27	44	A1
Brookthorpe Av *BNG/LEV* M19	116	B3
Brookway Cl *BNG/LEV* M19	126	B1
Brookwood Av *CHH* M8	52	B1
Broom Av *BNG/LEV* M19	105	D4
BRO M7	50	B1
RDSH SK5	120	A3
Broome Gv *FAIL* M35	57	C3
Broome St *CHAD* OL9	22	A3
Broomfield *SWIN* M27	47	C3
Broomfield Cl *RDSH* SK5	120	A3
Broomfield Dr *CHH* M8	51	C2
RDSH SK5	120	A3
Broomfield Rd *HTNM* SK4	128	B1
Broomhall Rd *BKLY* M9	14	B4
SWIN M27	47	C3
Broomhurst Av *OLDS* OL8	40	A1
Broom La *BNG/LEV* M19	118	A1
BRO M7	50	A1
Broom St *SWIN* M27	47	C3
Broomwood Wk *HULME* * M15	7	F5
Broseley Av *DID/WITH* M20	126	A2
Broseley Rd *OLDTF/WHR* M16	98	B3
Brotherton Cl *HULME* M15	6	A4
Brotherton Dr *CSLFD* M3	2	B2
Broughton La *BRO* M7	50	B4
Broughton Rd *RDSH* SK5	130	A1
SLFD M6	67	C1
Broughton Rd East *SLFD* M6	67	C1
Broughton St *CHH* M8	51	C4
Brow Av *MDTN* M24	18	A3
Browfield Av *ORD* M5	84	A2
Browmere Dr *DID/WITH* M20	124	A1
Brownacre St *DID/WITH* M20	115	C3
Browncross St *CSLFD* M3	2	C4
Brownhills Ct *CCHDY* * M21	112	A1
Brownhill St *OP/CLY* * M11	89	D1
Browning Av *DROY* M43	75	D4
Browning Rd *RDSH* SK5	106	A4
SWIN M27	44	B1
Browning St *CSLFD* M3	2	B3
HULME M15	85	C3
Brownlow Wk *BRUN/LGST* * M13	9	D4
Brown St *CHAD* OL9	20	B2
CSLFD M3	3	D3
FAIL M35	56	B2
OLD OL1	23	D2
SLFD M6	66	A4
STKP SK1	129	D4
Brownsville Rd *HTNM* SK4	118	A4
Brownwood Av *STKP* SK1	131	C4
Broxton St *NEWH/MOS* M40	72	A2
Broxwood Cl *GTN* * M18	91	C4
Brundrett's Rd *CCHDY* M21	112	A1
Brundrett St *STKP* SK1	133	C1
Brunel Av *ORD* M5	67	C4
Brunel Cl *STRET* M32	97	D3
Brunet Wk *WGTN/LGST* * M12	89	C3
Brunswick Rd *DID/WITH* M20	115	D3
Brunswick Sq *OLD* * OL1	23	C3

Brunswick St *BRUN/LGST* M13............9 D5
　　OLD OL1 ....22 B1
　　STREET M32 ....109 D1
Brunton Av *RDSH* SK5 ....120 A3
Brunt St *RUSH/FAL* M14 ....102 A2
Brussels St *EDGY/DAV* SK3 ....132 A3
Bruton Av *STRET* M32 ....96 A4
Bryan Rd *CCHDY* M21 ....99 C3
Bryant Cl *BRUN/LGST* M13 ....87 D4
Brydon Av *WGTN/LGST* M12 ....9 F3
Brydon Cl *SLFD* M6 ....66 A3
Brynden Av *DID/WITH* M20 ....115 D4
Bryn Dr *RDSH* SK5 ....120 A4
Brynford Av *BKLY* M9 ....14 B4
Brynorme Rd *CHH* M8 ....82 B3
Brynton Rd *BRUN/LGST* M13 ....103 D3
Buchanan St *SWIN* M27 ....26 A4
Buchan St *OP/CLY* M11 ....73 C5
Buckden Rd *HTNM* SK4 ....119 C2
Buckfast Cl *CCHDY* M21 ....99 C4
Buckfield Av *ORD* M5 ....84 A2
Buckhurst Rd *BNG/LEV* M19 ....104 B4
Buckingham Av *ORD* M5 ....65 C3
　　WHTF M45 ....11 C1
Buckingham Rd *CCHDY* M21 ....99 C4
　　DROY M43 ....74 B4
　　HTNM SK4 ....118 B4
　　PWCH * M25 ....30 A3
　　STRET M32 ....83 C4
　　SWIN M27 ....26 B3
Buckingham Rd West *HTNM* SK4 ....127 D1
Buckingham St *OFTN* * SK2 ....133 D2
　　ORD M5 ....66 A4
Buckland Av *BKLY* M9 ....32 B2
Buckland Rd *SLFD* M6 ....65 C1
Buckley Av *GTN* M18 ....105 D1
Buckley La *PWCH* M25 ....28 D2
Buckley Rd *GTN* M18 ....105 C1
Buckley St *BRO* M7 ....68 A1
　　CHAD OL9 ....20 B2
　　OP/CLY M11 ....91 D2
　　RDSH SK5 ....106 B3
Bucklow Av *RUSH/FAL* M14 ....102 A4
Buckthorn Cl *CCHDY* M21 ....113 C3
Buckthorn La *ECC* M30 ....60 D1
Buddleia Gv *BRO* M7 ....50 A3
Bude Av *RDSH* SK5 ....121 C4
Budsworth Av *DID/WITH* M20 ....115 C2
Buerton Av *BKLY* M9 ....14 B4
Bugle St *CMANE* * M1 ....7 D2
Buile Dr *BKLY* M9 ....35 C3
Buile Hill Dr *ORD* M5 ....65 C2
Buile St *BRO* M7 ....50 B2
Bulkeley St *EDGY/DAV* SK3 ....132 A2
Buller Rd *BRUN/LGST* M13 ....104 A3
Buller St *DROY* M43 ....93 C1
Bullock St *OFTN* SK2 ....133 C2
Bulteel St *ECC* M30 ....61 C2
Bunkers HI *PWCH* M25 ....28 B2
Bunsen St *CMANE* * M1 ....4 C4
Bunyard St *CHH* M8 ....52 A3
Burbridge Cl *OP/CLY* M11 ....88 D1
Burdale Dr *SLFD* M6 ....64 A1
Burder St *OLDS* OL8 ....39 D5
Burdett Wy *WGTN/LGST* M12 ....88 B4
Burdith Av *RUSH/FAL* M14 ....101 D3
Burford Av *OLDTF/WHR* M16 ....100 A3
　　URM M41 ....94 B1
Burford Dr *OLDTF/WHR* M16 ....100 A3
　　SWIN M27 ....25 D3
Burford Rd *OLDTF/WHR* M16 ....100 A3
Burgess Dr *FAIL* M35 ....57 D2
Burgin Wk *NEWH/MOS* M40 ....70 B1
Burland Cl *BRO* M7 ....50 A4
Burleigh Ms *CCHDY* M21 ....112 A3
Burleigh Rd *STRET* M32 ....97 D1
Burleigh St *BRUN/LGST* M13 ....87 C4
Burley Ct *HTNM* * SK4 ....128 B3

Burlington Av *OLDS* OL8 ....40 B1
Burlington Cl *HTNM* SK4 ....126 B3
Burlington Rd *DID/WITH* M20 ....115 D2
　　ECC M30 ....62 B1
Burlington St *HULME* M15 ....86 B4
Burman St *OP/CLY* M11 ....92 A2
Burnaby St *OLDS* * OL8 ....21 D4
Burnage Av *BNG/LEV* M19 ....117 C1
Burnage Hall Rd *BNG/LEV* M19 ....116 B2
Burnage La *BNG/LEV* M19 ....117 C4
　　HTNM SK4 ....126 A3
Burnage Range *BNG/LEV* M19 ....104 B4
Burnbray Av *BNG/LEV* M19 ....116 B3
Burnell Cl *NEWH/MOS* M40 ....5 F1
Burnett Av *ORD* M5 ....84 A1
Burnett Cl *NEWH/MOS* M40 ....53 C4
Burnfield Rd *GTN* M18 ....106 A2
Burnham Av *RDSH* SK5 ....107 C4
Burnham Dr *BNG/LEV* M19 ....117 C2
Burnham Rd *DTN/ASHW* M34 ....107 D2
Burnley St *CHAD* OL9 ....21 C2
　　FAIL M35 ....57 D2
Burnsall Av *WHTF* M45 ....10 A1
Burns Av *SWIN* M27 ....25 C4
Burns Cl *OP/CLY* M11 ....72 A4
Burns Gdns *PWCH* * M25 ....29 C2
Burns Gv *DROY* M43 ....75 D3
Burnside Av *HTNM* SK4 ....119 D3
　　SLFD M6 ....46 A4
Burnside Dr *BNG/LEV* M19 ....116 B2
Burnthorp Av *BKLY* M9 ....33 C2
Burrows Av *CCHDY* M21 ....112 A3
Burslem Av *DID/WITH* M20 ....114 B3
Burstead St *GTN* M18 ....91 D3
Burstock St *ANC* M4 ....70 A2
Burston St *GTN* M18 ....90 B3
Burton Av *DID/WITH* M20 ....115 C3
Burton Gv *WALK* M28 ....43 D1
Burton Rd *DID/WITH* M20 ....124 A1
Burton St *HTNM* SK4 ....129 D2
　　MDTN M24 ....17 C1
　　NEWH/MOS M40 ....70 A1
Burton Wk *CSLFD* M3 ....2 B2
　　HTNM SK4 ....129 D1
Burtree St *WGTN/LGST* * M12 ....89 D3
Bury Av *OLDTF/WHR* M16 ....100 A2
Bury New Rd *BRO* M7 ....50 A2
　　PWCH M25 ....11 D3
Bury Old Rd *PWCH* M25 ....11 D3
Bury Pl *OP/CLY* M11 ....21 D1
Bury St *CSLFD* M3 ....3 D2
　　RDSH SK5 ....130 A2
Bush St *NEWH/MOS* M40 ....53 D4
Busk Rd *CHAD* OL9 ....21 D1
Busk Wk *CHAD* * OL9 ....21 D1
Bute Av *OLDS* OL8 ....41 C2
Bute St *NEWH/MOS* M40 ....35 C4
　　ORD M5 ....65 C4
Butler Gn *CHAD* OL9 ....38 B1
Butler La *NEWH/MOS* M40 ....5 F1
Butler St *ANC* M4 ....5 F2
Butman St *GTN* M18 ....92 A3
Butter La *CSLFD* * M3 ....3 E4
Buttermere Av *SWIN* M27 ....45 C3
Buttermere Ct *STRET* M32 ....96 B2
Butterstile Av *PWCH* M25 ....29 C3
Butterstile Cl *PWCH* M25 ....29 C4
Butterstile La *PWCH* M25 ....29 C3
Butterwick Cl *WGTN/LGST* M12 ....105 C2
Butterworth La *CHAD* OL9 ....37 D2
Butterworth St *CHAD* * OL9 ....21 C2
　　MDTN M24 ....18 B2
　　OP/CLY M11 ....89 D1
Butt Hill Av *PWCH* M25 ....30 A2
Butt Hill Dr *PWCH* M25 ....30 A2
Butt Hill Rd *PWCH* M25 ....30 A2
Buttress St *GTN* M18 ....90 B3
Buxton Av *DID/WITH* M20 ....114 A3

Buxton La *DROY* M43 ....**91** D1
Buxton Pl *OLDS* * OL8 ....**22** B4
Buxton Rd *STRET* M32 ....**95** D2
Buxton St *CMANE* M1 ....**9** D1
Byrcland St *WGTN/LGST* M12 ....**88** B1
Byrom Av *BNG/LEV* M19 ....**105** D4
Byrom St *CSLFD* M3 ....**3** D1
   OLDTF/WHR M16 ....**100** A1
   ORD M5 ....**83** D1
Byron Av *DROY* M43 ....**75** D2
   PWCH M25 ....**29** C2
   SWIN M27 ....**44** B3
Byron Gv *RDSH* SK5 ....**106** B4
Byron Rd *STRET* M32 ....**97** D2
Byron St *ECC* M30 ....**62** A3
   OLDS OL8 ....**39** C3

C

Cablestead Wk *OP/CLY* M11.................**89** C1
Cable St *CSLFD* M3 ....**3** D2
Cabot Pl *RDSH* SK5................................**130** A1
Cabot St *BRUN/LGST* M13 ....**9** D5
Caddington Rd *CCHDY* M21 ....**112** B1
Cadogan Pl *BRO* * M7................................**31** D4
Cadogan St *RUSH/FAL* M14 ....**101** D1
Cadum Wk *BRUN/LGST* M13......................**9** E5
Caen Av *NEWH/MOS* M40 ....**36** B2
Cairn Dr *SLFD* M6 ....**49** D4
Cairn Wk *OP/CLY* * M11...........................**72** A4
Cairnwell Rd *CHAD* OL9 ....**20** B1
Caister Av *WHTF* M45 ....**11** D2
Caistor Cl *OLDTF/WHR* M16 ....**113** D1
Caistor St *STKP* SK1 ....**131** C1
Caistor Wk *OLD* OL1 ....**23** C1
Cakebread St *WGTN/LGST* M12 ....**9** E1
Calbourne Crs *WGTN/LGST* M12........**105** D2
Caldbeck Av *SALE* M33 ....**110** B4
Caldecott Rd *BKLY* M9 ....**14** B4
Calder Cl *RDSH* SK5..............................**120** B4
Calder Dr *SWIN* M27 ....**25** D4
Calder St *ORD* M5 ....**6** A2
Caldervale Av *CCHDY* M21 ....**122** B1
Caldon Cl *ECC* M30 ....**79** C1
Caldy Rd *SLFD* M6 ....**65** C1
Caledon Av *NEWH/MOS* M40 ....**54** B1
Caledonian Dr *ECC* M30 ....**79** C1
Caledonia Wy *STRET* M32 ....**80** B4
Cale Gn *EDGY/DAV* SK3 ....**133** C3
Cale St *OFTN* SK2 ....**133** C2
Caley St *CMANE* M1 ....**8** A2
Calgary St *GTN* M18 ....**90** B4
Calico Cl *CSLFD* M3 ....**8** A1
Callingham Rd *CCHDY* M21 ....**113** C4
Callum Wk *BRUN/LGST* * M13 ....**87** D3
Calluna Ms *DID/WITH* * M20 ....**124** B1
Calthorpe Av *BKLY* M9 ....**52** B2
Calton Av *BRO* M7 ....**48** B3
Calver Av *ECC* M30 ....**78** B1
Calverley Av *BNG/LEV* M19 ....**117** C3
Calverton Dr *NEWH/MOS* M40 ....**55** D2
Calvert St *ORD* M5 ....**65** C3
Calver Wk *NEWH/MOS* * M40 ....**5** F1
Calvine Wk *NEWH/MOS* * M40 ....**70** B2
Cambell Rd *ECC* M30 ....**61** C3
Cambert La *GTN* M18 ....**90** B4
Camberwell St *CHH* * M8 ....**69** D1
   OLDS * OL8 ....**40** B1
Camborne St *RUSH/FAL* M14 ....**102** A3
Cambo Wk *HTNM* SK4 ....**127** C1
Cambrai Crs *ECC* M30 ....**60** B1
Cambrian St *NEWH/MOS* M40 ....**71** D3
Cambridge Av *OLDTF/WHR* M16 ....**99** D1
Cambridge Dr *DTN/ASHW* M34 ....**107** D2
Cambridge Gv *ECC* M30 ....**63** C3
   WHTF M45 ....**11** D1

Cambridge Rd *BKLY* M9 ....**34** A4
   DROY M43 ....**75** C2
   FAIL M35 ....**57** C4
   HTNM SK4 ....**118** B4
Cambridge St *BRO* M7 ....**68** B1
   CHAD OL9 ....**39** D1
   HULME M15 ....**7** F3
   OFTN SK2 ....**133** D3
Camden Av *NEWH/MOS* M40 ....**73** D1
Camelford Cl *HULME* * M15 ....**86** B3
Camelia Rd *BKLY* M9 ....**52** B2
Cameron St *CMANE* * M1 ....**7** E2
Campbell Rd *BRUN/LGST* M13 ....**104** A3
   SWIN M27 ....**44** B3
Campbell St *RDSH* SK5 ....**107** C4
Camp St *BRO* M7 ....**67** D1
   CSLFD M3 ....**7** D1
Camrose Wk *BRUN/LGST* * M13............**88** A4
Canada St *NEWH/MOS* M40 ....**71** D1
   OFTN SK2 ....**133** D2
Canal Bank *ECC* M30 ....**61** D2
Canal Bridge La *OP/CLY* M11 ....**89** C1
Canal Cottages Yd *ANC* * M4 ....**5** F5
Canal Side *ECC* M30 ....**61** D2
Canal St *CHAD* OL9 ....**39** C2
   CMANE M1 ....**8** B1
   DROY M43 ....**75** D2
   ORD * M5 ....**67** D4
   STKP SK1 ....**133** D1
Canberra St *OP/CLY* M11 ....**73** D3
Candleford Rd *DID/WITH* * M20 ....**115** C3
Canisp Cl *CHAD* OL9 ....**20** B1
Canley Cl *STKP* SK1...............................**133** C1
Canning St *HTNM* SK4 ....**129** D3
Cannon St *ANC* M4 ....**4** A3
   CHAD OL9 ....**22** B2
   CSLFD M3 ....**2** A2
   ECC M30 ....**62** B4
Canon Green Dr *CSLFD* M3 ....**2** C1
Canons Gv *NEWH/MOS* M40 ....**53** D4
Canonsleigh Cl *CHH* M8 ....**50** B4
Canonway *SWIN* M27 ....**44** B2
Canon Tighe Ct *CHAD* * OL9 ....**20** B2
Canterbury Dr *PWCH* M25 ....**30** B3
Canterbury Gdns *ORD* M5 ....**63** D3
Canterbury Pk *DID/WITH* M20 ....**124** C2
Canterbury Rd *STKP* SK1 ....**131** C4
   URM M41 ....**94** A2
Canterfield Cl *DROY* M43 ....**77** C3
Cantrell St *OP/CLY* M11..........................**73** C4
Canute Rd *STRET* M32 ....**97** D2
Canute St *SLFD* * M6 ....**67** C3
Capella Wk *BRO* M7 ....**67** D1
Cape St *DID/WITH* M20 ....**115** D2
Capital Rd *OP/CLY* M11 ....**92** D1
Capricorn Wy *SLFD* * M6 ....**67** D1
Capstan St *BKLY* M9 ....**52** A4
Carberry Rd *GTN* M18 ....**91** D4
Carden Av *SWIN* M27 ....**44** C2
Carder Cl *SWIN* M27 ....**45** C2
Cardiff Cl *OLDS* OL8 ....**39** C3
Cardiff St *BRO* M7 ....**50** B2
Cardigan Rd *OLDS* OL8 ....**39** C3
Cardigan St *SLFD* * M6 ....**65** D4
Cardinal St *CHH* M8 ....**52** A3
   OLD OL1 ....**23** C2
Carding Gv *CSLFD* M3 ....**2** C1
Cardroom Rd *ANC* M4 ....**5** E4
Cardus St *BNG/LEV* M19 ....**104** B4
Cardwell Rd *ECC* M30 ....**60** B4
Cardwell St *OLDS* OL8 ....**41** C2
Carey Cl *BRO* * M7 ....**68** A1
Carey Wk *HULME* M15............................**86** A4
Carfax St *GTN* M18 ....**91** D4
Carill Av *NEWH/MOS* M40 ....**35** D4
Carill Dr *RUSH/FAL* M14.......................**116** A1
Carina Pl *BRO* M7 ....**67** D1
Carisbrook Av *WHTF* M45 ....**11** D2

Carisbrook Dr SWIN M27 ....45 D3
Carisbrook St BKLY M9 ....53 C2
Carlburn St OP/CLY M11 ....74 A3
Carley Gv BKLY M9 ....33 C1
Carlford Gv PWCH M25 ....29 C2
Carlile St EDGY/DAV SK3 ....132 B1
Carlingford Cl EDGY/DAV SK3 ....152 D8
Carlisle Cl WHTF M45 ....12 A2
Carlisle St CHAD OL9 ....65 D2
   SWIN M27 ....26 A3
Carloon Rd NTHM/RTH M23 ....122 A4
Carlton Av PWCH M25 ....31 D3
Carlton Crs STKP SK1 ....130 B3
Carlton Dr PWCH M25 ....31 D3
Carlton Range GTN * M18 ....107 C3
Carlton Rd HTNM SK4 ....127 D3
   OLDTF/WHR M16 ....100 A2
   SALE M33 ....108 B3
   SLFD M6 ....65 D1
Carlton St ECC M30 ....62 A2
   OLDTF/WHR M16 ....99 D1
Carlyle Cl CHH M8 ....51 D3
Carlyn Av SALE M33 ....110 A3
Carmel Av ORD M5 ....84 B3
Carmel Cl ORD M5 ....84 B1
Carmel Ct BKLY M9 ....34 A4
Carmichael St EDGY/DAV SK3 ....132 A1
Carmona Dr PWCH M25 ....29 D1
Carmoor Rd BRUN/LGST M13 ....87 D4
Carnaby St BKLY M9 ....35 C4
Carna Rd RDSH SK5 ....106 B3
Carnarvon St BRO * M7 ....50 B2
   CSLFD M3 ....69 C3
   OLDS OL8 ....39 C3
   STKP SK1 ....133 D1
Carnegie Av BNG/LEV M19 ....105 C4
Carnforth Av CHAD OL9 ....20 B3
Carnforth Rd HTNM SK4 ....118 B3
Carnforth St RUSH/FAL M14 ....102 A2
Carnoustie St NEWH/MOS M40 ....55 D2
Carnwood Cl NEWH/MOS M40 ....74 A1
Caroline Dr ANC M4 ....5 E4
Caroline St BRO M7 ....68 B1
   EDGY/DAV SK3 ....132 A2
Carpenters La ANC M4 ....4 B3
Carpenters Wk DROY M43 ....92 A1
Carr Av PWCH M25 ....29 C3
Carr Bank Av CHH M8 ....32 A2
Carrgreen Cl BNG/LEV M19 ....117 C3
Carriage Dr NEWH/MOS M40 ....53 C4
Carriage St OLDTF/WHR M16 ....85 C3
Carrigart PWCH M25 ....29 D2
Carrill Gv East BNG/LEV M19 ....104 B3
Carrington Field St OFTN SK2 ....133 C2
Carrington Rd RUSH/FAL M14 ....115 D1
   STKP SK1 ....130 B2
Carrington St CHAD OL9 ....19 C4
   SWIN M27 ....27 C4
Carrington Ter SWIN * M27 ....26 B4
Carron Av BKLY M9 ....34 B4
Carr St SWIN M27 ....44 A2
Carruthers St ANC M4 ....71 C4
Carslake Av NEWH/MOS M40 ....53 C4
Carson Rd BNG/LEV M19 ....117 D3
Carstairs Cl CHH M8 ....51 C2
Carter St BRO * M7 ....50 A4
   SALQ 64 B4
Carthage St OLDS OL8 ....41 C1
Cartmel Av HTNM SK4 ....119 C3
Cartmel Cl OLDS OL8 ....40 A2
Cartmel Crs CHAD OL9 ....38 A3
Cartmel Gv WALK M28 ....43 C2
Cartwright Rd CCHDY M21 ....111 C1
Carver Av PWCH M25 ....12 B4
Carver Cl OLDTF/WHR M16 ....84 A4
Carver St OLDTF/WHR M16 ....84 A4
Carver Wk HULME * M15 ....86 A4
Carville Rd BKLY M9 ....36 B2

Cascade Dr CHH M8 ....50 B4
Cash Gate Ct OLDS * OL8 ....40 A2
Cashmoor Wk WGTN/LGST M12 ....88 B3
Cass Av ORD M5 ....83 D1
Cassidy Cl ANC M4 ....5 D1
Casson St FAIL M35 ....57 C2
Castle Cl DROY M43 ....76 A3
Castledene Av SLFD M6 ....65 D2
Castlefield Av BRO M7 ....50 B1
Castlefield Br ORD M5 ....6 A1
Castle Hill Rd PWCH M25 ....31 C3
Castlemere Rd BKLY M9 ....33 D2
Castlemill St OLD OL1 ....3 F2
Castlemoor Av BRO M7 ....49 C1
Castle Quay HULME M15 ....6 C1
Castlerea Cl ECC M30 ....79 C1
Castle St CSLFD M3 ....3 F3
   ECC M30 ....63 C3
   EDGY/DAV SK3 ....132 A2
   MDTN M24 ....19 C2
   STKP SK1 ....130 A3
Castleton Av STRET M32 ....96 C3
Castleton Rd BRO M7 ....31 D4
   STRET M32 ....95 D1
Castleton St CHAD * OL9 ....19 C4
Castleton Wk OP/CLY * M11 ....72 A4
Castlewood Rd BRO M7 ....48 A1
Catchdale Cl BKLY M9 ....15 D4
Cateaton St CSLFD M3 ....3 F3
Caterham St ANC M4 ....71 C4
Catfield Wk HULME * M15 ....6 B4
Cathedral Ap CSLFD M3 ....3 F2
Cathedral Gdns CSLFD M3 ....3 F2
Cathedral Gates CSLFD * M3 ....3 F3
Cathedral St ANC M4 ....3 F3
Catherine Houses HTNM * SK4 ....127 C3
Catherine St CHH M8 ....31 D4
   SWIN M27 ....43 D2
Catherine St ECC M30 ....60 B2
   OP/CLY M11 ....91 D2
Catherston Cl OLDTF/WHR M16 ....100 B2
Catlow La ANC * M4 ....4 B3
Catlow St BRO M7 ....68 B1
Catterick Av DID/WITH M20 ....125 D2
Catterick Rd DID/WITH M20 ....125 D2
Cattlin Wy OLDS OL8 ....39 D3
The Causeway CHAD OL9 ....19 C4
Cavanagh Cl BRUN/LGST M13 ....88 A3
Cavell St CMANE * M1 ....4 C4
Cavell Wy SLFD M6 ....66 B4
Cavendish Av DID/WITH M20 ....114 A3
   SWIN M27 ....27 D2
Cavendish Gv ECC M30 ....62 B2
Cavendish Rd BRO M7 ....31 C4
   DID/WITH M20 ....114 A3
   ECC M30 ....62 B2
   HTNM SK4 ....127 C3
   STRET M32 ....97 D1
   URM M41 ....94 B3
   WALK M28 ....43 C3
Cavendish St CHAD OL9 ....22 B3
   HULME M15 ....8 A5
Caversham Dr BKLY M9 ....53 D1
Cawdor Rd RUSH/FAL M14 ....102 B4
Cawdor St ECC M30 ....61 D4
   HULME M15 ....6 A4
   SWIN M27 ....44 A1
Cawley Av PWCH M25 ....29 C3
Cawley Ter BKLY * M9 ....14 B4
Cawood Sq RDSH SK5 ....121 D3
Cawston Wk CHH M8 ....51 D3
Caxton Rd RUSH/FAL M14 ....102 A4
Caxton St CSLFD * M3 ....3 D3
Caxton Wy ORD M5 ....67 C4
Caygill St CSLFD M3 ....3 D2
Caythorpe St RUSH/FAL M14 ....101 D2

Cayton St *WGTN/LGST* M12 ....104 B2
Cecil Gv *GTN* M18 ....106 A1
Cecil Rd *BKLY* M9 ....34 A1
   ECC M30 ....62 B4
   STRET M32 ....96 B4
Cecil St *BRUN/LGST* M13 ....87 C4
   *EDGY/DAV * SK3 ....132 B2
Cedar Av *WHTF* M45 ....11 C3
Cedar Crs *CHAD* M9 ....21 C1
Cedar Dr *DROY* M43 ....76 A3
   SWIN M27 ....25 C1
Cedar Gv *HTNM* SK4 ....118 B4
   PWCH M25 ....11 D3
   RUSH/FAL M14 ....116 A1
Cedar Pl *BRO* M7 ....67 D1
Cedar Rd *FAIL* M35 ....57 C3
   MDTN M24 ....18 B1
Cedarwood Av *HTNM* SK4 ....127 D4
Cedric Rd *CHH* M8 ....31 D3
Cedric St *ORD* M5 ....65 C3
Celia St *CHH* M8 ....52 B1
Celtic St *STKP* SK1 ....133 C1
Cemetery Rd *DROY* M43 ....75 C4
   FAIL M35 ....57 C4
   ORD M5 ....65 C4
   SWIN M27 ....25 C4
Cemetery Rd North *SWIN* M27 ....25 D3
Centaur Cl *SWIN* M27 ....26 A3
Centenary Wy *SALQ* M50 ....63 D4
Central Av *BNG/LEV* M19 ....104 D3
   SLFD M6 ....47 D3
   SWIN M27 ....28 A3
Central Dr *CHH* M8 ....33 C4
   RDSH SK5 ....120 B4
   SWIN M27 ....46 A2
   URM M41 ....94 A3
Central Park Est *TRPK* * M17 ....81 D3
Central Rd *DID/WITH* M20 ....114 B4
Central St *CMANW* M2 ....3 F5
Centurion Gv *BRO* M7 ....50 B4
Ceylon St *NEWH/MOS* M40 ....54 B3
Chadderton Prec *CHAD* * OL9 ....21 C2
Chadderton St *ANC* M4 ....4 C2
Chadderton Wy *CHAD* OL9 ....22 A1
Chaddesley Wk *OP/CLY* * M11 ....89 D1
Chadwick Cl *RUSH/FAL* * M14 ....102 A2
Chadwick Rd *ECC* M30 ....62 B3
   URM M41 ....95 C3
Chadwick St *STKP* SK1 ....133 C1
   SWIN M27 ....45 C1
Chaffinch Cl *DROY* M43 ....76 B2
Chain Rd *BKLY* M9 ....16 A1
Chain St *CMANE* M1 ....4 A5
Chalcombe Gra *WGTN/LGST * M12 ....104 A1
Chale Cl *NEWH/MOS* M40 ....71 C2
Chale Dr *MDTN* M24 ....18 B3
Chalfont Av *URM* * M41 ....94 B3
Chalfont Dr *CHH* M8 ....51 D2
Challenor Sq *WGTN/LGST* M12 ....89 D1
Challum Dr *CHAD* OL9 ....20 B1
Chamber Hall Cl *OLDS* OL8 ....40 A1
Chamber Rd *OLDS* OL8 ....39 D2
Chambers Field Ct *ORD* M5 ....66 B4
Chancel Av *ORD* M5 ....84 B1
Chancellor La *WGTN/LGST* M12 ....88 A1
Chancel Ms *STKP* SK1 ....130 B4
Chancel Pl *CMANE* * M1 ....5 E5
Chancery La *CMANW* M2 ....3 F5
Chancery St *CHAD* OL9 ....21 D1
Chancery Wk *CHAD* OL9 ....21 D1
Chandos Gv *ORD* M5 ....65 C3
Chandos Rd *CCHDY* M21 ....99 D4
   HTNM SK4 ....118 A3
   PWCH M25 ....30 A3
Chandos Rd South *CCHDY* M21 ....99 D4
Change Wy *CSLFD* M3 ....2 C1
Chantry Cl *RDSH* SK5 ....119 D2
Chapelfield Rd *WGTN/LGST* M12 ....9 F2

Chapel Gv *URM* M41 ....94 B3
Chapelhill Dr *BKLY* M9 ....33 D2
Chapel La *BKLY* M9. ....33 C2
Chapel Pl *URM* M41 ....79 C1
Chapel Rd *OLDS* OL8 ....39 D2
   PWCH M25 ....29 C4
   SALE M33 ....109 C4
   SWIN M27 ....43 D2
Chapel St *BNG/LEV* M19 ....104 B4
   CSLFD M3 ....2 C3
   DROY M43 ....75 D4
   ECC M30 ....61 D4
   HTNM SK4 ....126 A3
   MDTN * M24 ....15 D2
   MDTN M24 ....17 C1
   PWCH M25 ....29 D1
   SWIN M27 ....26 B4
Chapeltown St *CMANE* M1 ....9 E1
Chapel Wks *CMANW* M2 ....3 F4
Chapman Ms *GTN* * M18 ....91 C4
Chapman St *GTN* M18 ....91 C3
Chappell Rd *DROY* M43 ....75 D3
Chapter St *NEWH/MOS* M40 ....72 A1
Charcoal Rd *NEWH/MOS* M40 ....56 A4
Chariot St *OP/CLY* M11 ....91 C1
Charlbury Av *PWCH* M25 ....11 C2
   RDSH SK5 ....120 A3
Charles Av *DTN/ASHW* M34 ....92 B2
Charles Halle Rd *HULME* M15 ....86 B4
Charles Morris Cl *FAIL* M35 ....58 B4
Charles St *CHAD* OL9 ....21 D3
   CMANE M1 ....8 A3
   DROY * M43 ....74 B4
   SLFD M6 ....66 A4
   STKP SK1 ....133 C2
   SWIN M27 ....25 C4
   WHTF M45 ....11 C2
Charleston St *OLDS* OL8 ....41 C1
Charlestown Rd *BKLY* M9 ....34 A3
Charlesworth St *OP/CLY* M11 ....89 D1
   STKP * SK1 ....133 C2
Charley Av *BRO* M7 ....68 A1
Charlotte St *CMANW* * M2 ....4 A5
   STKP SK1 ....131 C4
Chariton Av *ECC* M30 ....62 A4
   PWCH M25 ....30 A2
Chariton Dr *SWIN* M27 ....25 C3
Chariton Pl *CMANE* M1 ....9 D3
Chariton Rd *BNG/LEV* M19 ....105 C3
Charminster Dr *CHH* M8 ....52 A1
Charnley Cl *NEWH/MOS* M40 ....71 D2
Charnley St *WHTF* M45 ....11 C1
Charnwood Rd *BKLY* M9 ....16 B4
Charter St *CSLFD* M3 ....69 C2
   OLD OL1 ....23 D1
Chartwell Cl *SLFD* M6 ....66 A3
The Chase *WALK* M28 ....42 B4
Chaseley Rd *SLFD* M6 ....65 D1
Chasewood *BNG/LEV* * M19 ....104 B4
Chataway Rd *CHH* M8 ....52 A1
Chatburn Rd *CCHDY* M21 ....112 A1
Chatfield Rd *CCHDY* M21 ....112 A1
Chatford Cl *BRO* M7 ....68 B1
Chatham St *DID/WITH* * M20 ....114 B3
Chatham Gv *DID/WITH* M20 ....114 B3
Chatham Rd *GTN* * M18 ....106 B2
   OLDTF/WHR M16 ....99 C2
Chatham St *CMANE* M1 ....4 C5
   EDGY/DAV SK3 ....132 A1
Chatley Rd *ECC* M30 ....60 A4
Chatley St *CSLFD* M3 ....69 C1
Chatsworth Av *PWCH* M25 ....30 A3
Chatsworth Cl *DROY* M43 ....74 A2
   URM M41 ....94 B3
Chatsworth Gv *OLDTF/WHR* M16 ....100 A3
Chatsworth Rd *DROY* M43 ....74 B2

URM M41	94 B4
Churchgate Buildings *CMANE* * M1	9 E1
Church Gn *SLFD* * M6	66 A2
Churchill Crs *RDSH* SK5	106 B4
Churchill St *HTNM* SK4	129 C2
OLDE OL4	23 D3
Churchill St East *OLDE* OL4	23 D3
Churchill Wy *SLFD* M6	66 B3
TRPK M17	81 D2
Church La *BKLY* M9	53 C1
BNG/LEV M19	117 C3
BRO M7	30 A4
OLD OL1	23 C4
PWCH M25	29 D1
WHTF M45	10 B1
Church Rd *ECC* M30	63 C3
HTNM SK4	129 D3
MDTN M24	19 C2
URM * M41	94 A4
WYTH/NTH M22	125 C4
Churchside Cl *BKLY* M9	34 A3
Church St *ANC* M4	4 B3
DROY M43	75 D4
ECC M30	62 B3
FAIL M35	57 C1
HTNM SK4	129 D2
OLD OL1	23 C2
STRET M32	96 B4
SWIN M27	44 B1
SWIN M27	46 A1
Church Ter *SALE* * M33	108 B3
Church Wk *SWIN* M27	26 A1
Churchwood Rd *DID/WITH* M20	125 C2
Churnet St *NEWH/MOS* M40	53 C4
Churston Av *BKLY* M9	34 B1
Churton Rd *GTN* M18	105 C3
Churwell Av *HTNM* SK4	127 C1
Cicero St *BKLY* M9	53 D1
Cinder St *ANC* * M4	5 E2
Cipher St *ANC* M4	5 E1
Circle South *TRPK* M17	82 B5
The Circuit *DID/WITH* M20	115 C4
Circular Rd *DID/WITH* M20	115 C4
PWCH M25	30 A3
Circus St *CMANE* * M1	4 C5
Ciss La *URM* M41	94 B3
Citrus Wy *SLFD* M6	66 B3
City Rd *HULME* M15	85 C3
City Rd East *HULME* M15	7 E4
City Wk *SWIN* M27	46 A1
Clacton Wk *BRUN/LGST* M13	9 E5
Clague St *OP/CLY* M11	72 B3
Claife Av *NEWH/MOS* M40	36 A3
Clandon Av *ECC* M30	61 C3
Clapham St *NEWH/MOS* M40	55 D1
Clara St *CHAD* OL9	39 D1
Claremont Av *DID/WITH* M20	114 B4
HTNM SK4	118 B4
Claremont Gv *DID/WITH* M20	124 B2
Claremont Range *WI* M18	107 C1
Claremont Rd *RUSH/FAL* M14	102 A2
SALE M33	109 C4
SLFD M6	64 B1
Claremont St *FAIL* M35	57 C1
OLDS OL8	41 C3
SLFD M6	46 B3
Clarence Av *OLDS* OL8	40 A1
TRPK M17	80 A3
WHTF M45	11 D2
Clarence Rd *BRUN/LGST* M13	103 D2
HTNM SK4	118 A4
SWIN M27	43 D2
Clarence St *BRO* M7	68 A1
CMANW * M2	3 F5
Clarendon Av *HTNM* SK4	128 A2
Clarendon Crs *ECC* M30	63 C2
SALE M33	110 A4
Clarendon Rd *DTN/ASHW* M34	92 B2

ECC M30	63 C2
OLDTF/WHR M16	99 D3
SWIN M27	45 C1
Clarendon Rd West *CCHDY* M21	99 C3
Clarendon St *HULME* M15	7 D5
RDSH * SK5	130 A2
WHTF M45	11 C1
Clare Rd *BNG/LEV* M19	117 C3
RDSH * SK5	130 A1
Clare St *CMANE* M1	9 D3
ORD * M5	67 C2
Claribel St *OP/CLY* M11	88 B1
Claridge Rd *CCHDY* M21	98 B4
Clarion St *ANC* M4	5 E1
Clark Av *GTN* M18	91 D4
Clarke Av *ORD* M5	84 A2
Clark's Hi *PWCH* M25	29 D1
Clarkwell Cl *OLD* * OL1	22 B1
Claude Av *SWIN* M27	44 A1
Claude Rd *CCHDY* M21	111 D2
Claude St *CHH* M8	32 B4
ECC M30	61 C1
SWIN M27	44 A1
Claxton Av *BKLY* M9	34 A2
Clay Bank *DROY* M43	74 B4
Claybar Dr *ECC* M30	62 B2
Claybrook Wk *OP/CLY* * M11	72 B4
Clayburn Rd *HULME* M15	7 D5
Claycourt Av *ECC* M30	61 C1
Claygate Dr *BKLY* M9	16 A4
Claymore St *GTN* M18	91 D3
Clay St *OLDS* OL8	40 B1
Clayton Av *DID/WITH* M20	125 C2
Claytonbrook Rd *OP/CLY* M11	73 D3
Clayton Cl *HULME* M15	85 C4
Clayton Hall Rd *OP/CLY* M11	73 D3
Clayton La *OP/CLY* M11	90 A1
Clayton La South *OP/CLY* M11	89 D2
Clayton St *CHAD* OL9	38 B2
FAIL * M35	56 B2
OP/CLY M11	73 C2
Cleadon Av *GTN* M18	105 D1
Cleavley St *ECC* M30	61 C3
Clee Av *BRUN/LGST* M13	104 A3
Cleethorpes Av *BKLY* M9	33 C2
Clegg St *DROY* * M43	75 C4
OLDE OL4	23 D3
WHTF M45	11 C1
Clementine Cl *SLFD* M6	67 C3
Clement Stott Cl *BKLY* M9	35 C1
Clement St *BRO* M7	68 A1
HTNM SK4	129 D2
Cleminson St *CSLFD* M3	2 B3
Clevedon Av *URM* M41	95 D3
Clevedon St *BKLY* M9	53 D1
Cleveland Av *BNG/LEV* M19	105 C3
SLFD M6	64 B2
Cleveland Rd *CHH* M8	33 C3
HTNM SK4	127 D1
Cleveleys Av *CCHDY* M21	112 B2
Cleveleys Gv *BRO* M7	50 B2
Cleworth St *HULME* * M15	6 A4
Cleworth Wk *HULME* M15	6 A4
Clibran St *CHH* M8	52 A3
Cliff Av *GTN* M7	49 D3
Cliff Crs *BRO* M7	50 A2
Cliffdale Dr *CHH* M8	32 B4
Cliff Gv *HTNM* SK4	128 A1
Clifford St *ECC* M30	78 A1
SWIN M27	46 A1
Clifton Av *ECC* M30	62 A2
RUSH/FAL M14	116 A1
Clifton Cl *OLDTF/WHR* M16	85 C4
Clifton Dr *SWIN* M27	25 C4
Clifton Gv *OLDTF/WHR* M16	85 C4
SWIN M27	24 B3
Clifton House Rd *SWIN* M27	25 D1
Clifton Park Rd *OFTN* SK2	133 D4

Clifton Pl *PWCH* * M25 ....11 D4
Clifton Rd *CCHDY* M21 ....112 B1
  ECC M30 ....62 A2
  HTNM SK4 ....127 D1
  PWCH M25 ....28 B1
Clifton St *FAIL* M35 ....38 B4
  NEWH/MOS M40 ....72 A4
  OLDTF/WHR M16 ....85 C4
Clifton Vw *SWIN* M27 ....25 D1
Cliftonville Dr *SLFD* M6 ....46 A3
Clinton Av *RUSH/FAL* M14 ....101 D3
Clinton Gdns *RUSH/FAL* M14 ....101 D3
Clippers Quay *SALQ* M50 ....83 D3
Clitheroe Rd *BRUN/LGST* M13 ....104 A2
Clito St *BKLY* M9 ....54 A1
Clively Av *SWIN* M27 ....27 C4
Clive Av *FAIL* M35 ....56 B2
Clive St *ANC* M4 ....5 C3
  OLDS OL8 ....40 A3
Clivia Gv *BRO* * M7 ....50 A3
Cloak St *CMANE* M1 ....8 B3
Clock House Av *DROY* M43 ....74 B2
Clockhouse Ms *DROY* * M43 ....74 B2
Clock St *CHAD* OL9 ....39 C3
Cloister Rd *HTNM* SK4 ....126 A3
Cloister St *BKLY* M9 ....54 A1
Clopton Wk *HULME* M15 ....85 D3
Clothorn Rd *DID/WITH* M20 ....125 C1
The Clough *RDSH* SK5 ....121 C3
Clough Bank *BKLY* * M9 ....34 A3
Clough Dr *PWCH* M25 ....29 C1
Cloughfield Av *ORD* M5 ....84 A1
Clough Ga *OLDS* OL8 ....40 A3
Clough La *PWCH* M25 ....29 C1
Clough Rd *BKLY* M9 ....54 A1
  DROY M43 ....76 A3
  FAIL M35 ....57 D2
Cloughs Av *CHAD* OL9 ....19 C3
Clough St *NEWH/MOS* M40 ....73 D1
Clough Top Rd *BKLY* M9 ....35 D3
Clovelly Av *OLDS* OL8 ....39 D3
Clovelly Rd *CCHDY* M21 ....112 B1
  SWIN M27 ....43 D2
Clovelly St *NEWH/MOS* * M40 ....56 A4
Clover Av *EDGY/DAV* SK3 ....132 A4
Cloverbank Av *BNG/LEV* M19 ....126 A1
Clowes St *CHAD* OL9 ....38 B3
  CSLFD M3 ....3 D3
  WGTN/LGST M12 ....89 D3
Club St *OP/CLY* M11 ....92 A2
Clumber Rd *GTN* M18 ....107 C1
Clwyd Av *EDGY/DAV* SK3 ....132 A3
Clyde Av *WHTF* M45 ....11 C3
Clyde Rd *DID/WITH* M20 ....124 A1
Clydesdale St *OLDS* OL8 ....40 B1
Clyne St *STRET* M32 ....83 C4
Coalbrook Wk *WGTN/LGST* M12 ....88 A1
Coalburn St *WGTN/LGST* M12 ....89 D4
Coal Pit La *OLDS* OL8 ....59 C2
Coalshaw Green Rd *CHAD* OL9 ....38 B2
Coatbridge St *OP/CLY* M11 ....73 D4
Cobalt Av *URM* M41 ....80 A3
Cobb Cl *CHH* M8 ....31 D2
Cobble Bank *BKLY* M9 ....33 D2
Cobden St *BKLY* M9 ....34 B4
  CHAD OL9 ....21 C2
  SLFD M6 ....66 A1
Cob Hall Rd *STRET* M32 ....96 B4
Cobham Av *NEWH/MOS* M40 ....36 B3
Cobourg St *CMANE* M1 ....8 C1
Coburg Av *BRO* M7 ....68 C2
Cochrane Av *WGTN/LGST* M12 ....88 B4
Cockcroft St *BKLY* M9 ....34 A4
Coconut Gv *SLFD* * M6 ....67 C3
Coddington Av *OP/CLY* M11 ....91 D1
Coghlan Cl *OP/CLY* * M11 ....73 C3
Colborne Av *ECC* M30 ....61 C3

  RDSH * SK5 ....107 C2
Colbourne Av *CHH* M8 ....32 A4
Colchester Pl *HTNM* SK4 ....128 A2
Colchester Wk *OLD* * OL1 ....23 C2
Colclough Cl *NEWH/MOS* M40 ....55 C3
Coldhurst St *OLD* OL1 ....22 B1
Coldstream Av *BKLY* M9 ....34 A1
Colebrook Dr *NEWH/MOS* M40 ....54 B3
Coleby Av *OLDTF/WHR* M16 ....99 D1
Colemore Av *DID/WITH* M20 ....126 A2
Colenso Gv *HTNM* SK4 ....128 A2
Colenso St *OLDS* OL8 ....40 A2
Coleridge Cl *RDSH* SK5 ....106 B4
Coleridge Rd *OLDTF/WHR* M16 ....99 D2
  RDSH SK5 ....106 B4
Coleshill St *NEWH/MOS* M40 ....71 D2
Cole St *BKLY* M9 ....54 A1
Colgate Crs *RUSH/FAL* M14 ....115 C1
Colgate La *ORD* M5 ....83 D3
Colgrove Av *NEWH/MOS* M40 ....36 B3
Colina Dr *CHH* M8 ....32 A4
Colindale Av *BKLY* M9 ....34 B1
Colin Murphy Rd *HULME* M15 ....6 C4
Colin Rd *HTNM* SK4 ....129 D1
Coll Dr *URM* M41 ....79 C4
College Av *OLDS* OL8 ....40 A1
College Cl *OFTN* SK2 ....133 D3
College Dr *OLDTF/WHR* M16 ....99 D2
College Rd *ECC* M30 ....63 D3
  OLDS OL8 ....40 A1
  OLDTF/WHR M16 ....100 A3
Colley Av *STRET* M32 ....83 C4
Collie Av *SLFD* M6 ....49 D4
Collier Hl *OLDS* OL8 ....40 A2
Collier Hill Av *OLDS* OL8 ....39 D2
Collier St *CSLFD* M3 ....3 D2
  CSLFD M3 ....7 D2
  SLFD M6 ....48 A3
  SWIN M27 ....44 B2
Colliery St *OP/CLY* M11 ....72 B4
Collin Av *GTN* M18 ....105 D1
Collingburn Av *ORD* M5 ....84 A2
Collinge Av *MDTN* M24 ....19 D1
Collinge St *MDTN* M24 ....19 C2
Collingham St *CHH* M8 ....69 D1
Collington Cl *WGTN/LGST* M12 ....89 D4
Collingwood Av *DROY* M43 ....74 B2
Collingwood Dr *SWIN* M27 ....45 D2
Collingwood Rd *BNG/LEV* M19 ....104 A4
Collingwood Wy *OLD* * OL1 ....23 C1
Collyhurst Rd *NEWH/MOS* M40 ....52 B4
Collyhurst St *NEWH/MOS* M40 ....70 B1
Colman Gdns *ORD* M5 ....84 A2
Colmore Dr *BKLY* M9 ....35 D1
Colonial Rd *OFTN* SK2 ....133 D3
Colson Dr *MDTN* M24 ....17 C2
Columbia Av *GTN* M18 ....107 C1
Columbia St *OLDS* * OL8 ....41 C1
Columbine St *OP/CLY* M11 ....91 C2
Colwell Av *STRET* M32 ....96 A4
Colwyn Av *MDTN* M24 ....17 D3
  RUSH/FAL M14 ....116 B1
Colwyn Crs *RDSH* SK5 ....120 A4
Colwyn Rd *SWIN* M27 ....43 D3
Colwyn St *CHAD* OL9 ....22 C3
  SLFD M6 ....66 A2
Combe Cl *OP/CLY* M11 ....73 C2
Combermere Av *DID/WITH* M20 ....114 B2
Comet St *CMANE* M1 ....5 D5
Commercial Cl *OLD* OL1 ....23 C3
Commercial St *CHAD* OL9 ....21 D3
  HULME M15 ....7 D3
Como Wk *GTN* M18 ....90 A3
Compass St *OP/CLY* M11 ....90 B2
Compstall Av *RUSH/FAL* M14 ....102 A4
Compstall Gv *GTN* * M18 ....91 D3
Compton Wy *MDTN* M24 ....18 B2
Comus St *ORD* M5 ....84 B1

Concert La CMANW M2 ....4 A5
Concord Pl SLFD M6 ....48 B4
Condor Cl DROY * M43 ....76 B2
Condor Pl SLFD M6 ....48 B4
Condor Wk BRUN/LGST * M13 ....87 C3
Conewood Wk BRUN/LGST M13 ....87 D3
Congou St CMANE M1 ....9 E1
Congreave St OL1 ....22 B1
Coningsby Dr BKLY M9 ....53 C3
Conisborough Pl WHTF M45 ....12 A2
Coniston Av BKLY M9 ....53 C1
    OLDS OL8 ....40 A2
    WHTF M45 ....11 C1
Coniston Cl CHAD OL9 ....20 B2
Coniston Rd RDSH SK5 ....120 A3
    SWIN M27 ....96 B2
Coniston St NEWH/MOS M40 ....55 D4
    SLFD M6 ....67 C1
Conmere Sq HULME M15 ....7 F4
Connaught Av BNG/LEV M19 ....117 C2
    WHTF M45 ....11 D1
Connaught St CHAD OL9 ....9 D1
Connie St OP/CLY M11 ....90 B1
Connington Av BKLY M9 ....34 A4
Conran St BKLY M9 ....53 C2
Constable St GTN M18 ....91 D3
Constance Gdns SLFD M6 ....66 A4
Constance St HULME * M15 ....7 D3
Consul St WYTH/NTH M22 ....123 C4
Conway Av SWIN M27 ....27 C2
    WHTF M45 ....11 C2
Conway Cl MDTN M24 ....17 D2
    OLDTF/WHR * M16 ....98 B2
Conway Gv CHAD OL9 ....20 A1
Conway Rd URM M41 ....94 A1
Conway St RDSH SK5 ....129 D1
Conyngham Rd RUSH/FAL M14 ....103 C1
Cooke St FAIL M35 ....57 C1
Cook St CSLFD M3 ....2 C3
    ECC M30 ....61 D4
    EDGY/DAV * SK3 ....129 C4
Coomassie St SLFD * M6 ....66 A2
Co-operation St FAIL M35 ....33 A4
Co-operative St SLFD * M6 ....66 A3
Cooper La BKLY M9 ....16 A4
Cooper St CMANW M2 ....3 F5
    DROY * M43 ....74 B4
    STKP SK1 ....133 C2
    STRET M32 ....97 C4
Coop St ANC * M4 ....4 C2
Cope Cl OP/CLY * M11 ....91 D2
Copeland Av SWIN M27 ....27 C2
Copeman Cl BRUN/LGST M13 ....87 D5
Copenhagen St NEWH/MOS M40 ....54 B3
Copgrove Rd CCHDY M21 ....112 A2
Copley Rd CCHDY M21 ....98 B3
Copperas Ln DROY M43 ....91 D1
Copperas St ANC M4 ....4 B3
Copperbeech Cl WYTH/NTH M22 ....123 D4
The Coppice BKLY M9 ....35 D3
    PWCH M25 ....29 D1
    SWIN M27 ....43 D1
    WALK M28 ....42 A1
Coppice Dr WYTH/NTH M22 ....123 C4
Coppice St OLDS OL8 ....22 A4
Copping St WGTN/LGST M12 ....89 C3
Coppleridge Dr CHH M8 ....32 B3
Copson St DID/WITH M20 ....115 C2
Copster Av OLDS OL8 ....40 B2
Copster Hill Rd OLDS OL8 ....40 B2
Copster Pl OLDS OL8 ....40 B2
Copthall La CHH M8 ....51 C1
Copthorne Crs BRUN/LGST M13 ....103 D3
Coral St BRUN/LGST M13 ....9 E4
Coram St GTN M18 ....92 A3
Corbar Rd OFTN SK2 ....133 D4
Corbett St OP/CLY M11 ....72 B4

Corby St WGTN/LGST M12 ....89 D3
Cordingley Av DROY M43 ....92 A1
Cordova Av DTN/ASHW M34 ....107 C2
Corelli St NEWH/MOS M40 ....72 A1
Corinthian Av BRO M7 ....49 D4
Corkland Rd CCHDY M21 ....112 A1
Cork St WGTN/LGST M12 ....88 A1
Corley Wk OP/CLY * M11 ....72 A4
Cormallen Gv FAIL M35 ....57 D2
Cornbrook Arches HULME M15 ....84 B2
Cornbrook Ct HULME * M15 ....85 C3
Cornbrook Gv OLDTF/WHR M16 ....85 C4
Cornbrook Park Rd HULME M15 ....84 B3
Cornbrook Rd HULME * M15 ....84 B2
Cornbrook St OLDTF/WHR M16 ....85 C4
Cornbrook Wy OLDTF/WHR M16 ....85 C4
Corn Cl BRUN/LGST M13 ....87 D4
Cornell St ANC M4 ....5 D2
Cornet St BRO M7 ....50 A4
Cornford Av GTN M18 ....105 C2
Corn Hill La DTN/ASHW M34 ....92 B4
Corn St FAIL M35 ....55 D3
Cornwall Av BNG/LEV M19 ....118 A1
Cornwall Crs RDSH SK5 ....121 D3
Cornwall Rd DROY M43 ....75 D2
Cornwall St CHAD OL9 ....21 C4
    ECC M30 ....61 D4
    OP/CLY M11 ....91 C2
Corona Av OLDS OL8 ....40 A2
Coronation Rd DROY M43 ....75 C2
    FAIL M35 ....56 B4
Coronation Sq WGTN/LGST M12 ....9 F2
Coronation St OP/CLY * M11 ....90 B1
    ORD M5 ....84 A1
    RDSH SK5 ....129 D1
    SWIN M27 ....26 B4
Corporation St CMANW M2 ....3 F4
    MDTN M24 ....17 D1
    STKP SK1 ....130 A3
Corran Cl ECC M30 ....61 D3
Corrie Crs FWTH BL4 ....25 C1
Corrie Dr FWTH BL4 ....25 C1
Corrie Rd SWIN M27 ....26 B2
Corrigan St GTN M18 ....91 D3
Corringham Rd BNG/LEV M19 ....118 B2
Corriss Av BKLY M9 ....53 D1
Corwen Av BKLY M9 ....53 D1
Corwen Cl OLDS OL8 ....39 C3
Cosgrove Crs FAIL M35 ....56 B4
Cosgrove Rd FAIL M35 ....56 B4
Cotham St CSLFD M3 ....69 C2
Cotswold Av CHAD OL9 ....20 B4
Cotswold Cl PWCH M25 ....12 B4
Cotswold Dr SLFD M6 ....66 A2
Cotswold Rd HTNM SK4 ....129 C1
Cottam Gv SWIN M27 ....45 D2
Cottam St OLD OL1 ....22 A1
Cottenham La BRO M7 ....68 B1
Cottenham St BRUN/LGST M13 ....9 D5
Cotterdale Cl OLDTF/WHR * M16 ....100 A3
Cotterill St SLFD M6 ....66 B3
Cotter St WGTN/LGST M12 ....9 E3
Cottesmore Dr CHH M8 ....52 B1
Cottingham Rd WGTN/LGST M12 ....88 B3
Cottonfield Rd DID/WITH M20 ....115 D3
Cotton Hl DID/WITH M20 ....115 D4
Cotton La DID/WITH M20 ....115 D3
Cotton St ANC M4 ....5 D3
Cotton Tree St HTNM SK4 ....129 D4
Coulsden Dr BKLY M9 ....34 A2
Councillor St OP/CLY M11 ....90 A1
Countess Av BRO M7 ....50 A4
Countess Pl PWCH M25 ....30 B1
Countess Rd DID/WITH M20 ....125 C2
Countess St OFTN SK2 ....133 D4
Counthill Dr CHH M8 ....31 D3
County St CMANW M2 ....3 F5
    OLDS OL8 ....39 D3

Coupland St HULME M15	86	B4
Courier St M18	91	D1
Court Dr NEWH/MOS M40	74	B1
Courtfield Av BKLY * M9	34	A1
Courthill St STKP SK1	133	D1
Courts Vw SALE M33	109	D4
Covent Gdn STKP * SK1	130	A4
Covent Gdns STKP SK1	130	A4
Coverdale Crs WGTN/LGST M12	88	A3
Cowan St NEWH/MOS M40	71	C3
Cowburn St CSLFD M3	69	C2
Cowesby St RUSH/FAL M14	101	D2
Cow La FAIL M35	56	B2
ORD M5	67	D4
SALE M33	110	B3
Cowley St NEWH/MOS M40	55	D3
Cowling St BRO M7	48	A1
Cowper St MDTN M24	19	C2
Crabbe St ANC M4	69	D2
Crab La BKLY M9	33	C1
Crabtree La OP/CLY M11	74	A4
Cradley Av OP/CLY M11	91	C1
Cragie St CHH M8	51	C4
Craighall Av BNG/LEV M19	117	C1
Craigmore Av DID/WITH M20	123	C1
Craignair Ct SWIN * M27	46	A1
Craig Rd GTN M18	105	D1
HTNM SK4	127	D4
Craigslands Av NEWH/MOS M40	54	B3
Craig Wk OLDS * OL8	22	B4
Craigweil Av DID/WITH M20	125	D2
Craigwell Rd PWCH M25	31	C3
Cramer St NEWH/MOS * M40	54	A4
Crammond Cl NEWH/MOS M40	56	A3
Cranage Rd BNG/LEV M19	118	A3
Cranbourne Rd CCHDY M21	112	A1
HTNM SK4	128	A1
OLDTF/WHR M16	99	D1
Cranbourne St ORD M5	67	D4
Cranbrook Dr PWCH M25	30	B3
Cranbrook Rd ECC M30	60	B1
GTN M18	106	B2
Cranbrook Wk CHAD OL9	21	C3
Crane St WGTN/LGST M12	9	F2
Cranfield Cl NEWH/MOS M40	71	C3
Cranford Av DID/WITH M20	126	A3
SALE M33	109	D3
STRET M32	98	A2
Cranford Cl SLFD M6	46	A3
Cranleigh Av HTNM SK4	127	C1
Cranleigh Dr SALE M33	108	B4
Cranlington Dr CHH M8	51	C3
Cranmere Av BNG/LEV M19	105	D3
Cranmer Rd DID/WITH M20	125	C1
Cranswick St RUSH/FAL M14	101	C2
Crantock St WGTN/LGST M12	105	C3
Cranwell Dr BNG/LEV M19	126	B1
Craston Rd BRUN/LGST M13	103	D3
Craven Av ORD M5	84	A1
Craven Dr ORD M5	83	D3
Cravenhurst Av NEWH/MOS M40	73	C1
Craven Pl OP/CLY M11	73	D5
Craven Rd RDSH * SK5	120	A3
Craven St OLD OL1	22	B1
ORD M5	67	D4
Cravenwood Rd CHH M8	51	D1
Crawford Av WALK M28	42	A1
Crawford St ECC M30	63	D2
NEWH/MOS * M40	55	D4
Crawley Av ECC M30	61	D1
Craydon St OP/CLY M11	90	B1
Crayfield Rd BNG/LEV M19	118	A1
Crayford Rd NEWH/MOS M40	73	C1
Cray Wk BRUN/LGST M13	8	C4
Crediton Cl HULME M15	86	A1
Cresbury St WGTN/LGST * M12	88	A2
The Crescent BNG/LEV M19	104	B4

DROY M43	75	C4
MDTN M24	16	B1
PWCH M25	30	A1
Crescent Av CHH * M8	51	D1
PWCH M25	30	A3
SWIN M27	46	A1
Crescent Cl EDGY/DAV SK3	133	D4
Crescent Dr CHH M8	52	A1
Crescent Gv BNG/LEV * M19	104	B4
PWCH M25	30	A3
Crescent Pk NEWH/MOS M40	55	C4
Crescent Range RUSH/FAL M14	102	A1
Crescent Rd CHAD OL9	37	D3
CHH M8	51	D1
STKP SK1	131	C2
Crescent St CHH M8	52	B1
Crescent Wy EDGY/DAV SK3	133	D4
Cressfield Av CCHDY M21	111	C2
Cressingham Rd STRET M32	96	A4
Cressington Cl SLFD * M6	65	D3
Cresswell Gv DID/WITH M20	114	B4
The Crest DROY M43	92	B2
Crete St OLDS OL8	41	C1
Criccieth St OLDTF/WHR M16	101	C1
Crime La OLDS OL8	59	C2
Crimsworth Av OLDTF/WHR M16	99	C3
Crinan Wk NEWH/MOS M40	71	C2
Cringleford Wk WGTN/LGST M12	89	C4
Cringle Hall Rd BNG/LEV M19	117	C1
Cringle Rd BNG/LEV M19	118	A2
Criterion St RDSH SK5	107	C3
The Croft OLDS OL8	40	B3
Croft Av PWCH M25	14	A1
Croft Bank BRO * M7	49	D4
GTN M18	91	D4
Croft Brow OLDS OL8	40	B3
Croft Gates Rd MDTN M24	16	A2
Croft Hill Rd NEWH/MOS M40	35	D4
Crofton St OLDS OL8	41	C2
OLDTF/WHR M16	100	A1
RUSH/FAL M14	102	A2
Croft St BRO M7	49	D4
FAIL M35	56	B4
OP/CLY M11	73	C4
Cromarty Av CHAD OL9	38	A2
Cromarty Wk OP/CLY M11	72	A4
Cromer Av DID/WITH M20	115	C3
DTN/ASHW M34	107	D2
Cromer St OP/CLY * M11	74	A4
STKP SK1	130	B3
Cromford Av STRET M32	96	A2
Cromford St OLD OL1	23	D1
Cromhurst St CHH M8	32	B4
Crompton Rd BNG/LEV M19	117	C2
Crompton St CHAD OL9	21	D2
OLD OL1	22	B1
SWIN M27	44	B1
Cromwell Av OLDTF/WHR M16	99	D3
Cromwell Gv BNG/LEV M19	104	B4
BRO M7	49	D4
Cromwell Range RUSH/FAL M14	103	C3
Cromwell Rd ECC M30	61	D3
PWCH M25	30	B1
SLFD M6	49	D4
STRET M32	97	D4
SWIN M27	25	D4
Cromwell St HTNM SK4	129	C2
OLD OL1	23	C3
Crondall St RUSH/FAL M14	101	D2
Cronshaw St BNG/LEV M19	118	A1
Crookhill Dr CHH M8	51	C2
Crookilley Wy STKP SK1	131	C2
Croom Wk NEWH/MOS * M40	71	C3
Crosby Rd NEWH/MOS M40	56	A4
SLFD * M6	47	C4
Crosby St OFTN SK2	133	C2

Crosfield Gv GTN M18 ....106 A1
Cross Av PWCH M25 ....11 D3
Crossbank Cl BRUN/LGST M13 ....88 A4
Crossbank St OLDS OL8 ....22 B3
Crossby Cl MDTN M24 ....17 C4
Crosscliffe St OLDTF/WHR M16 ......101 C1
Crossdale Rd BKLY M9 ....34 B1
Crossfell Av BKLY M9 ....15 C4
Crossfield Dr SWIN M27 ....25 D3
    WALK M28 ....42 A2
Crossford Br SALE M33 ....109 D2
Crossford Ct SALE * M33 ....109 C5
Crossford St STRET M52 ....97 C4
Crossgate Ms HTNM SK4 ....126 B3
Crosshill St OLDTF/WHR M16 ....101 C1
Cross Keys St ANC M4 ....4 C2
Crossland Rd CCHDY M21 ....111 D1
    DROY M43 ....75 D3
Crosslands PWCH M25 ....29 D2
Cross La DROY M43 ....77 C1
    GTN M18 ....91 C4
    ORD M5 ....66 B4
Crossley Ct ANC M4 ....71 C4
Crossley Rd BNG/LEV M19 ....117 D2
    SALE M33 ....108 B3
Crossley St GTN M18 ....90 A3
Crossmead Dr BKLY M9 ....16 B4
Cross Rd CCHDY M21 ....112 A2
Cross St CSLFD M3 ....3 D3
    MDTN M24 ....17 C4
    OLDTF/WHR M16 ....85 C4
    SALE M33 ....109 C4
    STRET M32 ....97 C3
    SWIN M27 ....28 A3
    WALK M28 ....43 D2
Crossway DID/WITH M20 ....125 C2
Crossways OLDS OL8 ....41 D4
Croston Wk OP/CLY M11 ....74 D4
Croton St HTNM SK4 ....126 B3
Croughton Cl OP/CLY * M11 ....91 C2
Crowborough Wk HULME M15 ....86 A4
Crowcroft Rd BRUN/LGST M13 ....104 B3
Crowden Rd NEWH/MOS M40 ....36 A3
Crow Hl North MDTN M24 ....17 C3
Crow Hl South MDTN M24 ....17 C3
Crowley Rd BKLY M9 ....54 A1
Crowngreen Rd ECC M30 ....62 B4
Crownhill Dr DROY M43 ....75 D3
Crown La ANC M4 ....4 B1
Crown Point Av NEWH/MOS * M40 ....55 D4
Crown Sq CSLFD M3 ....3 D5
Crown St CSLFD M3 ....3 D2
    FAIL M35 ....57 C1
    HULME M15 ....6 C3
    NEWH/MOS M40 ....55 D4
Crowther Av ORD M5 ....83 D1
Crowther St GTN M18 ....91 C4
Crowthorn Rd HTNM SK4 ....119 C3
Croxdale Cl AULW OL7 ....59 D4
Croydon Dr NEWH/MOS M40 ....73 D1
Crumpsall La CHH M8 ....32 A4
Crumpsall V BKLY M9 ....33 D3
Crumpsall Wy CHH M8 ....33 C4
Cryer St DROY M43 ....76 B1
Cuba St MDTN M24 ....18 B1
Cubley Rd BRO M7 ....50 B1
Cuckoo Gv PWCH M25 ....12 A3
Cuckoo La PWCH M25 ....12 A3
Cuddington Av DID/WITH M20 ....114 B1
Cuddington Crs EDGY/DAV SK3 ....132 A3
Cudworth Rd BKLY M9 ....14 B4
Culand Cl WGTN/LGST M12 ....88 A3
Culbert Av DID/WITH M20 ....125 D2
Culcheth La NEWH/MOS M40 ....55 D4
Culford Cl WGTN/LGST M12 ....88 A3
Cullen Gv BKLY M9 ....34 B2
Cullercoats Wk WGTN/LGST * M12 ..105 C2
Culross Av NEWH/MOS M40 ....37 D4

Culvercliff Wk CSLFD M3 ....7 D1
Culver Rd EDGY/DAV SK3 ....132 A4
Culverwell Dr ORD M5 ....67 C3
Cumberland Av RDSH SK5 ....131 D1
    SWIN M27 ....26 A3
Cumberland Rd BKLY * M9 ....34 A4
Cumberland St BRO M7 ....68 A1
Cumbrae Gdns ORD M5 ....65 D4
Cumbrae Rd BNG/LEV M19 ....105 D4
Cumbrian Cl BRUN/LGST * M13 ....87 D3
Cumbria Wk SLFD M6 ....67 C3
Cummings St OLDS OL8 ....39 D3
Cunard Cl BRUN/LGST M13 ....9 E5
Cundiff Rd CCHDY M21 ....112 A3
Cunningham Wy OLD * OL1 ....22 B1
Curate St STKP SK1 ....130 B4
Curtels Cl WALK M28 ....43 D2
Curtis Rd BNG/LEV M19 ....105 D4
    HTNM SK4 ....127 D3
Curzon Av RUSH/FAL M14 ....103 D1
Curzon Rd BRO M7 ....50 A2
    SALE M33 ....109 C4
    STRET M32 ....95 D2
Curzon St OLD OL1 ....23 C2
Cuthbert Av BNG/LEV M19 ....105 C3
Cutland St NEWH/MOS M40 ....54 B3
Cutler Hill Rd FAIL M35 ....58 B2
Cutter Cl ORD M5 ....83 D1
Cycle St OP/CLY M11 ....90 A1
Cyclone St OP/CLY M11 ....89 C1
Cygnus Av BRO M7 ....67 D2
Cymbal Ct RDSH SK5 ....129 D1
Cypress Av CHAD OL9 ....21 C1
Cypress Rd DROY M43 ....75 D2
    ECC M30 ....60 B1
Cypress St MDTN M24 ....18 A1
Cyprus Cl ORD M5 ....66 A4
Cyprus St STRET M52 ....97 C3
Cyril St RUSH/FAL M14 ....102 A2
Cyrus St NEWH/MOS M40 ....71 C3

D

Daccamill Dr SWIN M27 ....45 C3
Dacre Av OLDTF/WHR M16 ....99 C3
Dagenham Rd RUSH/FAL * M14 ....102 B2
Dagnall Av CCHDY M21 ....112 A3
Daimler St CHH M8 ....51 D3
Daine Av NTHM/RTH M23 ....122 A4
Dainton St WGTN/LGST M12 ....88 A2
Daintry Cl HULME * M15 ....7 E5
Daintry Rd CHAD OL9 ....21 D2
Dairy St CHAD OL9 ....21 C2
Daisy Av BRUN/LGST M13 ....103 D1
Daisy Bank NEWH/MOS M40 ....55 D4
Daisy Bank Av SLFD M6 ....46 B3
Daisy Bank Rd RUSH/FAL M14 ....103 C1
Daisy St CHAD OL9 ....20 B1
    CHAD OL9 ....22 A3
    OFTN SK2 ....133 C2
Dakerwood Cl NEWH/MOS M40 ....55 D4
Dakley St OP/CLY M11 ....90 B2
Dakota Av SALO M50 ....82 B1
Dakota South SALO M50 ....83 C1
Dalbeattie St BKLY M9 ....53 D1
Dalberg St WGTN/LGST M12 ....88 A2
Dalbury Dr NEWH/MOS M40 ....52 B4
Dalby Av SWIN M27 ....44 B2
Dalby Gv STKP SK1 ....130 B4
Dale Av ECC M30 ....61 D2
Dalebeck Cl WHTF M45 ....12 A1
Dalebrook Ct HTNM * SK4 ....128 B4
Daleford Sq BRUN/LGST * M13 ....9 E5
Dales Av CHH M8 ....32 A3
Dales Brow SWIN * M27 ....44 A3
Dalesman Cl BKLY M9 ....54 A1

Dalesman Wk *HULME* M15 .... 8 A5
Dales Park Dr *SWIN* * M27 .... 44 A3
Dale St *ANC* M4 .... 4 B4
   EDGY/DAV SK3 .... 132 A2
   MDTN M24 .... 18 A2
   SWIN M27 .... 44 B3
Dalham Av *BKLY* M9 .... 35 D3
Dalkeith Rd *RDSH* SK5 .... 120 A2
Dalkeith St *GTN* M18 .... 90 A3
Dallas Ct *SALQ* M50 .... 82 B1
Dalley Av *BRO* M7 .... 68 A1
Dalmahoy Cl *NEWH/MOS* M40 .... 55 D1
Dalmain Cl *CHH* M8 .... 51 C3
Dalmorton Rd *CCHDY* M21 .... 113 C1
Dalny St *BNG/LEV* M19 .... 105 C3
Dalston Av *FAIL* M35 .... 58 A1
Dalston Dr *DID/WITH* M20 .... 125 D3
Dalton Av *RUSH/FAL* M14 .... 101 D3
   STRET M32 .... 95 C1
   WHTF M45 .... 11 D2
Dalton Dr *SWIN* M27 .... 47 C2
Dalton Gv *HTNM* SK4 .... 128 B1
Dalton Rd *BKLY* M9 .... 16 A4
   MDTN M24 .... 15 C3
Dalton St *ANC* M4 .... 70 A2
   CHAD OL9 .... 21 C3
   ECC M30 .... 62 A2
   FAIL M35 .... 56 B1
   SALE M33 .... 109 D3
Daltry St *OLD* OL1 .... 23 D1
Damask Av *CSLFD* M3 .... 2 A2
Dameral Cl *CHH* * M8 .... 51 D3
Dame St *CHAD* OL9 .... 22 A1
Dam Head Dr *BKLY* M9 .... 34 B2
Damien St *BNG/LEV* M19 .... 105 C3
Damson Gn *MDTN* M24 .... 18 B3
Danby Ct *OLD* * OL1 .... 22 B1
Dane Bank *MDTN* M24 .... 18 A1
Danebank Wk *BRUN/LGST* * M13 .... 9 D4
Danecroft Cl *BRUN/LGST* M13 .... 88 A4
Danefield Rd *SALE* M33 .... 109 D3
Daneholme Rd *BNG/LEV* M19 .... 116 B3
Dane Ms *SALE* * M33 .... 109 C3
Dane Rd *DTN/ASHW* M34 .... 107 C3
   SALE M33 .... 109 D3
Daneshill *PWCH* M25 .... 12 A3
Danesmoor Rd *DID/WITH* M20 .... 114 B4
Danes Rd *RUSH/FAL* M14 .... 103 C3
Dane St *OP/CLY* M11 .... 91 C3
Danesway *PWCH* M25 .... 31 C3
   SWIN M27 .... 46 B3
Daneswood Av *BKLY* * M9 .... 35 C1
Danett Cl *WGTN/LGST* M12 .... 89 C3
Dan Fold *OLD* * OL1 .... 22 B2
Danforth Gv *BNG/LEV* M19 .... 118 A3
Daniel Adamson Rd *SALQ* M50 .... 82 A1
Daniel's La *STKP* * SK1 .... 130 A3
Danson St *NEWH/MOS* M40 .... 71 D2
Dantall Av *BKLY* M9 .... 35 D3
Dante Cl *SLFD* M6 .... 63 D1
Dantzic St *ANC* M4 .... 4 B1
Dantzic St *ANC* M4 .... 70 A2
Darden Cl *HTNM* SK4 .... 126 B3
Darell Wk *CHH* M8 .... 52 A3
Darenth Cl *HULME* * M15 .... 86 A3
Daresbury Cl *EDGY/DAV* SK3 .... 132 A4
Daresbury Rd *CCHDY* M21 .... 98 A3
Daresbury St *CHH* M8 .... 51 D1
Dargai St *OP/CLY* M11 .... 74 A4
Dargle Rd *SALE* M33 .... 109 C3
Dark La *WGTN/LGST* M12 .... 88 A3
Darley Av *CCHDY* M21 .... 112 B5
   ECC M30 .... 78 B1
Darley St *OLDTF/WHR* M16 .... 99 D2
Darley St *OP/CLY* M11 .... 71 D4
   STRET M32 .... 97 C3
Darlington Rd *DID/WITH* M20 .... 114 B3
Darliston Av *BKLY* M9 .... 14 B4

Darnall Av *DID/WITH* M20 .... 114 B1
Darncombe Cl *OLDTF/WHR* M16 ...... 101 C1
Darnley St *OLDTF/WHR* M16 .... 100 A1
Darras Rd *GTN* M18 .... 105 D2
Dart Cl *CHAD* OL9 .... 20 A1
Dartford Av *ECC* M30 .... 61 C3
   RDSH SK5 .... 121 C3
Dartford Cl *WGTN/LGST* M12 .... 88 A3
Dartmouth Cl *OLDS* OL8 .... 41 C1
Dartmouth Crs *RDSH* SK5 .... 121 D4
Dartmouth Rd *CCHDY* M21 .... 112 B3
   WHTF M45 .... 11 D1
Darton Av *NEWH/MOS* M40 .... 71 C2
Darwell Av *ECC* M30 .... 78 B1
Darwen St *OLDTF/WHR* M16 .... 84 B4
Dashwood Rd *PWCH* M25 .... 11 D4
Dauntesy Av *SWIN* * M27 .... 47 C2
Davenfield Gv *DID/WITH* M20 .... 125 C2
Davenfield Rd *DID/WITH* M20 .... 125 C2
Davenham Rd *RDSH* SK5 .... 107 C3
Davenhill Rd *BNG/LEV* M19 .... 117 D1
Davenport Av *DID/WITH* M20 .... 115 C2
Davenport Park Rd *OFTN* SK2 .... 133 C4
Davenport Rd *DROY* * M43 .... 74 B4
Daventry Rd *CCHDY* M21 .... 113 C1
David's Farm Cl *MDTN* M24 .... 18 A2
Davidson Dr *MDTN* M24 .... 18 A2
David's La *MDTN* M24 .... 18 A2
David St *RDSH* SK5 .... 119 D1
Davies Sq *RUSH/FAL* M14 .... 101 D1
Davies St *OLD* OL1 .... 22 A1
Davis St *ECC* M30 .... 62 B4
Davy Av *SWIN* M27 .... 46 A1
Davyhulme Rd *STRET* M32 .... 96 B2
Davyhulme Rd East *STRET* M32 .... 97 C2
Davy St *NEWH/MOS* * M40 .... 70 A1
Dawlish Av *DROY* M43 .... 74 B3
   RDSH SK5 .... 121 C4
Dawlish Rd *CCHDY* M21 .... 112 B1
Dawnay St *OP/CLY* M11 .... 90 A2
Dawson Rd *CSLFD* * M3 .... 3 E2
   CSLFD M3 .... 6 B2
   STKP SK1 .... 131 C2
   SWIN M27 .... 45 D1
Day Dr *FAIL* M35 .... 57 C3
Deacons Cl *STKP* SK1 .... 130 B4
Deacons Dr *SLFD* M6 .... 47 C3
Deal Av *RDSH* SK5 .... 121 C3
Deal Cl *NEWH/MOS* M40 .... 56 A4
Deal St *CSLFD* * M3 .... 3 D1
Dean Av *NEWH/MOS* M40 .... 55 C2
   OLDTF/WHR M16 .... 99 C2
Deanbank Av *BNG/LEV* M19 .... 117 C1
Dean Brook Cl *NEWH/MOS* * M40 ...... 55 C2
Dean Cl *WHTF* M45 .... 10 A2
Dean Ct *HULME* * M15 .... 85 C3
Deanery Wy *STKP* SK1 .... 130 A3
Dean La *NEWH/MOS* M40 .... 55 C3
Dean Rd *CSLFD* M3 .... 3 D1
   GTN M18 .... 106 B1
Deanscourt Av *SWIN* M27 .... 44 B2
Deansgate *HULME* M15 .... 7 D3
Deanshut Rd *OLDS* OL8 .... 47 C5
Deans Rd *SWIN* M27 .... 44 B2
Dean St *CMANE* M1 .... 5 D4
   FAIL M35 .... 56 B2
Deansway *SWIN* M27 .... 44 B2
Deanswood Dr *BKLY* M9 .... 14 B4
Deanwater Cl *BRUN/LGST* M13 .... 9 D4
Deanwater Ct *STRET* * M32 .... 109 D1
Deanway *NEWH/MOS* M40 .... 54 B1
Dearden St *HULME* M15 .... 7 D5
Dearmans Pl *CSLFD* M3 .... 3 D3
Dearne Dr *STRET* M32 .... 97 D3
Debdale La *GTN* M18 .... 107 C1
Debenham Av *NEWH/MOS* M40 .... 73 D1
Debenham Rd *STRET* M32 .... 95 D4

Deepcar St *BNG/LEV* M19 ....104 B3
Deepdale Av *DID/WITH* M20 ....114 A1
Deepdale Cl *RDSH* SK5 ....107 C4
Deepdale Dr *URM* M41 ....47 C2
Deeping Av *OLDTF/WHR* M16 ....100 A3
Deerfold Cl *GTN* * M18 ....91 C4
Deerhurst Dr *CHH* M8 ....51 C3
Deeroak Cl *GTN* M18 ....90 A3
Deerpark Rd *OLDTF/WHR* M16 ....100 B2
Deer St *CMANE* M1 ....9 E1
Deganwy Gv *RDSH* SK5 ....120 A4
Delacourt Rd *RUSH/FAL* M14 ....114 B1
Delafield Av *WGTN/LGST* M12 ....104 A3
Delahays Range *GTN* M18 ....107 C1
Delaine Rd *DID/WITH* M20 ....115 D3
Delamere Av *SLFD* M6 ....46 B3
 STRET M32 ....97 C3
 SWIN M27 ....27 C3
 WHTF M45 ....10 B1
Delamere Rd *BNG/LEV* M19 ....117 D1
Delamere St *OP/CLY* M11 ....92 A2
Delaunays Rd *CHH* M8 ....33 C3
Dell Av *SWIN* M27 ....47 C2
Dellcot Cl *PWCH* M25 ....31 C3
 SLFD M6 ....46 A4
Dellcot La *WALK* M28 ....42 A4
The Delph *WALK* * M28 ....42 A3
Delside Av *NEWH/MOS* M40 ....54 B1
Delvino Wk *HULME* M15 ....101 C1
Demesne Rd *OLDTF/WHR* M16 ....100 B3
Denbigh Pl *SLFD* M6 ....66 B4
Denbigh Rd *SWIN* M27 ....26 B3
Denbigh St *HTNM* SK4 ....129 C2
 OLDS * OL8 ....41 C2
Denbigh Wk *HULME* M15 ....85 D4
Denby La *HTNM* SK4 ....129 C1
Dencombe St *BRUN/LGST* M13 ....104 A3
Dene Ct *HTNM* * SK4 ....128 B3
Dene Dr *MDTN* M24 ....17 C2
Deneford Rd *DID/WITH* M20 ....124 B3
Dene Hollow *RDSH* SK5 ....107 C4
Denehurst St *WGTN/LGST* * M12 ....89 C1
Dene Pk *DID/WITH* M20 ....124 B3
Dene Rd *DID/WITH* M20 ....124 B2
Dene Rd West *DID/WITH* M20 ....124 A2
Deneway *HTNM* SK4 ....128 B3
Deneway Cl *HTNM* SK4 ....128 B3
Deneway Ms *HTNM* * SK4 ....128 B3
Denewell Cl *BRUN/LGST* M13 ....88 A4
Denham St *BRUN/LGST* M13 ....103 C1
Denhill Rd *HULME* M15 ....101 C1
Denis Av *OLDTF/WHR* M16 ....100 B3
Denison Rd *RUSH/FAL* M14 ....103 C1
Denison St *RUSH/FAL* M14 ....102 B2
Deniston Rd *HTNM* SK4 ....118 A4
Denmark Rd *RUSH/FAL* M14 ....101 C1
 SALE M33 ....109 C3
Denmark St *CHAD* OL9 ....21 D1
Denmark Wy *CHAD* OL9 ....21 D1
Denmore Rd *NEWH/MOS* M40 ....36 B3
Dennison Av *DID/WITH* M20 ....115 D3
Denshaw Av *BNG/LEV* M19 ....126 B2
Densmead Wk *NEWH/MOS* M40 ....5 F1
Densmore St *FAIL* * M35 ....56 B2
Denstone Av *ECC* M30 ....62 B3
Denstone Rd *RDSH* SK5 ....107 C4
 SLFD M6 ....47 C2
Denton La *CHAD* OL9 ....20 B4
Denver Av *NEWH/MOS* M40 ....71 C2
Deramore St *RUSH/FAL* M14 ....102 A2
Derby Av *SLFD* M6 ....65 D3
Derby Ct *CHAD* OL9 ....21 D4
Derby Gv *BNG/LEV* M19 ....105 C4
Derby Range *HTNM* SK4 ....128 A1
Derby Rd *HTNM* SK4 ....128 B1
 RUSH/FAL M14 ....115 D2
 SLFD M6 ....65 D3
 URM M41 ....94 A2

WHTF M45 ....11 D3
Derbyshire Av *STRET* M32 ....96 A2
Derbyshire Crs *STRET* M32 ....96 A2
Derbyshire Gv *STRET* M32 ....95 D2
Derbyshire La *STRET* M32 ....96 B3
Derbyshire La West *URM* M41 ....41 C4
Derbyshire Rd *NEWH/MOS* M40 ....74 A1
 SALE M33 ....109 D3
Derbyshire St *OP/CLY* M11 ....90 B2
Derby St *CHAD* OL9 ....21 D4
 CHAD OL9 ....50 B4
 CHH M8 ....50 B4
 EDGY/DAV SK3 ....132 A1
 FAIL * M35 ....38 B4
 PWCH M25 ....29 D1
Derg St *SLFD* M6 ....66 A3
Derker St *OLD* OL1 ....23 D1
Dermot Murphy Cl *DID/WITH* M20 ....114 A3
Dernford Av *BNG/LEV* M19 ....117 C4
Derwen Rd *EDGY/DAV* SK3 ....132 B2
Derwent Av *CCHDY* M21 ....113 C4
 DROY M43 ....74 B4
 WHTF M45 ....12 A1
Derwent Cl *WHTF* M45 ....12 A2
Derwent Dr *CHAD* OL9 ....20 B2
Derwent Rd *STRET* M32 ....97 C3
Derwent St *CHH* M8 ....52 B3
 OP/CLY * M11 ....74 A4
 ORD M5 ....84 B1
Dettingen St *SLFD* M6 ....47 D3
Deva Sq *CHAD* * OL9 ....21 D4
Devas St *HULME* M15 ....87 C4
Deverill Av *GTN* M18 ....107 C1
Devine Cl *CSLFD* M3 ....2 A2
Devon Av *BNG/LEV* M19 ....117 C4
Devon Cl *RDSH* SK5 ....131 D1
 SLFD M6 ....63 D2
Devon Rd *DROY* M43 ....75 D2
 FAIL M35 ....56 B3
Devonshire Cl *URM* M41 ....94 B3
Devonshire Park Rd *OFTN* SK2 ....133 D4
Devonshire Pl *PWCH* M25 ....11 D4
Devonshire Rd *CCHDY* M21 ....112 B1
 ECC M30 ....62 B3
 HTNM SK4 ....128 A3
 SLFD M6 ....65 D2
Devonshire St *BRO* M7 ....50 B3
 WGTN/LGST M12 ....88 A3
Devonshire St East *NEWH/MOS* * M40 .....56 A4
Devonshire St North *WGTN/LGST* M12 ....88 A2
Devonshire St South *BRUN/LGST* M13 ....88 A4
Devon St *CHAD* OL9 ....39 C1
 SWIN M27 ....26 A3
Devon Wy *OLDS* OL8 ....39 D3
Dewar St *OP/CLY* M11 ....72 B2
Dewes Av *SWIN* M27 ....27 C3
Dewey St *OP/CLY* M11 ....91 C2
Dewhurst St *CHH* M8 ....69 C1
Dew Wy *CHAD* OL9 ....22 A2
Dexter Rd *BKLY* M9 ....14 B4
Deyne Av *PWCH* M25 ....30 A1
 RUSH/FAL M14 ....102 B1
Deyne St *SLFD* M6 ....65 D3
Diamond St *OFTN* SK2 ....133 D3
Dickenson Rd *RUSH/FAL* M14 ....103 C2
Dickens Rd *ECC* M30 ....62 A4
Dickinson St *CMANE* M1 ....8 A1
 CSLFD M3 ....68 B2
Didley Sq *WGTN/LGST* * M12 ....89 C3
Didsbury Pk *DID/WITH* M20 ....125 C3
Didsbury Rd *HTNM* SK4 ....126 B3
Dillmoss Wk *HULME* * M15 ....85 C3
Dillon Dr *WGTN/LGST* M12 ....88 B4
Dilston Cl *BRUN/LGST* M13 ....87 D3
Dilworth St *HULME* M15 ....87 C4
Dingle Dr *DROY* M43 ....76 A2
Dingle Rd *MDTN* M24 ....16 B3
Dinnington Dr *CHH* M8 ....51 C3
Dinorwic Cl *CHH* M8 ....32 B3

Dinting Av *DID/WITH* M20 ....**114** B2
Dinton St *HULME* M15 ....**84** B2
Discovery Pk *HTNM* * SK4 ....**118** D3
Disley Av *DID/WITH* M20 ....**114** A3
Dixon Av *BRO* M7 ....**50** A3
Dixon Dr *SWIN* M27 ....**25** D1
Dixon St *NEWH/MOS* M40 ....**55** C3
   SLFD M6 ....**48** A3
Dobcross Cl *BRUN/LGST* M13 ....**104** B3
Dobroyd St *CHH* M8 ....**51** D1
Dobson Cl *BRUN/LGST* M13 ....**88** A3
Doddington La *ORD* M5 ....**83** D1
Dodd St *ORD* M5 ....**65** C3
Dodge Hl *HTNM* SK4 ....**129** D3
Dodworth Cl *HULME* M15 ....**86** A3
Doe Brow *SWIN* M27 ....**25** D1
Dolbey St *ORD* M5 ....**65** D4
Dolefield *CSLFD* M3 ....**3** D1
Dollond St *BKLY* M9 ....**34** B4
Dolphin Pl *WGTN/LGST* M12 ....**9** F4
Dolphin St *WGTN/LGST* M12 ....**9** F4
Domett St *ORD* M5 ....**53** D3
Donald St *CMANE* * M1 ....**9** F4
Dona St *STKP* SK1 ....**133** D1
Don Av *SLFD* M6 ....**64** B3
Doncaster Av *DID/WITH* M20 ....**114** A4
Doncaster Wk *OLD* OL1 ....**23** C2
Donhead Wk *BRUN/LGST* * M13 ....**87** D3
Donleigh St *NEWH/MOS* M40 ....**56** A3
Donnington Rd *GTN* M18 ....**91** D4
Donnison St *WGTN/LGST* M12 ....**89** D3
Donovan Av *NEWH/MOS* M40 ....**70** B1
Dorchester Av *PWCH* M25 ....**30** B3
   URM M41 ....**95** C2
Dorchester St *SWIN* M27 ....**45** C3
Dorclyn Av *URM* M41 ....**94** A3
Doric Cl *OP/CLY* M11 ....**72** A4
Dorking Av *NEWH/MOS* M40 ....**72** B1
Dorlan Av *GTN* M18 ....**107** C1
Dorman St *OP/CLY* M11 ....**91** C2
Dorney St *GTN* M18 ....**91** C4
Dorning Rd *SWIN* M27 ....**45** D2
Dorning St *ECC* M30 ....**62** A4
Dorothy St *BRO* M7 ....**51** C2
Dorris St *BNG/LEV* M19 ....**118** A1
Dorset Av *DTN/ASHW* M34 ....**93** D1
   RDSH SK5 ....**111** D4
   RUSH/FAL M14 ....**101** C3
Dorset Rd *BNG/LEV* M19 ....**105** D4
   DROY M43 ....**75** C2
   FAIL M35 ....**57** C4
Dorset St *CHAD* OL9 ....**21** D4
   STRET M32 ....**97** C4
   SWIN M27 ....**26** A3
Dorsey St *ANC* * M4 ....**4** C3
Dorstone Cl *NEWH/MOS* M40 ....**73** D1
Dorwood Av *BKLY* M9 ....**15** C3
Dougall Wk *WGTN/LGST* M12 ....**89** D3
Doughty Av *ECC* M30 ....**63** C2
Douglas Gn *SLFD* M6 ....**48** B4
Douglas Rd *SWIN* M27 ....**43** D2
Douglas St *BRO* M7 ....**50** A3
   FAIL M35 ....**57** C2
   NEWH/MOS M40 ....**54** B2
   OLD OL1 ....**23** D1
   SWIN M27 ....**45** D2
Doulton St *NEWH/MOS* M40 ....**55** D1
Dounby Av *ECC* M30 ....**61** C2
Douro St *NEWH/MOS* M40 ....**54** A4
Dovecote *DROY* M43 ....**77** C2
Dovecote Ms *CCHDY* M21 ....**111** D1
Dovedale Av *DID/WITH* M20 ....**114** B2
   DROY M43 ....**74** B3
   ECC M30 ....**62** B2
   PWCH M25 ....**31** C2
   URM M41 ....**94** A3
Dovedale St *FAIL* M35 ....**56** B2

Dovehouse Cl *WHTF* M45 ....**10** A1
Doveleys Rd *SLFD* M6 ....**47** D4
Dovercourt Av *HTNM* * SK4 ....**127** C2
Doveridge Gdns *SLFD* M6 ....**66** A2
Dover Pk *URM* M41 ....**94** A1
Dover Rd *SWIN* M27 ....**26** B3
Dover St *BRUN/LGST* M13 ....**87** C3
   CHAD OL9 ....**21** D1
   ECC M30 ....**61** C3
   RDSH * SK5 ....**119** D2
Dovestone Wk *NEWH/MOS* * M40 ..**37** D4
Doveston Rd *SALE* M33 ....**109** C3
Downfields *RDSH* SK5 ....**107** D4
Downham Crs *PWCH* M25 ....**31** D2
Downham Gdns *PWCH* M25 ....**31** D2
Downham Rd *HTNM* SK4 ....**119** C2
Downing St *CMANE* M1 ....**9** D3
Downley Dr *ANC* M4 ....**5** F3
The Downs *MDTN* M24 ....**18** A3
   PWCH M25 ....**29** D2
Dowry St *OLDS* OL8 ....**23** C1
Drake Cl *OLD* OL1 ....**23** C1
Drake Ct *RDSH* SK5 ....**129** D1
Drayfields *DROY* M43 ....**77** C3
Drayton Wk *OLDTF/WHR* M16 ....**84** D4
Dresden St *NEWH/MOS* M40 ....**55** D1
Drewett St *NEWH/MOS* M40 ....**71** D1
Dreyfus Av *OP/CLY* M11 ....**73** D3
Driffield St *ECC* M30 ....**78** B1
   RUSH/FAL M14 ....**101** D2
Drill Wk *ANC* M4 ....**5** F4
Drinkwater Rd *PWCH* M25 ....**29** C3
Driscoll St *BRUN/LGST* M13 ....**104** A2
The Drive *BRO* M7 ....**30** B4
   DID/WITH M20 ....**125** D2
   PWCH M25 ....**30** A1
   RDSH SK5 ....**131** D1
Droitwich Rd *NEWH/MOS* M40 ......**71** C1
Dronfield Rd *SLFD* M6 ....**65** C1
Droughts La *PWCH* M25 ....**13** C1
Droylsden Rd *DTN/ASHW* M34 ......**76** A4
   NEWH/MOS M40 ....**56** A4
Drury La *CHAD* OL9 ....**38** B2
Drury St *BNG/LEV* M19 ....**104** B4
Dryad Cl *SWIN* M27 ....**26** A3
Drybrook Cl *BRUN/LGST* M13 ....**88** B4
Dryden Av *SWIN* M27 ....**26** A4
Dryden Rd *OLDTF/WHR* M16 ....**99** D2
Dryden St *BRUN/LGST* M13 ....**87** D3
Dryhurst Wk *HULME* M15 ....**86** B3
Drymoss *OLDS* OL8 ....**41** C4
Drywood Av *WALK* M28 ....**42** B4
Ducal St *ANC* M4 ....**70** A1
Duchess Rd *CHH* M8 ....**52** A1
Duchy Bank *SLFD* M6 ....**47** C3
Duchy Rd *SLFD* M6 ....**47** C3
Duchy St *EDGY/DAV* SK3 ....**132** A2
   SLFD M6 ....**66** A2
Ducie Gv *HULME* M15 ....**87** C4
Ducie St *CMANE* M1 ....**5** D5
   OLDS OL8 ....**41** C3
   WHTF M45 ....**11** C1
Duckworth Rd *PWCH* M25 ....**29** C2
Duddon Cl *WHTF* M45 ....**12** A1
Dudley Av *WHTF* M45 ....**11** C1
Dudley Cl *HULME* M15 ....**85** D4
Dudley Rd *OLDTF/WHR* M16 ....**100** A2
   SALE M33 ....**109** C3
   SWIN M27 ....**26** A4
Dudley St *CHH* M8 ....**51** C3
   ECC M30 ....**61** C3
Dudlow Wk *HULME* * M15 ....**85** C3
Duffield Ct *MDTN* * M24 ....**17** C4
Duffield Gdns *MDTN* M24 ....**17** C4
Duffield Rd *MDTN* M24 ....**17** C4
   SLFD M6 ....**47** C4
Dugdale Av *BKLY* M9 ....**34** B1
Duice Pl *ORD* M5 ....**67** D4

Duke Ct *OLDTF/WHR* M16 ....85 C4
Duke Pl *CSLFD* M3 ....6 C2
Duke St *BRO* M7 ....50 C4
   CSLFD M3 ....3 E2
   CSLFD M3 ....6 C2
   ECC M30 ....61 D1
   FAIL M35 ....57 D1
   STKP SK1 ....129 D4
Dulford Wk *BRUN/LGST* M13 ....87 C4
Dulgar St *OP/CLY* M11 ....90 A1
Dulverton St *NEWH/MOS* M40 ....55 C3
Dulwich St *ANC* M4 ....70 D4
Dumbarton Cl *RDSH* SK5 ....120 A3
Dumbarton Rd *RDSH* SK5 ....120 A3
Dumbell St *SWIN* M27 ....26 A3
Dumber La *SALE* M33 ....108 A3
Dunbar St *OLD* OL1 ....22 A1
Dunblane Av *HTNM* SK4 ....129 D1
Duncan Rd *DID/WITH* M20 ....125 D2
Duncan St *BRO* M7 ....49 D3
   ORD M5 ....84 B1
Dun Cl *CSLFD* M3 ....2 A3
Duncombe Dr *NEWH/MOS* M40 ....55 C3
Duncombe Rd *BRO* M7 ....50 B3
Dundonald Rd *DID/WITH* M20 ....125 D2
Dundonald St *OFTN* SK2 ....133 C4
Dunedin Dr *SLFD* M6 ....48 A4
Dunham St *HULME* M15 ....85 D3
Dunkerley Av *FAIL* M35 ....57 C2
Dunkirk Cl *DTN/ASHW* M34 ....107 D1
Dunkirk St *DROY* M43 ....76 A4
Dunley Cl *WGTN/LGST* M12 ....89 C4
Dunlop St *CSLFD* M3 ....3 E4
Dunoon Rd *RDSH* SK5 ....120 A2
Dunscar Cl *WHTF* M45 ....10 A2
Dunsley Av *NEWH/MOS* M40 ....37 C3
Dunsmore Cl *OLDTF/WHR* M16 ....100 A1
Dunstable *BNG/LEV* M19 ....105 C4
Dunster Av *BKLY* M9 ....34 B1
   RDSH SK5 ....121 D4
   SWIN M27 ....27 C3
Dunston St *OP/CLY* M11 ....90 B1
Dunton Gn *RDSH* SK5 ....121 C3
Dunworth St *RUSH/FAL* M14 ....102 A2
Durant St *ANC* M4 ....4 C1
Durban St *AULW* OL7 ....77 D4
   OLDS OL8 ....39 D2
Durham Av *URM* M41 ....94 B2
Durham Crs *FAIL* M35 ....57 D1
Durham Rd *SLFD* M6 ....46 B4
Durham St *BKLY* * M9 ....53 D2
   CHAD OL9 ....39 D1
   DROY M43 ....92 B1
   RDSH SK5 ....106 B3
Durley Av *CHH* M8 ....52 A2
Durling St *WGTN/LGST* M12 ....9 F4
Durnford Av *URM* M41 ....95 D3
Dutton St *CSLFD* M3 ....69 C2
Dyche St *ANC* M4 ....4 B2
Dyer St *OP/CLY* M11 ....89 D1
   ORD M5 ....84 B2
Dymchurch St *NEWH/MOS* M40 ....73 D1
Dyserth Gv *RDSH* SK5 ....120 A4

E

Eades St *SLFD* M6 ....66 B2
Eadington St *CHH* M8 ....32 B4
Eagar St *NEWH/MOS* M40 ....55 C3
Eagle Dr *SLFD* M6 ....48 B2
Eagle St *CHAD* OL9 ....22 B3
Ealing Av *RUSH/FAL* M14 ....102 A3
Ealinger Wy *SWIN* M27 ....26 A3
Ealing Pl *BNG/LEV* * M19 ....117 D3
Earby Gv *BKLY* M9 ....35 C2
Earl Rd *HTNM* SK4 ....128 B1
Earlston Av *DTN/ASHW* M34 ....107 D2
Earl St *BRO* M7 ....68 A1
   DTN/ASHW M34 ....107 D1
   EDGY/DAV SK3 ....132 A3
   PWCH M25 ....30 B1
Earls Wy *FAIL* M35 ....56 A3
Earl Wk *WGTN/LGST* * M12 ....89 C4
Earnshaw Av *STKP* SK1 ....131 C4
East Aisle Rd *TRPK* M17 ....96 B1
East Av *BNG/LEV* M19 ....117 C2
Eastburn Av *NEWH/MOS* M40 ....70 B2
East Central Dr *SWIN* M27 ....46 A2
Eastcombe Av *BRO* M7 ....49 C2
Eastcote Rd *RDSH* SK5 ....120 A4
East Dr *SLFD* M6 ....47 D4
   SWIN M27 ....46 A2
Eastern Av *SWIN* M27 ....28 A2
Eastern By-Pass *OP/CLY* M11 ....73 D3
Eastern Cir *BNG/LEV* M19 ....117 D3
Eastfield *SLFD* M6 ....65 D1
Eastfield Av *MDTN* M24 ....18 A4
   NEWH/MOS M40 ....71 D2
Eastford Sq *NEWH/MOS* M40 ....70 A1
East Gra *OP/CLY* M11 ....73 D3
East Gv *BRUN/LGST* M13 ....87 D4
Eastham Av *RUSH/FAL* M14 ....102 A4
Easthaven Av *OP/CLY* M11 ....73 D3
East Hill St *OLDE* * OL4 ....23 D3
Eastholme Dr *BNG/LEV* M19 ....118 A2
Easthope Cl *DID/WITH* M20 ....115 C2
Eastlands Rd *BKLY* M9 ....16 B4
Eastleigh Av *BRO* M7 ....50 B1
Eastleigh Dr *NEWH/MOS* M40 ....71 C2
Eastleigh Rd *PWCH* M25 ....31 D2
East Meade *CCHDY* M21 ....112 A2
   PWCH M25 ....31 C3
   SWIN M27 ....44 B3
Eastmoor Dr *NEWH/MOS* M40 ....74 A1
East Newton St *ANC* * M4 ....5 F1
Eastnor Cl *HULME* * M15 ....85 C3
Easton Cl *MDTN* M24 ....18 B2
Easton Rd *DROY* M43 ....74 B3
East Ordsall La *ORD* M5 ....2 A5
East Park Cl *BRUN/LGST* * M13 ....9 F5
Eastpark Cl *BRUN/LGST* M13 ....87 D3
East Philip St *CSLFD* M3 ....68 B2
East Rd *STRET* M32 ....96 A1
   WGTN/LGST M12 ....104 B2
Eastry Av *RDSH* SK5 ....121 C4
East Union St *OLDTF/WHR* M16 ....84 B3
East Vw *MDTN* M24 ....17 C1
Eastville Gdns *BNG/LEV* M19 ....116 B4
Eastwood Av *DROY* M43 ....74 B4
   NEWH/MOS M40 ....38 A4
   URM M41 ....94 A3
Eastwood Rd *NEWH/MOS* M40 ....38 A4
Eaton Rd *CHH* M8 ....32 A4
Eaves La *CHAD* OL9 ....20 B4
Ebbdale Cl *STKP* SK1 ....133 D1
Ebberstone St *RUSH/FAL* M14 ....101 D3
Ebden St *CMANE* * M1 ....8 C2
Ebenezer St *HULME* M15 ....7 F4
Ebsworth St *NEWH/MOS* M40 ....54 A1
Eccles Cl *OP/CLY* M11 ....90 B1
Eccles Fold *OP/CLY* M11 ....73 D4
Eccleshall St *OP/CLY* M11 ....73 D4
Eccles New Rd *ORD* M5 ....64 A3
Eccles Old Rd *SLFD* M6 ....64 B2
Eccles Rd *SWIN* M27 ....45 C3
Eccleston Av *RUSH/FAL* M14 ....101 D4
   SWIN M27 ....44 A2
Eccleston Pl *BRO* * M7 ....50 A1
Eccleston St *FAIL* * M35 ....57 D1
Echo St *CMANE* M1 ....8 C3
Eckford St *CHH* M8 ....52 A3
Edale Av *NEWH/MOS* M40 ....54 B1
   RDSH SK5 ....107 D3
Edale Rd *STRET* M32 ....96 A2
Edale St *SLFD* M6 ....49 C4

Edbrook Wk *BRUN/LGST* * M13 ....**88** A4
Eddie Colman Cl *NEWH/MOS* * M40 ....**55** C4
Eddisbury Av *DID/WITH* M20 ....**114** A1
Eddystone Cl *ORD* M5 ....**66** B4
Edenbridge Rd *NEWH/MOS* M40 ....**73** C1
Eden Cl *HULME* M15 ....**86** A3
STKP SK1 ....**133** D1
Edenfield La *WALK* M28 ....**60** A1
Edenfield Rd *PWCH* M25 ....**31** D2
Edenhall Av *BNG/LEV* M19 ....**117** C1
Eden St *OLD* OL1 ....**22** B2
Edgbaston Dr *OLDTF/WHR* M16 ....**99** D2
Edgedale Av *BNG/LEV* M19 ....**116** B4
Edgefield Av *BKLY* M9 ....**34** B1
Edgehill Cl *SLFD* M6 ....**66** A3
Edgehill Rd *SLFD* M6 ....**64** B2
Edgehill St *ANC* * M4 ....**4** B3
Edge La *OP/CLY* M11 ....**74** A3
STRET M32 ....**97** D4
Edge Lane Rd *OLD* OL1 ....**23** C5
Edge St *ANC* M4 ....**4** B3
Edgeware Av *PWCH* M25 ....**32** A1
Edgeware Rd *CHAD* OL9 ....**37** D2
ECC M30 ....**60** B1
Edgewater *ORD* M5 ....**65** C3
Edgeworth Dr *RUSH/FAL* M14 ....**116** B2
Edgware Rd *NEWH/MOS* M40 ....**73** C1
Edilom Rd *CHH* M8 ....**31** D3
Edinburgh Sq *NEWH/MOS* M40 ....**71** C1
Edison Rd *ECC* M30 ....**78** B1
Edison St *OP/CLY* M11 ....**91** D2
Edith Av *RUSH/FAL* M14 ....**101** D3
Edith Cavell Cl *OP/CLY* M11 ....**73** C4
Edith St *OLDS* OL8 ....**41** C2
Edlin Cl *WGTN/LGST* M12 ....**88** B3
Edmonton Rd *NEWH/MOS* M40 ....**72** B1
Edmund Cl *HTNM* SK4 ....**129** D2
Edmund St *CSLFD* * M3 ....**2** C1
DROY M43 ....**92** B3
FAIL * M35 ....**57** C1
SLFD M6 ....**65** D2
Edson Rd *CHH* M8 ....**32** A2
Edward Av *CCHDY* M21 ....**111** C1
SLFD M6 ....**64** B2
Edward Charlton Rd
OLDTF/WHR * M16 ....**99** C3
Edward Ms *CHAD* * OL9 ....**21** D4
Edward Rd *BKLY* M9 ....**16** A4
Edwards Dr *WHTF* M45 ....**12** A1
Edward St *BKLY* M9 ....**53** D1
BRO M7 ....**68** B3
CHAD OL9 ....**20** B2
CHAD OL9 ....**21** D3
DROY * M43 ....**92** B1
PWCH M25 ....**11** D4
STKP SK1 ....**133** C1
Edwin Rd *OP/CLY* M11 ....**71** D4
Eeasbrook *URM* M41 ....**94** A4
Egbert St *NEWH/MOS* M40 ....**55** C2
Egerton Crs *DID/WITH* * M20 ....**115** C2
Egerton Dr *SALE* M33 ....**109** C4
Egerton Ms *DROY* * M43 ....**92** B1
RUSH/FAL M14 ....**116** A1
Egerton Pk *WALK* M28 ....**43** C2
Egerton Rd *ECC* M30 ....**62** A1
RUSH/FAL M14 ....**116** A1
WHTF M45 ....**11** C2
Egerton Rd North *CCHDY* M21 ....**99** D3
HTNM SK4 ....**118** B3
Egerton Rd South *CCHDY* M21 ....**112** B1
HTNM SK4 ....**118** B4
Egerton St *DROY* M43 ....**76** A4
ECC M30 ....**61** C3
HULME M15 ....**6** B5
MDTN * M24 ....**15** D2
OLD OL1 ....**23** D2
PWCH M25 ....**30** B1
Egerton Ter *RUSH/FAL* M14 ....**116** A2
Eggington St *NEWH/MOS* M40 ....**52** B4
Egmont St *CHH* M8 ....**51** D1
SLFD M6 ....**47** D3
Egremont Av *DID/WITH* M20 ....**114** B2
Egremont Ct *BRO* * M7 ....**49** D1
Eida Wy *TRPK* M17 ....**81** D1
Eighth Av *OLDS* OL8 ....**40** A4
Eighth St *TRPK* M17 ....**81** D3
Eileen Gv *RUSH/FAL* M14 ....**102** B3
Eileen Gv West *RUSH/FAL* M14 ......**102** A3
Elaine Av *BKLY* M9 ....**36** A3
Elbe St *WGTN/LGST* * M12 ....**9** F2
Elbow St *BNG/LEV* M19 ....**104** B4
Elcot Cl *NEWH/MOS* * M40 ....**72** B1
Elder Gv *NEWH/MOS* M40 ....**38** A3
Eldermount Rd *BKLY* M9 ....**34** A3
Elderwood *CHAD* OL9 ....**19** D2
Eldon Pl *ECC* M30 ....**61** D4
Eldon Prec *OLDS* OL8 ....**22** B4
Eldon St *OLDS* OL8 ....**23** C4
Eldridge Dr *NEWH/MOS* M40 ....**54** B4
Eleanor Rd *CCHDY* M21 ....**111** C1
Eleanor St *OLD* OL1 ....**22** A1
Electo St *OP/CLY* M11 ....**91** D2
Elevator Rd *TRPK* M17 ....**82** B3
Eleventh St *TRPK* M17 ....**82** A3
Elf Mill Cl *EDGY/DAV* SK3 ....**132** B5
Elford Gv *GTN* M18 ....**107** D1
Elgar St *WGTN/LGST* M12 ....**104** B2
Elgin Av *DID/WITH* * M20 ....**126** A2
Elgol Cl *EDGY/DAV* SK3 ....**133** C4
Eliot Rd *ECC* M30 ....**62** A4
Eli St *CHAD* OL9 ....**38** B4
Eliza Ann St *ECC* M30 ....**61** D1
NEWH/MOS M40 ....**70** B1
Elizabeth Av *CHAD* OL9 ....**38** B1
STKP * SK1 ....**133** C5
Elizabeth Cl *STRET* M32 ....**97** C3
Elizabeth Ct *HTNM* SK4 ....**128** B3
RUSH/FAL M14 ....**116** A2
Elizabeth Slinger Rd *DID/WITH* M20 ..**123** D1
Elizabeth St *CHH* M8 ....**51** D1
SWIN M27 ....**26** A4
WHTF M45 ....**11** C2
Eliza St *HULME* M15 ....**6** C5
Elkanagh Gdns *SLFD* M6 ....**66** A2
Ellanby Cl *RUSH/FAL* M14 ....**102** A2
Ellaston Dr *URM* * M41 ....**94** A3
Ellastone Rd *SLFD* M6 ....**64** B1
Ellbourne Rd *BKLY* M9 ....**32** B1
Ellenbrook Cl *WGTN/LGST* M12 ......**90** A3
Ellen Gv *FWTH* BL4 ....**24** B1
Ellenhall Cl *BKLY* M9 ....**53** C1
Ellen St *CHAD* OL9 ....**22** C1
DROY M43 ....**93** C1
HTNM SK4 ....**129** C2
Ellen Wilkinson Crs *WGTN/LGST* M12 ..**89** D2
Elleray Rd *MDTN* M24 ....**17** C4
SLFD M6 ....**47** C4
Ellerby Av *SWIN* M27 ....**26** B2
Ellesmere Av *ECC* M30 ....**62** B3
Ellesmere Cir *URM* M41 ....**79** C2
Ellesmere Rd *CCHDY* M21 ....**99** D4
ECC M30 ....**62** B1
Ellesmere Rd North *HTNM* SK4 ....**118** B1
Ellesmere Rd South *CHDY* M21 ......**112** B1
Ellesmere St *ECC* M30 ....**62** A4
FAIL M35 ....**57** C1
HULME M15 ....**6** A4
SWIN M27 ....**26** B4
SWIN M27 ....**44** A2
Ellesmere Ter *RUSH/FAL* M14 ....**116** A2
Ellingham Cl *OP/CLY* M11 ....**72** A4
Elliot Sq *OLD* * OL1 ....**23** D1
Ellis Dr *CHH* M8 ....**33** C4
Ellis La *MDTN* M24 ....**15** C1
Ellis St *BRO* M7 ....**68** B1

HULME M15 ....85 D3
Elliston Sq *WGTN/LGST* M12 ....89 D3
Ellor St *SLFD* M6 ....66 A2
  SLFD M6 ....67 C3
Ellwood Rd *STKP* SK4 ....131 C4
Elmbank Av *DID/WITH* M20 ....123 D1
Elmbank Rd *MDTN* M24 ....18 B1
Elm Crs *WALK* M28 ....42 B2
Elmdale Wk *HULME* * M15 ....8 A5
Elm Dr *STRET* M32 ....96 A4
Elmfield Dr *DTN/ASHW* M34 ....93 D1
  EDGY/DAV SK3 ....133 C4
Elmfield St *CHH* M8 ....51 D3
Elmgate Gv *BNG/LEV* M19 ....104 B3
Elm Gv *DID/WITH* M20 ....125 C2
  DROY M43 ....74 A3
  PWCH M25 ....11 D3
  SALE M33 ....109 C3
  URM M41 ....94 B3
  WALK M28 ....24 A4
Elmham Av *NEWH/MOS* M40 ....70 B1
Elmhurst Dr *BNG/LEV* M19 ....117 C1
Elm Rd *DID/WITH* M20 ....124 B1
  DID/WITH M20 ....125 C1
  OLDS OL8 ....40 A4
Elmscott Wk *BRUN/LGST* M13 ......88 A4
Elmsdale Av *BKLY* M9 ....16 A4
Elmsmere Rd *DID/WITH* M20 ....126 A2
Elms Rd *HTNM* SK4 ....118 A4
Elmstead Av *DID/WITH* M20 ....114 B3
Elm St *ECC* M30 ....62 A4
  FAIL M35 ....57 C1
  MDTN M24 ....18 B1
  SWIN M27 ....25 D4
Elmswood Av *RUSH/FAL* M14 ......101 C3
Elmsworth Av *BNG/LEV* M19 ......105 C4
Elmton Rd *BKLY* M9 ....34 B2
Elm Tree Cl *FAIL* M35 ....58 A2
Elmtree Dr *HTNM* SK4 ....128 A3
Elm Tree Rd *MPL/ROM* SK6 ....131 C3
Elmwood Gv *BKLY* M9 ....54 A2
Elsa Rd *BNG/LEV* M19 ....105 D4
Elsdon Dr *GTN* M18 ....91 C3
Elsdon Rd *BRUN/LGST* M13 ....104 A3
Elsham Gdns *GTN* M18 ....105 C1
Elsie St *BKLY* M9 ....53 D1
Elsinore Cl *FAIL* M35 ....58 A2
Elsinore Rd *OLDTF/WHR* M16 ....98 B1
Elsma Rd *NEWH/MOS* M40 ....74 B1
Elsmore Rd *RUSH/FAL* M14 ....101 D4
Elstree Av *NEWH/MOS* M40 ....75 C1
Elstree Gv *EDGY/DAV* SK3 ....132 A1
Elswick Av *BNG/LEV* M21 ....123 C1
Elsworth St *CSLFD* M5 ....69 D2
Eltham Av *BNG/LEV* M19 ....104 B3
Elton Av *BNG/LEV* M19 ....117 D1
Elton Cl *WHTF* M45 ....11 C1
Elton St *BRO* M7 ....68 A2
  STRET M32 ....83 C3
Elton's Yd *BRO* M7 ....68 A2
Elvate Crs *CHH* M8 ....50 B3
Elverdon Cl *HULME* M15 ....85 C4
Elverston St *WYTH/NTH* M22 ......123 C4
Elverston Wy *CHAD* * OL9 ....21 D1
Elvey St *NEWH/MOS* M40 ....54 A4
Elwick Cl *OLDTF/WHR* M16 ....101 C2
Ely Av *STRET* M32 ....95 C3
Ely Crs *FAIL* M35 ....57 C4
Elysian St *OP/CLY* M11 ....90 B3
Ely St *CHAD* OL9 ....21 C4
Emaline Gra *SLFD* M6 ....65 D3
Ember St *OP/CLY* * M11 ....74 A3
Emerson Av *ECC* M30 ....63 D2
Emerson St *ORD* M5 ....65 C3
Emery Av *CCHDY* M21 ....112 B3
Emery Cl *HTNM* SK4 ....127 D1
Emily Beavan Cl *OP/CLY* M11 ....73 C4
Emily Pl *DROY* M43 ....75 C4
Emley St *BNG/LEV* M19 ....105 C4

Emlyn St *SWIN* M27 ....44 A1
Emma St *OLDS* OL8 ....41 C2
Emmett St East *NEWH/MOS* M40 ..53 D4
Emmott St *OLD* * OL1 ....23 C3
Emperor St *STKP* * SK1 ....130 B3
Empire St *CSLFD* M5 ....69 C1
Empress Dr *HTNM* SK4 ....129 C1
Empress St *CHH* M8 ....51 C1
  OLDTF/WHR M16 ....84 B3
Enbridge St *ORD* * M5 ....83 D1
Encombe Pl *CSLFD* M3 ....2 A3
Endcott Cl *GTN* M18 ....90 A3
Enderby Rd *NEWH/MOS* M40 ....36 B4
Endon Dr *OLDTF/WHR* M16 ....114 A1
Endsleigh Rd *DID/WITH* M20 ......115 D3
Energy St *NEWH/MOS* * M40 ....71 D2
Enfield Av *BNG/LEV* M19 ....117 D3
  OLDS OL8 ....40 B2
Enfield Cl *ECC* M30 ....79 C1
Enfield Dr *OP/CLY* M11 ....73 D5
Enfield Rd *ECC* M30 ....62 A1
  SWIN M27 ....44 B3
Engell Cl *GTN* M18 ....90 B4
Engine St *CHAD* OL9 ....39 C1
Enid Cl *BRO* M7 ....50 A4
Ennerdale Av *CCHDY* M21 ....123 C1
  SWIN M27 ....45 C3
Ennerdale Rd *STRET* * M32 ....96 B2
Ennismore Av *ECC* M30 ....63 D3
Enstone Dr *NEWH/MOS* M40 ....37 C4
Entwisle St *SWIN* M27 ....25 C4
Enver Rd *CHH* M8 ....52 A2
Enville Rd *NEWH/MOS* M40 ....36 A4
  SLFD M6 ....47 D3
Enville St *BKLY* M9 ....34 A2
Epping Cl *CHAD* OL9 ....19 D1
Epping St *HULME* M15 ....85 D5
Eppleworth Ri *SWIN* M27 ....26 B3
Epsley Cl *HULME* M15 ....86 B3
Epsom Av *BNG/LEV* M19 ....117 C3
Epworth St *CMANE* M1 ....5 F5
Ercall Av *WGTN/LGST* M12 ....88 B3
Erica Cl *RDSH* SK5 ....120 A1
Erica Dr *BNG/LEV* M19 ....126 B1
Eric Brook Cl *RUSH/FAL* M14 ......101 D2
Erin St *OP/CLY* * M11 ....91 D2
Erith Cl *RDSH* SK5 ....121 C3
Erlington Av *OLDTF/WHR* M16 ....99 C2
Ermen Rd *ECC* M30 ....78 B1
Ermington Dr *CHH* M8 ....51 C3
Emeley Gv *WGTN/LGST* M12 ......105 C2
Ernest St *OFTN* SK2 ....133 D3
  PWCH M25 ....29 C1
Ernocroft Gv *GTN* * M18 ....91 D3
Errington Dr *BRO* M7 ....68 A1
Errol Av *BKLY* M9 ....14 B4
Errwood Crs *BNG/LEV* M19 ....117 D1
Errwood Rd *BNG/LEV* M19 ....117 D3
Erskine Rd *BKLY* M9 ....16 B4
Erskine St *HULME* M15 ....85 C3
Erwin St *NEWH/MOS* M40 ....55 C3
Erwood Rd *HTNM* SK4 ....117 C3
Eryngo St *STKP* SK1 ....130 B4
Eskdale Av *DID/WITH* M20 ....114 B2
  OLDS OL8 ....40 A1
Eskrigge Cl *BRO* M7 ....51 C1
Esmond Rd *CHH* M8 ....51 D2
Essex Av *DID/WITH* M20 ....125 C1
  DROY M43 ....75 D2
Essex Cl *FAIL* M35 ....57 C4
Essex Rd *GTN* M18 ....107 C2
  RDSH SK5 ....121 D4
Essex St *CMANW* M2 ....3 F5
Essex Wy *HULME* M15 ....85 C4
Estate St *OLDS* OL8 ....41 C1
Estate St South *OLDS* * OL8 ....41 C1
Estonfield Dr *URM* M41 ....95 C3
Eston St *BRUN/LGST* M13 ....105 C1

Eswick St *OP/CLY* M11 ....**73** D4
Etchells St *STKP* * SK1 ....**130** A4
Etchell St *NEWH/MOS* * M40 ....**52** B4
Ethel Av *BKLY* M9 ....**16** A4
   SWIN M27 ....**46** A1
Ethel St *OLDS* OL8 ....**41** C2
Ethel Ter *BNG/LEV* M19 ....**104** B4
Etherow Av *NEWH/MOS* * M40 ....**38** A3
Etherstone St *CHH* M8 ....**52** B1
Eton Av *OLDS* OL8 ....**40** B2
Eton Cl *OLDTF/WHR* M16 ....**85** C2
Eton Ct *OLDTF/WHR* * M16 ....**85** C2
Etruria Cl *BRUN/LGST* M13 ....**88** B4
Ettrick Cl *OP/CLY* M11 ....**91** C2
Euclid Cl *OP/CLY* M11 ....**71** D4
Europa Ga *TRPK* M17 ....**82** A4
Europa Wy *TRPK* M17 ....**82** A4
Euston Av *BKLY* M9 ....**35** D2
Evan Cl *DID/WITH* M20 ....**124** B2
Evans Cl *DID/WITH* M20 ....**124** B2
Evans Rd *ECC* M30 ....**60** B4
Evans St *CSLFD* M3 ....**3** D1
   MDTN M24 ....**18** A1
   OLD OL1 ....**23** C1
Evan St *NEWH/MOS* M40 ....**53** D4
Eva St *RUSH/FAL* M14 ....**102** B2
Evelyn St *RUSH/FAL* M14 ....**116** A1
Evening St *FAIL* M35 ....**57** C1
Evenley Cl *GTN* * M18 ....**91** D3
Everard St *ORD* M5 ....**84** B2
Everglade *OLDS* OL8 ....**41** D4
Everleigh Dr *CHH* M8 ....**51** C3
Eversden Ct *BRO* * M7 ....**68** B3
Eversley Rd *DID/WITH* M20 ....**124** B2
Everton Rd *OLDS* OL8 ....**40** A1
   RDSH SK5 ....**107** C3
Everton St *SWIN* M27 ....**44** B3
Every St *CMANE* M4 ....**71** C4
Evesham Av *HTNM* SK4 ....**128** A2
Evesham Cl *MDTN* M24 ....**18** A4
Evesham Gdns *MDTN* * M24 ....**17** D4
Evesham Rd *BKLY* M9 ....**35** D3
   MDTN M24 ....**17** D4
Evesham Wk *MDTN* M24 ....**18** A4
   OLDS * OL8 ....**22** B4
Eve St *OLDS* OL8 ....**41** C3
Ewan St *GTN* M18 ....**91** C3
Ewart Av *ORD* M5 ....**66** B4
Ewhurst Av *SWIN* M27 ....**44** A3
Ewing Cl *CHH* M8 ....**32** B4
Exbury Cl *RUSH/FAL* M14 ....**116** A2
Exchange Quay *ORD* M5 ....**83** D3
Exchange Sq *CSLFD* M3 ....**3** F3
Exchange St *CMANW* * M2 ....**3** F4
   EDGY/DAV SK3 ....**129** D4
Exeter Av *ECC* M30 ....**63** D1
Exeter Rd *RDSH* SK5 ....**121** D4
   URM M41 ....**94** A1
Exeter St *SLFD* M6 ....**65** D3
Exford Cl *NEWH/MOS* M40 ....**71** C2
   RDSH SK5 ....**121** D4
Exmouth Av *RDSH* SK5 ....**121** D4
Exmouth Wk *OLDTF/WHR* M16 ....**100** B2
Eynford Av *RDSH* SK5 ....**121** C3
Eyre St *HULME* M15 ....**86** B4

F

Faber St *ANC* M4 ....**69** D2
Factory Brow *MDTN* M24 ....**15** D2
Factory La *BKLY* M9 ....**34** A4
   ORD * M5 ....**2** A4
Factory St *MDTN* M24 ....**17** C1
Failsworth Rd *FAIL* M35 ....**58** A3
Fairbottom St *OLD* OL1 ....**23** C2
Fairbourne Rd *BNG/LEV* M19 ....**105** D4

Fairbrook Dr *SLFD* M6 ....**65** D3
Fairbrother St *ORD* M5 ....**84** B2
Fairclough St *OP/CLY* M11 ....**72** B3
Fairfax Av *DID/WITH* M20 ....**125** C1
Fairfax Rd *PWCH* M25 ....**11** D4
Fairfield Av *DROY* M43 ....**92** B1
Fairfield Sq *DROY* M43 ....**92** B1
   OP/CLY M11 ....**91** D2
Fairfields *OLDS* OL8 ....**41** D3
Fairfield Sq *DROY* M43 ....**92** B1
Fairfield St *CMANE* M1 ....**9** D2
   SLFD M6 ....**47** C4
Fairford Cl *RDSH* SK5 ....**120** A4
Fairford Wy *RDSH* SK5 ....**120** A4
Fairhaven Av *CCHDY* M21 ....**112** A2
   WHTF M45 ....**10** A2
Fairhaven St *WGTN/LGST* M12 ....**89** C3
Fairholme Rd *DID/WITH* M20 ....**115** D3
   HTNM SK4 ....**128** B2
Fairhope Av *SLFD* M6 ....**64** A1
Fairisle Cl *OP/CLY* M11 ....**92** A3
Fairlawn *HTNM* SK4 ....**129** C2
Fairlawn Cl *RUSH/FAL* M14 ....**101** D1
Fairlea *DID/WITH* M20 ....**125** D3
Fairlee Av *DTN/ASHW* M34 ....**93** D1
Fairleigh Av *SLFD* M6 ....**66** B2
Fairless Rd *ECC* M30 ....**61** C4
Fairman St *OLDTF/WHR* M16 ....**85** D4
Fairmead Rd *NTHM/RTH* M23 ....**122** B4
Fairmount Rd *SWIN* M27 ....**43** C5
Fair Oak Rd *BNG/LEV* M19 ....**117** C4
Fairstead Wk *OP/CLY* M11 ....**92** A2
Fair St *CMANE* M1 ....**5** E5
   SWIN M27 ....**26** B4
Fairview Av *BNG/LEV* M19 ....**104** A3
   DTN/ASHW M34 ....**107** D4
Fairview Cl *CHAD* OL9 ....**19** D1
Fairview Rd *DTN/ASHW* M34 ....**107** D3
The Fairway *NEWH/MOS* M40 ....**56** A1
Fairway *DROY* M43 ....**92** B1
   PWCH M25 ....**31** C3
   SWIN M27 ....**46** B2
The Fairways *WHTF* M45 ....**11** C3
Fairy La *CHH* M8 ....**50** B4
   SALE M33 ....**122** A2
Falcon Av *URM* M41 ....**94** B3
Falcon Crs *SWIN* M27 ....**27** C3
Falcon Dr *CHAD* OL9 ....**21** D1
Falcon St *OLDS* OL8 ....**22** B4
Falfield Dr *CHH* M8 ....**52** A4
Falkland Av *NEWH/MOS* M40 ....**71** C1
Fallons Rd *WALK* M28 ....**24** B4
Fallowfield Av *ORD* M5 ....**84** B4
Fallow Fields Dr *RDSH* SK5 ....**107** D4
The Fallows *CHAD* OL9 ....**20** B1
Falmer St *GTN* M18 ....**92** A3
Falmouth Crs *RDSH* SK5 ....**107** D4
Falmouth St *NEWH/MOS* M40 ....**72** A1
   OLDS OL8 ....**41** C1
Falsgrave Cl *NEWH/MOS* M40 ....**54** B4
Falston Av *NEWH/MOS* M40 ....**37** C3
Faraday Av *CHH* M8 ....**51** D3
   SWIN M27 ....**28** A3
Faraday St *CMANE* M1 ....**4** C4
Far La *GTN* M18 ....**106** A1
Farley Av *GTN* M18 ....**107** D1
Farley Wy *RDSH* SK5 ....**106** B4
Farm Av *STRET* M32 ....**95** D1
Farm Cl *HTNM* SK4 ....**118** B3
Farmer St *HTNM* SK4 ....**129** C2
Farm Hl *PWCH* * M25 ....**11** D4
Farm La *PWCH* M25 ....**13** D1
   WALK M28 ....**42** A4
Farm Rd *OLDS* OL8 ....**58** B1
Farmstead Cl *FAIL* M35 ....**58** B3
Farm St *FAIL* M35 ....**56** A3
Farmway *MDTN* M24 ....**17** C2
Farm Yd *BNG/LEV* M19 ....**104** B4

Farn Av *RDSH* SK5........................106 B3
Farnborough Rd *NEWH/MOS* M40.......71 C2
Farndon Rd *RDSH* SK5.....................106 B3
Farnham Av *BKLY* M9........................16 A4
Farnley St *WGTN/LGST* * M12............89 D3
Farnworth Dr *RUSH/FAL* M14............102 B3
Farrand Rd *OLDS* OL8.......................39 C3
Farrant Rd *WGTN/LGST* M12.............104 B2
Farrar Rd *DROY* M43.........................92 A1
Farrell St *CSLFD* M3..........................8 B2
Farrer Rd *BRUN/LGST* M13...............104 A3
Farringdon St *SLFD* * M6...................65 D2
Farr St *EDGY/DAV* SK3....................132 A1
Farwood Cl *OLDTF/WHR* M16............84 B4
Fastnet St *OP/CLY* M11.....................89 D1
Faulkner Rd *STRET* M32.....................97 D3
Faulkner St *CMANE* M1.......................8 A1
Faversham Brow *OLD* * OL1...............22 B1
Faversham St *NEWH/MOS* M40..........55 C2
Fay Av *BKLY* M9...............................36 A3
Featherstall Rd North *CHAD* OL9........22 A2
Featherstall Rd South *CHAD* OL9.......22 A3
Federation St *ANC* M4........................4 A2
   PWCH M25................................11 C4
Fellbrigg Cl *GTN* M18.......................105 D2
Fellitop Dr *RDSH* SK5......................120 B1
Felthorpe Dr *CHH* M8.......................51 C3
Fencegate Av *HTNM* SK4..................119 C3
Fenchurch Av *NEWH/MOS* M40...........73 D1
Fencot Dr *WGTN/LGST* M12..............104 B1
Fenella St *BRUN/LGST* M13..............103 D1
Fenham Cl *NEWH/MOS* * M40.............52 B4
Fenmore Av *GTN* M18......................105 C2
Fennel St *ANC* M4............................3 F2
Fenney St *BRO* M7...........................50 A4
Fenney St East *BRO* M7....................50 B3
Fenn St *HULME* M15...........................6 C5
Fenwick Dr *HTNM* SK4.....................126 B2
Fenwick St *HULME* M15......................8 A5
Ferdinand St *NEWH/MOS* * M40.........71 C1
Fernacre *SALE* M33.........................109 D4
Fern Bank *NEWH/MOS* * M40.............55 D2
Fernbray Av *BNG/LEV* M19...............126 A1
Fernbrook Cl *BRUN/LGST* M13...........88 A4
Fern Cl *MDTN* M24............................19 C1
Fernclough Rd *BKLY* M9....................53 C3
Ferndale Gdns *BNG/LEV* M19............116 B3
Ferndene Rd *DID/WITH* M20.............115 C4
   WHTF M45.................................12 B2
Ferndown Av *CHAD* OL9....................19 C2
Ferney Field Rd *CHAD* OL9................20 A2
Ferngate Dr *DID/WITH* M20..............115 C3
Fernhill Dr *GTN* M18........................105 C1
Fernholme Ct *OLDS* OL8....................39 D1
Fernhurst Rd *DID/WITH* M20............115 C4
Fernie St *ANC* * M4..........................69 D2
Fernlea Crs *SWIN* M27......................44 B2
Fernleigh Av *BNG/LEV* M19..............105 D4
Fernleigh Dr *OLDTF/WHR* * M16........84 B4
Fernside Av *DID/WITH* M20..............116 A4
Fern St *CHAD* OL9............................20 B1
   CHH M8....................................69 D1
   OLDS OL8.................................22 A4
Fernwood Av *GTN* M18....................106 A2
Ferring Wk *CHAD* * OL9.....................21 C3
Ferris St *OP/CLY* M11.......................91 C1
Ferry St *OP/CLY* M11........................88 B1
Fettler Cl *SWIN* M27.........................44 B2
Field Bank Gv *BNG/LEV* M19............105 C3
Fielden Av *CCHDY* M21......................99 C3
Fielden Rd *DID/WITH* M20...............114 A4
Fielders Wy *SWIN* M27......................25 D3
Fieldfare Av *NEWH/MOS* M40.............73 C1
Fielding St *ECC* M30.........................61 D1
Field Pl *DID/WITH* M20....................125 C2
Fields New Rd *CHAD* OL9..................20 B4
Field St *DROY* M43............................92 A1
   FAIL M35...................................56 B2

GTN M18...91 D3
   SLFD M6.....................................66 A3
Fieldsway *OLDS* OL8.........................40 B3
Field Vale Dr *RDSH* SK5...................107 D4
Field View Wk *OLDTF/WHR* M16........101 C3
Fife Av *CHAD* OL9.............................38 A1
Fifield Cl *OLDS* OL8..........................41 D2
Fifth Av *OLDS* OL8...........................39 D3
   OP/CLY M11.............................73 D3
   TRPK M17.................................81 D4
Fifth St *TRPK* M17...........................81 D4
Filby Wk *NEWH/MOS* M40.................71 D1
Fildes St *MDTN* M24.........................19 C2
Filey Av *OLDTF/WHR* M16................100 A3
Filey Dr *SLFD* M6.............................47 D2
Filey Rd *RUSH/FAL* M14...................116 A1
Finborough Cl *OLDTF/WHR* M16.......100 B1
Finchley Av *NEWH/MOS* M40.............73 C1
Finchley Gv *NEWH/MOS* M40.............35 C4
Finchley Rd *RUSH/FAL* M14.............115 C1
Finishing Wk *ANC* M4.........................7 D4
Finland St *EDGY/DAV* SK3...............132 A2
Finney Dr *CCHDY* M21......................111 D2
Finningley Rd *BKLY* M9.....................15 C3
Finny Bank Rd *SALE* M33.................108 B3
Finsbury Av *NEWH/MOS* M40.............73 D1
Finsbury Rd *RDSH* SK5....................119 D1
Finstock Cl *ECC* M30........................61 C4
Fintry Gv *ECC* M30...........................62 A4
Firbeck Dr *ANC* M4...........................71 C3
Fircroft Rd *OLDS* OL8.......................41 D3
Firdale Av *NEWH/MOS* M40...............37 D4
Firdale Wk *CHAD* OL9.......................21 D2
Firefly Cl *CSLFD* M3...........................2 A4
Fir Gv *BNG/LEV* M19.......................104 B3
   CHAD OL9.................................21 D2
Fir Rd *SWIN* M27.............................56 B2
Firs Av *FAIL* M35..............................56 B2
   OLDTF/WHR M16......................99 C3
Firsby St *BNG/LEV* M19..................104 B4
First Av *OLDS* OL8...........................40 A3
   OP/CLY M11.............................74 A3
   SWIN M27................................44 A4
   TRPK M17.................................82 A4
Fir St *ECC* M30................................62 A4
   FAIL M35...................................56 B2
   HTNM SK4...............................129 D3
   NEWH/MOS M40.......................71 C1
   OLDTF/WHR * M16.....................99 C1
   SLFD M6...................................66 A3
Firswood Dr *SWIN* M27.....................44 B4
Firth St *OLD* OL1..............................23 C3
Fir Tree Av *OLDS* OL8.......................41 C3
Firwood Av *URM* M41........................95 D4
Firwood Pk *CHAD* OL9......................19 C3
Fishbourne Sq *RUSH/FAL* * M14.......102 B2
Fisher St *OLD* OL1............................23 C1
Fitton Av *CCHDY* M21......................112 A3
Fitton Crs *SWIN* M27.........................26 A2
Fitton Hill Rd *OLDS* OL8....................41 D1
Fitzgeorge St *NEWH/MOS* M40..........52 B4
Fitzgerald Cl *PWCH* M25....................29 C3
Fitzgerald Wy *SLFD* * M6...................66 A2
Fitzroy St *DROY* M43........................93 C1
Fitzwarren St *SLFD* M6......................66 A3
Fitzwilliam St *BRO* M7.......................68 A1
Flag Rw *ANC* * M4............................70 A2
Flagship Av *ORD* * M5.......................84 A1
Flamborough Rd *RUSH/FAL* * M14.....102 A2
Flamingo Av *WGTN/LGST* M12...........89 D3
Flashfields *PWCH* M25.......................29 C4
Flash St *NEWH/MOS* M40...................55 D3
Flatley Cl *HULME* M15.......................86 B3
Flavian Wk *OP/CLY* * M11..................90 A1
Flaxpool Cl *OLDTF/WHR* M16...........100 B1
Flax St *CSLFD* M3..............................2 B1

Frostlands Rd OLDTF/WHR M16 .... 100 B1
Frostlands St OLDTF/WHR * M16 .... 100 B1
Frost St ANC * M4 .... 71 C4
   OLDS OL8 .... 40 B1
Froxmer St GTN M18 .... 90 B3
Fulford St OLDTF/WHR M16 .... 99 D1
Fulham Av NEWH/MOS M40 .... 55 C4
Fullerton Rd HTNM SK4 .... 128 A3
Fulmer Dr ANC M4 .... 5 F2
Fulmere Ct SWIN M27 .... 44 A3
Fulneck Sq DROY M43 .... 92 B1
Fulwood Av BKLY M9 .... 35 C1
Furness Av WHTF M45 .... 11 D1
Furness Gv HTNM SK4 .... 127 D4
Furness Quay SALQ M50 .... 83 D2
Furness Rd RUSH/FAL M14 .... 102 B4
   URM M41 .... 94 A2
Furnival Cl DTN/ASHW M34 .... 107 D3
Furnival St GTN M18 .... 90 B3
Furnival St RDSH SK5 .... 106 B3
Furrow Dr ECC M30 .... 61 C1
Fushia Gv BRO * M7 .... 50 A3
Fylde Rd HTNM SK4 .... 127 D3

G

Gable St OP/CLY M11 .... 89 D1
Gabriels Ter MDTN M24 .... 18 B2
Gaddum Rd DID/WITH M20 .... 125 D2
Gail Av HTNM SK4 .... 129 C3
Gail Cl FAIL M35 .... 56 B4
Gainford Gdns NEWH/MOS M40 .... 36 A4
Gainford Rd RDSH SK5 .... 107 C4
Gainsborough Av DID/WITH * M20 ..... 115 D3
   OLDS OL8 .... 40 B1
   STRET * M32 .... 98 C3
Gainsborough Rd CHAD OL9 .... 19 D1
   DTN/ASHW M34 .... 77 C4
Gainsborough St BRO M7 .... 50 B2
Gairloch Av STRET M32 .... 96 A3
Gair Rd RDSH SK5 .... 130 A1
Gaitskell Cl WGTN/LGST M12 .... 71 D4
Galbraith Rd DID/WITH M20 .... 125 D2
Galbraith St CMANE * M1 .... 8 A3
Gale Rd PWCH M25 .... 29 C2
Galgate Cl HULME M15 .... 6 B1
Galloway Dr SWIN M27 .... 26 A1
Galloway Rd SWIN * M27 .... 44 A3
Galston St OP/CLY M11 .... 89 D1
Galsworthy Av CHH M8 .... 51 D4
Galvin Rd BKLY M9 .... 33 C2
Galway St OLD OL1 .... 23 C3
Gamma Wk OP/CLY M11 .... 73 C3
Gantock Wk RUSH/FAL M14 .... 102 B3
Ganton Av WHTF M45 .... 10 A1
Garbrook Av BKLY M9 .... 15 D4
Garden Av DROY M43 .... 76 B3
   STRET M32 .... 97 C3
Garden La CSLFD M3 .... 3 D2
Garden St ECC M30 .... 62 B4
   OLD OL1 .... 23 C3
Garden Wall Cl ORD M5 .... 84 B1
Gardner Rd PWCH M25 .... 29 C1
Gardner St SLFD M6 .... 66 B1
   WGTN/LGST M12 .... 90 A3
Garfield Av BNG/LEV M19 .... 105 C4
Garfield St STKP * SK1 .... 130 B3
Garforth Av ANC M4 .... 5 F2
Garforth St CHAD * OL9 .... 21 D2
Gargrave St BRO M7 .... 48 A1
Garlick St CHAD * OL9 .... 22 B3
   GTN M18 .... 91 D3
Garnant Cl BKLY M9 .... 54 A1
Garner Dr ECC * M30 .... 61 C1
   SLFD M6 .... 65 C2
Garner's La EDGY/DAV SK3 .... 133 C4

Garnett St STKP SK1 .... 130 A4
Garratt Wy GTN M18 .... 90 B4
Garston Cl HTNM SK4 .... 128 B2
Garswood Rd RUSH/FAL M14 .... 101 C3
The Garth ORD M5 .... 65 C3
Garthorne Cl OLDTF/WHR M16 .... 100 A1
Garthwaite Av OLDS OL8 .... 40 B2
Gartside St AULW * OL7 .... 77 D4
   CSLFD M3 .... 3 D5
Garwood St HULME M15 .... 7 D4
Gascoyne St RUSH/FAL M14 .... 102 A3
Gaskell Rd ECC M30 .... 62 A4
Gaskell St NEWH/MOS M40 .... 55 D4
   SWIN M27 .... 26 A3
Gas St HTNM SK4 .... 129 D4
Gatcombe Sq RUSH/FAL M14 .... 102 B2
Gateshead Cl RUSH/FAL M14 .... 102 A1
Gate St OP/CLY M11 .... 90 B1
Gateway Crs CHAD OL9 .... 37 D1
Gateway Rd GTN * M18 .... 90 B3
The Gateways SWIN M27 .... 26 A4
Gathurst St GTN M18 .... 91 D3
Gatley Av RUSH/FAL M14 .... 101 C4
Gatley Brow OLD * OL1 .... 22 B1
Gatling Av WGTN/LGST M12 .... 104 B3
Gavin Av ORD M5 .... 66 B3
Gawsworth Av DID/WITH M20 .... 125 D4
Gawsworth Cl EDGY/DAV SK3 .... 132 B3
Gaythorn St ORD M5 .... 67 D4
Gee La ECC M30 .... 61 C2
Gee St EDGY/DAV SK3 .... 132 A3
Gemini Rd SLFD M6 .... 67 D1
Geneva Wk CHAD * OL9 .... 21 D3
Genista Gv BRO * M7 .... 50 A3
George Leigh St ANC M4 .... 4 C3
George's Rd HTNM SK4 .... 129 C3
George St CHAD OL9 .... 20 B2
   CMANE M1 .... 8 A5
   ECC M30 .... 61 D4
   FAIL M35 .... 57 C1
   OLD OL1 .... 22 B3
   PWCH M25 .... 30 A4
   STKP SK1 .... 130 B4
   URM M41 .... 94 B3
George St North BRO M7 .... 51 C1
George St South BRO M7 .... 50 B1
Georgette Dr CSLFD M3 .... 3 D1
Gerald Av CHH M8 .... 51 D1
Gerald Rd SLFD M6 .... 48 B3
Germain Cl BKLY M9 .... 15 D4
Gerrard Rd SLFD M6 .... 66 B2
Gertrude Cl ORD M5 .... 83 D1
Gervis Cl NEWH/MOS * M40 .... 53 C4
Gibbon St OP/CLY M11 .... 72 B3
Gibb Rd WALK M28 .... 43 C2
Gibbs St CSLFD M3 .... 2 A1
Gibson Av GTN M18 .... 92 A2
Gibson Pl ANC M4 .... 69 D2
Gibsons Rd HTNM SK4 .... 128 A1
Gidlow St GTN M18 .... 91 D3
Gifford Av BKLY M9 .... 35 C1
Gilbert St ECC M30 .... 78 A1
   HULME M15 .... 6 B5
   ORD * M5 .... 66 A4
Gilda Brook Rd ECC M30 .... 63 D3
Gilda Crs ECC M30 .... 63 D2
Gildenhall FAIL M35 .... 57 D2
Gildersdale Dr BKLY M9 .... 15 C3
Gildridge Rd OLDTF/WHR M16 .... 100 B4
Gilesgate RUSH/FAL M14 .... 102 B2
Giles St WGTN/LGST M12 .... 104 B1
Gillbrook Rd DID/WITH M20 .... 125 D3
Gilford Av BKLY M9 .... 54 A1
Gillingham Rd ECC M30 .... 61 C3
Gillingham Sq OP/CLY M11 .... 89 C1
Gill St BKLY M9 .... 35 C4
   STKP SK1 .... 131 C2
Gilman Cl BKLY * M9 .... 33 D3

Gilman St *BKLY* M9 ....33 D3
Gilmerton Dr *NEWH/MOS* * M40 ....55 C4
Gilmore Dr *PWCH* M25 ....12 A4
Gilmore St *EDGY/DAV* SK3 ....132 B2
Gilmour St *MDTN* M24 ....17 D1
Gilmour Ter *BKLY* M9 ....35 C4
Gilpin Rd *URM* M41 ....95 C4
Giltbrook St *NEWH/MOS* M40 ....71 C1
Girton St *BRO* M7 ....68 B1
Girvan Av *NEWH/MOS* M40 ....37 C3
Gisborn Dr *SLFD* M6 ....48 A4
Gisburne Av *NEWH/MOS* M40 ....37 C3
Givendale Dr *CHH* M8 ....52 B3
The Glade *HTNM* SK4 ....127 D4
Gladstone Ct *HULME* M15 ....100 B1
Gladstone Gv *HTNM* SK4 ....127 D2
Gladstone Ms *HTNM* * SK4 ....129 D2
Gladstone Rd *ECC* M30 ....62 B3
  URM M41 ....94 B3
Gladstone St *SWIN* M27 ....45 D3
Gladwyn Av *DID/WITH* M20 ....123 D1
Glamis Av *OP/CLY* M11 ....73 D2
  STRET M32 ....95 D3
Glamorgan Pl *CHAD* * OL9 ....21 D4
Glanford Av *NEWH/MOS* M40 ....32 B2
Glasshouse St *ANC* M4 ....5 E1
Glasson Wk *CHAD* OL9 ....20 B3
Glastonbury Rd *STRET* M32 ....95 C2
Glaswen Gv *RDSH* SK5 ....130 A1
Gleaves Rd *ECC* M30 ....62 B4
Gleave St *SALE* M33 ....109 C3
Glebelands Rd *PWCH* M25 ....11 D4
  SALE M33 ....108 B3
Glebe Rd *URM* M41 ....94 B3
Glebe St *CHAD* OL9 ....38 B2
  STKP SK1 ....130 B4
Gleden St *NEWH/MOS* M40 ....71 C1
Gledhill Av *ORD* M5 ....85 C2
Gledhill St *DID/WITH* M20 ....115 C2
Glemsford Cl *NEWH/MOS* * M40 ....55 C3
The Glen *MDTN* M24 ....18 A3
Glenacre Gdns *GTN* M18 ....106 B2
Glenart *ECC* M30 ....62 B2
Glen Av *BKLY* M9 ....34 B4
  SALE M33 ....108 B3
  SWIN M27 ....44 B1
  WALK M28 ....42 B1
Glenbarry Cl *BRUN/LGST* M13 ....87 C3
Glenbarry St *WGTN/LGST* M12 ....88 B1
Glenbrook Rd *BKLY* M9 ....14 B4
Glencastle Rd *GTN* M18 ....90 B4
Glencoe St *OLDS* * OL8 ....39 D3
Glencross Av *CCHDY* M21 ....98 B3
Glendale *SWIN* M27 ....27 C4
Glendale Av *BNG/LEV* M19 ....117 D3
Glendale Ct *OLDS* OL8 ....41 C1
Glendale Rd *ECC* M30 ....63 D2
Glendene Av *DROY* M43 ....76 B2
Glendevon Pl *WHTF* M45 ....12 A2
Glendinning St *SLFD* M6 ....65 D3
Glendore *ORD* M5 ....64 B3
Glendower Dr *NEWH/MOS* M40 ....52 B4
Glenfield Rd *HTNM* SK4 ....129 C1
Glenfyne Rd *SLFD* M6 ....47 C4
Glen Gv *MDTN* M24 ....18 B3
Glenhurst Rd *BNG/LEV* * M19 ....116 B3
Glenmere Cl *WHTF* M45 ....11 C3
Glenmoor Rd *STKP* SK1 ....133 D1
Glenmore Av *DID/WITH* M20 ....123 D1
Glenmore Dr *CHH* M8 ....52 A2
  FAIL M35 ....58 A1
Glenolden St *OP/CLY* M11 ....74 A3
Glensdale Dr *NEWH/MOS* M40 ....37 D4
Glenside Av *GTN* M18 ....106 A2
Glenside Gv *FAIL* M35 ....57 D2
Glen St *SALO* M50 ....83 D2
Glenthorn Av *BKLY* M9 ....16 A3
Glenwood Dr *BKLY* M9 ....53 D2

Glenwyn Av *BKLY* M9 ....34 B1
Globe Cl *OLDTF/WHR* M16 ....85 C4
Gloucester Av *BNG/LEV* M19 ....118 A1
  WHTF M45 ....11 C1
Gloucester Pl *SLFD* M6 ....66 B2
Gloucester Rd *DROY* M43 ....75 D2
  DTN/ASHW M34 ....107 D3
  MDTN M24 ....17 D3
  SLFD M6 ....64 B1
  URM M41 ....94 A4
Gloucester St *CMANE* M1 ....7 F3
  ORD M5 ....84 B1
  SLFD M6 ....66 B2
Gloucester St North *CHAD* * OL9 ....21 D4
Glynrene Dr *SWIN* M27 ....24 B3
Godbert Av *CCHDY* M21 ....112 B4
Goddard St *OLDS* OL8 ....41 C1
Godfrey Av *DROY* M43 ....74 B1
Godfrey Range *GTN* M18 ....107 C1
Godfrey Rd *SLFD* M6 ....46 B1
Godlee Dr *SWIN* M27 ....44 B2
Godley Cl *OP/CLY* M11 ....90 B2
Godwin St *GTN* M18 ....91 D3
Golborne Av *DID/WITH* M20 ....114 A2
Goldenhill Av *OP/CLY* M11 ....73 D2
Golden St *ECC* M30 ....62 A4
Goldfinch Wy *DROY* M43 ....76 B2
Goldsmith Av *ORD* M5 ....65 C3
Goldsmith Rd *RDSH* SK5 ....106 A4
Gold St *CMANE* * M1 ....4 B5
Golfview Dr *ECC* M30 ....62 A1
Goodiers Dr *ORD* M5 ....83 D1
Goodier St *NEWH/MOS* M40 ....53 D4
Goodman St *BKLY* M9 ....34 B4
Goodwill Cl *SWIN* M27 ....45 C2
Goodwin Sq *BKLY* * M9 ....53 C2
Goodwood Dr *SWIN* M27 ....46 A3
Goole St *OP/CLY* M11 ....89 D1
Goostrey Av *DID/WITH* M20 ....114 A4
Gordon Av *BNG/LEV* M19 ....105 C4
  CHAD OL9 ....38 C3
Gordon Pl *DID/WITH* M20 ....115 C4
Gordon Rd *ECC* M30 ....62 A4
  SALE M33 ....109 C3
  SWIN M27 ....43 D3
Gordon St *BRO* M7 ....68 A1
  CHAD OL9 ....38 A1
  GTN M18 ....91 D3
  HTNM SK4 ....129 D3
  OLDTF/WHR M16 ....100 A1
Gordon Ter *BKLY* * M9 ....53 D1
Gore Av *FAIL* M35 ....58 A3
  ORD M5 ....65 C3
Gorebrook Ct *WGTN/LGST* M12 ......104 B1
Gore Crs *ORD* M5 ....65 C2
Goredale Av *GTN* M18 ....106 B2
Gore Dr *SLFD* M6 ....65 C2
Gorelan Rd *GTN* * M18 ....91 C4
Gore St *CMANE* M1 ....4 C5
  CSLFD M3 ....2 C4
  SLFD M6 ....66 B2
Goring Av *GTN* M18 ....91 C3
Gorse Av *DROY* M43 ....76 B3
  STRET M32 ....98 A2
Gorse Crs *STRET* M32 ....98 A2
Gorse Dr *STRET* M32 ....98 A2
Gorsefield Dr *SWIN* M27 ....45 C2
Gorse La *STRET* M32 ....98 A2
Gorse Rd *SWIN* M27 ....44 B3
Gorses Rd *CHAD* OL9 ....38 A1
  STRET M32 ....97 D2
Gorseway *RDSH* SK5 ....131 C1
Gorsey Brow *STKP* SK1 ....130 B4
Gorseyfields *DROY* M43 ....92 B1
Gorsey Mount St *STKP* SK1 ....130 B4
Gorton La *WGTN/LGST* M12 ....89 D3
Gorton Rd *OP/CLY* M11 ....89 C2
  RDSH SK5 ....120 A1

Gorton St *CHAD* OL9	21	C3
CSLFD * M3	3	E2
ECC M30	60	B4
NEWH/MOS M40	70	B1
Gortonvilla Wk *WGTN/LGST* M12	89	C3
Gosport Sq *BRO* M7	50	A4
Gotha Wk *BRUN/LGST* M13	9	F5
Gough St *EDGY/DAV* SK3	129	C4
Goulden Rd *DID/WITH* M20	114	B4
Goulden St *ANC* M4	4	C2
SLFD M6		
Goulder Rd *GTN* M18	106	B2
Gould St *ANC* M4	70	A2
Govan St *WYTH/NTH* M22	123	D4
Gowan Rd *OLDTF/WHR* M16	100	B4
Gowerdale Rd *RDSH* SK5	121	D4
Gower Rd *HTNM* SK4	129	C1
Gower St *OLD* OL1	23	C4
SWIN M27	26	B4
Goyt Crs *STKP* SK1	131	C2
Goyt Rd *STKP* SK1	131	C2
Grace Wk *ANC* M4	71	C4
Gradwell St *EDGY/DAV* SK3	132	A1
Grafton Av *ECC* M30	63	C1
Grafton St *BRUN/LGST* M13	87	C4
FAIL M35	57	C1
HTNM SK4	129	C2
Graham Rd *SLFD* M6	64	B1
Graham St *OP/CLY* M11	89	D1
Grainger Av *WGTN/LGST* M12	104	B2
Grain Vw *ORD* * M5	83	D1
Grammar School Rd *OLDS* OL8	39	C4
Grampian Cl *CHAD* OL9	20	B4
Granada Ms *OLDTF/WHR* * M16	100	B4
Granada Rd *DTN/ASHW* M34	107	C2
Granary La *WALK* M28	60	A1
Granby Rd *STRET* M32	97	C4
SWIN M27	43	D2
Granby Rw *CMANE* M1	7	H5
Granby St *CHAD* OL9	38	B3
Grandale St *RUSH/FAL* * M14	102	B2
Grand Central Sq *EDGY/DAV* * SK3	132	B1
Grand Union Wy *ECC* M30	79	C1
The Grange *RUSH/FAL* M14	102	B2
Grange Av *BNG/LEV* M19	117	C1
ECC M30	62	A1
HTNM SK4	118	B3
OLDS OL8	39	D1
STRET M32	97	C2
SWIN M27	25	C3
Grange Ct *OLDS* * OL8	39	D1
ECC M30	62	A1
Grange Dr *BKLY* M9	35	C2
ECC M30	62	A1
Grangeforth Rd *CHH* M8	51	C1
Grange Gv *WHTF* M45	11	C1
Grange La *DID/WITH* M20	125	C3
Grangepark Rd *BKLY* M9	35	C2
Grange Rd *CCHDY* M21	98	B3
ECC M30	60	A1
Grange St *CHAD* OL9	22	B2
FAIL M35	56	A3
SLFD M6	65	D3
Grangethorpe Dr *BNG/LEV* M19	116	B3
Grangethorpe Rd *RUSH/FAL* M14	102	B3
Grangewood Dr *BKLY* M9	53	C2
Gransden Dr *CHH* M8	52	B3
Granshaw St *NEWH/MOS* M40	71	D2
Gransmoor Av *OP/CLY* M11	92	A2
Gransmoor Rd *OP/CLY* M11	92	A2
Grant Cl *BKLY* M9	34	A3
Grantham Rd *HTNM* SK4	128	B3
Grantham St *OLDE* OL4	23	D4
Granville Av *BRO* M7	50	B1
Granville Cl *CHAD* OL9	21	D1
Granville Gdns *DID/WITH* M20	124	B3
Granville St *DTN/ASHW* M34	76	A4
RUSH/FAL M14	115	D1
URM M41	94	B2
Granville St *CHAD* * OL9	21	D1
ECC M30	62	A2
Granville Wk *CHAD* OL9	21	D1
Grasmere Av *HTNM* SK4	119	D3
Grasmere Crs *ECC* M30	61	C1
Grasmere Rd *STRET* M32	97	C2
SWIN M27	45	C3
Grasmere St *WGTN/LGST* M12	105	C2
Grasscroft *RDSH* SK5	121	D3
Grasscroft Cl *RUSH/FAL* M14	101	C3
Grassfield Av *BRO* M7	49	D5
Grassingham Gdns *SLFD* M6	66	A2
Grassington Av *NEWH/MOS* M40	35	D4
Gratrix Av *ORD* M5	84	A2
Gratrix St *GTN* M18	106	B1
Gravel La *CSLFD* M3	3	E2
Gravenmoor Dr *BRO* M7	50	B3
Graver La *NEWH/MOS* M40	56	A4
Grayson Av *WHTF* M45	11	D2
Graythorpe Wk *ORD* * M5	66	B4
Graythorp Wk *RUSH/FAL* M14	102	A2
Greame St *OLDTF/WHR* M16	101	C2
Great Ancoats St *ANC* M4	5	F5
Great Bridgewater St *CMANW* M2	7	E2
Great Cheetham St East *BRO* M7	50	B3
Great Cheetham St West *BRO* M7	49	D4
Great Clowes St *BRO* M7	49	D5
Great Ducie St *CSLFD* M3	3	F1
Great Egerton St *STKP* SK1	129	D4
Great Gable Cl *OLD* OL1	23	D1
Great George St *CSLFD* M3	2	A3
Great Heaton Cl *MDTN* * M24	15	D2
Great Jackson St *HULME* M15	6	C3
Great John St *CSLFD* M3	6	C1
Great Jones St *WGTN/LGST* M12	89	D1
Great Marlborough St *CMANE* M1	7	F2
Great Newton St *NEWH/MOS* M40	55	D4
Great Portwood St *STKP* SK1	130	B5
Great Southern St *RUSH/FAL* M14	102	A2
Great Stone Rd *STRET* M32	98	A1
Great St *CMANE* M1	9	D1
Great Underbank *STKP* SK1	129	D4
Great Western St *OLDTF/WHR* M16	100	B1
Greaves Av *FAIL* M35	56	B3
Greaves St *OLD* OL1	23	C3
Grecian St *BRO* M7	49	D4
Grecian St North *BRO* M7	49	D4
Grecian Ter *BRO* * M7	49	D3
Gredle Cl *URM* M41	8	C4
Greek St *CMANE* M1	8	C4
EDGY/DAV SK3	132	B3
The Green *HTNM* SK4	128	B3
OLDS OL8	27	D3
SWIN M27	45	D2
WALK M28	42	A4
Greenacre La *WALK* M28	60	A1
Greenacres Dr *BNG/LEV* M19	126	B3
Green Av *SWIN* M27	45	C2
Greenbank Av *HTNM* SK4	126	B3
SWIN * M27	44	A3
Greenbank Rd *SLFD* M6	65	D2
Green Bank Ter *HTNM* * SK4	129	D3
Greencroft Rd *ECC* M30	61	C1
Greendale Dr *BKLY* M9	34	B2
Green Dr *BNG/LEV* M19	100	A4
Green End *BNG/LEV* M19	116	B4
Greenfield Av *URM* M41	94	A3
Greenfield Cl *EDGY/DAV* SK3	132	B3
Green Fold *GTN* M18	93	D2
Greenford Rd *CHH* M8	51	D2
Greengate *CSLFD* M3	3	E2
MDTN M24	18	B4
Greengate East *NEWH/MOS* M40	56	B1
Greengate La *PWCH* M25	29	D1
Greengate St *OLDE* OL4	23	D4
Greengate West *CSLFD* M3	2	C1

Greenhalgh St FAIL M35 ....55 D3
  HTNM SK4 ....129 D3
Greenhalgh Wk ANC M4 ....5 E3
Greenheys DROY M43 ....75 D3
Greenheys La HULME M15 ....86 A4
Greenheys La West HULME M15 ....86 A4
Greenhill PWCH M25 ....29 D1
Greenhill Av SALE M33 ....108 B3
Greenhill Pas OLD OL1 ....23 D3
Greenhill Rd CHH M8 ....51 D2
  MDTN M24 ....18 B2
Green Hill St EDGY/DAV SK3 ....132 A2
Greenhill Ter EDGY/DAV SK3 ....152 A2
Greenhill Ter OLDE * OL4 ....23 D3
Greenholm Cl NEWH/MOS M40 ....37 C4
Greenhow St DROY M43 ....92 A1
Greenhurst Crs OLDS OL8 ....41 D3
Greening Rd BNG/LEV M19 ....105 C5
Greenland St CHH M8 ....51 C2
  SLFD * M6 ....65 D3
Green La ECC M30 ....61 D5
  FAIL M35 ....74 B1
  GTN M18 ....91 C3
  HTNM SK4 ....128 B3
  MDTN M24 ....19 C2
  OLDS OL8 ....40 B3
Greenlea Av GTN M18 ....106 A2
Greenleach La WALK M28 ....42 A1
Greenpark Rd WYTH/NTH M22 ....123 C4
Green Pastures HTNM SK4 ....126 B4
Greenside WALK M28 ....42 B4
Greenside Crs DROY M43 ....75 C3
Greenside La DROY M43 ....74 B2
Greenside St OP/CLY M11 ....73 C3
Greenside Wk MDTN M24 ....18 B4
Green & Slater Homes HTNM * SK4 ....127 D2
Greenson Dr MDTN M24 ....16 B2
Greenstead Av CHH M8 ....51 D2
Greenstone Dr SLFD M6 ....48 A4
Green St ECC M30 ....78 A1
  EDGY/DAV SK3 ....133 C5
  OLDS * OL8 ....22 A3
  RUSH/FAL M14 ....87 C5
  STRET M32 ....109 D1
Greenthorne Av HTNM SK4 ....119 C2
Green Wk OLDTF/WHR M16 ....99 D3
  STRET M32 ....96 A3
Green Wks PWCH M25 ....30 B2
Greenwatch Cl ECC M30 ....61 D5
Greenway MDTN M24 ....16 B4
Greenway Av BNG/LEV M19 ....118 C3
Greenways NEWH/MOS M40 ....37 C4
Greenwich Cl NEWH/MOS M40 ....74 A1
Greenwood Av SWIN M27 ....27 C4
Greenwood St OLDS * OL8 ....41 C4
  SLFD M6 ....66 A1
Greer St OP/CLY M11 ....90 B1
Greetland Dr BKLY M9 ....35 C1
Gregory St OLDS OL8 ....39 D2
  WGTN/LGST M12 ....89 D3
Gregory Wy RDSH SK5 ....120 A3
Gregson Rd RDSH SK5 ....119 D3
Gregson St OLD OL1 ....23 C3
Greg St RDSH SK5 ....119 D3
Grelley Wk RUSH/FAL M14 ....102 A1
Grendale Av STKP SK1 ....131 C4
Grendon Av OLDS OL8 ....40 B2
Grendon Wk WGTN/LGST M12 ....89 D3
Grenfell Rd DID/WITH M20 ....124 B2
Grenham Av HULME M15 ....6 A5
Grenville St EDGY/DAV SK3 ....132 A1
Gresford Cl CCHDY M21 ....111 D1
Gresham St WHTF M45 ....10 A1
Gresham Dr CHAD OL9 ....21 D2
Gresham Wk HTNM SK4 ....129 D2
Greton Cl BRUN/LGST M13 ....103 D1
Greville St BRUN/LGST M13 ....103 D2
Greyhound Dr SLFD M6 ....49 C4
Grey Mare La OP/CLY M11 ....72 B4
Greystoke Av BNG/LEV M19 ....105 D4
Greystoke La FAIL M35 ....56 A3
Greystoke St STKP SK1 ....130 B4
Greystone Av OLDTF/WHR M16 ....114 A1
Grey St PWCH M25 ....30 B1
  WGTN/LGST M12 ....88 B3
Greyswood Av CHH M8 ....51 C3
Greytown Cl SLFD M6 ....48 A4
Grierson St OLDTF/WHR M16 ....100 B3
Griffin Ct CSLFD * M3 ....2 C3
Griffin Gv BNG/LEV M19 ....117 D1
Griffin Rd FAIL M35 ....56 A2
Griffin St BRO * M7 ....49 D3
Griffiths Cl BRO * M7 ....68 A1
Griffiths St NEWH/MOS M40 ....55 D4
Grimscott Cl BKLY * M9 ....54 C4
Grimshaw La MDTN M24 ....18 A2
  NEWH/MOS M40 ....54 A4
Grimshaw St FAIL * M35 ....56 B1
  STKP * SK1 ....130 B1
Grindall Av BKLY M9 ....36 A3
Grindley Av CCHDY M21 ....113 C4
Grindlow St BRUN/LGST M13 ....88 B3
Grindon Av BRO M7 ....48 B2
Grinton Av BRUN/LGST M13 ....103 D3
Grisebeck Wy OLD * OL1 ....22 B3
Grizebeck Cl GTN M18 ....90 B3
Groby Rd CCHDY M21 ....112 A1
Groby St OLDS OL8 ....41 C2
Groom St CMANE * M1 ....8 C4
Grosvenor Av WHTF M45 ....10 B1
Grosvenor Gdns BRO M7 ....68 A1
Grosvenor Rd ECC M30 ....60 B2
  HTNM SK4 ....127 D2
  OLDTF/WHR M16 ....100 A3
  SALE M33 ....108 A4
  SWIN M27 ....46 A2
Grosvenor Sq BRO M7 ....68 A1
Grosvenor St CMANE M1 ....8 B4
  PWCH M25 ....30 B1
  STKP SK1 ....133 C2
  STRET M32 ....97 C3
  SWIN M27 ....26 A3
The Grove DID/WITH M20 ....125 C4
  ECC M30 ....63 C4
  EDGY/DAV SK3 ....132 B2
Grove Av FAIL M35 ....56 B4
Grove Cl RUSH/FAL M14 ....102 B2
Grovehurst SWIN M27 ....43 C3
Grove La DID/WITH M20 ....125 C3
Grove Rd AULW OL7 ....59 D4
  BRO M7 ....50 B4
  DROY M43 ....92 A1
  OLD OL1 ....23 D2
Grovewood Cl AULW OL7 ....59 D4
Grundy Av PWCH M25 ....28 B3
Grundy St HTNM SK4 ....126 B3
Guernsey Cl BNG/LEV * M19 ....117 D3
Guest Rd PWCH M25 ....11 D3
Guide Post Sq BRUN/LGST * M13 ....88 A3
Guide Post Rd BRUN/LGST M13 ....88 A3
Guide St SALQ M50 ....64 B4
Guido St FAIL M35 ....56 B2
Guildford Rd BNG/LEV M19 ....105 C3
  SLFD M6 ....64 A1
  URM M41 ....94 B1
Guildhall Cl HULME M15 ....86 B4
Guilford Rd ECC M30 ....61 C4
Guinness Rd TRPK M17 ....80 B1
Gullane Cl NEWH/MOS M40 ....55 D1
Gulvain Pl CHAD OL9 ....20 A1
Gunson St NEWH/MOS M40 ....5 F1
Gun St ANC M4 ....4 C3
Gurner Av ORD M5 ....84 A2
Gurney St ANC M4 ....71 C4
Guy Fawkes St ORD M5 ....84 A2

Guy St *BRO* M7 ....**51** C2
Gwelo St *OP/CLY* M11 ....**72** B3
Gwenbury Av *STKP* SK1 ....**131** C3
Gwendor Av *CHH* M8 ....**32** A2
Gyte's La *BNG/LEV* M19 ....**105** D3

H

Hacking St *BRO* M7 ....**50** B3
    PWCH M25 ....**29** D1
Hackle St *OP/CLY* M11 ....**73** D3
Hackleton Cl *ANC* M4 ....**71** C4
Hackness Rd *CCHDY* M21 ....**111** C1
Hackney Av *NEWH/MOS* M40 ....**73** D3
Haddington Dr *BKLY* M9 ....**34** B2
Haddon Av *NEWH/MOS* M40 ....**37** D3
Haddon Gv *RDSH* SK5 ....**119** D2
Haddon Hall Rd *DROY* M43 ....**74** B3
Haddon Rd *CCHDY* M21 ....**113** C4
    ECC M30 ....**78** B1
    SWIN M27 ....**43** D4
Haddon St *SLFD* M6 ....**49** C4
    STRET M32 ....**97** C1
Hadfield Av *CHAD* OL9 ....**21** C4
Hadfield St *BRO* M7 ....**50** B3
    OLDS OL8 ....**40** B2
    OLDTF/WHR M16 ....**84** B3
Hadley Av *BRUN/LGST* M13 ....**103** D3
Hadley St *SLFD* M6 ....**49** C4
Hadlow Gn *RDSH* SK5 ....**121** C3
Hadlow Wk *NEWH/MOS* * M40 ....**71** D2
Hafton Rd *BRO* M7 ....**49** C3
Hagley Rd *ORD* M5 ....**83** D3
Hague Rd *DID/WITH* M20 ....**114** B3
Hague St *NEWH/MOS* M40 ....**54** A4
Haig Av *HTNM* SK4 ....**119** D4
Haigh Pk *HTNM* SK4 ....**119** D4
Haig Rd *STRET* M32 ....**97** C2
Haldon Rd *DID/WITH* M20 ....**116** A4
Hale La *FAIL* M35 ....**55** D2
Hales Cl *DROY* M43 ....**75** C2
Halesden Rd *HTNM* SK4 ....**119** C3
Halesworth Wk *NEWH/MOS* * M40 ....**70** B1
Haley Cl *RDSH* SK5 ....**120** A1
Haley St *CHH* M8 ....**51** D2
Half Edge La *ECC* M30 ....**63** C2
Halford Dr *NEWH/MOS* M40 ....**55** C1
Half St *CSLFD* * M3 ....**3** D1
Hallam Rd *NEWH/MOS* M40 ....**55** C4
Hallam St *OFTN* SK2 ....**133** D3
Hallas Gv *NTHM/RTH* M23 ....**122** A4
Hall Av *RUSH/FAL* M14 ....**103** C3
Hall Bank *ECC* M30 ....**61** D3
Hall Dr *MDTN* M24 ....**17** C3
Hall Gv *RUSH/FAL* M14 ....**103** C2
Halliday Rd *NEWH/MOS* M40 ....**73** C3
Halliford Rd *NEWH/MOS* M40 ....**54** A4
Halliwell Av *OLDS* OL8 ....**40** B3
Halliwell La *CHH* M8 ....**51** C2
Halliwell Rd *PWCH* M25 ....**29** C4
Halliwell St *CHAD* * OL9 ....**38** B4
Halliwell St West *CHH* * M8 ....**51** C2
Hall Moss Rd *BKLY* M9 ....**35** D2
Hallows Av *CCHDY* M21 ....**112** B4
Hall Rd *RUSH/FAL* M14 ....**103** C3
Hallroyd Brow *OLD* * OL1 ....**22** D1
Hall St *CMANW* M2 ....**7** F1
    FAIL M35 ....**56** A3
    MDTN * M24 ....**17** D1
    STKP SK1 ....**130** B4
    SWIN M27 ....**26** A3
Hallsville Rd *BNG/LEV* M19 ....**105** D4
Hallsworth Rd *ECC* M30 ....**60** D3
Hallwood Av *SLFD* M6 ....**64** B1
Hallworth Av *DTN/ASHW* M34 ....**76** A4

Hallworth Rd *CHH* M8 ....**52** A1
Halmore Rd *NEWH/MOS* M40 ....**71** C3
Halsbury Cl *WGTN/LGST* M12 ....**88** B3
Halsey Cl *CHAD* OL9 ....**37** D2
Halsmere Dr *BKLY* M9 ....**34** B2
Halstead Av *CCHDY* M21 ....**111** D2
    SLFD M6 ....**47** D4
Halstock Wk *NEWH/MOS* M40 ....**53** C4
Halston Cl *RDSH* SK5 ....**130** B3
Halston St *HULME* M15 ....**85** D3
Halton Bank *SLFD* M6 ....**66** A1
Halton Rd *OP/CLY* M11 ....**73** D3
Halvis Gv *OLDTF/WHR* M16 ....**99** C2
Hambridge Cl *CHH* M8 ....**51** D2
Hamer Dr *OLDTF/WHR* M16 ....**85** C4
Hamer Hl *BKLY* M9 ....**33** D2
Hamerton Rd *NEWH/MOS* M40 ....**70** B1
Hamilcar Av *ECC* M30 ....**62** B3
Hamilton Cl *PWCH* M25 ....**29** D2
Hamilton Crs *HTNM* SK4 ....**128** A4
Hamilton Gv *OLDTF/WHR* M16 ....**85** C4
Hamilton Ms *ECC* * M30 ....**61** C2
    PWCH * M25 ....**29** D2
Hamilton Rd *BRUN/LGST* M13 ....**104** A2
    PWCH M25 ....**29** D2
    WHTF M45 ....**10** B1
Hamilton Sq *HTNM* SK4 ....**129** D2
Hamilton St *BRO* * M7 ....**50** A2
    CHAD OL9 ....**20** B2
    ECC M30 ....**61** C2
    OLDTF/WHR M16 ....**85** C4
    SWIN M27 ....**25** C4
Hammerstone Rd *GTN* M18 ....**90** B3
Hammett Rd *CCHDY* M21 ....**111** D1
Hammond Av *HTNM* SK4 ....**119** D4
Hamnett St *OP/CLY* M11 ....**74** A4
Hampden Crs *GTN* M18 ....**90** B4
Hampden Gv *ECC* M30 ....**62** A3
Hampden Rd *PWCH* M25 ....**30** A1
Hampshire Rd *CHAD* OL9 ....**21** C4
    DROY M43 ....**75** D2
    RDSH SK5 ....**121** D4
Hampshire St *BRO* M7 ....**50** A3
Hampson Cl *ECC* M30 ....**61** C4
Hampson Rd *STRET* M32 ....**96** B3
Hampson St *DROY* M43 ....**75** D3
    ECC M30 ....**61** C4
    NEWH/MOS * M40 ....**71** C1
    ORD M5 ....**2** A5
    SWIN M27 ....**26** B4
Hampton Rd *CCHDY* M21 ....**98** A4
    FAIL M35 ....**57** D1
    URM M41 ....**94** A4
Hampton St *OLDS* OL8 ....**40** A1
Hamsell Rd *BRUN/LGST* M13 ....**9** E4
Hancock Cl *RUSH/FAL* M14 ....**102** A3
Hancock St *STRET* M32 ....**110** A1
Handforth Gv *BRUN/LGST* M13 ....**103** D3
Handforth Rd *RDSH* SK5 ....**120** A4
Handley Av *RUSH/FAL* M14 ....**102** A4
Handsworth Wy *WGTN/LGST* M12 ....**88** B3
Hankinson Wy *SLFD* M6 ....**66** B2
Hanley Cl *MDTN* M24 ....**17** D4
Hanlith Ms *BNG/LEV* M19 ....**117** C1
Hanlon St *CHH* M8 ....**51** C1
Hannah Baldwin Cl *OP/CLY* M11 ....**89** C1
Hannah St *WGTN/LGST* M12 ....**104** B3
Hanover Ct *BRO* M7 ....**50** A2
    WALK * M28 ....**43** C3
Hanover Crs *RUSH/FAL* M14 ....**103** C3
Hanover Gdns *BRO* M7 ....**50** B1
Hanover St *ANC* M4 ....**4** A2
Hansdon Cl *CHH* M8 ....**51** D3
Hanson Ms *STKP* SK1 ....**131** C3
Hanson Pk *MDTN* * M24 ....**18** B1
Hanson Rd *NEWH/MOS* M40 ....**54** A4
Hanson St *MDTN* M24 ....**17** D1
Hanworth Cl *BRUN/LGST* M13 ....**9** D4
Hapton Av *STRET* M32 ....**97** C4

Hapton Pl *HTNM* * 129 D2
Hapton St *BNG/LEV* M19 ....104 B4
Harbern Cl *ECC* M30 ....62 A1
Harbord St *MDTN* M24 ....17 D1
Harcombe Rd *DID/WITH* M20 ....115 D3
Harcourt Av *URM* M41 ....95 C4
Harcourt Cl *URM* M41 ....95 C4
Harcourt Rd *SALE* M33 ....108 B3
Harcourt St *RDSH* SK5 ....120 A1
    STRET M32 ....97 D2
Hardcastle Av *CCHDY* M21 ....112 B3
Hardcastle Rd *EDGY/DAV* SK3 ......132 A2
Hardcastle St *OLD* * OL1 ....23 D2
Hardfield Rd *MDTN* M24 ....17 D4
Hardicker St *BNG/LEV* M19 ....118 A3
Harding St *ANC* M4 ....71 C4
    CSLFD M3 ....5 E2
    SLFD M6 ....66 B1
    STKP SK1 ....131 C4
Hardman Av *PWCH* M25 ....31 D3
Hardman La *FAIL* M35 ....56 B1
Hardman Rd *RDSH* SK5 ....120 A1
Hardman's Rd *WHTF* M45 ....11 C3
Hardman St *CHAD* OL9 ....39 C2
    CSLFD M3 ....3 D1
    EDGY/DAV SK3 ....129 C4
    FAIL M35 ....56 A2
Hardon Gv *BRUN/LGST* M13 ....104 A3
Hardrush Fold *FAIL* M35 ....57 D3
Hardshaw Cl *BRUN/LGST* * M13 ......9 D5
Hardwood Cl *CHH* M8 ....51 D2
Hardy Av *CCHDY* M21 ....111 D1
Hardy Gv *SWIN* M27 ....44 A4
    WALK M28 ....42 A1
Hardy La *CCHDY* M21 ....112 B3
Hardy St *ECC* M30 ....61 C4
    OLDE OL4 ....23 D4
Haredale Dr *CHH* M8 ....52 A3
Harefield Dr *DID/WITH* M20 ....124 B3
Harehill Cl *BRUN/LGST* M13 ....9 D5
Hare St *ANC* * M4 ....4 B5
Harewood Ct *RDSH* SK5 ....119 D1
Harewood Wy *SWIN* M27 ....26 A3
Hargrave Cl *BKLY* M9 ....15 D3
Hargreave's St *ANC* M4 ....69 D2
    CHAD OL9 ....21 D3
    OLD * OL1 ....23 C2
Harkness St *WGTN/LGST* M12 ....9 E1
Harland Dr *CHH* M8 ....52 A3
Harlech Av *WHTF* M45 ....12 A3
Harley Av *RUSH/FAL* M14 ....103 D2
Harley Rd *SALE* M33 ....109 D4
Harley St *OP/CLY* M11 ....91 C3
Harlow Dr *GTN* M18 ....106 A2
Harmer Cl *NEWH/MOS* M40 ....54 A4
Harmony St *OLDE* OL4 ....23 D3
Harmsworth Dr *HTNM* SK4 ....118 A4
Harmsworth St *SLFD* M6 ....65 D3
Harold Av *GTN* M18 ....107 C3
Harold Priestnall St *NEWH/MOS* M40 ...55 C4
Harold St *CHAD* OL9 ....22 A2
    FAIL * M35 ....56 B2
    OLDTF/WHR M16 ....84 B3
    PWCH M25 ....29 C1
Harper Ct *EDGY/DAV* SK3 ....132 B2
Harper St *EDGY/DAV* * SK3 ....132 B2
    OLDS OL8 ....40 C3
Harp Rd *TRPK* M17 ....80 B1
Harp St *OP/CLY* M11 ....91 C2
Harpurhey Rd *CHH* M8 ....52 B1
Harriett St *ANC* M4 ....5 F2
Harringay Rd *NEWH/MOS* M40 ....55 D4
Harrington St *GTN* M18 ....91 D4
Harris Av *URM* M41 ....79 C4
Harrison Av *BNG/LEV* M19 ....105 C3
Harrison St *ANC* M4 ....71 C4
    BRO M7 ....68 A1
    OFTN SK2 ....133 C2

OLD * OL1 ....23 C3
Harris St *CHH* M8 ....68 B1
Harrogate Av *PWCH* M25 ....31 C3
Harrogate Ct *OP/CLY* M11 ....91 D2
Harrogate Dr *RDSH* SK5 ....119 D1
Harrogate Rd *RDSH* SK5 ....106 B4
Harrop Fold *OLDS* OL8 ....41 D4
Harrop St *GTN* M18 ....92 A3
Harrow Av *BNG/LEV* M19 ....117 D3
    OLDS OL8 ....40 A2
Harrowby Dr *NEWH/MOS* M40 ....53 C4
Harrowby Rd *SWIN* M27 ....44 B2
Harrow St *CHH* M8 ....33 C4
Harry Hall Gdns *BRO* * M7 ....67 D1
Harry Rd *RDSH* SK5 ....120 A1
Harry St *CHAD* OL9 ....21 D3
Harry Thorneycroft Wk *OP/CLY* M11 ...88 B1
Hart Av *DROY* M43 ....76 A4
Harter St *CMANE* M1 ....6 E4
Hartfield Cl *BRUN/LGST* M13 ....9 E5
Hartford Av *HTNM* SK4 ....119 C3
Hartford Rd *URM* M41 ....94 B1
Hartford Sq *CHAD* * OL9 ....21 D3
Hart Hill Dr *ORD* M5 ....65 C2
Harthill St *CHH* M8 ....52 B1
Hartington Cl *URM* M41 ....94 B3
Hartington Dr *OP/CLY* M11 ....73 C2
Hartington Rd *CCHDY* M21 ....112 A1
    ECC M30 ....60 B2
Hartington St *RUSH/FAL* M14 ....101 C2
Hartis Av *BRO* M7 ....50 B3
Hartlepool Cl *RUSH/FAL* M14 ....102 A2
Hartley Av *PWCH* M25 ....30 D2
Hartley Hall Gdns *OLDTF/WHR* M16 ...100 B4
Hartley Rd *CCHDY* M21 ....98 B3
Hartley St *EDGY/DAV* * SK3 ....132 A1
    NEWH/MOS M40 ....54 A1
Harton Av *GTN* M18 ....105 D2
Hart Rd *RUSH/FAL* M14 ....102 A4
Hartshead Cl *OP/CLY* M11 ....92 B2
Hartshead Crs *FAIL* M35 ....58 B3
Hart St *CMANE* M1 ....8 B1
    DROY M43 ....75 D3
Hartswood Rd *DID/WITH* M20 ......116 A3
Hartwell Cl *OP/CLY* M11 ....89 C1
Harvard Gv *SLFD* M6 ....64 B2
Harvest Cl *SLFD* M6 ....47 D4
Harvey St *STKP* SK1 ....130 A4
Harwich Cl *BNG/LEV* * M19 ....104 B4
    RDSH SK5 ....121 D3
Harwood Ct *SLFD* M6 ....67 C1
Harwood Rd *BNG/LEV* M19 ....116 B3
    HTNM SK4 ....126 B3
Harwood St *HTNM* SK4 ....129 D2
Haslam Rd *EDGY/DAV* SK3 ....132 B3
Haslam St *MDTN* * M24 ....18 B2
Haslemere Rd *DID/WITH* M20 ....116 A3
Hasper Av *DID/WITH* M20 ....114 B2
Hassall Av *DID/WITH* M20 ....114 A1
Hassop Av *BRO* M7 ....48 B2
Hassop Cl *OP/CLY* M11 ....71 D4
Hassop Rd *RDSH* SK5 ....107 C4
Hastings Av *CCHDY* M21 ....111 D1
    WHTF M45 ....12 A2
Hastings Cl *WHTF* M45 ....12 A2
Hastings Rd *ECC* M30 ....60 B1
    PWCH M25 ....12 B4
Hatfield Av *BNG/LEV* M19 ....117 C3
Hatherley Rd *DID/WITH* M20 ....116 A3
Hatherop Cl *ECC* M30 ....61 C2
Hathersage Rd *BRUN/LGST* M13 ..102 B3
Hathersage St *CHAD* OL9 ....21 D3
Hathershaw La *OLDS* OL8 ....41 C2
Hatro Ct *URM* M41 ....95 D4
Hatter St *ANC* M4 ....4 C2
Hatton Av *BRO* M7 ....68 A2
Hattons Ct *STRET* M32 ....96 B2
Hattons Rd *TRPK* M17 ....81 C3

Hatton St *STKP* SK1 ....**129** D3
Haughton Dr *WYTH/NTH* M22 ....**123** C4
Havana Cl *OP/CLY* M11 ....**72** A4
Havelock Dr *BRO* M7.........................**68** A4
Havelock St *OLDS* OL8 ....**23** C4
Haven Dr *DROY* M43 ....**74** B3
Havencroft Av *ECC* M30 ....**79** C1
Haven St *SLFD* M6 ....**65** D3
Haverfield Rd *BKLY* M9 ....**34** B2
Haverford St *WGTN/LGST* M12 .....**89** C3
Haversham Dr *CHH* M8 ....**51** D3
Havers Rd *GTN* M18 ....**91** D4
Hawarden Av *OLDTF/WHR* M16 .....**99** D3
Hawes Av *RUSH/FAL* M14 ....**116** B2
 SWIN * M27 ....**45** C3
Hawes Cl *OFTN* SK2 ....**133** C4
Haweswater Cl *DTN/ASHW* M34 ..**107** D3
Haweshead Rd *CHH* M8 ....**52** A3
Hawkhurst Rd *BRUN/LGST* M13 ..**104** A2
Hawkins St *RDSH* SK5 ....**129** D1
Hawkshaw St *ORD* M5 ....**66** B4
Hawksley St *OLDS* OL8 ....**39** C3
Hawkstone Av *DROY* M43 ....**74** B2
 WHTF M45 ....**10** A1
Hawley St *BNG/LEV* M19 ....**118** A1
Haworth Dr *STRET* M32 ....**95** C2
Haworth Rd *GTN* M18 ....**105** D1
Hawthorn Av *ECC* M30 ....**128** A2
 URM M41 ....**95** C4
Hawthorn Dr *BNG/LEV* M19 ....**117** C2
 SLFD M6 ....**63** D1
 SWIN M27 ....**46** B2
Hawthorne Crs *OLDS* OL8 ....**41** C3
Hawthorne Dr *WALK* M28 ....**42** B2
Hawthorn Gv *CHAD* OL9 ....**21** C1
Hawthorn Gv *HTNM* SK4 ....**128** A2
Hawthorn La *CCHDY* * M21 ....**111** C3
Hawthorn Rd *DROY* M43 ....**76** B3
 HTNM SK4 ....**126** B3
 NEWH/MOS M40 ....**37** D4
 OLDS OL8 ....**39** C3
 STRET M32 ....**110** B1
Hawthorn Rd South *DROY* M43 ......**76** B3
Hawthorn St *GTN* M18 ....**91** C3
Hawthorn Ter *HTNM* * SK4 ....**128** B2
Haxby Rd *GTN* M18 ....**106** A2
Haydn Av *RUSH/FAL* M14 ....**102** A1
Hayfield Cl *WGTN/LGST* M12 ....**88** B3
Hayfield Rd *SLFD* M6 ....**64** A1
Hayley St *BRUN/LGST* * M13 ....**103** D1
Haymans Wk *BRUN/LGST* M13 ....**9** D5
Haymarket Cl *BRUN/LGST* M13 .....**87** D4
Haymond Cl *SLFD* M6 ....**48** B3
Hazel Av *OLDTF/WHR* M16 ....**100** A3
 SWIN M27 ....**45** D2
Hazelbank Av *DID/WITH* M20 ....**115** D4
Hazelbottom Rd *CHH* M8 ....**52** A2
Hazel Cl *DROY* M43 ....**76** B3
Hazeldene Rd *NEWH/MOS* M40 ....**37** D4
Hazelfields *WALK* M28 ....**43** C2
Hazel Gv *CHAD* OL9 ....**21** C1
 ORD M5 ....**64** B3
 URM M41 ....**94** B3
Hazelhurst Fold *WALK* M28 ....**43** D2
Hazelhurst Rd *WALK* M28 ....**43** C2
Hazel La *OLDS* OL8 ....**40** A3
Hazelmere Av *ECC* M30 ....**61** C1
Hazelmere Cl *ECC* M30 ....**79** C1
Hazel Rd *WHTF* M45 ....**12** A1
Hazel Ter *BKLY* * M9 ....**34** A1
Hazelwood *CHAD* OL9 ....**19** D2
Headingley Dr *OLDTF/WHR* M16 ...**98** D1
Headingley Rd *RUSH/FAL* M14......**116** A2
Headlands Dr *PWCH* M25 ....**29** D4
Heald Av *RUSH/FAL* M14 ....**102** A2
Heald Gv *RUSH/FAL* M14 ....**102** A1
Heald Pl *RUSH/FAL* M14 ....**102** A2
Heald St *STKP* SK1 ....**130** B3

Healey Cl *BRO* M7 ....**49** D1
Heap St *WHTF* * M45 ....**11** C2
The Heath *MDTN* M24 ....**18** A3
Heath Av *BRO* M7 ....**67** D1
Heathbank Rd *BKLY* M9 ....**33** D1
Heathcote Av *HTNM* SK4 ....**128** D2
Heathcote Rd *GTN* M18 ....**105** D1
Heath Crs *EDGY/DAV* SK3 ....**133** C4
Heather Av *DROY* M43 ....**76** B3
Heatherdale Dr *CHH* M8 ....**51** D3
Heather Gv *DROY* M43 ....**93** C1
Heatherside *RDSH* SK5 ....**107** D4
Heather St *OP/CLY* M11 ....**73** C3
Heathfield *WALK* M28 ....**42** A4
Heathfield Av *HTNM* SK4 ....**118** B4
Heathfield Dr *SWIN* M27 ....**45** D2
Heathfield Rd *OFTN* SK2 ....**133** C5
Heathfield St *NEWH/MOS* M40 ......**55** D4
Heathland Av *BRO* M7 ....**49** C1
Heathlands Dr *PWCH* M25 ....**29** D4
Heath Rd *EDGY/DAV* SK3 ....**133** C3
Heathside Rd *DID/WITH* M20 ....**115** D4
Heath St *CHH* M8 ....**51** C2
Heathwood Rd *BNG/LEV* M19 ......**126** B1
Heaton Cl *HTNM* SK4 ....**127** D2
Heaton La *HTNM* SK4 ....**129** D4
Heaton Moor Rd *HTNM* SK4 ....**128** A2
Heaton Park Rd *BKLY* M9 ....**14** B4
Heaton Park Rd West *BKLY* M9 ......**14** B4
Heaton Rd *DID/WITH* M20 ....**115** D2
 HTNM SK4 ....**129** C2
Heaton St *BRO* M7 ....**50** B2
 PWCH M25 ....**30** B1
Heavily Gv *OFTN* SK2 ....**133** D3
Hebburn Wk *RUSH/FAL* M14 ....**102** A1
Hebden Av *SLFD* M6 ....**64** B2
Hebden Wk *HULME* M15 ....**86** A4
Hector Rd *BRUN/LGST* M13 ....**104** A2
Heddon Cl *HTNM* SK4 ....**126** B2
Hedges St *FAIL* M35 ....**57** D1
Helena St *SLFD* M6 ....**64** B4
Helen St *BRO* M7 ....**49** D4
 ECC M30 ....**78** A1
Helensville Av *SLFD* M6 ....**48** A4
Helga St *NEWH/MOS* M40 ....**71** C1
Helmet St *CMANE* M1 ....**9** F2
Helmshore Wk *BRUN/LGST* M13 .....**9** D4
Helsby Wk *WGTN/LGST* M12 ....**88** B1
Helston St *NEWH/MOS* M40 ....**72** A1
Hembury Av *BNG/LEV* M19 ....**117** C3
Hemlock Av *OLDS* OL8 ....**40** B2
Hemming Dr *ECC* M30 ....**62** B4
Hemmington Dr *BKLY* M9 ....**53** C2
Hemmons Rd *WGTN/LGST* M12 ...**105** C3
Hempshaw La *STKP* SK1 ....**133** D2
Hemsley St *BKLY* M9 ....**34** B4
Hemsley St South *BKLY* M9 ....**53** D1
Hemswell Cl *SLFD* M6 ....**65** D1
Hemsworth Rd *GTN* M18 ....**106** A2
Henbury Dr *RUSH/FAL* M14...........**101** C2
Henbury St *RUSH/FAL* M14...........**101** C2
Henderson Av *SWIN* M27 ....**26** A4
Henderson St *BNG/LEV* M19 ....**118** A1
Hendham V *BKLY* M9 ....**52** B2
Hendon Rd *BKLY* M9 ....**33** D1
Hengist St *GTN* M18 ....**106** A1
Henley Av *OLDTF/WHR* M16 ....**99** C2
Henley Pl *BNG/LEV* M19 ....**117** D3
Henley St *CHAD* OL9 ....**38** B2
 OLD OL1 ....**22** A1
Henniker St *SWIN* M27 ....**44** B3
Henrietta St *OLDTF/WHR* M16 ......**84** B4
Henry St *ANC* M4 ....**4** C3
 DROY M43 ....**75** D4
 ECC M30 ....**61** D4
 FAIL M35 ....**40** C4
 MDTN M24 ....**17** C1

OLDTF/WHR M16	84	B4
PWCH M25	12	B4
Henshaw Ct OLDTF/WHR M16	99	C1
Henshaw La CHAD OL9	38	A3
Henshaw St OLD OL1	22	B2
STRET M32	97	C3
Henton Wk NEWH/MOS M40	70	B4
Henwood Rd DID/WITH M20	115	D4
Hepple Cl HTNM SK4	127	C2
Heppleton Rd NEWH/MOS M40	37	C3
Hepple Wk AULW * OL7	59	D4
Hepton St OLD OL1	22	B1
Herbert St CHAD OL9	21	C2
CHH * M8	51	C1
DROY M43	75	C4
EDGY/DAV SK3	132	A2
PWCH M25	29	C1
STRET M32	97	C3
Hereford Dr PWCH M25	30	B3
SWIN M27	45	C3
Hereford Rd ECC M30	45	D4
RDSH SK5	121	D4
Hereford St CHAD OL9	21	C4
SALE M33	109	C4
Heritage Gdns DID/WITH M20	125	C3
Hermitage Rd CHH M8	32	B4
Hermon Av OLDS OL8	40	B3
Herne St OP/CLY M11	89	D1
Heron Ct SLFD M6	64	A2
Herondale Rd NEWH/MOS M40	55	C4
Heron Dr DTN/ASHW M34	76	B4
Heron Ml OLDS * OL8	40	A2
Heron St EDGY/DAV SK3	132	A1
HULME M15	85	D4
OLDS OL8	39	D2
SWIN M27	26	B4
Herristone Rd CHH M8	32	B3
Herrod Av HTNM SK4	119	D4
Herschel St NEWH/MOS M40	54	D4
Hersey St SLFD * M6	65	D3
Hertford Rd BKLY M9	34	A4
Hesford Av BKLY M9	54	A2
Hesketh Av DID/WITH M20	124	B2
Hesketh Rd HTNM SK4	129	D1
Hessel St SALO M50	65	C4
Hester Wk HULME * M15	86	A3
Heston Av BRUN/LGST M13	103	D3
Heswall Av DID/WITH M20	115	C2
Heswall Rd RDSH SK5	107	C3
Hetherington Wk WGTN/LGST M12	104	A1
Hethorn St NEWH/MOS M40	55	D4
Hetton Av BRUN/LGST M13	103	D3
Hewart Cl NEWH/MOS M40	70	B1
Hewitt Av DTN/ASHW M34	107	C2
Hewitt St CSLFD M3	7	D3
Hewlett Rd CCHDY M21	98	B4
Hexham Cl CHAD OL9	21	D4
Hexham Rd GTN M18	105	C1
Hexon St SLFD M6	65	D2
Heybrook Cl WHTF M45	12	B1
Heybury Cl OP/CLY M11	89	C1
Heyford Av NEWH/MOS M40	37	C3
Heyridge Dr WYTH/NTH M22	123	C4
Heyrod St CMANE M1	9	E1
Heyrose Wk HULME M15	85	C3
The Heys PWCH M25	12	A4
RDSH SK5	107	D4
Heys Av SWIN M27	24	B3
Heys Cl North SWIN M27	24	B3
Heyscroft Rd DID/WITH M20	115	D3
HTNM SK4	127	D3
Heysham Av DID/WITH M20	114	A2
Heys Rd PWCH M25	12	A4
Heys Vw PWCH M25	30	A1
Heywood Av SWIN M27	27	C3
Heywood Gdns PWCH M25	30	A1
Heywood Gv SALE M33	108	B3
Heywood Old Rd MDTN M24	14	B1
Heywood Rd PWCH M25	12	A3
Heywood St CHH M8	51	D3
FAIL M35	56	A2
SWIN M27	44	B1
Heywood Wy SLFD M6	66	A2
Heyworth St ORD * M5	65	D4
Hibbert Crs FAIL M35	57	D2
Hibbert St HTNM SK4	119	D4
RUSH/FAL M14	102	B2
Hibernia Wy STRET M32	80	B4
Higginson Rd RDSH SK5	119	D2
Higham Vw SLFD M6	66	B2
High Bank GTN M18	91	D4
High Bank Crs PWCH M25	30	B2
High Bank Gv PWCH M25	30	B2
High Bank Rd DROY M43	92	A1
SWIN M27	46	A1
High Bank Side STKP * SK1	130	A4
High Barn Rd MDTN M24	17	D2
Highbury Rd HTNM SK4	118	B3
OLDTF/WHR M16	100	B4
Highclere Av CHH M8	51	C3
Highclere Rd CHH M8	32	A3
Highcliffe Rd BKLY M9	32	B3
Highcroft Av DID/WITH M20	123	D1
Higher Ardwick WGTN/LGST M12	9	F4
Higher Barlow Rw STKP SK1	133	D1
Higher Bury St HTNM SK4	129	C3
Higher Cambridge St HULME M15	8	A5
Higher Chatham St HULME M15	8	A5
Higher Cft ECC M30	78	B1
Higher Hillgate STKP SK1	133	C2
Higher House Cl CHAD OL9	38	B1
Higher La WHTF M45	10	B1
Higher Lime Rd OLDS OL8	58	B1
Higher Ormond St HULME * M15	8	B5
Higher Rd URM M41	94	A3
Higher York St BRUN/LGST M13	8	C5
Highfield Cl STRET M32	109	D1
Highfield Dr ECC M30	62	A2
MDTN M24	17	C2
SWIN M27	46	B2
Highfield Pk HTNM SK4	127	C3
Highfield Pl GTN * M18	107	C1
Highfield Range GTN * M18	107	C1
Highfield Rd BNG/LEV M19	105	D4
ECC M30	62	A1
HTNM SK4	118	B3
PWCH M25	11	D3
SLFD M6	66	A2
STRET M32	109	D1
Highfield St BRO M7	51	C1
CHAD OL9	22	A2
MDTN M24	18	A1
Highfield Ter BKLY M9	53	C1
Highgate Crs GTN M18	106	A1
High Gates SALE M33	110	B4
High Hurst Cl MDTN * M24	15	D2
High La CCHDY M21	112	A1
High Legh Rd OP/CLY M11	91	C1
Highmead St GTN M18	107	C1
Highmead Wk OLDTF/WHR M16	85	C4
Highmore Dr BKLY M9	53	C1
High Peak St NEWH/MOS M40	55	C3
Highshore Dr CHH M8	52	A3
Highstone Dr CHH M8	52	B3
High St ANC M4	3	G4
DROY M43	75	D4
OLD OL1	22	C3
STKP SK1	130	A4
Highworth Dr NEWH/MOS M40	37	C3
Higson Av CCHDY M21	112	A2
ECC M30	78	B1
Hilary Av OLDS OL8	41	C4
Hilary Cl HTNM SK4	129	C3
Hilbury Av BKLY M9	34	A4
Hilda Gv RDSH SK5	130	A1
Hilda St CHAD OL9	22	A2

Hilden Ct *OLDTF/WHR* M16..............100 A1
Hillam Cl *CHH* M8..............95 C4
Hillbrook Av *NEWH/MOS* * M40.......36 A3
Hillcote Wk *GTN* * M18..............90 A3
Hillcourt St *CMANE* M1..............8 B4
Hill Crs *BKLY* M9..............32 B2
Hillcrest *SLFD* * M6..............63 D2
Hill Crest Av *HTNM* SK4..............17 D3
Hillcrest Dr *BNG/LEV* M19..............118 B3
Hillcrest Rd *PWCH* M25..............29 C3
Hillcroft *CHH* M8..............51 D1
Hilldale Av *BKLY* M9..............34 A1
Hillfield *ORD* M5..............65 C3
Hillfield Cl *BRUN/LGST* M13..............88 A4
Hillfoot Wk *HULME* * M15..............85 C3
Hillgate *ORD* M5..............84 A2
Hillier St *BKLY* M9..............53 D1
Hillier St North *BKLY* M9..............53 D1
Hillingdon Cl *OLDS* OL8..............39 C4
Hillingdon Dr *NEWH/MOS* M40..............36 A3
Hillingdon Rd *STRET* M32..............97 D4
Hillkirk St *OP/CLY* M11..............71 D4
Hill La *BKLY* M9..............34 A2
Hillman Cl *NEWH/MOS* M40..............53 C4
Hillside Av *BRO* M7..............48 B1
Hillside Cl *NEWH/MOS* M40..............35 D4
Hillside Dr *SWIN* M27..............47 C3
Hill St *BRO* M7..............50 A1
    DID/WITH M20..............115 C2
Hill Top Av *PWCH* M25..............30 A1
Hilltop Av *BKLY* M9..............34 A2
    WHTF M45..............12 A1
Hilltop Gv *WHTF* M45..............12 A1
Hillview Rd *DTN/ASHW* M34..............107 D4
Hillwood Av *CHH* M8..............32 A2
Hilrose Av *URM* M41..............95 C3
Hilton Av *URM* M41..............94 A3
Hilton Cl *EDGY/DAV* * SK3..............132 B1
Hilton Dr *PWCH* M25..............30 A3
Hilton La *PWCH* M25..............29 D3
Hiltons Cl *OLDS* OL8..............22 B4
Hilton Sq *SWIN* M27..............26 B4
Hilton St *ANC* M4..............4 B3
    BRO M7..............50 A3
    EDGY/DAV SK3..............132 A1
Hilton St North *BRO* M7..............50 A3
Hilton Wk *MDTN* M24..............15 C1
Himley Rd *OP/CLY* M11..............73 D2
Hinchley Rd *BKLY* M9..............36 A2
Hinchley Wy *SWIN* M27..............26 A3
Hinckley St *OP/CLY* M11..............89 C1
Hindburn Cl *WHTF* M45..............12 A1
Hinde St *NEWH/MOS* M40..............54 B1
Hindley St *STKP* SK1..............133 C1
Hinton St *ANC* * M4..............5 D1
    OLDS OL8..............23 C4
Hitchen Wk *BRUN/LGST* M13..............87 D4
Hive St *OLDS* OL8..............39 C3
Hobart St *GTN* M18..............91 C4
Hobson St *FAIL* M35..............56 A3
    OLD OL1..............23 C3
    OP/CLY M11..............92 B2
    RDSH SK5..............107 C3
Hodder Wy *WHTF* M45..............12 B1
Hoddesdon St *CHH* M8..............52 A2
Hodge La *SLFD* M6..............66 A3
Hodge St *BKLY* M9..............35 C4
Hodgson St *CHH* M8..............51 C4
Hodson Fold *OLDS* OL8..............41 D4
Hodson Rd *SWIN* M27..............25 D3
Holbeck Gv *RUSH/FAL* M14..............103 D1
Holbeton Cl *CHH* M8..............50 B4
Holborn Av *FAIL* M35..............58 A2
Holborn Dr *CHH* M8..............52 A4
Holborn St *STKP* * SK1..............130 A4
Holbrook St *CMANE* * M1..............8 B2
Holcombe Cl *SLFD* M6..............66 B3
Holcombe Rd *RUSH/FAL* M14..............116 B2

Holden Rd *BRO* M7..............31 C4
Holden St *OLDS* OL8..............41 C2
Holdgate Cl *HULME* M15..............85 D4
Holdsworth St *SWIN* M27..............44 A2
Holford Av *RUSH/FAL* M14..............102 A3
Holford St *BRUN/LGST* M13..............67 D1
Holker Cl *BRUN/LGST* M13..............88 A4
Holkham Cl *ANC* * M4..............5 F3
Holland Rd *CHH* M8..............32 A3
Holland St *NEWH/MOS* M40..............71 C3
    SLFD M6..............48 B4
The Hollies *DID/WITH* M20..............124 A3
Hollin Bank *HTNM* SK4..............119 C2
Hollingworth Av *NEWH/MOS* M40......38 A3
Hollingworth St *STKP* * SK1..............133 C1
Hollingworth St *CHAD* OL9..............39 C2
Hollins Gv *WGTN/LGST* M12..............104 B2
Hollins Rd *OLDS* OL8..............39 D3
    OLDS OL8..............41 C2
Hollinwood Av *NEWH/MOS* M40..............37 C3
Holloway Dr *WALK* M28..............24 B4
Hollow End *RDSH* SK5..............121 C1
Hollow Vale Dr *RDSH* SK5..............107 D4
Holly Bank *NEWH/MOS* * M40..............55 D2
Hollybush St *GTN* M18..............91 D3
Hollyedge Dr *PWCH* M25..............29 D3
Holly Gv *CHAD* OL9..............21 C1
Hollyhey Dr *NTHM/RTH* M23..............122 A4
Hollyhurst *WALK* M28..............43 C3
Holly La *OLDS* OL8..............39 D3
Holly Rd *HTNM* SK4..............118 B4
    SWIN M27..............44 A3
Holly Royde Cl *DID/WITH* M20..............114 B3
Holly St *DROY* M43..............74 A3
    OP/CLY M11..............88 B1
    STKP SK1..............130 B4
Hollywood Wy *HTNM* SK4..............129 C4
Holmbrook Wk *CHH* M8..............51 D3
Holm Ct *SLFD* * M6..............66 B2
Holmcroft Rd *GTN* M18..............106 A3
Holmdale Av *BNG/LEV* M19..............116 B4
Holme Park Wy *FAIL* M35..............58 B3
Holme Rd *DID/WITH* M20..............124 A2
Holmes St *EDGY/DAV* * SK3..............132 B2
Holmfield Av *BKLY* M9..............54 A3
    PWCH M25..............30 B2
Holmfield Av West *NEWH/MOS* M40......54 A3
Holmfield Cl *HTNM* SK4..............129 C2
Holmfirth St *BRUN/LGST* M13..............104 A1
Holmlea Rd *DROY* M43..............74 B3
Holmleigh Av *BKLY* M9..............34 B4
Holmpark Rd *OP/CLY* M11..............91 C2
Holmside Gdns *BNG/LEV* M19..............126 A1
Holmwood Rd *DID/WITH* M20..............115 C4
Holroyd St *OP/CLY* * M11..............89 D1
Holst Av *CHH* M8..............51 D3
Holtby St *BKLY* M9..............34 B4
Holt La *FAIL* M35..............58 A2
Holt Lane Ms *FAIL* M35..............57 D2
Holt St *ECC* M30..............78 B1
    NEWH/MOS M40..............54 A4
    STKP SK1..............133 C1
    SWIN M27..............26 A3
Holt Town *NEWH/MOS* M40..............71 D3
Holwood Dr *OLDTF/WHR* M16..............113 D1
Holyoake St *DROY* M43..............76 B3
Holyoak St *NEWH/MOS* M40..............55 D3
Holyrood Cl *PWCH* M25..............12 B3
Holyrood Dr *PWCH* M25..............12 B3
    SWIN M27..............43 D2
Holyrood Gv *PWCH* M25..............12 A3
Holyrood Rd *PWCH* M25..............12 B4
Holyrood St *NEWH/MOS* M40..............74 A1
Holywood Dr *OP/CLY* * M11..............73 C3
Homebury Dr *OP/CLY* * M11..............73 C3
Home Dr *MDTN* M24..............17 C2
Homerton Rd *NEWH/MOS* M40..............73 C1
Homestead Crs *BNG/LEV* M19..............126 A2

Hometel *RUSH/FAL* M14 .... **102** B4
Homewood Av *WYTH/NTH* M22 .... **123** C4
Homewood Rd *WYTH/NTH* M22 .... **122** B4
Honduras St *OLDE* OL4 .... **23** D2
Honey St *CHH* M8 .... **69** D1
Honeywell La *OLDS* OL8 .... **41** C2
Honister Rd *BKLY* M9 .... **54** A2
Honor St *BRUN/LGST* M13 .... **103** D2
Hood St *ANC* M4 .... **5** D3
Hooley Range *HTNM* SK4 .... **128** A2
Hooley St *OLDE* OL8 .... **23** D3
  STKP SK1 .... **129** D4
  WGTN/LGST M12 .... **88** A1
Hooton St *NEWH/MOS* M40 .... **71** D2
Hopcroft Cl *BKLY* M9 .... **15** C3
Hope Av *STRET* M32 .... **96** A2
Hopecourt Cl *SLFD* M6 .... **64** A1
Hopedale Rd *RDSH* SK5 .... **120** A3
Hopelea St *DID/WITH* M20 .... **115** C2
Hope Park Cl *PWCH* M25 .... **30** A1
Hope Park Rd *PWCH* M25 .... **30** A2
Hope Rd *PWCH* M25 .... **29** D3
  RUSH/FAL M14 .... **103** C1
Hopes Carr *STKP* SK1 .... **130** A4
Hope St *BRO* M7 .... **50** A2
  CMANE M1 .... **4** C3
  HTNM SK4 .... **129** C4
  ORD M5 .... **67** D4
  SWIN M27 .... **45** D1
Hope Ter *EDGY/DAV* SK3 .... **132** B1
Hopkinson Rd *BKLY* M9 .... **16** A4
Hopkin St *OLD* OL1 .... **23** C1
Hoppet La *DROY* M43 .... **76** B3
Hopwood Av *ECC* M30 .... **62** A2
Hopwood St *CSLFD* * M3 .... **3** D2
  NEWH/MOS M40 .... **55** C3
  SWIN M27 .... **45** D1
Horace Barnes Cl *RUSH/FAL* M14 ..... **101** D2
Horace Gv *HTNM* SK4 .... **129** D1
Horatio St *GTN* * M18 .... **92** A3
Horbury Av *GTN* M18 .... **106** A2
Hornbeam Ct *SLFD* M6 .... **66** B2
Hornbeam Rd *BNG/LEV* M19 .... **105** C3
Hornby Av *BKLY* M9 .... **16** B4
Hornby Rd *STRET* M32 .... **98** A3
Hornby St *CHH* M8 .... **69** C1
  MDTN M24 .... **17** D1
  OLDS * OL8 .... **22** A4
Horncastle Rd *NEWH/MOS* M40 .... **36** A4
Hornchurch St *HULME* M15 .... **85** D3
Horne Dr *ANC* M4 .... **5** E3
Hornsea Wk *OP/CLY* * M11 .... **72** B4
Horsedge St *OLD* OL1 .... **23** C1
Horsefield Cl *CCHDY* M21 .... **113** C2
Horseshoe La *CHAD* OL9 .... **20** A3
Horsham St *SLFD* M6 .... **65** D3
Horstead Wk *BNG/LEV* M19 .... **104** B3
Horton Rd *RUSH/FAL* M14 .... **101** D3
Horton St *OFTN* SK2 .... **133** C2
Hortree Rd *STRET* M32 .... **97** D3
Horwood Crs *DID/WITH* M20 .... **116** A4
Hoscar Dr *BNG/LEV* M19 .... **116** B2
Hoskins Cl *WGTN/LGST* M12 .... **89** D4
Hospital Rd *SWIN* M27 .... **46** A2
Hothersall Rd *RDSH* SK5 .... **120** A2
Hothersall St *BRO* M7 .... **68** B2
Hotspur Cl *DID/WITH* M20 .... **114** B1
Hough Cl *OLDS* OL8 .... **41** D3
Hough End Av *CCHDY* M21 .... **112** B3
Houghend Crs *CCHDY* M21 .... **113** D2
Hough Hall Rd *NEWH/MOS* M40 .... **54** A1
Houghton Av *OLDS* OL8 .... **40** A3
Houghton La *SWIN* M27 .... **44** A4
Houghton Rd *CHH* M8 .... **32** B4
Houghton St *SWIN* M27 .... **47** C3
Hough Wk *BRO* M7 .... **67** D2
Houldsworth Ml *RDSH* * SK5 .... **119** D2
Houldsworth St *CMANE* M1 .... **4** C3

RDSH SK5 .... **119** D2
Houseley Av *CHAD* OL9 .... **38** B2
Houson Pk *SALQ* M50 .... **66** A4
Hoveden St *CHH* M8 .... **69** C1
Hove Dr *RUSH/FAL* M14 .... **116** B2
Hovey Cl *CHH* * M8 .... **51** C2
Hovis St *OP/CLY* M11 .... **90** B1
  HTNM SK4 .... **118** B5
Howard Av *ECC* M30 .... **62** A2
Howard Rd *WYTH/NTH* M22 .... **123** C4
Howard St *CHH* M8 .... **68** B1
  ORD M5 .... **83** D1
  STKP SK1 .... **130** A3
  STRET M32 .... **97** C3
Howarth Av *WALK* M28 .... **43** D2
Howarth St *OLDTF/WHR* M16 .... **99** D1
Howbro Dr *AULW* OL7 .... **59** D4
Howden Cl *RDSH* SK5 .... **106** B3
Howden Rd *BKLY* M9 .... **15** D4
Howe St *BRO* M7 .... **49** D2
Howgill Crs *OLDS* OL8 .... **40** B2
Howgill St *OP/CLY* M11 .... **74** A4
Howton Cl *WGTN/LGST* M12 .... **104** B1
Hoy Dr *URM* M41 .... **79** C3
Hoylake Cl *NEWH/MOS* M40 .... **56** A1
Hoyland Cl *WGTN/LGST* M12 .... **89** C3
Hoyle Av *OLDS* OL8 .... **22** B4
Hoyle St *WGTN/LGST* M12 .... **9** F2
Hoyle Wk *BRUN/LGST* M13 .... **9** E5
Huddart Cl *ORD* M5 .... **84** A1
Hudson St *CHAD* OL9 .... **38** B3
Hudswell Cl *WHTF* M45 .... **10** B1
Hughes Av *FAIL* M35 .... **56** B1
Hughes St *OP/CLY* M11 .... **88** B1
Hugh Oldham Dr *BRO* M7 .... **49** D3
Hugo St *NEWH/MOS* M40 .... **54** B2
Hull Sq *CSLFD* M3 .... **2** A2
Hulme Hall La *NEWH/MOS* M40 .... **71** D1
Hulme Hall Rd *HULME* M15 .... **6** A3
Hulme Pl *ORD* * M5 .... **67** C4
Hulme Rd *NEWH/MOS* M40 .... **56** B4
Hulme St *HULME* M15 .... **7** D4
  OLDS OL8 .... **40** B1
  ORD M5 .... **67** D4
Hulton Dr *OLDTF/WHR* M16 .... **100** B1
Hulton St *FAIL* M35 .... **56** A2
  ORD M5 .... **83** D2
Humberstone Av *HULME* M15 .... **7** D4
Humber St *CHH* M8 .... **51** D2
  SALQ M50 .... **65** C2
Hume St *BNG/LEV* * M19 .... **118** A1
Humphrey Crs *URM* M41 .... **95** D3
Humphrey La *URM* M41 .... **95** D3
Humphrey Pk *URM* M41 .... **95** D3
Humphrey Rd *OLDTF/WHR* M16 .... **84** A4
Humphrey St *CHH* M8 .... **51** C1
Huncoat Av *HTNM* SK4 .... **119** C3
Huncote St *BKLY* M9 .... **34** B4
Hunmanby Av *HULME* M15 .... **7** E4
Hunter's La *OLD* OL1 .... **23** C2
Hunterston Av *ECC* M30 .... **63** D3
Huntingdon Av *CHAD* OL9 .... **21** C4
Huntingdon Crs *RDSH* * SK5 .... **121** D4
Huntingdon Rd *DID/WITH* M20 .... **114** B2
Hunt La *CHAD* OL9 .... **20** A1
Huntley Rd *CHH* M8 .... **31** D3
Hunts Bank *CSLFD* M3 .... **3** F1
Hunts Rd *SLFD* M6 .... **47** C4
Hunt St *BKLY* M9 .... **34** A4
Hurdlow Av *BRO* M7 .... **48** B2
Hurford Av *GTN* M18 .... **91** C3
Hurstbank Av *BNG/LEV* * M19 .... **126** A1
Hurstbourne Av *OP/CLY* M11 .... **73** C2
Hurstbrook Dr *STRET* M32 .... **95** C3
Hurstfold Av *BNG/LEV* M19 .... **126** A2

Hursthead Wk *BRUN/LGST* M13 ....9 D4
Hurst St *CHAD* OL9 ....22 A2
   RDSH SK5 ....119 D2
Hurstville Rd *CCHDY* M21 ....112 A3
Hurstway Dr *BKLY* M9 ....34 B2
Hus St *DROY* M43 ....92 A1
Huxley Av *CHH* M8 ....51 D3
Hyacinth Cl *EDGY/DAV* SK3 ....132 A4
Hyde Fold Cl *BNG/LEV* M19 ....117 C3
Hyde Gv *BRUN/LGST* M13 ....87 D4
Hyde Pl *BRUN/LGST* M13 ....87 D4
Hyde Rd *GTN* M18 ....107 C1
   MDTN M24 ....19 D3
   WGTN/LGST M12 ....88 A3
Hyde Sq *MDTN* M24 ....16 B1
Hyde St *DROY* M43 ....76 B1
   HULME M15 ....85 C4
Hythe Cl *RUSH/FAL* M14 ....102 B2
Hythe Wk *CHAD* * OL9 ....21 C3

I

Iceland St *SLFD* M6 ....65 D3
Ilex Gv *BRO* M7 ....50 A3
Ilford St *OP/CLY* M11 ....73 C3
Ilfracombe St *NEWH/MOS* M40 ....56 A3
Ilkley Cl *CHAD* OL9 ....21 C3
Ilkley Crs *RDSH* SK5 ....119 D3
Ilkley St *NEWH/MOS* M40 ....35 D4
Ilk St *OP/CLY* M11 ....73 C3
Illona Dr *BRO* M7 ....48 B1
Imperial Ter *SALE* * M33 ....108 B1
Ince Cl *DID/WITH* M20 ....115 C2
   HTNM SK4 ....129 D2
Ince St *HTNM* SK4 ....129 D2
Inchcape Dr *BKLY* M9 ....33 C1
Inchfield Rd *NEWH/MOS* M40 ....35 D4
Inchley Rd *BRUN/LGST* M13 ....8 C3
Incline Rd *OLDS* OL8 ....39 C3
Indigo St *SLFD* M6 ....48 A4
Industry St *CHAD* OL9 ....38 B1
Infant St *PWCH* * M25 ....30 B1
Ingham St *NEWH/MOS* * M40 ....74 B1
Inghamwood Cl *BRO* M7 ....51 C2
Ingleby Av *BKLY* M9 ....35 C1
Ingleby St *STRET* M32 ....97 D3
Ingledene Av *BRO* M7 ....31 C3
Ingleton Av *CHH* M8 ....33 C3
Inglewood Wk *BRUN/LGST* * M13 ......9 E5
Ingoldsby Av *BRUN/LGST* M13 ....103 C1
Ingram Dr *HTNM* SK4 ....126 B2
Inkerman St *NEWH/MOS* M40 ....53 C4
Innes St *WGTN/LGST* M12 ....105 C2
Innis Av *NEWH/MOS* M40 ....55 D4
Instow Cl *BRUN/LGST* M13 ....88 A4
Invar Rd *WALK* M28 ....25 C4
Inverness Av *BKLY* M9 ....35 D1
Inwood Wk *CHH* M8 ....52 B3
Iona Wy *URM* M41 ....79 C4
Ionian Gdns *BRO* M7 ....49 D4
Iqbal Cl *WGTN/LGST* M12 ....89 D4
Iredine St *OP/CLY* M11 ....73 C4
Iris St *OLDS* OL8 ....41 C5
Irkdale St *CHH* M8 ....52 B3
Irk St *ANC* * M4 ....69 D2
Irlam Av *ECC* M30 ....63 D1
Irlam Rd *SALE* M33 ....109 D4
Irlam Sq *SLFD* M6 ....47 C4
Irlam St *NEWH/MOS* M40 ....53 D4
Iron St *NEWH/MOS* M40 ....71 D4
Irving St *OLDS* OL8 ....39 C5
Irvin St *NEWH/MOS* M40 ....55 D3
Irwell Av *ECC* M30 ....63 C4
Irwell Gv *ECC* M30 ....63 C4
Irwell Pl *ECC* M30 ....63 C3
   ORD M5 ....67 D4

Irwell St *CHH* M8 ....68 B1
   CSLFD M3 ....2 C4
   SLFD M6 ....48 B3
Isaac Cl *ORD* M5 ....83 D1
Isabella Cl *OLDTF/WHR* M16 ....99 D1
Isaiah St *OLDS* * OL8 ....41 C1
Isca St *OP/CLY* M11 ....72 A4
Isis Cl *BRO* M7 ....48 B1
Islington St *CSLFD* M3 ....2 B3
Islington Wy *CSLFD* M3 ....2 A3
Isobel Cl *ECC* M30 ....62 A4
   OLDTF/WHR M16 ....101 C1
Ivybridge Cl *BRUN/LGST* M13 ....88 A1
Ivy Cl *OLDS* OL8 ....41 C1
Ivy Dr *MDTN* M24 ....17 C3
Ivygreen Rd *CCHDY* M21 ....111 C1
Ivyleaf Sq *BRO* M7 ....50 B3
Ivylea Rd *BNG/LEV* M19 ....126 B1
Ivy St *ECC* M30 ....62 A4
   NEWH/MOS M40 ....54 B1

J

Jack La *DROY* M43 ....76 B3
   URM M41 ....94 B3
Jackroom Dr *ANC* * M4 ....5 E4
Jackson Cl *OLDS* OL8 ....22 B4
Jackson Crs *HULME* M15 ....7 D4
Jackson's Rw *CSLFD* M3 ....3 E5
Jackson St *FAIL* M35 ....56 A3
   SALE M33 ....110 A4
   STRET M32 ....96 B4
   WHTF M45 ....11 C2
Jacobite Cl *BRO* M7 ....30 B4
James Brindley Basin *CMANE* M1 ......5 E5
James Corbett Rd *SALQ* M50 ....64 B3
James Henry Av *ORD* M5 ....84 A1
James Leigh St *CMANE* M1 ....8 A2
James St *DROY* M43 ....76 A3
   EDGY/DAV SK3 ....132 B2
   FAIL M35 ....57 D1
   NEWH/MOS M40 ....71 C2
   ORD M5 ....2 A4
   PWCH M25 ....11 D4
James St South *CHAD* * OL9 ....20 B2
Jammy La *CHAD* OL9 ....21 D3
Jane St *CHAD* OL9 ....21 C3
Japan St *BRO* M7 ....51 C2
Jardine Wy *CHAD* OL9 ....38 A1
Jarvis St *OLDE* OL4 ....23 D3
Jasmine Av *DROY* M43 ....76 B3
Jason St *ANC* M4 ....70 A2
Jean Cl *BNG/LEV* M19 ....104 A3
Jehlum Cl *CHH* M8 ....52 A2
Jenkinson St *HULME* M15 ....8 B4
Jenner Cl *HULME* M15 ....7 D5
Jennings Av *ORD* M5 ....83 D1
Jennings Cl *ORD* M5 ....83 D1
Jennison St *EDGY/DAV* SK3 ....132 A2
Jennison Cl *WGTN/LGST* M12 ....90 A3
Jenny St *OLDS* OL8 ....39 D3
Jepson St *OFTN* SK2 ....133 D3
Jersey Rd *RDSH* SK5 ....130 A1
Jersey St *ANC* M4 ....5 D3
Jerusalem Pl *CMANW* * M2 ....7 E1
Jesmond Av *PWCH* M25 ....30 A3
Jespersen St *OLD* OL1 ....23 C2
Jessamine Av *BRO* M7 ....68 A1
Jessel Cl *BRUN/LGST* M13 ....9 E5
Jessie St *NEWH/MOS* M40 ....54 B3
Jessop St *GTN* M18 ....91 C4
Jetson St *GTN* M18 ....92 A3
Jimmy McMullen Wk *RUSH/FAL* * M14 ..101 D2
Jinnah Cl *OP/CLY* M11 ....90 B1
J J Thomson Ms *RUSH/FAL* * M14 ....102 B4
Joan St *NEWH/MOS* M40 ....54 E1

Jobling St OP/CLY M11 ....89 C1
Jocelyn St NEWH/MOS M40 ....53 D3
Joddrell St CSLFD M3 ....3 D1
John Atkinson Ct ORD * M5 ....65 C3
John Beeley Av OP/CLY M11 ....91 C1
John Clynes Av NEWH/MOS * M40 ..70 B2
John Dalton St CMANW M2 ....3 E5
John Foran Cl NEWH/MOS M40 ......55 C3
John Gilbert Wy TRPK M17 ....82 B4
John Heywood St OP/CLY M11 ......75 C3
John Nash Crs HULME M15 ....85 D3
Johnny King Cl NEWH/MOS M40 ....53 C4
Johns Cl CCHDY M21 ....112 A1
John Smeaton Ct CMANE M1 ....5 E5
Johnson's Sq NEWH/MOS M40 ......71 C1
Johnson St CSLFD M3 ....3 D5
    HULME M15 ....85 C3
    SWIN M27 ....47 C3
John St ANC M4 ....4 B3
    BRO M7 ....68 A1
    CHAD OL9 ....22 B3
    CSLFD M3 ....3 D2
    DROY M43 ....92 A1
    ECC M30 ....61 C4
    FAIL M35 ....38 A4
    PWCH M25 ....13 C1
    SALE M33 ....109 C4
    STKP SK1 ....130 A4
    SWIN M27 ....45 D1
John William St ECC M30 ....63 C3
    OP/CLY * M11 ....73 D4
Joiner St ANC M4 ....4 B4
    ORD M5 ....67 D4
Jonas St BKLY M9 ....53 D3
    BRO * M7 ....69 E2
Jones Ga STKP SK1 ....133 C2
Jones St OLD OL1 ....23 D1
    SLFD M6 ....66 A2
Jordan St HULME M15 ....7 D3
Josephine Dr SWIN M27 ....45 D2
Joseph Johnson Ms
    WYTH/NTH * M22 ....123 D4
Joseph St ECC M30 ....61 C4
    FAIL M35 ....57 D1
Joshua La MDTN M24 ....19 C2
Josslyn Rd ORD M5 ....65 C2
Jo St ORD M5 ....66 B4
Joule Cl ORD M5 ....83 D1
Joules Ct STKP SK1 ....130 A4
Joule St BKLY M9 ....34 B4
Jowett St RDSH SK5 ....130 A1
Joyce St NEWH/MOS M40 ....55 C2
Joynson Av BRO M7 ....68 A4
Joynson St SALE M33 ....109 C4
Jubilee St SLFD M6 ....66 A3
Judson Av CCHDY M21 ....112 A1
Judy St BKLY M9 ....54 A1
Julia St CSLFD M3 ....69 C2
Julius St BNG/LEV M19 ....118 C1
Junction Rd OFTN SK2 ....133 C2
Junction St MDTN M24 ....19 C3
    OLDS * OL8 ....40 B1
June Av HTNM * SK4 ....128 B3
Juniper Bank RDSH SK5 ....120 B1
Juniper Cl SALE M33 ....108 A3
Jura Dr URM M41 ....79 D4
Jurby Av BKLY M9 ....33 D3
Jury St CHH M8 ....69 C1
Justin Cl BRUN/LGST M13 ....8 C4
Jutland St CMANE M1 ....5 D5

K

Kale St BRUN/LGST M13 ....9 D4
Kalima Gv BRO M7 ....50 A3
Kansas Av SALQ M50 ....82 B1
Kara St SLFD M6 ....65 D3
Kathleen Gv RUSH/FAL M14 ......102 B3
Kay's Av STKP SK1 ....131 C5
Kays Gdns CSLFD M3 ....2 B2
Kay St OP/CLY M11 ....89 C2
    SLFD M6 ....48 A3
Keadby Cl ECC M30 ....79 C1
Kearsley Rd CHH M8 ....32 B3
Kearsley St ECC M30 ....61 C5
Kearton Dr ECC M30 ....63 D4
Keary Cl GTN M18 ....91 C3
Keaton Cl SLFD M6 ....65 D4
Keats Av DROY M43 ....75 D3
Keats Rd ECC M30 ....62 A4
Keble Av OLDS OL8 ....40 B2
Kedleston Av RUSH/FAL M14 ......103 D1
Keele Cl NEWH/MOS M40 ....70 B2
Keele St NEWH/MOS M40 ....70 B2
Keighley Av DROY M43 ....75 D3
Keith Wk NEWH/MOS M40 ....71 C2
Kelbrook Rd OP/CLY M11 ....90 A1
Kelling Wk HULME M15 ....6 B4
Kellbrook Crs BRO * M7 ....48 B1
Kelmarsh Cl OP/CLY * M11 ....91 C1
Kelsall Crs EDGY/DAV SK3 ....132 A3
Kelsall Dr DROY M43 ....75 D2
Kelsall St CHAD OL9 ....22 A3
    WGTN/LGST M12 ....89 C3
Kelso Cl OLDS OL5 ....41 C4
Kelstern Av BRUN/LGST M13 ......103 D2
Kelstern Sq BRUN/LGST M13 ......103 D2
Kelton Cl RDSH SK5 ....120 A4
Kelvin Av MDTN M24 ....15 C2
Kelvin Gv CHH M8 ....51 D3
Kelvington Dr BKLY M9 ....53 C3
Kelvin St ANC M4 ....4 B3
Kemble Av NTHM/RTH M23 ....122 B4
Kempsey Ct CHAD OL9 ....20 B2
Kempsey St CHAD OL9 ....21 C2
Kempster St BRO M7 ....68 A1
Kemp St MDTN M24 ....17 C1
Kempton Cl DROY M43 ....76 B3
Kempton Wy CHAD OL9 ....21 D2
Kemsing Wk ORD * M5 ....66 B3
Kenchester Av OP/CLY M11 ....91 C1
Kendal Gv WHTF M45 ....11 C1
Kendall Rd CHH M8 ....32 A2
Kendal Rd SLFD M6 ....46 B4
    STRET M32 ....97 C2
Kenilworth Av DID/WITH M20 ......114 A4
    SWIN M27 ....27 C3
    WHTF M45 ....11 D3
Kenilworth Gv DTN/ASHW M34 ......93 D1
Kenmere Gv NEWH/MOS M40 ......36 A4
Kenmore Cl WHTF M45 ....12 A1
Kenmore Rd WHTF M45 ....12 A1
Kenmore Wy WHTF M45 ....12 A1
Kennard Cl BKLY M9 ....53 C4
Kennedy Rd ORD M5 ....64 B3
Kennedy St CMANW M2 ....3 F5
    OLDS * OL8 ....22 B4
Kennedy Wy HTNM SK4 ....128 B3
Kennerley Rd OFTN SK2 ....133 D4
Kenneth Sq BRO M7 ....50 B3
Kennington Av NEWH/MOS M40 ....75 C1
Kensington Av CHAD OL9 ....19 D1
    RUSH/FAL M14 ....103 C1
Kensington Dr ORD M5 ....65 C2
Kensington Rd CCHDY M21 ....98 B3
    FAIL M35 ....58 A1
    OLDS OL8 ....40 A1
Kensington St RUSH/FAL M14 ....101 D2
Kenslow Av CHH M8 ....32 A3
Kent Av CHAD OL9 ....20 B3
    DROY M43 ....74 B3
Kentford Dr NEWH/MOS M40 ......70 B1
Kentmore Cl HTNM SK4 ....126 B3
Kenton Av GTN M18 ....105 D2

Kent Rd *DTN/ASHW* M34 ....107 D3
   FAIL M35...56 B3
Kent Rd East *RUSH/FAL* M14 ....103 C3
Kent Rd West *RUSH/FAL* M14 ....102 B2
Kentstone Av *HTNM* SK4 ....126 A2
Kent St *BRO* M7 ....68 A1
   CMANW * M2 ....3 F4
   OLDS OL8 ....41 C1
   SWIN M27 ....26 A3
Kenwick Dr *NEWH/MOS* M40 ....37 D3
Kenwood Av *BNG/LEV* M19 ....117 C3
Kenwood Cl *STRET* M32 ....97 D3
Kenwood La *WALK* M28 ....42 A4
Kenwood Rd *RDSH* SK5 ....106 B3
   STRET M32 ....97 D3
Kenworthy La *WYTH/NTH* M22 ....123 C3
Kenwright St *ANC* M4 ....4 B2
Kenwyn St *NEWH/MOS* M40 ....71 D2
Kenyon Av *OLDS* OL8 ....41 C2
Kenyon La *MDTN* M24 ....18 B1
   NEWH/MOS M40 ....54 B1
   PWCH M25 ....30 B1
Kenyon St *SWIN* M18 ....91 D3
Keppel Rd *CCHDY* M21 ....99 C5
Kerrera Dr *ORD* * M5 ....65 C4
Kerr St *BKLY* M9 ....34 A2
Kersal Av *SWIN* M27 ....46 B1
Kersal Bank *BRO* M7 ....49 D3
Kersal Cl *PWCH* M25 ....29 D4
Kersal Crag *BRO* M7 ....30 B3
Kersal Hall Av *BRO* M7 ....48 B1
Kersal Rd *PWCH* M25 ....29 D4
Kersal Vale Rd *SWIN* M27 ....29 C4
Kersal Wy *BRO* M7 ....49 C3
Kersh Av *BNG/LEV* M19 ....118 A1
Kershaw Av *PWCH* M25 ....29 C3
Kershaw Dr *MDTN* M24 ....37 C1
Kershaw Gv *DTN/ASHW* M34 ....93 C1
Kershaw La *DTN/ASHW* M34 ....93 C2
Kershaw Rd *FAIL* M35 ....57 C1
Kershaw St *DROY* M43 ....75 C4
Kershaw Wk *WGTN/LGST* M12 ....88 A3
Kershope Gv *ORD* M5 ....83 D1
Kerwin Wk *OP/CLY* * M11 ....89 D1
Kesteven Rd *BKLY* M9 ....53 C2
Keston Av *BKLY* M9 ....35 D2
   DROY M43 ....74 B4
Keston Crs *RDSH* SK5 ....121 C3
Kestrel Av *DTN/ASHW* M34 ....76 B4
   SWIN M27 ....27 C3
Kestrel Cl *PWCH* M25 ....11 C3
Kestrel Rd *TRPK* M17 ....80 A1
Kestrel Wk *WGTN/LGST* M12 ....89 C1
Keswick Av *CHAD* OL9 ....20 B2
   OLDS OL8 ....41 C4
Keswick Cl *BRUN/LGST* M13 ....103 C1
Keswick Gv *SLFD* M6 ....66 A2
Keswick Rd *HTNM* SK4 ....119 C2
   STRET M32 ....96 B2
Kettering Rd *BNG/LEV* M19 ....105 C3
Ketton Cl *OP/CLY* M11 ....91 D2
Kevin St *BNG/LEV* M19 ....118 A1
Kew Gdns *NEWH/MOS* M40 ....35 D4
Kew Rd *FAIL* M35 ....57 D1
Keymer St *OP/CLY* M11 ....71 D5
Keynsham Rd *OP/CLY* M11 ....73 C2
Keystone Cl *SLFD* M6 ....65 D1
Key Wost Cl *OP/CLY* M11 ....72 A4
Keyworth Wk *NEWH/MOS* M40 ....71 D1
Khartoum St *OLDTF/WHR* M16 ....100 A1
   OP/CLY M11 ....74 A3
Kibworth Cl *WHTF* M45 ....10 A1
Kiel Cl *ECC* M30 ....79 D1
Kilburn Av *BKLY* M9 ....16 A4
Kildare Rd *CCHDY* M21 ....113 C1
   SWIN M27 ....44 B1
Kilmington Dr *CHH* M8 ....51 C3
Kilner Wk *NEWH/MOS* M40 ....70 B1

Kilnside Dr *BKLY* M9 ....53 C2
Kilnwick Cl *GTN* M18 ....105 C2
Kilrush Av *ECC* M30 ....79 C1
Kilsby Wk *NEWH/MOS* M40 ....71 C1
Kilton Wk *NEWH/MOS* * M40 ....70 B1
Kilvert Dr *SALE* M33 ....108 A4
Kilvert St *TRPK* M17 ....83 D4
Kimberley St *BRO* * M7 ....50 B2
   EDGY/DAV SK3 ....132 B2
   OLDS OL8 ....39 D2
Kimberley Wk *HULME* M15 ....6 B4
Kimbolton Cl *WGTN/LGST* M12 ....89 D2
Kinburn Rd *BNG/LEV* M19 ....126 A3
Kincardine Rd *BRUN/LGST* M13 ....8 C1
Kincraig Cl *OP/CLY* M11 ....73 D1
Kinder St *EDGY/DAV* SK3 ....132 B2
Kinderton Av *DID/WITH* M20 ....115 C2
Kineton Wk *BRUN/LGST* M13 ....87 D3
King Edward St *BNG/LEV* M19 ....105 C4
   ECC M30 ....61 D3
   ORD M5 ....84 A1
Kingfisher Av *DTN/ASHW* M34 ....76 B4
Kingfisher Cl *WGTN/LGST* M12 ....88 B4
Kingham Dr *ANC* M4 ....5 F2
King St Rbt *OLDS* OL8 ....22 B3
King St *ORD* M5 ....65 C3
Kingsbridge Rd *BKLY* M9 ....52 B2
Kingsbrook Rd *OLDTF/WHR* M16 ....113 D1
Kingsbury Rd *OP/CLY* M11 ....73 D3
Kingscliffe St *BKLY* M9 ....53 D2
King's Cl *GTN* M18 ....92 A3
   PWCH M25 ....12 B4
Kings Ct *RDSH* SK5 ....130 A2
Kings Crs *OLDTF/WHR* M16....................99 C2
Kingsdale Rd *DTN/ASHW* M34 ....107 C3
King's Dr *HTNM* SK4 ....127 D2
   MDTN M24 ....16 A1
Kingsfield Dr *DID/WITH* M20 ....125 D3
Kingsfold Av *NEWH/MOS* * M40 ....70 B1
Kingsford St *ORD* M5 ....65 C3
King Sc *STRET* M32 ....98 A2
Kingsheath Av *OP/CLY* M11 ....73 C2
Kingshill Rd *CCHDY* M21 ....111 D1
Kingsland Cl *NEWH/MOS* M40 ....71 C2
Kings La *STRET* M32 ....98 A2
Kingslea Rd *DID/WITH* M20 ....115 D4
Kingsleigh Rd *HTNM* SK4 ....127 C1
Kingsley Av *BKLY* M9 ....54 A2
   BRO M7 ....48 B2
   HTNM SK4 ....129 D1
   STRET M32 ....98 A2
   WHTF M45 ....10 A2
Kingsley Gv *DTN/ASHW* M34 ....93 D1
Kingsley Rd *SWIN* M27 ....25 C3
King's Lynn Cl *DID/WITH* M20 ....125 C2
Kingsmead Ms *BKLY* M9 ....15 D4
Kingsmere Av *BNG/LEV* M19 ....104 A4
Kingsmill Av *BNG/LEV* M19 ....118 A1
Kings Rd *CCHDY* M21 ....113 C1
   CHAD OL9 ....37 D2
   DTN/ASHW M34 ....92 B4
   OLDS OL8 ....23 C4
   PWCH M25 ....30 B3
   STRET M32 ....97 D3
Kings Ter *STRET* M32 ....98 A2
Kingston Av *CHAD* OL9 ....38 B1
   DID/WITH M20 ....125 C4
Kingston Cl *BRO* M7 ....50 A1
Kingston Dr *SALE* M33 ....110 A4
Kingston Gv *BKLY* M9 ....35 C4
Kingston Ml *EDGY/DAV* * SK3 ....129 C4
Kingston Rd *DID/WITH* M20 ....125 C4
   FAIL M35 ....58 A2
Kingston St *EDGY/DAV* SK3 ....129 C4
King St *BRO* M7 ....50 B2
   CHAD OL9 ....22 B3
   CMANW M2 ....3 F4
   CSLFD M3 ....3 D2

DROY M43	92	B1
ECC M30	63	C4
FAIL M35	56	A4
SLFD M6	47	C4
King St East *STKP* SK1	130	A4
King St West *CSLFD* M3	3	E4
EDGY/DAV SK3	132	C3
HTNM SK4	129	C4
Kings Vw *HTNM* * SK4	128	B4
Kingsway *BNG/LEV* M19	104	A4
DID/WITH M20	126	A5
MDTN M24	17	C3
STKP SK1	130	A3
STRET M32	96	B4
SWIN M27	46	B5
Kingsway Av *BNG/LEV* M19	104	A4
Kingsway Cl *OLDS* OL8	58	B4
Kingsway Crs *BNG/LEV* M19	116	B4
Kingsway Pk *URM* M41	94	A1
Kingswood Gv *RDSH* SK5	107	C4
Kingswood Rd *ECC* M30	61	C1
PWCH M25	11	C4
RUSH/FAL M14	116	B2
King William St *ECC* M30	60	B2
ORD M5	83	D1
Kinley Cl *WGTN/LGST* M12	89	C3
Kinloch St *OLDS* OL8	41	D1
OP/CLY M11	72	B5
Kinmel Av *RDSH* SK5	131	D1
Kinnaird Rd *DID/WITH* M20	115	C4
Kinross Rd *RUSH/FAL* M14	103	D2
Kintyre Av *ORD* M5	65	C4
Kintyre Cl *OP/CLY* * M11	73	D4
Kinver Rd *NEWH/MOS* M40	36	B3
Kipling Av *DROY* M43	75	D2
Kipling St *BRO* M7	50	A3
Kippax St *RUSH/FAL* M14	102	A2
Kirby Av *CHAD* OL9	37	C2
SWIN M27	44	D1
Kirkbank St *OLDS* OL9	22	A2
Kirkby Av *NEWH/MOS* M40	55	C2
Kirkdale Av *NEWH/MOS* M40	37	C3
Kirkgate Cl *NEWH/MOS* * M40	5	F1
Kirkham Av *GTN* M18	91	C3
Kirkham St *CHAD* OL9	22	A2
ORD M5	65	D4
Kirkhaven Sq *NEWH/MOS* M40	71	C4
Kirklinton Dr *BKLY* M9	53	C3
Kirkman Av *ECC* M30	78	B3
Kirkman Cl *GTN* M18	106	A1
Kirkmanshulme La *WGTN/LGST* M12	104	B1
Kirk Rd *BNG/LEV* M19	118	A2
Kirkstall Rd *URM* M41	94	B3
Kirkstall Sq *BRUN/LGST* M13	87	D3
Kirkstead Cl *OP/CLY* M11	89	D1
Kirkstile Pl *SWIN* M27	25	D1
Kirkstone Rd *NEWH/MOS* M40	36	B3
Kirk St *GTN* M18	91	C4
Kirkway *BKLY* M9	35	D1
MDTN M24	17	D3
Kirkwood Dr *NEWH/MOS* M40	70	B1
Kirtley Av *ECC* M30	62	A2
Kitepool St *ECC* * M30	60	B2
Kitty Wheeldon Gdns *SALE* * M33	108	B4
Kiwi St *SLFD* M6	66	B3
Knaresborough Cl *RDSH* SK5	106	B4
Knightley Av *NEWH/MOS* M40	53	C4
Knightsbridge *STKP* SK1	130	A3
Knightsbridge Cl *BRO* M7	50	A1
Knight's Cl *PWCH* M25	12	A4
Knight St *DID/WITH* M20	125	C3
Kniveton Cl *WGTN/LGST* M12	89	C3
Kniveton Rd *WGTN/LGST* M12	89	C3
Knoll St *BRO* M7	50	B4
Knott Lanes *OLDS* OL8	59	D1
Knott St *ORD* M5	65	C4
Knowl Cl *DTN/ASHW* M34	107	D3
Knowldale Wy *WGTN/LGST* M12	88	B4
Knowle Dr *PWCH* M25	29	D3
The Knowles *OLDS* OL8	39	C4
Knowles Pl *HULME* M15	7	F4
Knowl St *OLDS* OL8	39	D3
Knowsley Av *ORD* M5	84	A1
Knowsley Dr *SWIN* M27	25	D3
Knowsley Gn *ORD* * M5	84	A1
Knowsley Rd *WHTF* M45	11	C1
Knowsley St *CHH* M8	69	D1
Knutsford Av *HTNM* SK4	119	C2
Knutsford Rd *GTN* M18	105	D1
Knutsford St *SLFD* M6	65	D3
Krokus Sq *CHAD* * OL9	20	B2

L

Labrador Quay *SALQ* M50	83	C2
Labtec St *SWIN* M27	27	C4
Laburnum Av *DTN/ASHW* M54	76	B4
FAIL M35	57	C3
SWIN M27	44	B3
WHTF * M45	11	C3
Laburnum Gv *PWCH* M25	11	D4
Laburnum Rd *DTN/ASHW* M54	107	C2
GTN M18	106	A1
MDTN M24	18	B1
OLDS OL8	58	B1
Laburnum St *SLFD* M6	66	A3
Lackford Dr *NEWH/MOS* M40	70	B1
Lacrosse Av *OLDS* OL8	39	C4
Lacy Gv *STRET* M32	97	C1
Lacy St *STKP* SK1	133	C1
STRET M32	97	C1
Lacy Wk *WGTN/LGST* M12	88	A1
Ladybarn Crs *RUSH/FAL* M14	116	A2
Ladybarn La *RUSH/FAL* M14	116	A1
Ladybarn Rd *RUSH/FAL* M14	116	A1
Ladyshore Cl *ORD* M5	66	A4
Ladysmith Rd *DID/WITH* M20	125	D3
Ladysmith St *EDGY/DAV* SK3	132	C4
OLDS OL8	39	D2
Ladythorn Ct *PWCH* M25	29	D3
Ladythorne Av *PWCH* M25	29	D3
Ladythorne Dr *PWCH* M25	29	D3
Lagos Cl *RUSH/FAL* M14	101	D1
Laindon Rd *RUSH/FAL* M14	103	D2
Lake Dr *MDTN* M24	17	C2
Lake Rd *TRPK* M17	97	C4
Lakeside Cl *GTN* M18	92	A3
Lake Vw *BKLY* M9	53	D3
Lakin St *NEWH/MOS* M40	54	B2
Lamb Cl *WGTN/LGST* * M12	89	C4
Lamb Ct *CSLFD* * M3	2	C3
Lambeth Av *FAIL* M35	57	C2
Lambeth Rd *NEWH/MOS* M40	73	D1
RDSH SK5	120	A2
Lamb La *CSLFD* M3	2	C3
Lambs Fold *HTNM* SK4	119	C4
Lambton Rd *WALK* M28	43	D3
Lambton St *ECC* M30	61	C1
Lamburn Av *NEWH/MOS* * M40	37	C1
Lamorna Cl *BRO* M7	49	C1
Lamplight Wy *SWIN* M27	47	D2
Lamport Cl *CMANE* M1	8	C3
Lamport St *CMANE* * M1	8	C3
Lampson St *CHH* M8	68	B1
Lamsholme Cl *BNG/LEV* M19	104	B3
Lanbury Dr *CHH* M8	51	C2
Lancashire Ct *CHAD* * OL9	21	D4
Lancashire Hl *RDSH* SK5	129	D2
Lancashire St *NEWH/MOS* M40	54	A4
Lancaster Av *FAIL* M35	56	B2
MDTN M24	18	B2
URM M41	94	B2
WHTF M45	11	D2
Lancaster Dr *PWCH* M25	30	B3

Lancaster Rd DID/WITH M20	124	B2
DROY M43	75	C2
SLFD M6	46	A4
Lancaster St CHAD OL9	38	B2
STKP SK1	130	B3
Lanchester St NEWH/MOS M40	71	D2
Lancing Av DID/WITH M20	126	A3
Lancing Wk CHAD * OL9	20	B3
Landcross Rd RUSH/FAL M14	102	B4
Lander Gv BKLY M9	35	C2
Landos Rd NEWH/MOS M40	5	F1
Landsberg Rd FAIL M35	58	A1
Landseer St OLDS OL8	23	D4
Lands End Rd MDTN M24	15	C2
Lane End ECC M30	63	C4
Lane End Rd BNG/LEV M19	126	A1
Lanfield Dr CHH M8	51	C2
Langcroft Dr NEWH/MOS M40	55	D3
Langdale Av BNG/LEV M19	118	A1
OLDS OL8	40	A1
Langdale Dr HTNM SK4	118	B3
RUSH/FAL M14	103	C1
STRET * M32	96	B2
Langfield Av OLDTF/WHR M16	100	C1
Langfield Crs DROY * M43	76	B3
Langford Rd DID/WITH M20	114	B3
HTNM SK4	128	B1
Langham Ct STRET M32	95	D2
Langham Rd HTNM SK4	128	A4
OLDS OL8	40	B1
SLFD M6	66	A3
Langholme Cl HULME * M15	6	
Langholme Pl ECC M30	61	C3
Langland Cl RDSH SK5	106	A3
Langland Dr ECC M30	78	B2
Langley Av PWCH M25	12	A4
Langley Cl URM M41	95	C3
Langley Gdns PWCH M25	12	A3
Langley Hall Rd PWCH M25	12	A3
Langley Rd PWCH M25	11	D4
RUSH/FAL M14	102	B4
SWIN M27	48	A1
Langley Rd South SLFD M6	48	A1
Langness St OP/CLY M11	73	D4
Lango St OLDTF/WHR * M16	84	A4
Langport Av WGTN/LGST M12	88	B4
Langsett Av SLFD M6	64	B2
Langshaw St ORD M5	66	A4
Langside Av BKLY M9	34	B1
Langston St CSLFD * M3	69	C2
Langthorne St BNG/LEV M19	118	A1
Langton Cl FAIL M35	58	A1
Langton St MDTN M24	17	D1
SLFD M6	65	D3
Langworthy Rd NEWH/MOS M40	54	B2
SLFD M6	66	A2
Lanhill Dr CHH M8	52	B3
Lankro Wy ECC M30	63	C4
Lansdale Gdns BNG/LEV M19	116	B3
Lansdowne DTN/ASHW M34	76	B4
Lansdowne Ct CHAD OL9	21	C3
Lansdowne Rd CHAD OL9	21	C3
CHH M8	51	D1
ECC M30	62	A2
SALE M33	108	B3
Lanstead Dr NEWH/MOS M40	71	D3
Lapwing La DID/WITH M20	114	B4
RDSH SK5	121	D3
Larch Av STRET M32	97	C4
SWIN M27	43	D3
Larch Cl FAIL M35	57	C3
Larch Gv CHAD OL9	21	C3
SWIN M27	24	A3
Larch Rd ECC M30	60	B1
Larch St OLDS OL8	22	A3
Larchview Rd MDTN M24	18	B1
Larchwood CHAD OL9	19	D2
Larchwood Av BKLY M9	54	A2
Larkhill Wk CHH M8	52	A3
Larks Ri DROY M43	77	C2
Larmuth Av CCHDY M21	112	B3
Larne Av STRET M32	96	B3
Larne St OP/CLY M11	89	D1
Larwood Av HTNM SK4	127	D4
Lascar Av ORD M5	83	D1
Lashbrook Cl NEWH/MOS M40	71	C1
Lassell St OP/CLY * M11	92	A2
Lastingham St NEWH/MOS M40	55	D3
Latchmere Rd RUSH/FAL M14	115	C1
Latham St OP/CLY M11	92	A2
Lathbury Rd BKLY M9	55	C3
Lathom Rd DID/WITH M20	116	A2
Latimer St OLDE OL4	23	D3
Latrobe St DROY M43	92	B1
Lauderdale Crs BRUN/LGST M13	87	D3
Laundry St SLFD M6	66	A1
Laurel Av CHAD OL9	19	C1
RUSH/FAL M14	101	D3
Laurel Bank Gdns BKLY M9	34	A1
Laurel End La HTNM SK4	127	D2
Laurel Gv ORD * M5	84	B3
Laurel Rd HTNM SK4	128	A1
Laurel St HTNM SK4	128	A1
MDTN M24	19	C1
Laurence Cl WGTN/LGST M12	89	D3
Lausanne Rd DID/WITH M20	115	C2
Lavenders Brow STKP SK1	130	A4
Lavenham Av OP/CLY M11	74	A4
Lavington Gv GTN M18	106	A3
Lavinia St ECC M30	61	C3
Lavister Av BNG/LEV M19	126	A2
Lawers Av CHAD OL9	20	B1
Lawler Av ORD M5	84	A3
Lawn Dr SWIN M27	44	B2
Lawngreen Av CCHDY M21	111	D2
Lawnside Ms DID/WITH M20	114	B4
Lawnswood Dr SWIN M27	45	D3
Lawnswood Park Rd SWIN M27	45	D3
Lawrence St STKP SK1	129	D4
Lawson Cl WALK M28	43	D2
Lawson Gv SALE M33	108	B3
Lawson Gv BKLY M9	33	D3
Lawton Rd HTNM SK4	128	B1
Lawton St DROY M43	76	A3
OP/CLY M11	91	C2
Laxey St NEWH/MOS * M40	55	C3
Laycock Crs FAIL M35	57	C3
Laycock Gv FAIL M35	57	C2
Laystall St CMANE M1	5	D4
Layton Cl STKP SK1	133	D1
Layton St NEWH/MOS M40	71	C3
Leabank St BNG/LEV M19	104	B4
Leabrook Dr NEWH/MOS M40	56	B1
Leaburn Dr BNG/LEV M19	126	B1
Leach St GTN M18	90	A4
PWCH M25	12	A4
Leaconfield Dr WALK M28	42	A2
Lea Ct FAIL M35	56	B2
Leacroft Av CCHDY M21	113	C4
Lea Dr BKLY M9	35	C2
Leafield Av DID/WITH M20	126	A1
Leaf St HULME M15	7	E5
RDSH SK5	119	D2
Leagate URM M41	94	B4
Leaholme Cl NEWH/MOS M40	56	A4
Leak St OLDTF/WHR M16	84	B3
Leamington Av DID/WITH M20	124	C1
Leamington Rd ECC M30	61	C2
RDSH SK5	119	D2
Leamington St OP/CLY M11	91	C2
Leander Cl BKLY M9	34	B3
Lea Rd HTNM SK4	128	A1
Leaside Dr DID/WITH M20	116	A4
Lecester Rd CHH M8	52	A3
Leconfield Dr BKLY M9	34	B2
Leconfield Rd ECC M30	60	A1

Ledbrooke Cl *ORD* M5 .... 84 A2
Ledburn Rd *HULME* M15 .... 6 B1
Ledbury Cl *MDTN* M24 .... 17 D3
Ledbury Rd *FAIL* * M35 .... 74 B1
Ledsham Av *BKLY* M9 .... 14 A3
Lee Crs *STRET* M32 .... 97 D3
Leegate Cl *HTNM* SK4 .... 127 C1
Leegate Dr *BKLY* M9 .... 35 C1
Leegate Gdns *HTNM* SK4 .... 127 C1
Leegate Rd *HTNM* SK4 .... 127 D1
Leegrange Rd *BKLY* M9 .... 34 B4
Lees Hall Crs *RUSH/FAL* M14 .... 116 A1
Leeside *HTNM* SK4 .... 127 C1
Lees Park Av *DROY* M43 .... 76 B3
Lees Rd *OLDE* OL4 .... 23 D2
Lees St *DROY* M43 .... 76 A3
  GTN M18 .... 91 D3
  MDTN M24 .... 19 C2
  SWIN M27 .... 26 A4
Lee St *OLDS* OL8 .... 22 A3
Leeswood Av *CCHDY* M21 .... 112 B3
Leewood *SWIN* M27 .... 25 C1
Left Bank *CSLFD* M5 .... 3 D4
Legh Dr *DTN/ASHW* M34 .... 76 A4
Legh Rd *BRO* M7 .... 50 A1
Legh St *BRO* M7 .... 50 A1
  ECC M30 .... 61 D4
Legion Gv *BRO* M7 .... 50 B3
Leicester Av *BRO* * M7 .... 51 C1
  DROY M43 .... 75 C2
Leicester Rd *BRO* M7 .... 50 B2
  FAIL M35 .... 57 D4
  SALE M33 .... 109 C4
Leicester Rd *RDSH* SK5 .... 106 B3
Leigh Av *SWIN* M27 .... 44 A4
Leighbrook Rd *RUSH/FAL* M14 .... 115 C1
Leigh St *BRO* M7 .... 50 A2
Leighton Rd *OLDTF/WHR* M16 .... 99 D1
Leighton St *NEWH/MOS* M40 .... 54 B1
Leinster Rd *SWIN* M27 .... 44 B2
Lemnos St *OLD* OL1 .... 23 D2
Lena St *CMANE* M1 .... 4 C5
Len Cox Wk *ANC* * M4 .... 4 C3
Leng Rd *NEWH/MOS* M40 .... 56 A4
Lenham Cl *RDSH* SK5 .... 119 D2
Lentmead Dr *NEWH/MOS* M40 .... 35 D4
Leominster Rd *MDTN* * M24 .... 18 D3
Leopold Av *DID/WITH* M20 .... 114 B4
Leroy Dr *BKLY* M9 .... 34 A3
Lesley Rd *STRET* M32 .... 95 D4
Leslie Av *CHAD* OL9 .... 39 C3
Leslie Hough Wy *SLFD* M6 .... 67 C1
Leslie St *RUSH/FAL* M14 .... 102 A3
Lester St *STRET* M32 .... 97 C3
Letchworth St *RUSH/FAL* M14 .... 102 A3
Letham St *OLDS* OL8 .... 41 C3
Levedale Rd *BKLY* M9 .... 34 B1
Levenhurst Rd *SLFD* M6 .... 66 A1
Levens Rd *NEWH/MOS* M40 .... 54 B2
  SLFD M6 .... 49 C4
Levens Wk *CHAD* OL9 .... 20 B3
Lever Av *SWIN* M27 .... 27 C3
Lever St *CMANE* M1 .... 4 C4
Lever Wk *MDTN* M24 .... 17 C2
Lewis Av *BKLY* M9 .... 34 B3
  URM M41 .... 79 C4
Lewisham Av *NEWH/MOS* M40 .... 73 C1
Lewis Rd *DROY* M43 .... 74 B3
  RDSH SK5 .... 107 C4
Lewis St *ECC* M50 .... 62 A4
  NEWH/MOS M40 .... 71 C2
Lewtas St *ECC* M30 .... 62 B4
Lexton Av *CHH* M8 .... 33 C3
Leybourne Av *BNG/LEV* M19 .... 105 D3
Leyburn Av *STRET* M32 .... 96 A3
Leyburn Cl *WHTF* M45 .... 10 B1
Leyburn Rd *NEWH/MOS* M40 .... 36 B3
Leycroft St *CMANE* * M1 .... 9 D1
Leyland Av *DID/WITH* M20 .... 126 A2
Leyland St *HTNM* * SK4 .... 129 D4
Leyton Av *NEWH/MOS* M40 .... 55 C2
Leywell Rd *BKLY* M9 .... 54 A1
Library La *CHAD* OL9 .... 22 A1
Lichens Crs *OLDS* OL8 .... 41 D2
Lichfield Av *RDSH* SK5 .... 119 D2
Lichfield Dr *CHH* M8 .... 52 A2
  PWCH M25 .... 30 B3
  SWIN M27 .... 45 C3
Lichfield Rd *ECC* M30 .... 63 C1
  URM M41 .... 94 A1
Lichfield St *SLFD* M6 .... 48 B4
Lidbrook Wk *WGTN/LGST* M12 .... 88 B3
Lidgate Gv *CHH* M8 .... 32 B4
Lifton Av *NEWH/MOS* M40 .... 71 D1
Lightbourne Av *SWIN* M27 .... 45 C2
Lightbowne Rd *NEWH/MOS* M40 .... 54 B3
Light Oaks Rd *SLFD* M6 .... 46 A4
Lignum Av *CHAD* OL9 .... 21 C1
Lilac Av *SWIN* M27 .... 45 D1
Lilac Ct *SLFD* M6 .... 66 B3
Lilac Gv *CHAD* OL9 .... 21 D4
  NEWH/MOS M40 .... 35 D4
  PWCH M25 .... 11 D3
Lilac La *OLDS* OL8 .... 40 A3
Lilac St *OFTN* SK2 .... 133 C3
Lila St *BKLY* M9 .... 54 A3
Lilford Cl *WGTN/LGST* M12 .... 89 D3
Lillian Gv *RDSH* SK5 .... 120 A3
Lillian St *OLDTF/WHR* M16 .... 99 D1
Lilmore Av *NEWH/MOS* M40 .... 55 D3
Lily Cl *EDGY/DAV* SK3 .... 132 A4
Lily La *BKLY* M9 .... 54 A2
Lily St *ECC* M30 .... 61 C4
  MDTN M24 .... 18 B1
Limbert Cir *CHH* M8 .... 33 D4
Lime Av *SWIN* M27 .... 43 D3
  WHTF M45 .... 11 C2
Lime Bank St *WGTN/LGST* M12 .... 88 B1
Limebrook Cl *OP/CLY* M11 .... 91 D2
Lime Cl *SLFD* M6 .... 66 B2
Lime Cl *SLFD* * M6 .... 66 B2
Lime Crs *OLDTF/WHR* M16 .... 99 C1
Limeditch Rd *FAIL* M35 .... 58 B4
Limefield *MDTN* M24 .... 16 B2
Limefield Rd *BRO* M7 .... 31 C4
Limefield Ter *BNG/LEV* M19 .... 104 B4
Lime Gdns *MDTN* M24 .... 16 B1
Lime Ga *OLDS* OL8 .... 39 D3
Lime Gn *OLDS* OL8 .... 40 A4
Lime Green Rd *OLDS* OL8 .... 58 B1
Lime Gv *OLDTF/WHR* M16 .... 99 C1
  PWCH M25 .... 11 D3
Limehurst Av *DID/WITH* M20 .... 114 A1
Limekiln La *WGTN/LGST* M12 .... 88 A1
Lime La *OLDS* OL8 .... 39 D4
Lime Rd *STRET* M32 .... 97 C4
Limerston Dr *NEWH/MOS* M40 .... 54 A4
Limeside Rd *OLDS* OL8 .... 39 D3
Limestead Av *CHH* M8 .... 51 D1
Lime St *ECC* M30 .... 62 A4
  NEWH/MOS M40 .... 71 C2
Lime Tree Cl *URM* M41 .... 94 B4
Lime Tree Gv *FAIL* M35 .... 58 A2
Limetrees Rd *MDTN* M24 .... 17 C1
Limley Gv *CCHDY* M21 .... 112 B2
Linby St *HULME* M15 .... 6 C4
Lincoln Av *BNG/LEV* M19 .... 105 C4
  DROY M43 .... 75 D2
  STRET M32 .... 95 C2
Lincoln Gv *BRUN/LGST* M13 .... 87 D4
Lincoln Rd *FAIL* M35 .... 57 D3
  MDTN M24 .... 18 B4
Lincoln St *BRUN/LGST* M13 .... 104 A1
  CHAD OL9 .... 21 C4

ECC M30 ....61 D4
Lindale Av CHAD OL9 ....20 B3
   NEWH/MOS M40 ....37 C5
Linden Av SLFD M6 ....47 D3
   SWIN M27 ....44 A2
Linden Dr ORD M5 ....83 D1
Linden Gv RUSH/FAL M14 ....116 A1
Linden Pk BNG/LEV M19 ....117 C1
Linden Rd DID/WITH M20 ....124 B1
Lindenwood CHAD OL9 ....19 D1
Lindeth Av GTN M18 ....106 A1
Lindfield Rd RDSH SK5 ....107 C4
Lindinis Av SLFD M6 ....66 B3
Lindisfarne Rd AULW OL7 ....59 D4
Lindleywood Rd RUSH/FAL M14 ....116 B1
Lindon Wy DROY M43 ....91 D1
Lindow Rd OLDTF/WHR M16 ....99 C3
Lindrick Av WHTF M45 ....10 A3
Lindrick Cl NEWH/MOS M40 ....55 D2
Lindsay Av BNG/LEV M19 ....104 A4
   SWIN M27 ....44 A2
Lindsay Rd BNG/LEV M19 ....117 C3
Lind St NEWH/MOS M40 ....71 D3
Lindum Av OLDTF/WHR M16 ....99 D1
Lindum St RUSH/FAL M14 ....102 A2
Lindwall Cl NTHM/RTH M23 ....122 A3
Linehan Cl HTNM SK4 ....126 A3
Linen Ct CSLFD M3 ....2 A1
Lines Rd DROY M43 ....76 A4
Linfield St OP/CLY M11 ....73 C4
Linford Av NEWH/MOS M40 ....36 B3
Lingard Rd WYTH/NTH M22 ....123 C4
Lingard St RDSH SK5 ....120 A1
Lingcrest Rd BNG/LEV M19 ....118 B2
Lingfield Rd OP/CLY M11 ....73 D3
Lingmoor Wk HULME * M15 ....86 A4
Linhope St HTNM SK4 ....126 B2
The Link RDSH SK5 ....121 D3
Link Av URM M41 ....95 D4
Link La OLDS OL8 ....40 B3
The Links NEWH/MOS M40 ....55 D2
Links Av FAIL M35 ....57 C4
Links Dr PWCH M25 ....15 D3
Links Vw PWCH M25 ....29 D4
Links Wy CHAD OL9 ....21 D1
Linksway PWCH M25 ....31 C3
   SWIN M27 ....45 D3
Linksway Cl HTNM SK4 ....117 D4
Linley Rd SALE M33 ....109 C4
Linnet Cl DTN/ASHW M34 ....76 B3
   WGTN/LGST M12 ....104 A1
Linn St CHH M8 ....32 B4
Linsley St CSLFD * M3 ....3 D2
Linstead Dr CHH * M8 ....51 C3
Linton Av DTN/ASHW M34 ....107 C3
Linton Cl ANC M4 ....88 A1
Linton Rd SALE M33 ....109 D3
Linwood Gv WGTN/LGST M12 ....104 B3
Linwood St FAIL M35 ....55 D5
Lion Brow BKLY M9 ....34 A3
Lion Fold La BKLY M9 ....34 A3
Lions Dr SWIN M27 ....45 D2
Lion St BKLY M9 ....34 A3
Lisburn Av CCHDY M21 ....99 D4
Lisburn Rd NEWH/MOS M40 ....54 B1
Liscard Av RUSH/FAL M14 ....102 A4
Lismore Av URM M41 ....79 C3
Lissadel St SLFD M6 ....66 B1
Lister Rd MDTN M24 ....15 C3
Litcham Cl CMANE M1 ....8 C3
Litchfield Gv WALK M28 ....43 C2
Little Ancoats St CMANE M1 ....4 C1
Little David St CMANE M1 ....8 B1
Little Ees La SALE M33 ....108 A2
Little Egerton St STKP SK1 ....129 D3
Littlegreen Gdns SLFD M6 ....66 A2
Littlehaven Cl WGTN/LGST M12 ....88 B4
Little Holme St ANC M4 ....71 C4
Little John St CSLFD M3 ....6 C1
Little Lever St CMANE M1 ....4 C4
Little Moss La SWIN M27 ....26 A3
Littlemoss Rd DROY M43 ....76 B2
Little Nelson St ANC * M4 ....4 B1
Little Peter St HULME M15 ....7 D3
Little Quay St CSLFD M3 ....3 E5
Littleton Rd BRO M7 ....48 B1
Little Underbank STKP * SK1 ....130 A3
Littlewood St SLFD M6 ....65 D3
Liverpool Cl RDSH SK5 ....119 D2
Liverpool Rd CSLFD M3 ....6 D1
   ECC M30 ....61 C4
Liverpool St RDSH SK5 ....119 D2
   SLFD M6 ....66 D5
Liverstudd Av RDSH SK5 ....120 A1
Livesey St ANC M4 ....70 B2
   BNG/LEV M19 ....118 A1
Livsey St WHTF M45 ....11 C1
Lizard St CMANE M1 ....4 C4
Lizmar Ter BKLY M9 ....54 A1
Lloyd Rd BNG/LEV M19 ....118 A2
Lloyd St CMANW M2 ....3 F5
   HTNM SK4 ....129 C1
Lloyd St South RUSH/FAL M14 ....101 D4
Lockett Gdns CSLFD M3 ....2 B2
Lockett St CHH M8 ....68 B1
   SLFD M6 ....48 B4
Lockhart Cl WGTN/LGST M12 ....89 D4
Locksley St HTNM SK4 ....128 B3
Lockton Cl CMANE M1 ....9 D3
   RDSH SK5 ....119 D3
Lockton Ct CMANE M1 ....8 C3
Lockwood St WGTN/LGST M12 ....105 C3
Lodge Av URM M41 ....94 B3
Lodge Ct HTNM SK4 ....127 C3
Lodge Fold DROY M43 ....76 A3
Lodgeside Cl DROY M43 ....76 A3
Lodge St NEWH/MOS M40 ....53 D4
Lodge Vw DROY M43 ....76 A3
Loganberry Av SLFD M6 ....66 B2
Lois St CHAD OL9 ....38 B3
Lomas Cl BNG/LEV M19 ....126 A2
Lomas St EDGY/DAV SK3 ....132 A2
   FAIL M35 ....55 D4
Lomax St CMANE M1 ....5 E4
Lombard Gv RUSH/FAL M14 ....115 D2
Lombard St OLD OL1 ....22 B1
Lombardy Ct SLFD * M6 ....66 B2
Lomond Av STRET M32 ....97 C2
London Pl STKP SK1 ....130 A4
London Rd CMANE M1 ....9 D2
London Sq STKP SK1 ....130 A4
London St SLFD M6 ....67 C3
   WHTF M45 ....11 C2
Longacre St CMANE M1 ....9 E1
Longbow Ct BRO * M7 ....68 A1
Longbridge Rd TRPK M17 ....80 B3
Longcrag Wk HULME * M15 ....86 A4
Longcroft Gv DTN/ASHW M34 ....93 C1
Longden Rd WGTN/LGST M12 ....104 B3
Longfellow St SLFD M6 ....67 D1
Longford Av STRET M32 ....97 D3
Longford Cl STRET M32 ....97 D2
Longford Pk STRET M32 ....98 A3
Longford Pl RUSH/FAL M14 ....103 D2
Longford Rd CCHDY M21 ....98 B4
   RDSH SK5 ....107 C4
   STRET M32 ....97 D2
Longford Rd West RDSH SK5 ....106 A4
Longford St GTN M18 ....91 C3
Longham Cl OP/CLY M11 ....71 D4
Longhurst Rd BKLY M9 ....33 C1
Long La CHAD OL9 ....38 A2
Longley Dr WALK M28 ....43 C4
Longley St OLD * OL1 ....23 C3
Longmead Rd SLFD M6 ....47 C4

Long Millgate *ANC* M4.....................3 F2
Longport Av *DID/WITH* M20.....114 B2
Longshaw Av *SWIN* M27.............26 A4
Longshut La *STKP* SK1.................133 C2
Longshut La West *OFTN* SK2.....133 D2
Longsight Rd *DROY* M43.............105 C2
Longsight St *HTNM* SK4.............129 C3
Long St *GTN* M18.........................91 D3
  MDTN M24...............................17 C1
  SWIN M27................................45 C2
Longton Av *DID/WITH* M20.......114 B4
Longton Rd *BKLY* M9..................33 D1
  SLFD M6..................................46 B3
Longview Dr *SWIN* M27..............24 B4
Longwood Rd *TRPK* M17.............81 C3
Longworth St *CSLFD* M3...............7 D1
Lonsdale Av *RDSH* SK5..............107 C2
  SWIN M27................................44 A4
Lonsdale Rd *BNG/LEV* M19.......105 C3
  OLDS OL8..................................39 C3
Lonsdale St *NEWH/MOS* M40.....55 D3
Loom St *ANC* M4............................8 A1
Lord Byron Sq *SALQ* M50............83 C1
Lord La *FAIL* M35.........................74 B1
Lord Napier Dr *ORD* M5..............83 D2
Lord North St *NEWH/MOS* M40...71 C1
Lord's Av *ORD* * M5.....................65 C3
Lordship Cl *BKLY* M9...................35 C4
Lordsmead St *HULME* M15.............6 A4
Lord St *CSLFD* M3........................69 C1
  DTN/ASHW M34.....................107 C1
  OLD OL1..................................23 C2
  STKP SK1..............................129 D4
Loretto Rd *URM* M41...................95 C4
Loring St *NEWH/MOS* M40..........55 D4
  URM M41................................94 B3
Lorne Gv *EDGY/DAV* SK3..........132 B2
  URM M41................................94 B3
Lorne Rd *RUSH/FAL* M14..........115 C3
Lorne St *BRUN/LGST* M13...........87 C4
  ECC M30.................................78 A1
  OLDS OL8................................40 B1
Lostock Av *BNG/LEV* M19.........105 C3
Lostock Gv *STRET* M32................96 A2
Lostock Rd *ORD* M5....................65 D3
  URM M41................................94 A1
Lostock St *NEWH/MOS* M40.......71 C2
Lothian Av *ECC* M30....................61 C2
Lottery St *EDGY/DAV* SK3.........129 C4
Lottie St *SWIN* M27.....................45 D1
Louisa St *OP/CLY* M11.................91 C1
Louvain St *FAIL* M35....................56 B2
Love La *HTNM* SK4....................129 C3
Lowcock St *BRO* M7.....................68 B1
Lowcroft St *CHAD* OL9.................20 A1
Lowcross Rd *NEWH/MOS* M40.....54 B3
Lower Albion St *CMANE* M1...........8 C2
Lower Brook La *WALK* * M28........42 B4
Lower Brook St *CMANE* * M1..........8 C1
Lower Broughton Rd *BRO* M7.......49 D4
  BRO M7..................................67 D3
Lower Bury St *HTNM* SK4..........129 C3
Lower Byrom St *CSLFD* M3............7 C3
Lower Carrs *STKP* SK1...............130 A4
Lower Chatham St *HULME* M15......8 A4
Lower Edge Av *OLD* OL1..............22 B3
Lower Gn *MDTN* M24...................17 C2
Lower Hardman St *CSLFD* M3........2 C5
Lower Hillgate *STKP* SK1...........130 A4
Lower Lime Rd *OLDS* OL8............58 B1
Lower Moat Cl *HTNM* SK4..........129 D2
Lower Monton Rd *ECC* M30.........62 B3
Lower Mosley St *CMANW* M2........7 E2
Lower Moss La *HULME* M15...........6 B4
  WHTF M45..............................11 C1
Lower Ormond St *HULME* M15.......8 A4
Lower Park Rd *RUSH/FAL* M14...102 B1
Lower Seedley Rd *SLFD* M6.........65 D2
Lower Sutherland St *SWIN* M27...44 B1

Lower Vickers St *NEWH/MOS* M40...71 C2
Lower Victoria St *CHAD* OL9........21 C2
Lowestead Rd *OP/CLY* M11..........73 D3
Lowestoft St *RUSH/FAL* M14.....102 A3
Lowe St *STKP* SK1.....................130 A4
Lowfield Av *DROY* M43................75 C2
Lowfield Gv *OFTN* SK2...............133 C2
Lowfield Rd *EDGY/DAV* SK3.......132 B3
Lowlands Cl *MDTN* M24...............36 B1
Lowndes Wk *BRUN/LGST* * M13...87 D3
Lowry Dr *SWIN* M27.....................26 A4
Lowry Houses *ECC* * M30............62 B3
Lowther Av *GTN* M18.................105 C2
Lowther Cl *PWCH* M25................29 D2
Lowther Rd *CHH* M8....................32 B4
  PWCH M25..............................29 C2
Lowthorpe St *RUSH/FAL* M14....101 D3
Lowton Av *BKLY* M9....................54 A2
Low Wood Rd *DTN/ASHW* M34...107 D1
Loxford Ct *HULME* M15..................7 F4
Loxford St *HULME* M15..................7 F5
Lubeck St *BKLY* M9.....................53 D1
Lucas Wk *OP/CLY* M11................89 C1
Lucerne Cl *CHAD* OL9..................21 D3
Lucien Cl *WGTN/LGST* M12.........88 B4
Lucy St *BRO* M7..........................50 A4
  EDGY/DAV SK3.....................132 B1
  HULME M15............................85 C3
Ludgate Hl *ANC* M4.......................4 C1
Ludgate Rd *NEWH/MOS* M40.......73 C1
Ludgate St *ANC* M4.......................4 B1
Ludlow Av *SWIN* M27...................26 B3
  WHTF M45..............................12 A3
Luke Rd *DROY* M43.....................76 A4
Lullington Rd *SLFD* M6................65 C1
Lulworth Crs *FAIL* M35................58 A1
Lulworth Rd *ECC* M30..................61 D3
Lumb La *DROY* M43.....................59 C4
  DTN/ASHW M34......................76 B4
Lumley Cl *RUSH/FAL* M14.........102 A1
Lumn's La *SWIN* M27...................27 D3
Luna St *ANC* M4............................4 C3
Lund St *OLDTF/WHR* M16...........84 B3
Lune Cl *WHTF* M45......................11 D1
Lune Dr *WHTF* M45......................11 D1
Lune St *OLDS* OL8.......................80 B1
Lune Wy *RDSH* SK5...................120 A4
Lunn Av *GTN* M18........................92 A3
Lupton St *CSLFD* * M3...................2 B5
Lurden Wk *CHAD* * OL9................38 B1
Luton Rd *RDSH* SK5...................120 A1
Luxhall Wk *NEWH/MOS* M40........55 C2
Luxor Gv *DTN/ASHW* M34..........107 C2
Lyceum Pl *HULME* * M15...............8 A4
Lychgate Ms *HTNM* * SK4..........126 B3
Lydden Av *OP/CLY* * M11.............73 D3
Lydford *SLFD* M6..........................67 C1
Lydford Wk *BRUN/LGST* * M13....87 D3
Lydgate Cl *WHTF* M45.................11 D1
Lydgate Rd *DROY* M43................74 B2
Lyme Gv *DROY* M43.....................92 A1
  OFTN SK2..............................133 C2
Lyme St *HTNM* SK4....................126 B3
Lymington Cl *MDTN* M24.............18 A4
Lymm Cl *EDGY/DAV* SK3...........132 A3
Lyndale Av *RDSH* SK5...............107 C2
  SWIN M27................................44 A3
Lyndene Av *WALK* M28................42 B1
Lyndhurst Av *CHAD* OL9..............20 A4
  PWCH M25..............................31 D2
Lyndhurst Rd *DID/WITH* M20.....124 B3
  OLDS OL8................................40 A2
  RDSH * SK5..........................119 D2
  STRET M32.............................96 A3
Lyndhurst St *SLFD* M6.................65 D3
Lynmouth Av *DID/WITH* M20.....114 B3
  OLDS OL8................................41 C2
  RDSH SK5.............................119 D2

Lynmouth Gv *PWCH* M25 ....29 C2
Lynn Av *SALE* M33 ....110 A3
Lynn Dr *DROY* M43 ....74 B3
Lynn St *CHAD* OL9 ....39 D1
Lynnwood Rd *BNG/LEV* M19 ....126 A3
Lynthorpe Rd *NEWH/MOS* M40 ....37 C3
Lynton Av *OLDS* M30 ....39 D3
  SWIN M27 ....26 A4
Lynton Dr *BNG/LEV* M19 ....117 C2
  PWCH M25 ....12 B3
Lynton Rd *CCHDY* M21 ....98 B4
  HTNM SK4 ....118 A4
  SWIN M27 ....26 A4
Lynton St *RUSH/FAL* M14 ....102 A3
Lynway Dr *DID/WITH* M20 ....115 C4
Lynwell Rd *ECC* M30 ....62 A3
Lynwood Av *ECC* M30 ....62 A3
  OLDTF/WHR M16 ....99 D3
Lynwood Gv *DTN/ASHW* M34 ....76 B3
  HTNM SK4 ....118 B3
  SALE M33 ....109 D4
Lyon Gv *WALK* M28 ....42 B1
Lyons Fold *SALE* M33 ....109 C3
Lyons Rd *TRPK* M17 ....80 C3
Lyon St *SWIN* M27 ....44 B2
Lysander Cl *RUSH/FAL* M14 ....114 B1
Lytham Av *CCHDY* M21 ....112 B2
Lytham Rd *RUSH/FAL* M14 ....104 A4
Lytham St *EDGY/DAV* SK3 ....133 C3
Lyth St *RUSH/FAL* M14 ....116 A2
Lytton Av *CHH* M8 ....51 D3
Lytton Rd *DROY* M43 ....75 D3

M

Mabel Av *WALK* M28 ....42 B2
Mabel Rd *FAIL* M35 ....38 B4
Mabel St *NEWH/MOS* M40 ....56 A4
Mabfield Rd *RUSH/FAL* M14 ....102 B4
Macauley Rd *OLDTF/WHR* M16 ....99 C3
  RDSH SK5 ....106 A4
Macdonald St *OLDS* OL8 ....41 C1
Macefin Av *CCHDY* M21 ....123 C3
Mackenzie Rd *BRO* M7 ....49 C3
Mackenzie St *WGTN/LGST* M12 ....104 C3
Mackintosh Wy *OLD* OL1 ....23 C2
Maclaren Dr *CHH* M8 ....31 D3
Maddison Rd *DROY* M43 ....75 C4
Madeley Dr *CHAD* OL9 ....21 C3
Maden Wk *CHAD* OL9 ....21 C1
Madison Av *DTN/ASHW* M34 ....93 C3
Madison St *GTN* M18 ....91 D3
Mafeking St *OLDS* OL8 ....39 D2
Magdala St *OLD* OL1 ....22 B1
Magnolia Dr *CHH* M8 ....51 D3
Magpie Cl *BRO* M7 ....76 B2
Magpie Wk *OP/CLY* M11 ....72 A4
Maher Gdns *HULME* M15 ....100 B1
Mahood St *EDGY/DAV* SK3 ....152 A2
Maida St *BNG/LEV* M19 ....105 C3
Maidford Cl *ANC* M4 ....71 C4
  STRET M32 ....97 D3
Maidstone Av *CCHDY* M21 ....98 B4
Maidstone Ms *CCHDY* M21 ....98 B4
Maidstone Rd *HTNM* SK4 ....126 A2
Main Av *BNG/LEV* M19 ....117 C3
  TRPK M17 ....96 B3
Maine Rd *RUSH/FAL* M14 ....101 D3
Mainprice Cl *SLFD* M6 ....66 A1
Mainway *MDTN* M24 ....17 C3
Mainway East *MDTN* M24 ....18 B3
Maitland Av *CCHDY* M21 ....122 B1
Maitland Wk *CHAD* OL9 ....21 C1

Major St *CMANE* M1 ....8 B1
Makin St *CMANE* M1 ....8 B1
Makkah Cl *NEWH/MOS* M40 ....54 B4
Malbrook Wk *BRUN/LGST* M13 ....9 E5
Malby St *OLD* OL1 ....23 C1
Malcolm Av *SWIN* M27 ....26 B3
Malcolm Dr *SWIN* M27 ....26 B3
Maldon Crs *SWIN* M27 ....45 C3
Maldon Dr *ECC* M30 ....62 B1
Maldwyn Av *CHH* M8 ....32 B3
Maleham St *BRO* M7 ....50 B3
Malham Dr *WHTF* M45 ....11 D1
Mallard Cl *OLDS* OL8 ....40 A3
Mallard St *CMANE* M1 ....8 A3
Mallow St *HULME* M15 ....6 C5
Malpas St *OLD* OL1 ....23 C2
  WGTN/LGST M12 ....89 D3
Malpas Wk *OLDTF/WHR* M16 ....85 C4
Malta Cl *MDTN* M24 ....19 C1
Malta St *ANC* M4 ....71 C4
Malton Av *CCHDY* M21 ....112 A1
Malton Rd *HTNM* SK4 ....127 D1
Malton St *OLDS* OL8 ....22 A4
Malt St *HULME* M15 ....6 A4
Malus Ct *SLFD* M6 ....66 B2
Malvern Av *DROY* M43 ....76 B3
Malvern Cl *HTNM* SK4 ....129 C2
  PWCH M25 ....12 B4
  SWIN M27 ....47 C3
Malvern Dr *SWIN* M27 ....47 C3
Malvern Gv *DID/WITH* M20 ....114 B3
  SLFD M6 ....64 B2
Malvern Rd *MDTN* M24 ....17 D4
Malvern Rw *HULME* * M15 ....84 B3
Malvern St *HULME* * M15 ....85 C3
  OLDS OL8 ....22 A4
Manby Rd *GTN* M18 ....105 C1
Manby Sq *GTN* M18 ....105 C1
Manchester Chambers *OLD* * OL1 ....22 B2
Manchester New Rd *MDTN* M24 ....17 C1
Manchester Old Rd *MDTN* M24 ....15 D1
Manchester Rd *CCHDY* M21 ....111 D1
  DROY M43 ....74 B4
  DTN/ASHW M34 ....107 D1
  HTNM SK4 ....119 C4
  OLDS OL8 ....39 D1
  SWIN M27 ....26 A2
Manchester St *OLDTF/WHR* M16 ....84 B4
Mancroft Wk *CMANE* * M1 ....8 C3
Mancunian Wy *WGTN/LGST* M12 ....9 F3
Mandarin Wk *SLFD* * M6 ....66 B3
Mandeville St *BNG/LEV* M19 ....118 A1
Mandley Av *NEWH/MOS* * M40 ....37 C3
Mandley Park Av *BRO* M7 ....50 B2
Manet Cl *BRO* M7 ....49 C1
Mangle St *CMANE* M1 ....4 C4
Mango Pl *SLFD* M6 ....66 B3
Manifold St *SLFD* M6 ....49 C4
Manilla Wk *OP/CLY* M11 ....72 A4
Manipur St *OP/CLY* M11 ....89 C1
Manley Av *SWIN* M27 ....26 A1
Manley Rd *CCHDY* M21 ....99 D4
  OLDS OL8 ....40 B1
Manley St *BRO* M7 ....50 A3
Mannington Dr *BKLY* M9 ....52 B3
Mannock St *OLDS* OL8 ....22 A3
Manor Av *OLDTF/WHR* M16 ....100 A3
  URM M41 ....94 A4
Manor Cl *CHAD* OL9 ....21 D1
Manor Ct *STRET* M52 ....96 A4
Manor Dr *CCHDY* M21 ....123 C1
Manor Ml *CHAD* * OL9 ....21 D1
Manor Pk *URM* * M41 ....94 A4
Manor Rd *BNG/LEV* M19 ....105 C3
  DROY M43 ....74 B4
  DTN/ASHW M34 ....93 C2
  MDTN M24 ....17 C3
  RDSH SK5 ....121 C4

SALE M33 ....**109** C4
SLFD M6 ....**65** C1
STRET M32 ....**96** A4
SWIN M27 ....**45** C3
Manor St *WGTN/LGST* M12 ....**9** E3
Mansfield Av *BKLY* M9 ....**34** A1
Mansfield Dr *BKLY* M9 ....**34** B1
Mansfield Rd *BKLY* M9 ....**34** A1
Mansford Dr *NEWH/MOS* M40 ....**54** A4
Manshaw Crs *OP/CLY* M11 ....**92** B2
Manshaw Rd *OP/CLY* M11 ....**92** B2
Manson Av *HULME* M15 ....**7** E5
Manstead Wk *NEWH/MOS* * M40 ....**71** D5
Manswood Dr *CHH* M8 ....**51** D2
Manton Av *BKLY* M9 ....**36** A2
DTN/ASHW M34 ....**107** D2
Manton Cl *CHH* M8 ....**51** C3
Manvers St *RDSH* SK5 ....**129** D1
Manwaring St *FAIL* M35 ....**56** B1
Maple Av *CCHDY* M21 ....**112** A4
DTN/ASHW M34 ....**76** A4
ECC M30 ....**60** B1
STRET M32 ....**97** C4
WHTF M45 ....**11** C1
Maple Cl *MDTN* M24 ....**19** C1
SLFD M6 ....**66** A2
Mapledon Rd *BKLY* M9 ....**54** A1
Maple Gv *FAIL* M35 ....**56** B4
NEWH/MOS M40 ....**37** D3
PWCH M25 ....**11** D3
Maple Rd *SWIN* M27 ....**44** B3
Maple St *OLDS* OL8 ....**39** D2
Maplin Cl *BRUN/LGST* M13 ....**9** E4
Marble St *CMANW* M2 ....**4** A4
Marcer Rd *NEWH/MOS* M40 ....**71** D4
March Av *HTNM* SK4 ....**128** A3
Marchioness St *GTN* * M18 ....**92** A4
Marchmont Cl *BRUN/LGST* * M13 ....**88** C3
Marchwood Av *CCHDY* M21 ....**100** A4
Marcliffe Dr *BNG/LEV* M19 ....**105** D4
Marcliff Gv *HTNM* SK4 ....**128** A3
Marcus Gv *RUSH/FAL* M14 ....**102** B3
Mardale Av *DID/WITH* M20 ....**115** C3
SWIN M27 ....**24** B3
Mardale Cl *PWCH* M25 ....**12** B1
Mardale Dr *SWIN* M27 ....**44** A3
Marfield *BKLY* * M9 ....**34** B4
Marfield Av *CHAD* OL9 ....**20** B4
Margaret Ashton Cl *BKLY* M9 ....**54** A4
Margaret Rd *DROY* M43 ....**74** B3
Margaret St *OLDS* OL8 ....**39** C3
RDSH SK5 ....**119** D2
Margate Av *NEWH/MOS* M40 ....**55** D4
Margate Rd *RDSH* SK5 ....**120** A2
Margrove Cl *FAIL* M35 ....**58** B2
Margrove Rd *SLFD* M6 ....**64** B1
Marguerita Rd *NEWH/MOS* M40 ....**71** D4
Marham Cl *CCHDY* * M21 ....**113** D3
Marie St *BRO* * M7 ....**50** B2
Mariman Dr *CHH* M8 ....**32** B3
Marina Crs *OP/CLY* M11 ....**73** C2
Marina Rd *DROY* M43 ....**76** A3
Marion St *OLDS* OL8 ....**41** C2
Marjorie Cl *GTN* M18 ....**90** A3
Mark Av *SLFD* M6 ....**67** C1
Market Pl *OLD* * OL1 ....**22** B2
STKP SK1 ....**130** A4
Market St *CMANE* M1 ....**4** A4
DROY M43 ....**76** A3
SWIN M27 ....**26** B3
Market Wy *SLFD* M6 ....**66** A2
Markfield Av *BRUN/LGST* M13 ....**88** B4
Markham Cl *WGTN/LGST* M12 ....**88** A1
Markington St *RUSH/FAL* M14 ....**101** D3
Mark St *CHAD* OL9 ....**22** A2
Marland Av *OLDS* OL8 ....**41** D4

Marland Crs *RDSH* SK5 ....**120** A1
Marland Fold La *OLDS* OL8 ....**41** C4
Marland St *CHAD* OL9 ....**38** B2
Marlborough Av *CCHDY* M21 ....**99** D2
Marlborough Dr *FAIL* M35 ....**56** B3
HTNM * SK4 ....**129** C1
Marlborough Rd *BRO* M7 ....**51** C3
ECC M30 ....**63** D1
STRET M32 ....**96** B2
Marlborough St *OLDE* OL4 ....**23** D3
Marlcroft Av *HTNM* SK4 ....**128** A3
Marley Dr *SALE* M33 ....**108** B5
Marleyer Cl *NEWH/MOS* M40 ....**55** D2
Marley Rd *BNG/LEV* M19 ....**118** D1
Marlfield St *BKLY* M9 ....**34** B4
Marlinford Dr *NEWH/MOS* M40 ....**55** D4
Marlow Dr *SWIN* M27 ....**44** B3
Marlowe Dr *DID/WITH* M20 ....**125** C1
Marlow Rd *BKLY* M9 ....**35** C5
Marmion Dr *CCHDY* M21 ....**111** D1
Marple Cl *OLDS* OL8 ....**40** A3
Marple Gv *STRET* M32 ....**96** B2
Marple St *HULME* M15 ....**85** C4
Marquis St *BNG/LEV* M19 ....**106** A4
Marriotts Ct *CMANW* M2 ....**4** A4
Marriott St *DID/WITH* M20 ....**115** C3
STKP SK1 ....**133** C1
Marron Pl *CMANW* * M2 ....**7** E1
Marsden Cl *AULW* OL7 ....**59** D4
Marsden St *CMANW* M2 ....**3** F4
ECC M30 ....**61** D2
Marshall Ct *OLD* * OL1 ....**22** B1
Marshall Rd *BNG/LEV* M19 ....**104** B4
Marshall Stevens Wy *TRPK* M17 ......**81** C4
Marshall St *ANC* M4 ....**4** C2
WGTN/LGST M12 ....**9** F5
Marsham Cl *BRUN/LGST* M13 ....**103** D1
Marshbrook Dr *CHH* M8 ....**33** D4
Marsh Cl *EDGY/DAV* SK3 ....**132** A3
Marshfield Wk *BRUN/LGST* M13 ....**87** D3
Marsland St *STKP* SK1 ....**130** A2
Marsland St North *BRO* M7 ....**51** C2
Marsland St South *BRO* M7 ....**51** C2
Mars St *CHAD* OL9 ....**38** B2
Marston Cl *FAIL* M35 ....**58** A3
WHTF M45 ....**11** D1
Marston Dr *BRO* M7 ....**50** B1
STRET M32 ....**97** D3
Marsworth Dr *ANC* * M4 ....**5** F3
Martha St *OLD* OL1 ....**22** A1
Martindale Crs *WGTN/LGST* M12 ......**88** B3
Martingale Wy *DROY* M43 ....**77** C2
Martin Rd *SWIN* M27 ....**27** C3
Martin St *ORD* M5 ....**85** D3
Martlesham Wk *ANC* * M4 ....**4** B5
Martlet Cl *RUSH/FAL* M14 ....**101** D4
Marton Av *DID/WITH* M20 ....**125** D3
Marton Gra *PWCH* M25 ....**31** C3
Marton Gn *EDGY/DAV* SK3 ....**132** A4
Marton Gv *HTNM* SK4 ....**119** D3
Maryfield Ct *OLDTF/WHR* * M16 ....**113** D1
Mary France St *HULME* M15 ....**6** C5
Mary St *CSLFD* M3 ....**69** C2
DROY M43 ....**76** A4
STKP SK1 ....**130** B3
Masboro St *CHH* M8 ....**51** C3
Masefield Av *PWCH* M25 ....**29** C2
Masefield Crs *DROY* M43 ....**75** D2
Masefield Dr *HTNM* SK4 ....**127** D3
Masefield Gv *RDSH* SK5 ....**106** B4
Masefield Rd *DROY* M43 ....**75** D2
Mason St *ANC* M4 ....**4** C2
Massey Av *FAIL* M35 ....**58** A1
Massey St *ORD* M5 ....**67** D4
STKP SK1 ....**130** A4
Matham Wk *HULME* M15 ....**8** A4
Mather Av *ECC* M30 ....**62** B3
PWCH M25 ....**30** B4

Mather Rd *ECC* M30....................62 B3
Mather St *FAIL* M35....................56 A2
Mather Wy *SLFD* * M6...................66 B2
Matisse Wy *BRO* M7....................9 C1
Matley Gn *RDSH* SK5..................121 D3
Matlock Av *BRO* M7.....................48 B2
  DID/WITH M20......................114 A3
Matlock Rd *RDSH* SK5.................107 D4
  STRET M32.........................95 D2
Matlock St *ECC* M30...................78 B1
Matt Busby Cl *SWIN* M27...............46 A2
Matthews La *BNG/LEV* M19.............105 C3
Matthew's St *WGTN/LGST* M12...........89 C2
Mattison St *OP/CLY* M11................91 D2
Mauldeth Cl *HTNM* SK4.................127 D2
Mauldeth Rd *BNG/LEV* M19..............127 C1
  DID/WITH M20......................115 D2
Mauldeth Rd West *CCHDY* M21..........113 D1
Maureen Av *CHH* M8.....................51 D1
Maurice Dr *SLFD* M6....................66 A1
Maurice St *SLFD* M6....................66 A1
Mawdsley Dr *CHH* M8....................52 B1
Max Woosnam Wk *RUSH/FAL* M14.........101 D2
Mayan Av *CSLFD* M3......................2 A2
May Av *HTNM* * SK4....................128 B3
Mayberth Av *CHH* M8....................32 B3
Mayburn Cl *MDTN* M24...................18 B4
Maybury St *GTN* M18....................91 D3
Maycroft Av *DID/WITH* M20.............115 D4
May Dr *BNG/LEV* M19...................117 C3
Mayes Gdns *ANC* M4.....................71 C4
Mayes St *ANC* M4........................4 B2
Mayfair Av *SLFD* M6....................64 A2
  WHTF * 11 C5
Mayfair Crs *FAIL* M35..................58 A1
Mayfair Ms *DID/WITH* * M20............124 A1
Mayfair Pk *DID/WITH* * M20............124 A1
Mayfield Av *RDSH* SK5.................120 A4
  STRET M32.........................96 A4
  SWIN M27..........................43 D3
Mayfield Gv *GTN* M18..................107 C3
  RDSH SK5.........................120 A4
Mayfield Rd *BRO* M7....................30 A4
  OLDTF/WHR M16....................100 B2
Mayflower Av *ORD* M5...................83 C1
Mayford Rd *BNG/LEV* M19...............104 B3
Maygate *OLD* OL1.......................22 A1
May Gv *BNG/LEV* M19...................118 A1
Mayhill Dr *SLFD* M6....................63 D1
  WALK M28..........................42 B1
Mayhurst Av *CCHDY* M21................123 C2
Mayorlowe Av *RDSH* SK5...............131 D1
Mayor St *CHAD* OL9.....................21 D2
Mayo St *WGTN/LGST* M12.................88 A1
Maypool Dr *RDSH* SK5.................120 A3
May Rd *OLDTF/WHR* M16.................100 A2
  SWIN M27..........................46 A3
May St *ECC* M30........................61 D1
  NEWH/MOS M40......................55 D4
  OLDS OL8..........................39 C1
Mayton St *OP/CLY* M11..................89 D2
Mayville Dr *DID/WITH* M20.............115 C4
Mayor Dr *CHAD* OL9.....................21 D2
Mead Gv *BNG/LGST* M13.................104 A2
Meade Hill Rd *PWCH* M25................31 D3
Meadfoot Av *PWCH* M25..................30 B2
Meadfoot Rd *GTN* M18...................91 C3
Meadow Av *NEWH* M27....................27 C4
Meadow Bank *CCHDY* M21................111 D2
  HTNM SK4.........................128 A3
Meadowbank Cl *FAIL* M35................57 D3

Meadow Bank Ct *STRET* M32.............96 A4
Meadow Cl *STRET* M32...................97 D4
Meadow Ct *CCHDY* M21..................111 C1
Meadowgate *URM* M41....................94 A4
  WALK M28..........................42 A1
Meadowgate Rd *SLFD* M6.................64 B2
Meadow La *OLDS* OL8....................40 B3
  WALK M28..........................42 A4
Meadow Rd *BRO* M7......................67 D2
  MDTN M24..........................16 B3
  URM M41...........................94 A4
The Meadows *MDTN* M24..................18 A3
  PWCH M25..........................30 A1
Meadows Rd *HTNM* SK4..................118 B3
  SALE M33.........................109 D3
Meadow Wy *NEWH/MOS* M40...............35 D4
The Meads *OLD* OL9.....................20 B3
Meadway *CHAD* OL9......................37 D3
Mealhouse Brow *STKP* * SK1...........130 A4
Meal St *HTNM* SK4.....................129 D2
Measham Ms *CMANE* * M1..................8 A3
Medlock Dr *OLDS* OL8...................41 D4
Medlock Rd *FAIL* M35...................57 D4
Medlock St *DROY* M43...................75 D3
  HULME M15.........................7 E3
  OLD OL1...........................20 B1
Medlock Wy *WHTF* M45...................12 B1
Medway Cl *OLDS* OL8....................39 D2
  ORD M5............................65 C2
Medway Rd *OLDS* OL8....................39 D2
Medway Wk *NEWH/MOS* M40................71 C3
Meech St *OP/CLY* M11...................90 B1
Mee's Sq *ECC* M30......................79 C1
Megna Cl *CHAD* OL9.....................22 A2
Melanie Dr *RDSH* SK5.................120 A1
Melba St *OP/CLY* M11...................91 D1
Melbourne Av *CHAD* OL9.................20 B2
  STRET M32.........................97 C3
Melbourne St *BKLY* M9..................53 D1
  BRO M7............................50 A4
  CHAD OL9..........................21 C2
  HULME M15..........................7 D4
  RDSH SK5.........................120 A1
  SWIN M27..........................46 A1
Melbury Av *DID/WITH* M20..............126 A1
Meldon Rd *BRUN/LGST* M13..............103 D3
Meldrum St *OLDS* OL8...................41 C1
Melford Av *NEWH/MOS* M40...............37 D4
Melfort Av *STRET* M32..................97 D4
Melksham Cl *ORD* M5....................67 C3
Melland Av *CCHDY* M21.................112 B4
Melland Rd *GTN* M18...................105 D2
Meller Rd *BRUN/LGST* M13..............104 A3
Melling Av *HTNM* SK4..................119 D3
Melling St *WGTN/LGST* M12.............89 C2
Mellors Rd *TRPK* M17...................81 C2
Mellor St *DROY* M43....................75 C4
  ECC M30...........................62 A4
  FAIL M35..........................56 A2
  NEWH/MOS M40......................71 C2
  PWCH M25..........................29 C1
  STRET M32.........................97 C1
Mellor Wy *CHAD* OL9....................39 C1
Mellowstone Dr *OLDTF/WHR* M16.........114 A1
Melloy Pl *CHH* M8......................69 D1
Melon Pl *SLFD* M6......................67 C3
Melrose Av *DID/WITH* M20..............125 D2
  ECC M30...........................60 B1
Melrose Ct *CHAD* * OL9.................38 B1
Melrose St *NEWH/MOS* M40...............55 D4
Meltham Av *DID/WITH* M20..............114 B3
Meltham Cl *HTNM* SK4..................126 B4
Meltham Rd *HTNM* SK4..................126 B4
Melton Av *DTN/ASHW* M34...............107 D2
Melton Cl *CHH* M8......................31 D4
Melton St *BKLY* M9.....................35 C4
  RDSH SK5.........................130 A1
Melverley Rd *BKLY* M9..................14 B4

Melville Cl *OP/CLY* M11 ....91 D2
Melville Rd *STRET* M32 ....96 A2
Melville St *CSLFD* M3 ....2 B5
Memorial Cottages *SWIN* M27 ....26 A2
Menai Rd *EDGY/DAV* SK3 ....132 B3
Mendip Cl *CHAD* * OL9 ....20 B1
  HTNM SK4 ....129 D2
Mendip Pl *OLDS* OL8 ....40 A2
Menston Av *NEWH/MOS* M40 ....37 D4
Mentone Rd *HTNM* SK4 ....128 A2
Mentor St *BRUN/LGST* M13 ....48 A3
Mercer Rd *GTN* M18 ....91 C4
Mercer St *BNG/LEV* M19 ....105 C4
  DROY M43 ....76 A3
Merchants Quay *SALQ* M50 ....83 D3
Mercian Wy *EDGY/DAV* SK3 ....132 B2
Mercury Pk *URM* * M41 ....80 A3
Mercury Wy *URM* M41 ....80 A3
Mere Av *DROY* M43 ....91 D1
  MDTN M24 ....17 D3
  SLFD M6 ....65 D3
Meredew Av *SWIN* M27 ....44 B3
Meredith St *RUSH/FAL* M14 ....116 A2
Mere Dr *DID/WITH* M20 ....125 C1
  SWIN M27 ....26 B3
Mereland Av *DID/WITH* M20 ....125 C1
Meridian Pl *DID/WITH* M20 ....124 B1
Merlewood Av *BNG/LEV* M19 ....118 B3
  DTN/ASHW * M34 ....76 A4
Merlewood Dr *SWIN* M27 ....43 D5
Meyn Av *DID/WITH* M20 ....125 D1
  SALE M33 ....109 D3
Merrill St *ANC* M4 ....71 C4
Merriman St *OLDTF/WHR* M16 ....100 B1
Merrow Wk *CMANE* M1 ....8 C3
Merrybower Rd *BRO* M7 ....50 B1
Merrydale Av *ECC* M30 ....62 B3
Merseybank Av *CHDY* M21 ....123 C1
Mersey Crs *DID/WITH* M20 ....123 D4
Mersey Mdw *DID/WITH* M20 ....124 A2
Mersey Rd *DID/WITH* M20 ....124 A2
  HTNM SK4 ....127 C3
  SALE M33 ....109 D3
Mersey Rd North *FAIL* M35 ....38 B4
Mersey Sq *STKP* SK1 ....129 D4
Mersey St *OP/CLY* M11 ....91 D1
  STKP SK1 ....130 B3
Merseyway *STKP* * SK1 ....129 C3
Merton Av *OLDS* OL8 ....40 A2
Merton Dr *DROY* M43 ....74 B4
Merton Gv *CHAD* OL9 ....37 C3
Merton Rd *PWCH* M25 ....12 B4
  SALE M33 ....108 B4
Merville Av *NEWH/MOS* M40 ....35 C4
Mervyn Rd *BRO* M7 ....48 B3
Merwood Gv *RUSH/FAL* M14 ....103 D1
Mesnefield Rd *BRO* M7 ....48 B1
Methuen St *WGTN/LGST* M12 ....105 C2
The Mews *NEWH/MOS* M40 ....30 A2
  PWCH M25 ....30 A2
  WHTF * M45 ....10 A1
Meyer St *EDGY/DAV* * SK3 ....133 C3
Meyrick Rd *SLFD* M6 ....66 B2
Michael St *MDTN* M24 ....17 C1
Michigan Av *SALQ* M50 ....83 C1
Mickleby Wk *NEWH/MOS* * M40 ....5 F1
Micklehurst Av *DID/WITH* M20 ....123 D1
Middlebourne St *SLFD* M6 ....65 D3
Middlegate *NEWH/MOS* M40 ....37 C3
Middle Ga *OLDS* OL8 ....40 A3
Middleham St *RUSH/FAL* M14 ....101 D3
Middle Hillgate *STKP* SK1 ....130 A4
Middlesex Rd *BKLY* M9 ....34 A3
  RDSH SK5 ....121 D3
Middlesex St *CHAD* * OL9 ....22 A3
Middlestone Dr *BKLY* M9 ....53 D3
Middleton Av *FAIL* M35 ....57 C2
Middleton Old Rd *BKLY* M9 ....34 A3

Middleton Rd *BKLY* M9 ....14 A4
  CHAD OL9 ....20 A1
  CHAD OL9 ....22 A2
  CHH M8 ....32 A3
  RDSH SK5 ....107 C3
Middleton Rd West *CHAD* OL9 ....19 D1
Middlewood Dr *HTNM* SK4 ....127 D4
Middlewood Gn *CHAD* OL9 ....20 B2
Middlewood St *ORD* M5 ....2 A5
Midford Av *OLDS* OL8 ....61 C3
Midgley Av *GTN* M18 ....91 D3
Midgley St *SWIN* M27 ....44 A3
Midhurst Av *NEWH/MOS* * M40 ....73 C1
Midland Rd *RDSH* SK5 ....107 C3
Midland St *WGTN/LGST* M12 ....88 A2
Midlothian St *OP/CLY* M11 ....73 D2
Midville Rd *OP/CLY* M11 ....73 D2
Midway St *BNG/LEV* M19 ....104 B3
Milan St *BRO* M7 ....50 B3
Milburn Av *NTHM/RTH* M23 ....122 A3
Milden Cl *DID/WITH* * M20 ....125 D1
Mildred Av *PWCH* M25 ....30 B3
Mildred St *BRO* M7 ....49 D4
Miles St *WGTN/LGST* M12 ....89 D2
Milford Av *OLDS* OL8 ....39 D3
Milford Dr *BNG/LEV* M19 ....118 B3
Milford St *BKLY* M9 ....33 C2
  SLFD M6 ....4 A4
Milk St *CMANE* M2 ....6 D4
Milkwood Gv *GTN* M18 ....106 A1
Millais St *NEWH/MOS* M40 ....35 D4
Millard St *CHAD* OL9 ....20 B2
Millbank St *CMANE* M1 ....5 E5
Millbeck Rd *HULME* M15 ....8 A5
Millbrook St *STKP* SK1 ....133 C1
Mill Brow *BKLY* M9 ....33 D3
  WALK M28 ....42 A3
Miller Rd *OLDS* OL8 ....40 B2
Millers Ct *ORD* M5 ....63 D3
Millers St *ECC* M30 ....61 D4
Miller St *ANC* M4 ....4 B2
Mill Fold Rd *MDTN* M24 ....17 C2
Mill Ga *OLDS* OL8 ....40 A2
Millgate *ANC* * M4 ....4 A3
  STKP SK1 ....130 A3
Millgate La *DID/WITH* M20 ....125 C4
Mill Green St *WGTN/LGST* * M12 ....88 A2
Millhall Cl *HULME* M15 ....85 D4
Millhead Av *NEWH/MOS* M40 ....71 D3
Millington Wk *HULME* * M15 ....6 B5
Mill La *CHAD* OL9 ....39 D1
  FAIL M35 ....56 A3
  RDSH SK5 ....107 D4
  WYTH/NTH M22 ....123 D4
Milom Av *NTHM/RTH* M23 ....122 A4
Millow St *ANC* M4 ....4 A1
Mills Farm Cl *OLDS* OL8 ....41 D4
Millstream La *DROY* M43 ....74 B2
Mill St *FAIL* M35 ....55 D2
  OP/CLY M11 ....90 B1
  SLFD M6 ....66 B1
Millwall Cl *GTN* M18 ....91 C4
Millwright St *NEWH/MOS* M40 ....55 C4
Milne Cl *WGTN/LGST* M12 ....89 D3
Milner Av *OLDTF/WHR* M16 ....100 A1
  SWIN M27 ....45 D1
Milne St *CHAD* OL9 ....21 C2
Milnrow Cl *CMANE* M1 ....9 D3
Milnthorpe St *SLFD* M6 ....48 B4
Milnthorpe Wy *WGTN/LGST* M12 ....88 B3
Milo St *BKLY* * M9 ....34 A2
Milton Av *DROY* M43 ....75 D4
  ORD * M5 ....65 C3
Milton Cl *STRET* M32 ....97 D2
Milton Ct *BNG/LEV* M19 ....126 B1
Milton Dr *CHAD* OL9 ....20 B3
  SALE M33 ....108 B3

Milton Gv *OLDTF/WHR* M16 ....99 D3
  SALE M33 ....108 B3
Milton Pl *SLFD* M6 ....66 B2
Milton Rd *DTN/ASHW* M34 ....77 C4
  PWCH M25 ....12 B4
  STRET M32 ....97 D2
  SWIN M27 ....25 C4
Milton St *BRO* M7 ....68 B1
  ECC M30 ....62 A3
Milverton Rd *RUSH/FAL* M14 ....103 C2
Milwain Dr *HTNM* SK4 ....118 B3
Milwain Rd *BNG/LEV* M19 ....117 C1
  STRET M32 ....96 B4
Mimosa Dr *SWIN* M27 ....26 A3
Mincing St *ANC* * M4 ....4 B1
Minden Cl *DID/WITH* M20 ....125 D1
Minden St *SLFD* M6 ....47 D3
Minehead Av *DID/WITH* M20 ....114 A4
Minoan Gdns *BRO* M7 ....49 D4
Minor St *FAIL* M35 ....38 B4
  OLDS OL8 ....22 B4
Minshull St *CMANE* M1 ....4 B5
Minshull St South *CMANE* M1 ....8 C1
Minster Rd *BKLY* M9 ....54 A1
Minstrel Cl *SWIN* M27 ....44 A2
Minton St *NEWH/MOS* M40 ....55 D1
  OLDE OL4 ....23 D4
Mirabel St *CSLFD* M3 ....3 E1
Mirfield Av *BKLY* M9 ....34 A1
  HTNM SK4 ....128 A3
  OLDS OL8 ....40 B1
Mirfield Dr *ECC* M30 ....62 A1
Mirfield Rd *BKLY* M9 ....34 A1
Miriam St *NEWH/MOS* M40 ....56 A3
Missouri Av *ORD* M5 ....65 D4
Mistletoe Gv *CSLFD* * M3 ....2 D1
Mitcham Av *BKLY* M9 ....35 D1
Mitchells Quay *FAIL* M35 ....56 B2
Mitchell St *ECC* M30 ....61 D2
  NEWH/MOS M40 ....55 C4
  OLD OL1 ....22 A4
  OP/CLY * M11 ....89 C2
Mitcheson Gdns *SLFD* M6 ....66 B2
Mitford Rd *RUSH/FAL* M14 ....115 D2
Mitford St *STRET* M32 ....96 B4
Mitre Rd *BRUN/LGST* M13 ....104 A1
Mitre St *FAIL* M35 ....57 C1
Mobberley Cl *WHTF* M45 ....12 B1
Mocha Pde *BRO* M7 ....68 A2
Mode Hill La *WHTF* M45 ....12 B1
Mode Wheel Rd South *ORD* M5 ....65 C4
Modwen Rd *ORD* * M5 ....84 A3
Mold St *OLD* OL1 ....22 A1
Molyneux Rd *BNG/LEV* M19 ....105 D4
Mona Av *STRET* M32 ....96 B2
Monaco Dr *WYTH/NTH* M22 ....115 C2
Monart Rd *BKLY* M9 ....34 B4
Mona St *SLFD* M6 ....66 B1
Monica Av *CHH* M8 ....32 A3
Monica Gv *BNG/LEV* M19 ....117 C1
Monks Hall Gv *ECC* M30 ....63 C3
Monkton Av *GTN* M18 ....105 D2
Monkwood Dr *BKLY* * M9 ....53 D1
Monmouth Av *SALE* M33 ....108 A4
Monmouth St *CHAD* OL9 ....21 D4
  GTN M18 ....91 D3
  MDTN M24 ....18 B2
Monroe Cl *SLFD* M6 ....65 D1
Monsal Av *BRO* M7 ....48 B2
Monsall Rd *NEWH/MOS* M40 ....53 D3
Monsall St *NEWH/MOS* M40 ....53 C4
  OLDS OL8 ....40 B2
Montague Rd *OLDTF/WHR* M16 ....83 D4
Montana Sq *OP/CLY* M11 ....91 D2
Montcliffe Crs *OLDTF/WHR* M16 ....101 C4
Monteagle St *BKLY* M9 ....33 C1
Montford St *SALQ* M50 ....66 A4
Montgomery Rd *BRUN/LGST* M13 ....104 A3
Montgomery St *OLDS* OL8 ....39 C3
Monton Av *ECC* M30 ....62 B2
Montondale *ECC* M30 ....61 D2
Montonfields Rd *ECC* M30 ....61 D2
Monton Gn *ECC* M30 ....62 B1
Monton La *ECC* M30 ....62 B3
Monton Mill Gdns *ECC* M30 ....61 D2
Monton Rd *ECC* M30 ....62 A2
  RDSH SK5 ....131 D1
Monton St *RUSH/FAL* M14 ....101 D1
Montreal St *BNG/LEV* M19 ....105 C4
  OLDS OL8 ....41 C1
Montrose Av *DID/WITH* M20 ....114 A4
  STRET M32 ....96 A3
Montrose Crs *BNG/LEV* M19 ....104 B4
Moon Gv *RUSH/FAL* M14 ....103 C2
Moon St *CHAD* * OL9 ....21 D2
Moorby Av *BNG/LEV* M19 ....126 B1
Moorclose St *MDTN* M24 ....18 A1
Moorcock Av *SWIN* M27 ....46 A1
Moorcroft Dr *BNG/LEV* M19 ....127 C1
Moorcroft St *DROY* * M43 ....75 D4
  OLDS OL8 ....39 D3
Moordale St *DID/WITH* M20 ....114 B4
Moordown Cl *CHH* M8 ....52 A3
Moore End *BRO* M7 ....49 D1
Moorfield *WALK* M28 ....42 A1
Moorfield Av *RUSH/FAL* M14 ....115 D2
Moorfield Cl *SWIN* M27 ....44 A3
Moorfield Gv *HTNM* SK4 ....128 A1
Moorfield Rd *DID/WITH* M20 ....124 A1
  OLDS OL8 ....39 C3
  SLFD M6 ....47 C4
Moorfield St *DID/WITH* * M20 ....115 C2
Moorgate Av *DID/WITH* M20 ....114 A3
Moorhead St *ANC* M4 ....5 D1
The Moorings *WALK* M28 ....42 B4
Moorings Rd *TRPK* M17 ....81 C1
Moorland Av *CHH* M8 ....32 A3
  DROY M43 ....74 B4
Moorland Rd *DID/WITH* M20 ....125 C2
Moor La *BRO* M7 ....48 B1
Moor Park Rd *DID/WITH* * M20 ....125 D4
Moorsholme Av *NEWH/MOS* M40 ....54 B2
Moorside Av *DROY* M43 ....76 B3
Moorside Crs *DROY* M43 ....76 B3
Moorside Rd *BRO* M7 ....30 B4
  CHH M8 ....32 B4
  HTNM SK4 ....127 D3
  SWIN M27 ....44 A1
Moorside St *DROY* M43 ....76 A3
Moorsley Dr *BKLY* M9 ....35 C1
Moor St *ECC* M30 ....61 C4
  SWIN M27 ....45 C2
Moorton Av *BNG/LEV* M19 ....117 C2
Moorton Pk *BNG/LEV* M19 ....117 C2
Moortop Cl *BKLY* M9 ....15 D4
Moor Top Pl *HTNM* SK4 ....128 A2
Moorville Rd *SLFD* M6 ....46 B4
Moorway Dr *BKLY* M9 ....35 D1
Moran Wk *HULME* M15 ....86 A3
Mora St *BKLY* M9 ....54 A1
Moravian Fld *DROY* * M43 ....92 B1
Moray Rd *CHAD* OL9 ....38 B1
Morbourne Cl *WGTN/LGST* M12 ....88 B3
Morecambe Cl *NEWH/MOS* M40 ....54 B2
Moreton Av *STRET* M32 ....97 C3
Moreton St *CHAD* OL9 ....20 A1
Morgan Pl *RDSH* SK5 ....130 A1
Morland Rd *OLDTF/WHR* M16 ....99 D1
Morley Av *RUSH/FAL* M14 ....101 D4
  SWIN M27 ....44 A2
Morley St *WHTF* M45 ....11 C1
Morna Wk *WGTN/LGST* M12 ....88 A1
Morningside Cl *DROY* M43 ....92 A2
Mornington Crs *RUSH/FAL* M14 ....114 B1
Mornington Rd *SALE* M33 ....110 A4

Morpeth Cl *AULW* OL7 ....77 D1
  WGTN/LGST M12 ....88 B4
Morpeth St *SWIN* M27 ....44 B3
Morris St *DID/WITH* M20 ....115 C2
  OLDE OL4 ....23 A3
Morrowfield Av *CHH* M8 ....51 C2
Morse Rd *NEWH/MOS* M40 ....55 C5
Mortimer Av *BKLY* M9 ....34 B1
Mortlake Dr *NEWH/MOS* M40 ....55 C4
Morton St *FAIL* M35 ....55 D2
  HTNM SK4 ....129 D1
Morville Rd *CCHDY* M21 ....100 A4
Morville St *CMANE * M1 ....9 E1
Moscow Rd *EDGY/DAV* SK3 ....132 A2
Moscow Rd East *EDGY/DAV* SK3 ....132 A2
Moseley Rd *RUSH/FAL* M14 ....116 B1
Moseley St *EDGY/DAV* SK3 ....132 B1
Mosley Rd *TRPK* M17 ....81 D3
Mosley Rd North *TRPK* M17 ....81 D1
Mosley St *CMANW* M2 ....4 A5
The Moss *MDTN* M24 ....18 A3
Moss Bank *CHH* M8 ....51 D1
Moss Bank *DROY* M43 ....76 B3
Moss Bank Ct *DROY* * M43 ....76 B3
Moss Bank Gv *SWIN* M27 ....24 B3
Moss Bank Wy *SWIN* M27 ....25 C3
Mossbray Av *BNG/LEV* M19 ....126 A1
Moss Brook Rd *BKLY* M9 ....53 C2
Mossclough Ct *BKLY* M9 ....53 D2
Moss Colliery Rd *SWIN* M27 ....25 C2
Mosscot Wk *BRUN/LGST* M13 ....9 D3
Mossfield Cl *HTNM* SK4 ....128 B3
Mossfield Dr *BKLY* M9 ....35 D1
Mossfield Rd *SWIN* M27 ....25 D3
Moss Grange Av *OLDTF/WHR * M16 ....100 A2
Mosshall Cl *HULME* M15 ....85 C3
Moss Hey Dr *NTHM/RTH* M23 ....122 A4
Moss House Ter *BKLY* * M9 ....33 D4
Moss La *AULW* OL7 ....77 D3
  MDTN M24 ....17 C4
  SWIN M27 ....25 C4
  URM M41 ....79 C4
  WHTF M45 ....11 C1
Moss La East *OLDTF/WHR * M16 ....100 B1
Moss La West *HULME* M15 ....100 B1
Mosslee Av *CHH* M8 ....32 A2
Moss Meadow Rd *SLFD* * M6 ....64 B1
Moss Park Rd *STRET* M32 ....95 D3
Moss Rd *STRET* M32 ....96 B2
Moss St *BRO* M7 ....50 A4
  DTN/ASHW M34 ....76 A4
Moss Vale Crs *STRET* M32 ....95 C1
Moss Vale Rd *URM* M41 ....94 B3
Mossway *MDTN* M24 ....17 C4
Mossylea Cl *MDTN* M24 ....18 A4
Moston Bank Av *BKLY* M9 ....53 D2
Moston La *BKLY* M9 ....53 D1
  NEWH/MOS M40 ....35 D4
Moston La East *NEWH/MOS* M40 ....37 C3
Moston Rd *MDTN* M24 ....19 C3
Moston St *BRO* M7 ....51 C2
Mostyn Av *RUSH/FAL* M14 ....116 B1
Motherwell Av *BNG/LEV* M19 ....104 B3
Mottram Av *CCHDY* M21 ....112 B4
Mottram Fold *STKP* SK1 ....133 C1
Mottram St *STKP* SK1 ....133 C1
Mough La *CHAD* OL9 ....37 C2
Mouldsworth Av *DID/WITH* M20 ....114 B2
  HTNM SK4 ....119 C3
Moulton St *CHH* M8 ....68 B1
Mouncey St *CMANE * M1 ....8 A3
Mountain St *NEWH/MOS* M40 ....74 A1
  STKP * SK1 ....130 B3
Mountbatten St *GTN* M18 ....90 B4
Mount Carmel Crs *ORD* * M5 ....84 B2
Mount Dr *URM* M41 ....95 C3
Mountfield *PWCH* M25 ....30 A1
Mountfield Wk *OP/CLY* M11 ....72 A4

Mount Fold *MDTN* M24 ....17 D2
Mountford Av *CHH * M8 ....32 A3
Mount Pleasant *MDTN* M24 ....15 D1
  PWCH M25 ....13 D1
Mount Rd *GTN* M18 ....90 B4
  HTNM SK4 ....128 B3
  MDTN M24 ....17 D2
  PWCH M25 ....12 B2
Mountside Crs *PWCH* M25 ....29 C1
Mount St *CMANW* M2 ....2 F1
  CSLFD M3 ....2 B2
  ECC M30 ....70 B1
  SWIN M27 ....45 C2
Mousell St *CHH* M8 ....69 D1
Mowbray Av *PWCH* M25 ....30 B3
Mowbray St *OLD* * OL1 ....23 C3
  STKP SK1 ....133 C1
Moxley Rd *CHH* M8 ....31 D4
Mozart Cl *ANC* M4 ....5 F2
Muirfield Cl *NEWH/MOS* M40 ....55 C5
Mulberry Ct *SLFD* * M6 ....66 B2
Mulberry Ms *HTNM* SK4 ....129 D3
Mulberry Mount St *EDGY/DAV* SK3 ....132 B1
Mulberry Rd *SLFD* M6 ....66 B3
Mulberry St *CMANW* M2 ....3 E5
Mulberry Wk *DROY* M43 ....91 D1
Mulgrave Rd *WALK* M28 ....42 B1
Mulgrave St *SWIN* M27 ....25 C4
Mull Av *WGTN/LGST* M12 ....88 B4
Mullion Cl *RDSH* SK5 ....106 A3
Mullion Wk *CHH* M8 ....69 D1
Mulmount Cl *OLDS* OL8 ....39 D2
Munday St *ANC* M4 ....71 C4
Munn Rd *BKLY* M9 ....15 C4
Munster St *ANC* * M4 ....4 A1
Muriel St *BRO* M7 ....50 A4
Murray St *ANC* M4 ....5 E3
  BRO M7 ....50 A3
Museum St *CMANW* M2 ....2 F1
Muslin St *ORD* M5 ....67 D4
Myerscroft Cl *NEWH/MOS* M40 ....56 A1
Myrtle Bank *PWCH* M25 ....29 D4
Myrtle Cl *OLDS* OL8 ....22 B4
Myrtle Gv *DROY* M43 ....76 B3
  DTN/ASHW M34 ....107 C2
  PWCH M25 ....30 A3
Myrtleleaf Gv *ORD* * M5 ....65 C3
Myrtle Pl *BRO* M7 ....65 C4
Myrtle St *OLDTF/WHR * M16 ....99 D1
  OP/CLY M11 ....88 B1
My St *ORD* M5 ....65 D4
Mytton St *HULME* M15 ....85 D4

N

Naburn Cl *RDSH* SK5 ....121 D3
Naburn St *BRUN/LGST* M13 ....103 C1
Nada Rd *CHH* M8 ....32 A4
Nadine St *SLFD* M6 ....65 D2
Nadin St *OLDS* OL8 ....40 B2
Nairn Cl *NEWH/MOS* * M40 ....71 C4
Nall St *BNG/LEV* M19 ....118 A2
Nameplate Cl *ECC* M30 ....61 C3
Nancy St *HULME* M15 ....85 C4
Nangreave Rd *OFTN* SK2 ....133 D3
Nansen Av *ECC* M30 ....61 D2
Nansen Cl *STRET* M32 ....97 D1
Nansen St *OP/CLY* M11 ....88 B1
  SLFD M6 ....65 D3
  STRET M32 ....97 C2
Nantwich Rd *RUSH/FAL* M14 ....101 D4
Napier Ct *HULME* * M15 ....84 B3
Napier Gn *ORD* M5 ....84 B2
Napier Rd *CCHDY* M21 ....112 A1
  ECC M30 ....61 D2
  HTNM SK4 ....128 A2

Napier St *SWIN* M27.....................................44 A2
Napier St East *OLDS* OL8.........................22 A4
Napier St West *OLDS* OL8........................21 D4
Naples St *ANC* M4...4 C1
Narbonne Av *ECC* M30..............................62 A3
Narburth Dr *CHH* M8...................................51 C2
Naseby Av *BKLY* M9......................................35 C1
Naseby Pl *PWCH* M25.................................12 B4
Naseby Rd *RDSH* SK5.................................119 D1
Naseby Wk *WHTF* M45................................12 B1
Nash Rd *TRPK* M17..79 D1
Nash St *HULME* M15.....................................85 D3
Nasmyth Rd *ECC* M30..................................78 B1
Nasmyth St *CHH* M8.....................................52 B4
Nately Rd *OLDTF/WHR * M16....................98 B3
Nathan Dr *CSLFD* M3.....................................2 C2
National Dr *CHAD* OL9.................................83 D1
Naunton Rd *MDTN* M24...............................18 A2
Naval St *ANC* M4..5 E3
Nave Ct *SLFD* M6..66 A1
Navenby Av *OLDTF/WHR* M16..................99 D1
Naylor St *NEWH/MOS* M40.......................71 C2
    OLD OL1...22 B2
Nazeby Wk *CHAD* * OL9.............................21 D4
Naze Ct *OLD* * OL1.......................................22 B1
Neale Rd *CCHDY* M21.................................111 D2
Neary Wy *URM* M41.......................................78 A2
Neath Cl *WHTF* M45......................................12 B1
Neath St *CHAD* OL9......................................22 A2
Neden Cl *OP/CLY* M11..................................90 A1
Needham Av *CCHDY* M21..........................112 A1
Needwood Cl *NEWH/MOS* M40................53 C4
Neenton Sq *WGTN/LGST* M12...................89 D2
Neild St *CMANE* M1...9 D2
    OLDS OL8...40 B1
Neill St *BRO* M7..68 B1
Neilson Cl *MDTN* M24...................................18 A2
Nell La *CCHDY* M21.....................................113 C2
Nelson Av *ECC* M30......................................62 A2
Nelson Dr *DROY* M43....................................74 A3
Nelson Fold *SWIN* M27.................................26 B4
Nelson Rd *BKLY* M9......................................16 A4
Nelson St *BRO* M7...50 A4
    BRUN/LGST M13....................................87 C4
    ECC M30..62 A3
    MDTN M24..18 A2
    NEWH/MOS M40.....................................71 C1
    ORD M5...65 D4
    STRET M32..97 C4
Nelson Wy *CHAD* * OL9...............................38 B1
Nelstrop Crs *HTNM* SK4............................119 C3
Nelstrop Rd *HTNM* SK4..............................119 C3
Nelstrop Rd North *RDSH* SK5...................119 C4
Nepaul Rd *BKLY* M9......................................34 B2
Neptune Gdns *BRO* M7................................67 D1
Neston Av *DID/WITH* M20..........................114 B3
Neston Gv *EDGY/DAV* SK3.......................132 A4
Neston St *OP/CLY* M11.................................92 A2
Netherbury Cl *GTN* M18.............................105 D2
Netherfield Cl *OLDS* OL8............................39 D1
Netherland St *SALQ* M50.............................66 A4
Nether St *WGTN/LGST* * M12......................9 E2
Netherton Rd *RUSH/FAL* M14..................101 D4
Nethervale Dr *BKLY* M9................................53 D2
Netherwood *OLDS* OL8................................58 A1
Nettleford Rd *CCHDY* M21........................113 D1
Nettleton Gv *BKLY* M9.................................35 C4
Nevile Rd *BRO* M7...49 C1
Neville Cardus Wk *RUSH/FAL* M14.......102 B3
Neville St *CHAD* OL9....................................21 D2
Nevin Rd *NEWH/MOS* M40.........................37 C4
New Allen St *NEWH/MOS* M40..................70 B2
Newall St *CHAD* OL9....................................39 C3
Newark Av *RUSH/FAL* M14.......................102 A3
Newark Rd *RDSH* SK5................................120 A4
    SWIN M27..27 C3
New Bailey St *CSLFD* M3..............................2 C4
Newbank Cha *CHAD* M9..............................20 B1

New Bank St *WGTN/LGST* M12..................88 B4
New Barn Rd *OLDS* OL8...............................41 D3
New Barns Av *CCHDY* M21........................112 B3
New Barton St *SLFD* M6...............................46 B4
Newbeck St *ANC* * M4.....................................4 D2
New Beech Rd *HTNM* SK4.........................126 B3
Newberry Gv *EDGY/DAV* SK3..................132 A4
New Bridge La *STKP* SK1...........................130 B3
New Bridge St *CSLFD* M3...............................3 E2
Newbrook Av *CCHDY* M21........................123 C2
Newburn Av *BKLY* M9..................................35 C1
Newbury Dr *ECC* M30...................................61 C2
    URM M41..78 B4
Newbury Wk *CHAD* * OL9...........................21 D2
Newby Rd *HTNM* SK4.................................128 B3
Newcastle St *HULME* M15.............................7 F4
New Church Ct *WHTF* * M45......................11 C1
Newchurch St *OP/CLY* M11........................89 C1
Newcliffe Rd *BKLY* M9..................................35 C1
Newcombe Cl *OP/CLY* M11.........................72 A4
Newcombe St *CSLFD* * M3..........................69 C3
Newcroft *FAIL* M35...58 A3
Newcroft Crs *URM* M41.................................95 C4
Newcroft Dr *EDGY/DAV* SK3....................132 A3
    URM M41..95 C4
Newcroft Rd *URM* M41..................................95 C4
New Cross St *SLFD* M6.................................64 B3
    SWIN M27..45 D2
Newdale Rd *BNG/LEV* M19........................105 C3
New Elizabeth St *CHH* M8............................51 D4
New Elm Rd *CSLFD* M3...................................6 B2
Newgate *ANC* M4..4 B2
New Hall Av *BRO* M7.....................................50 A1
New Hall La *BRO* M7......................................50 A1
Newhall Rd *RDSH* SK5...............................107 D3
Newhaven Av *OP/CLY* M11.........................92 A2
New Herbert St *SLFD* M6..............................46 B4
Newholme Rd *DID/WITH* M20...................113 D4
Newington Av *CHH* M8..................................32 A2
New Islington *ANC* M4.....................................5 F3
New Kings Head Yd *CSLFD* * M3.................2 E2
Newlands *FAIL* M35..74 B1
Newlands Dr *PWCH* M25..............................11 D4
    SWIN M27..46 B3
Newland St *CHH* M8......................................33 C4
New La *ECC* M30..61 C3
New Lawns *RDSH* SK5................................107 D4
Newlyn St *RUSH/FAL* M14........................102 A3
New Market *CMANW* M2.................................3 F4
Newmarket Gv *AULW* OL7...........................59 D4
Newmarket Rd *AULW* OL7...........................59 D4
New Mount St *ANC* * M4.................................4 B1
New Park Rd *ORD* M5...................................84 A2
Newport Av *RDSH* SK5...............................119 D2
Newport Rd *CCHDY* M21.............................98 B2
Newport St *OLDS* OL8..................................22 A4
    RUSH/FAL M14.....................................102 A2
    SLFD M6..65 D3
Newquay Av *RDSH* SK5.............................119 D2
New Quay St *CSLFD* M3.................................2 C4
New Rd *OLDS* OL8...40 B1
Newry Rd *ECC* M30.......................................79 D1
Newsham Rd *EDGY/DAV* SK3..................132 B3
Newsham Wk *WGTN/LGST* * M12............105 C2
Newsholme St *CHH* M8.................................51 C2
Newstead Av *DID/WITH* M20....................116 A4
Newstead Rd *URM* M41................................94 B2
New St *DROY* M43..92 B1
    ECC M30..61 D1
    NEWH/MOS M40.....................................71 D1
    SWIN M27..26 B4
New Thomas St *SLFD* * M6..........................66 B1
Newton Av *DID/WITH* M20........................114 B3
    WGTN/LGST M12..................................104 A1
Newton Rd *FAIL* M35.....................................56 B4
    MDTN M24..15 C2

Newton St *CMANE* M1......................4 C4
   DROY M43.............................76 B2
   EDGY/DAV SK3.................132 B1
   FAIL * M35...........................55 D3
   STRET M32..........................97 C3
Newtown Cl *OP/CLY* M11...............90 A1
   SWIN M27..............................26 A3
Newtown St *PWCH* M25.................30 B1
New Union St *ANC* M4......................5 E3
New Viaduct St *OP/CLY* M11..........71 D3
Newville Dr *DID/WITH* M20...........116 A4
New Vine St *HULME* M15...................7 E5
New Wakefield St *CMANE* M1...........8 A3
New Welcome St *HULME* M15............7 E5
New Zealand Rd *STKP* SK1.............130 B4
Niagara St *OFTN* SK2....................133 D3
Nicholas Cft *ANC* M4........................4 A3
Nicholas Owen Cl *OP/CLY* M11.......90 B1
Nicholas St *CMANW* M2....................4 A5
Nicholls St *SLFD* * M6.....................66 B2
Nicholson St *HTNM* SK4................129 D3
Nichols St *SLFD* M6.......................67 C4
Nicolas Rd *CCHDY* M21..................98 B4
Nigel Rd *BKLY* M9...........................54 A2
Nightingale Dr *DTN/ASHW* M34......76 B3
Nile St *OLD* OL1............................22 C1
Nile Ter *BRO* M7............................50 A4
Nimble Nook *CHAD* OL9..................20 B4
Nina Dr *NEWH/MOS* M40.................36 B2
Nine Acre Dr *ORD* M5.....................84 A2
Ninth Av *OLDS* OL8........................40 A4
Niven St *EDGY/DAV* SK3....................9 E5
Nixon St *EDGY/DAV* SK3................132 B1
   FAIL M35.............................56 B2
No 11 Pas *DID/WITH* * M20...........114 A4
Noble St *OLDS* OL8.........................41 C1
Nolan St *BKLY* M9...........................53 D2
Nona St *SLFD* M6............................65 D3
The Nook *ECC* M30.........................60 B2
   URM M41.............................94 A4
Norbet Wk *BKLY* M9........................53 D2
Norbreck Av *CCHDY* M21...............112 A2
Norburn Rd *BRUN/LGST* M13.........104 A3
Norbury Av *SLFD* M6......................47 C4
Norbury Cl *NEWH/MOS* * M40........71 C1
Norbury Gv *SWIN* M27....................26 A4
Norbury St *BRO* M7.........................50 B3
   STKP SK1...........................130 A4
Norcot Wk *HULME* * M15...................6 B5
Norden Av *DID/WITH* M20.............114 B3
Nordens Rd *CHAD* OL9....................20 A1
Nordens St *CHAD* OL9.....................20 B1
Noreen Av *PWCH* M25.....................12 B4
Norfolk Av *DROY* M43.....................75 C2
   DTN/ASHW M34................107 D3
   GTN * M18..........................105 D1
   HTNM SK4.........................118 B3
   WHTF M45............................11 D1
Norfolk Crs *FAIL* M35......................56 B3
Norfolk Rd *GTN* M18......................105 D1
Norfolk St *CHAD* OL9......................39 C1
   CMANW M2............................3 F4
   SLFD M6..............................48 B4
Norgate St *DID/WITH* M20.............125 C2
Norley Av *STRET* M32......................98 A2
Norley Dr *BNG/LEV* M19................105 D3
Normanby Gv *SWIN* M27..................25 D4
Normanby Rd *RUSH/FAL* M14.........101 C3
   SWIN M27............................25 D4
Norman Gv *RDSH* SK5....................119 D2
   WGTN/LGST M12................104 B3
Norman Rd *BRO* * M7.....................50 B3
   HTNM SK4.........................128 A3
   RUSH/FAL M14..................103 C3
Norman Rd West *BKLY* * M9...........54 A2
Norman St *CHAD* OL9.....................22 A1
   FAIL M35.............................38 B4
   WGTN/LGST M12.................90 A4

Normanton Av *SLFD* M6..................64 B2
Normanton Dr *BKLY* M9..................34 B1
Norris Av *HTNM* SK4.....................128 B3
Norris Bank Ter *HTNM* SK4...........128 B4
Norris Hill Dr *HTNM* SK4...............128 B3
Northallerton Rd *BRO* M7................49 C3
Northampton Rd *NEWH/MOS* M40...53 D3
North Av *BNG/LEV* M19.................117 C2
   URM M41.............................79 D2
Northbank Gdns *BNG/LEV* M19......116 B5
North Blackfield La *BRO* M7............49 D1
Northbourne St *SLFD* M6................65 D3
Northbrook Av *CHH* M8...................32 A1
North Broughton St *CSLFD* M3..........2 C3
North Cir *WHTF* M45.......................11 D3
North Clifden La *BRO* M7................50 B3
Northcombe Rd *EDGY/DAV* SK3......132 B4
North Crs *NEWH/MOS* M40..............37 C2
   OP/CLY M11........................74 A2
North Cft *OLDS* OL8........................41 D2
Northdale Rd *BKLY* M9....................15 C4
North Dean St *SWIN* M27................26 B4
Northdown Av *HULME* M15................6 A5
North Dr *DTN/ASHW* M34.................76 B4
   SWIN M27............................46 A2
Northen Gv *DID/WITH* M20.............124 A1
Northern Av *SWIN* M27....................27 D1
Northfield Av *NEWH/MOS* M40.........38 A3
Northfield Rd *NEWH/MOS* M40.........38 A3
North Ga *OLDS* OL8.........................40 B2
North George St *CSLFD* M3...............2 A2
North Gv *BRUN/LGST* M13...............88 A4
North Harvey St *STKP* * SK1..........130 A4
North Hill St *CSLFD* M3....................2 B1
Northland Rd *BKLY* M9....................35 D2
Northleigh Dr *PWCH* * M25.............31 C2
Northleigh Rd *OLDTF/WHR* M16......99 C1
North Lonsdale St *STRET* * M32.......97 D2
North Md *CCHDY* M21....................112 A1
Northmoor Rd *WGTN/LGST* M12....104 B3
Northolme Gdns *BNG/LEV* M19......126 B1
Northolt Ct *OP/CLY* * M11................74 A3
North Pde *CSLFD* M3.........................3 E4
North Phoebe St *ORD* M5................84 A1
North Pl *STKP* SK1........................130 A4
Northridge Rd *BKLY* M9...................16 A3
North Rd *DTN/ASHW* M34................77 C4
   OP/CLY M11........................73 D3
   PWCH M25...........................11 C4
   STRET M32.........................96 A1
   TRPK M17............................81 D4
North Star Dr *CSLFD* M3...................2 D4
North St *CHH* M8............................51 D4
Northumberland Cl
   OLDTF/WHR M16................84 B4
Northumberland Crs
   OLDTF/WHR * M16.............84 B4
Northumberland Rd
   OLDTF/WHR M16................99 D1
   RDSH SK5.........................121 C3
Northumberland St *BRO* M7............50 A2
Northurst Dr *CHH* M8......................32 A2
Northway *DROY* M43.......................92 B1
North Wy *RDSH* SK5......................121 D3
North Western St *BNG/LEV* M19.....117 D1
   WGTN/LGST M12..................9 F2
Northwold Dr *BKLY* M9....................36 A2
Norton Av *DTN/ASHW* M34............107 D2
   URM M41.............................94 A1
   WGTN/LGST M12................105 C2
Norton Gra *PWCH* M25....................31 C2
Norton Gv *HTNM* SK4....................128 A4
Norton St *BRO* M7..........................50 B2
   CMANE * M1..........................5 F5
   CSLFD M3.............................3 E2
   NEWH/MOS M40.................71 C2
Norville Av *NEWH/MOS* M40...........37 C2
Norway Gv *RDSH* * SK5.................130 A1

Norway St *OP/CLY* M11	88	B1
SLFD M6	65	D3
STRET M32	97	D2
Norwich Rd *STRET* M32	95	C2
Norwood *PCWH* M25	30	A3
Norwood Av *BRO* M7	49	C1
DID/WITH M20	126	A1
Norwood Dr *SWIN* M27	43	D2
Norwood Rd *STRET* M32	97	D4
Nottingham Av *RDSH* SK5	121	D3
Nottingham Dr *FAIL* M35	57	D2
	RDSH SK5	121	D3
Nuneaton Dr *NEWH/MOS* M40	71	C2
Nuneham Av *DID/WITH* M20	115	D2
Nunfield Cl *NEWH/MOS* M40	36	A3
Nunthorpe Dr *CHH* M8	52	B1
Nursery Rd *FAIL* M35	57	D3
HTNM SK4	128	B3
PWCH M25	11	D3
Nursery St *OLDTF/WHR* M16	101	C2
SLFD M6	66	A1
Nuthurst Rd *NEWH/MOS* M40	36	B4
Nutsford V *WGTN/LGST* M12	104	B1
Nuttall Ms *WALK* M45	11	C1
Nuttall St *OLDTF/WHR* M16	84	B4
OP/CLY M11	89	D2
Nutt La *PWCH* M25	13	D1

O

Oadby Cl *WGTN/LGST* M12	104	B1
Oak Av *CCHDY* M21	112	A1
GTN M18	107	C1
HTNM SK4	128	A3
MDTN M24	17	D2
WHTF M45	11	C1
Oak Bank *BKLY* M9	53	C1
PWCH M25	29	C4
Oak Bank Av *BKLY* M9	35	C4
Oakbank Av *CHAD* OL9	19	D1
Oak Bank Cl *WHTF* M45	12	A1
Oakdale Cl *WHTF* M45	10	A1
Oakdale Dr *DID/WITH* M20	125	D4
Oakdene *SWIN* M27	43	D3
Oakdene Av *HTNM* SK4	119	C4
Oakdene Rd *MDTN* M24	18	B3
Oakdene St *BKLY* M9	54	A1
Oak Dr *DTN/ASHW* M34	107	C4
RUSH/FAL M14	103	C4
Oaker Av *DID/WITH* M20	123	D1
Oakfield *PWCH* M25	31	C2
SALE M33	108	B4
Oakfield Av *DROY* M43	75	C4
OLDTF/WHR M16	98	B2
OLDTF/WHR M16	100	A3
Oakfield Gv *GTN* M18	106	A1
Oakfield Rd *DID/WITH* M20	124	B2
EDGY/DAV SK3	133	C4
Oakfield St *CHH* M8	51	D3
Oakford Av *NEWH/MOS* M40	55	F1
Oak Gv *ECC* M30	61	C4
URM M41	94	B3
Oakham Ms *BRO* M7	30	B4
Oakhill Wy *CHH* M8	51	C2
Oakhouse Dr *CCHDY* M21	112	A2
Oakington Av *RUSH/FAL* M14	102	A2
Oakland Av *BNG/LEV* M19	126	B1
SLFD M6	63	D1
Oaklands Dr *PWCH* M25	12	A1
SALE M33	108	B4
Oaklands Rd *BRO* M7	48	B2
SWIN M27	43	D3
Oak La *WHTF* M45	12	A1
Oakleigh Av *BNG/LEV* M19	117	C2
Oakley Cl *NEWH/MOS* M40	55	D4

Oakley St *ORD* M5	65	C4
Oakley Vis *HTNM* SK4	128	A2
Oakmere Av *ECC* M30	61	D1
Oakmoor Dr *BRO* M7	48	B1
Oak Rd *BRO* M7	49	D3
DID/WITH M20	115	C4
FAIL M35	57	C3
OLDS OL8	59	D3
Oak Shaw Cl *BKLY* M9	33	D3
Oak St *ANC* M4	4	B3
ECC M30	62	A4
MDTN * M24	19	C2
SWIN M27	26	B4
Oakville Dr *SLFD* M6	63	D1
Oakville Ter *NEWH/MOS* M40	35	C4
Oakwell Dr *CHH* M8	31	D4
Oakwell Man *BRO* M7	31	D4
Oakwood *CHAD* OL9	19	D2
Oakwood Av *NEWH/MOS* M40	37	C4
SWIN M27	25	D1
Oakwood Dr *SLFD* M6	46	A4
Oakworth St *BKLY* M9	33	D2
Oat St *STKP* SK1	133	D2
Oban Av *NEWH/MOS* M40	73	C1
Ockendon Dr *BKLY* M9	53	D3
Octavia Dr *NEWH/MOS* M40	73	D1
Odell St *OP/CLY* * M11	90	A2
Odessa Av *SLFD* M6	46	A4
Odette St *GTN* M18	105	D1
Offerton St *STKP* SK1	131	C3
Ogbourne Wk *BRUN/LGST* M13	87	D3
Ogden La *OP/CLY* M11	91	C2
Ogden Rd *FAIL* M35	57	C3
Ogden St *CHAD* OL9	21	C1
DID/WITH M20	125	C2
MDTN M24	17	D1
PWCH M25	30	B3
SWIN M27	45	C2
Ogwen Dr *PWCH* M25	12	A4
Ohio Av *SALQ* M50	83	C1
Okeover Rd *BRO* M7	50	A1
Old Bank *CMANW* M2	3	F4
Old Barton Rd *TRPK* M17	78	B2
Old Birley St *HULME* M15	86	A4
Old Broadway *DID/WITH* M20	115	C4
Oldbury Cl *NEWH/MOS* M40	71	C2
Oldcastle Av *DID/WITH* M20	114	B2
Old Chapel La *EDGY/DAV* SK3	132	B2
Old Church St *NEWH/MOS* M40	55	D3
Old Clough La *WALK* M28	42	A1
Old Elm St *BRUN/LGST* * M13	9	F5
Oldershaw Dr *BKLY* M9	53	D3
Old Farm Crs *DROY* M43	92	A1
Oldfield Gv *SALE* M33	109	D4
Oldfield Rd *ORD* M5	84	B3
PWCH M25	12	D4
SALE M33	109	D4
Oldfield St *OP/CLY* M11	73	C4
Old Gardens St *STKP* * SK1	133	C4
Oldgate Wk *HULME* * M15	85	C3
Old Hall Dr *GTN* M18	106	A1
Old Hall La *BRUN/LGST* M13	103	D3
PWCH M25	14	A3
Old Hall Rd *BRO* M7	50	A1
NEWH/MOS M40	55	C2
STRET M32	95	D1
Old Hall St *MDTN* M24	17	D1
OP/CLY * M11	91	D2
Oldham Av *STKP* SK1	131	C4
Oldham Rd *ANC* M4	5	D2
FAIL M35	38	B4
FAIL M35	56	B2
MDTN M24	17	C1
NEWH/MOS M40	54	A4
Oldham St *CMANE* M1	4	B4
DROY M43	76	A3
ORD M5	2	A5

RDSH * SK5 .....119 D2	
Oldham Wy *OLD* OL1 .....23 C3	
Old La *CHAD* OL9 .....39 C1	
OP/CLY M11 .....91 C2	
Old Lansdowne Rd *DID/WITH* M20 .....124 A1	
Old Malt La *DID/WITH* M20 .....114 B2	
Old Market St *BKLY* M9 .....33 D3	
Old Medlock St *CSLFD* * M3 .....6 B1	
Old Mill Cl *SWIN* M27 .....46 A4	
Old Mill St *ANC* M4 .....5 F4	
Old Moat La *DID/WITH* M20 .....115 C3	
Old Mount St *ANC* M4 .....8 B1	
Old Oak St *DID/WITH* M20 .....125 C2	
Old Park La *TRPK* M17 .....78 B3	
Old Parrin La *ECC* M30 .....61 C2	
Old Rd *BKLY* M9 .....34 A3	
FAIL M35 .....56 B2	
HTNM SK4 .....129 D2	
Old School Dr *BKLY* * M9 .....33 D3	
Old Shaw St *ORD* * M5 .....83 D1	
Old Station St *ECC* M30 .....61 D4	
Old Wellington Rd *ECC* M30 .....62 B3	
Old York St *HULME* M15 .....6 C5	
Olebrook Cl *WGTN/LGST* M12 .....88 A3	
Olga Ter *BKLY* * M9 .....34 A3	
Oliver St *EDGY/DAV* SK3 .....133 C1	
OP/CLY * M11 .....89 C1	
Olive Shapley Av *DID/WITH* M20 .....125 C2	
Olive St *FAIL* M35 .....56 B1	
Olivia Gv *RUSH/FAL* M14 .....103 C2	
Ollier Av *WGTN/LGST* M12 .....88 B3	
Olney St *BRUN/LGST* M13 .....103 C1	
Olwen Crs *RDSH* SK5 .....120 A1	
Olympic Ct *SALQ* M50 .....83 C1	
Omer Av *BRUN/LGST* M13 .....104 A3	
Omer Dr *BNG/LEV* M19 .....116 B2	
Onslow Av *NEWH/MOS* M40 .....37 D4	
Onslow Cl *OLD* OL1 .....22 B1	
Opal Ct *RUSH/FAL* * M14 .....116 A1	
Opal St *BNG/LEV* M19 .....118 A1	
Orama Av *SLFD* M6 .....63 D1	
Orange Hill Rd *PWCH* M25 .....12 B4	
Orange St *SLFD* M6 .....66 B2	
Orchard Av *GTN* M18 .....106 B1	
Orchard Gv *DID/WITH* M20 .....114 A4	
Orchard Pl *SALE* M33 .....109 C4	
Orchard Rd *FAIL* M35 .....57 C1	
Orchard Rd East *WYTH/NTH* M22 .....123 C3	
Orchard Rd West *WYTH/NTH* M22 .....123 C3	
Orchard St *DID/WITH* M20 .....114 A4	
SLFD M6 .....48 B4	
STKP SK1 .....130 A4	
Orchid St *BKLY* M9 .....53 D2	
Ordsall Dr *ORD* M5 .....84 A2	
Ordsall La *ORD* M5 .....6 A1	
ORD M5 .....83 D3	
Oregon Cl *BRUN/LGST* M13 .....9 E5	
Orford Rd *NEWH/MOS* M40 .....55 D3	
PWCH M25 .....11 D4	
Oriel Av *OLDS* OL8 .....40 B1	
Oriel Cl *CHAD* OL9 .....38 B1	
Oriel Rd *DID/WITH* M20 .....124 A1	
Orient Rd *SLFD* M6 .....63 D1	
Orient St *BRO* M7 .....51 C2	
Orion Pl *BRO* * M7 .....67 D1	
Orkney Dr *URM* M41 .....79 C3	
Orlanda Av *SLFD* M6 .....63 D1	
Orlanda Dr *BRO* M7 .....51 C3	
Orleans Wy *OLD* * OL1 .....22 B2	
Orme Av *MDTN* M24 .....17 C2	
SLFD M6 .....46 A4	
Orme Cl *OP/CLY* M11 .....71 C4	
URM M41 .....95 C3	
Orme St *OLDE* OL4 .....23 D4	
STKP * SK1 .....131 C3	
Ormonde Av *SLFD* M6 .....64 A1	
Ormsby Av *GTN* M18 .....105 C1	
Ormsgill Cl *HULME* M15 .....86 A3	

Ormsgill St *HULME* M15 .....86 A3	
Ormskirk Av *DID/WITH* M20 .....114 A3	
Ormskirk Rd *RDSH* SK5 .....120 A3	
Orphanage St *HTNM* SK4 .....129 D2	
Orpington Rd *BKLY* M9 .....53 D2	
Orrell St *OP/CLY* * M11 .....91 C1	
Orrel St *SLFD* M6 .....65 C1	
Orsett Cl *NEWH/MOS* M40 .....70 B2	
Orthes Gv *HTNM* SK4 .....119 C4	
Orvietto Av *SLFD* M6 .....63 D1	
Orville Dr *BNG/LEV* M19 .....117 C2	
Orwell Av *DTN/ASHW* M34 .....107 C2	
Osborne Dr *SWIN* M27 .....46 B2	
Osborne Rd *BKLY* * M9 .....53 D2	
BNG/LEV M19 .....104 A4	
OFTN SK2 .....133 C2	
OLDS OL8 .....22 A4	
SLFD * M6 .....63 D2	
Osborne St *CHAD* OL9 .....21 D1	
MPL/ROM SK6 .....131 D2	
NEWH/MOS M40 .....70 B2	
SLFD M6 .....66 A2	
Osbourne St *DID/WITH* M20 .....124 B2	
Oscar St *NEWH/MOS* M40 .....54 B2	
Oscroft Cl *CHH* M8 .....51 C3	
Osprey Cl *HULME* M15 .....85 D4	
Osprey Dr *DROY* M43 .....76 B2	
Osprey Wk *BRUN/LGST* * M13 .....87 D3	
Ossory St *RUSH/FAL* M14 .....102 A2	
Osterley Rd *BKLY* M9 .....35 D2	
Ostlers Ga *DROY* M43 .....77 C3	
Ostrich La *PWCH* M25 .....30 B2	
Oswald Cl *SLFD* M6 .....48 B4	
Oswald La *CCHDY* M21 .....99 C3	
Oswald Rd *CCHDY* M21 .....99 C3	
Oswald St *ANC* M4 .....4 A1	
CHAD OL9 .....22 A1	
RDSH SK5 .....107 C2	
Othello Dr *ECC* M30 .....62 A3	
Otley Av *SLFD* M6 .....63 D1	
Otley Cl *CHAD* OL9 .....21 C3	
Otterburn Cl *HULME* M15 .....86 A3	
Otter Dr *CHH* M8 .....50 B4	
Oulton Av *SALE* M33 .....110 B4	
Oulton Wk *NEWH/MOS* M40 .....71 C3	
Oundle Cl *RUSH/FAL* M14 .....102 B2	
Ouse St *SALQ* M50 .....82 B2	
Outram Sq *DROY* * M43 .....92 B1	
Outrington Dr *OP/CLY* M11 .....89 C2	
Outwood Av *SWIN* M27 .....25 C1	
Outwood Gv *BRO* M7 .....68 B1	
Overbridge Rd *BRO* M7 .....68 B1	
Overbrook Av *NEWH/MOS* M40 .....53 C4	
Overbrook Dr *PWCH* M25 .....30 A2	
Overdale *SWIN* M27 .....45 D3	
Overhill Rd *CHAD* OL9 .....20 A1	
Overlea Dr *BNG/LEV* M19 .....116 B4	
Overlinks Dr *SLFD* M6 .....46 A4	
Overstone Dr *CHH* M8 .....51 C2	
Owens Cl *CHAD* OL9 .....19 D1	
Owens Pk *RUSH/FAL* * M14 .....103 C4	
Owen St *ECC* M30 .....61 C4	
EDGY/DAV SK3 .....129 C4	
SLFD M6 .....48 B4	
Owler La *CHAD* OL9 .....37 C2	
Oxbrow Wy *WHTF* M45 .....11 D1	
Oxford Av *DROY* M43 .....75 C2	
WHTF M45 .....11 D1	
Oxford Ct *CMANE* * M1 .....7 F2	
OLDTF/WHR * M16 .....85 C4	
Oxford Pl *RUSH/FAL* M14 .....102 B1	
Oxford Rd *BRUN/LGST* M13 .....87 C4	
CMANE M1 .....8 A3	
SLFD M6 .....63 D1	
Oxford St *CHAD* OL9 .....7 D1	
CMANW M2 .....7 F1	
ECC M30 .....62 B4	
Oxford Wy *HTNM* SK4 .....129 C2	

Oxley St *OP/CLY* M11 ....72 B3
Oxney Rd *RUSH/FAL* M14 ....102 A1
Oxton St *OP/CLY* M11 ....92 A2

P

Pacific Wy *SALQ* M50 ....81 D1
Packwood Cha *CHAD* OL9 ....20 A1
Paddington Av *NEWH/MOS* * M40 ......55 C4
Paddington Cl *SLFD* M6 ....66 B3
Paddison St *SWIN* M27 ....44 B2
Paddock La *FAIL* M35 35
The Paddocks *EDGY/DAV* SK3 ....133 D4
Paddock St *WGTN/LGST* M12 ....9 E3
Padstow St *NEWH/MOS* * M40 ....71 D2
Paget St *NEWH/MOS* M40 ....53 C4
Pagnall Ct *CHAD* * OL9 ....21 C4
Paignton Av *BNG/LEV* M19 ....117 C3
Paignton Gv *HTNM* SK4 ....119 D2
Pailin Dr *DROY* M43 ....76 B3
Palace Rd *SALE* M33 ....108 B4
Palace St *CHAD* OL9 ....21 D3
Palatine Av *DID/WITH* M20 ....115 C3
Palatine Crs *DID/WITH* M20 ....115 C3
Palatine Rd *DID/WITH* M20 ....114 B3
  WYTH/NTH M22 ....123 C4
Palfrey Pl *WGTN/LGST* M12 ....9 F3
Pall Ml *CMANW* M2 ....3 F5
Palmer Cl *OLDS* OL8 ....41 C1
Palmerston Av *OLDTF/WHR* M16 ....100 A3
Palmerston Crs *WGTN/LGST* M12 ....88 A1
Palmer St *BRO* M7 ....49 C3
Palm Gv *CHAD* OL9 ....21 C1
Palm St *BRUN/LGST* M13 ....104 A2
  DROY M43 ....74 A3
Pandora St *DID/WITH* M20 ....114 B4
Pangbourne Av *URM* M41 ....94 B2
Pankhurst Wk *RUSH/FAL* M14 ....102 A2
Panmure St *OLDS* OL8 ....41 C1
Parbold St *DID/WITH* M20 ....114 B2
Paris Av *ORD* M5 ....84 A3
Parish Vw *ORD* M5 ....84 A1
Park Av *BNG/LEV* M19 ....104 A4
  BRO M7 ....51 C1
  FAIL M35 ....56 A1
  OLDTF/WHR M16 ....84 B4
  PWCH M25 ....30 A1
  SALE M33 ....108 B3
  WHTF M45 ....10 A3
Park Brow Cl *CCHDY* M21 ....112 B2
Park Cl *WHTF* M45 ....11 C3
Park Crs *RUSH/FAL* M14 ....102 B2
Parkdale Av *GTN* M18 ....90 B4
Park Dr *ECC* M30 ....62 A1
  HTNM SK4 ....128 A3
  OLDTF/WHR M16 ....99 D3
Parker St *CMANE* M1 ....4 E5
Parkfield *ORD* M5 ....65 C3
Parkfield Av *OLDS* OL8 ....39 C3
  PWCH M25 ....31 C2
  RUSH/FAL M14 ....102 A2
Parkfield Dr *MDTN* M24 ....16 B1
Parkfield Rd North *NEWH/MOS* M40 ....37 D3
Parkfield Rd South *DID/WITH* M20 ....124 B1
Parkfield St *RUSH/FAL* M14 ....102 A2
Park Gate Av *DID/WITH* M20 ....115 C3
Parkgate Dr *SWIN* M27 ....46 A2
Park Gv *BNG/LEV* M19 ....104 B3
  HTNM SK4 ....128 A1
Park Hl *PWCH* * M25 ....31 C3
Parkhill Av *CHH* M8 ....33 C3
Park Hill Dr *WHTF* M45 ....10 B1
Park House Bridge Est *SLFD* * M6 ....48 B1
Park House Bridge Rd *SLFD* M6 ....48 B1
Parkhouse St *OP/CLY* M11 ....90 A1
Parkhurst Av *NEWH/MOS* M40 ....37 D4

Parkin St *WGTN/LGST* M12 ....104 B2
Parklake Av *BRO* M7 ....50 A1
The Parklands *HTNM* SK4 ....129 D1
Parklands *WHTF* M45 ....10 B1
Park La *BRO* M7 ....50 A1
  OLDS OL8 ....41 C3
  SLFD M6 ....46 B4
  WHTF M45 ....10 B2
Park Lane Ct *WHTF* * M45 ....10 A1
Park La West *SWIN* M27 ....47 C2
Parkleigh Dr *NEWH/MOS* M40 ....37 D3
Park Ldg *BNG/LEV* M19 ....104 B4
Park Ms *OLDTF/WHR* M16 ....99 D3
Parkmount Rd *BKLY* M9 ....34 B4
Park Pl *ANC* M4 ....69 D2
  HTNM SK4 ....127 C3
  PWCH M25 ....12 B4
  SLFD M6 ....63 D2
Park Range *RUSH/FAL* M14 ....103 C2
Park Rd *ECC* M30 ....62 A1
  HTNM SK4 ....118 A4
  MDTN M24 ....17 C1
  OLDS OL8 ....23 C4
  PWCH M25 ....25 C2
  SALE M33 ....108 B3
  SLFD M6 ....63 D1
  STRET M32 ....96 B2
Park Rw *HTNM* SK4 ....127 C4
Park Seventeen *WHTF* M45 ....11 C1
Parkside Av *BRO* M7 ....50 B1
  ECC M30 ....61 D4
  FAIL M35 ....56 B4
Parkside Rd *RUSH/FAL* M14 ....101 C3
Parkside St *WGTN/LGST* * M12 ....9 F3
Park Sq *OLDTF/WHR* M16 ....98 B3
Parkstead Dr *BKLY* M9 ....53 C3
Parkstone Av *GTN* M18 ....92 A3
  WHTF M45 ....10 A3
Parkstone Dr *SLFD* M6 ....46 A3
Parkstone La *WALK* M28 ....60 A1
Park St *BRO* M7 ....49 D1
  CSLFD M3 ....2 A4
  DROY M43 ....76 B3
  OLDS OL8 ....22 B4
  PWCH M25 ....30 B1
  STKP SK1 ....130 A3
  SWIN M27 ....45 D2
Parksway *BKLY* M9 ....15 C3
  PWCH M25 ....36 B3
  SWIN M27 ....46 B3
Park Vw *BKLY* M9 ....52 B3
  RUSH/FAL * M14 ....116 B2
Park View Ct *PWCH* * M25 ....30 A2
Park View Rd *PWCH* M25 ....30 A2
Parkville Rd *DID/WITH* M20 ....115 C3
  PWCH M25 ....12 B3
Park Wy *STRET* M32 ....95 C1
Parlane St *ANC* * M4 ....69 D2
Parrenthorn Rd *PWCH* M25 ....12 B1
Parrfield Rd *WALK* M28 ....42 B2
Parrin La *ECC* M30 ....61 D2
Parrot St *OP/CLY* M11 ....73 D4
Parr St *ECC* M30 ....61 D2
  OP/CLY * M11 ....91 D2
Parrs Wood Av *DID/WITH* M20 ....125 D4
Parrs Wood La *DID/WITH* M20 ....126 A4
Parrs Wood Rd *DID/WITH* M20 ....125 D4
Parslow Av *CHH* M8 ....51 D1
Parsonage Cl *ORD* M5 ....84 B1
Parsonage Gdns *CSLFD* * M3 ....3 E4
Parsonage La *CSLFD* * M3 ....3 E3
Parsonage Rd *DID/WITH* M20 ....115 D2
  HTNM SK4 ....128 A1
Parsonage St *CHH* M8 ....32 A4
  HTNM SK4 ....129 D3
  HULME M15 ....85 D4

Parsons Fld *SLFD* * M6 ....48 B4
Parsons St *CHAD* OL9 ....21 D3
Partington La *SWIN* M27 ....44 B2
Partington Pl *SALE* M33 ....109 C4
Partington St *ECC* M30 ....62 A2
  FAIL M35...57 C2
  NEWH/MOS M40 ....54 A4
  OLD OL1 ....23 D2
  WALK M28 ....43 D1
Partridge Ri *DROY* M43 ....77 C2
Partridge Rd *FAIL* M35 ....58 B3
Partridge St *STRET* M32 ....83 C4
Partridge Wy *DROY* M43 ....19 C1
Parvet Av *DROY* M43 ....75 C2
Pascal St *BNG/LEV* M19 ....117 D1
Pass St *CHAD* OL9 ....22 A3
Patchett St *WGTN/LGST* M12 ....89 C3
Patey St *WGTN/LGST* M12 ....104 B2
Paton Ct *BRO* M7 ....67 D1
Paton St *CMANE* M1 ....4 C5
Patten St *DID/WITH* M20 ....115 C3
Patterson Av *CCHDY* M21 ....98 C3
Pattishall Cl *ANC* M4 ....71 C4
Paulden Dr *FAIL* M35 ....57 D2
Paulhan Rd *DID/WITH* M20 ....126 A1
Peace Cl *FAIL* * M35 ....38 B3
Peaceville Rd *BNG/LEV* M19 ....104 A4
Peach Bank *MDTN* M24 ....17 D1
Peach St *PWCH* M25 ....12 B4
Peach Tree Cl *BRO* * M7 ....51 D3
Peach Tree Ct *SLFD* * M6 ....66 B3
Peacock Av *SLFD* M6 ....47 D4
Peacock Cl *GTN* M18 ....90 B3
Peacock Gv *GTN* M18 ....106 A1
Peakdale Av *CHH* M8 ....32 A1
Peakdale Rd *DROY* M43 ....74 B2
Peaknaze Cl *SWIN* M27 ....46 A1
Peak St *CHAD* OL9 ....21 D3
  CMANE M1 ....5 D5
  STKP SK1 ....130 B4
Pear Cl *MDTN* M24 ....18 A3
Pearl Av *BRO* M7 ....31 D4
Pearn Rd *BNG/LEV* M19 ....117 D1
Pearson St *RDSH* SK5 ....130 A3
Pear Tree Cl *SLFD* M6 ....66 B3
Pear Tree Ct *SLFD* M6 ....66 B3
Peary St *ANC* M4 ....70 A2
Peatfield Av *NEWH/MOS* M40 ....25 C3
Peatfield Wk *HULME* * M15 ....86 A4
Pebworth Cl *MDTN* M24 ....17 C4
Peckford Dr *NEWH/MOS* M40 ....54 A4
Pedley Wk *BRUN/LGST* M13 ....9 D3
Peebles Dr *NEWH/MOS* M40 ....74 A1
Peel Cir *URM* M41 ....79 D3
Peel Cross Rd *ORD* M5 ....66 B4
Peel Green Rd *ECC* M30 ....78 A1
Peel Gv *WGTN/LGST* M12 ....104 B3
Peel La *CHH* M8 ....69 D1
Peel Moat Rd *HTNM* SK4 ....118 C3
Peel Mt *SLFD* M6 ....67 C2
Peel St *CHAD* OL9 ....21 C2
  DROY M43 ....92 A1
  ECC M30 ....63 C3
  FAIL M35 ....56 A3
  OFTN SK2 ....133 C3
Pegasus Sq *BRO* M7 ....67 D2
Pegwell Dr *BRO* M7 ....50 B4
Pelham Pl *CHH* M8 ....33 C3
Pelham St *OLDS* OL8 ....41 C3
Pellowe Rd *OLDS* OL8 ....40 B2
Pelton Av *SWIN* M27 ....25 C3
Pembridge Fold *MDTN* M24 ....18 A3
Pembridge Rd *BKLY* M9 ....35 C1
Pembroke Av *ECC* M30 ....62 A3
  SALE M33 ....108 A3
Pembroke Cl *BRUN/LGST* M13 ....88 A3
Pembroke St *BRO* M7 ....50 B3
  OLDS OL8 ....22 A3

  SLFD M6 ....65 D4
Pembry Cl *RDSH* SK5 ....121 D3
Pencarrow Cl *DID/WITH* M20 ....124 A2
Pencombe Cl *WGTN/LGST* M12 ....104 B3
Pencroft Wy *HULME* M15 ....86 B4
Pendennis Rd *HTNM* SK4 ....128 B2
Pendlebury Cl *PWCH* M25 ....29 C3
Pendlebury Rd *SWIN* M27 ....45 D1
Pendlecroft Av *SWIN* M27 ....46 B2
Pendlegreen Cl *OP/CLY* M11 ....89 C1
Pendleton On *SLFD* M6 ....66 A2
Pendleton Wy *SLFD* M6 ....66 B2
Pendleway *SWIN* M27 ....26 B4
Pendragon Pl *FAIL* M35 ....57 D2
Penelope Rd *SLFD* M6 ....47 C4
Penketh Av *GTN* M18 ....105 C1
Pennant Dr *PWCH* M25 ....11 C4
Pennell St *OP/CLY* M11 ....74 A4
Pennine Av *CHAD* OL9 ....20 B4
Pennine Cl *BKLY* M9 ....35 C1
Pennington St *CHAD* OL9 ....39 C2
  WGTN/LGST M12 ....104 B3
Pennon Cl *BRO* M7 ....50 B3
Penn St *NEWH/MOS* M40 ....54 A1
  OLDS OL8 ....22 A4
Penny La *RDSH* SK5 ....130 A3
Penrhyn Av *MDTN* M24 ....17 D2
Penrhyn Rd *PWCH* M25 ....30 A1
Penrith Av *OLDS* OL8 ....39 D2
  RDSH SK5 ....107 C4
  WHTF M45 ....13 D1
Penrod Pl *SLFD* M6 ....67 C1
Penroy Av *DID/WITH* M20 ....123 C2
Penruddock Wk *BRUN/LGST* * M13 ....104 A3
Pensarn Av *RUSH/FAL* M14 ....116 B3
Pensarn Gv *RDSH* SK5 ....130 A1
Pensby Cl *SWIN* M27 ....46 B2
Penshurst Rd *RDSH* SK5 ....121 D3
Pentland Av *NEWH/MOS* M40 ....36 B3
Pentlands Av *BRO* M7 ....50 A3
Penwortham St *NEWH/MOS* M40 ....72 A1
Penzance St *NEWH/MOS* M40 ....71 D2
Pepler Av *NTHM/RTH* M23 ....122 A3
Pepperhill Rd *OLDTF/WHR* M16 ....101 C1
Percival Cl *BRO* * M7 ....51 C3
Percival Rd *DROY* M43 ....76 A4
Percy Dr *ORD* M5 ....84 A2
Percy St *HULME* M15 ....85 C3
  STKP * SK1 ....130 A3
Peregrine Crs *DROY* M43 ....76 B2
Peregrine St *HULME* M15 ....86 A4
Perrygate Av *DID/WITH* M20 ....114 B3
Perrymead *PWCH* M25 ....12 A3
Perth Av *CHAD* OL9 ....38 B1
Perth St *SWIN* M27 ....44 A2
Peru St *SLFD* M3 ....2 A2
Peterborough St *GTN* M18 ....92 A3
Peterhead Wk *ORD* * M5 ....66 B4
Peterloo Ct *SLFD* * M6 ....65 D3
Peter Moss Wy *BNG/LEV* M19 ....105 C3
Peter St *CMANW* M2 ....7 E1
  ECC M30 ....62 A4
  OLD OL1 ....23 C4
  STKP SK1 ....130 B3
Petrel Cl *DROY* M43 ....76 B2
  EDGY/DAV SK3 ....132 A3
Petrock Wk *NEWH/MOS* M40 ....55 D4
Petworth Rd *CHAD* OL9 ....21 C3
Pevensey Rd *SLFD* M6 ....47 D4
Pevensey Wk *CHAD* * OL9 ....12 B2
Peveril Cl *WHTF* M45 ....12 B2
Peveril Rd *ORD* M5 ....65 C3
Pheasant Dr *CCHDY* M21 ....113 C2

Phelan Cl NEWH/MOS M40	52	B4
Philips Dr WHTF M45	10	A3
Philips Park Rd OP/CLY M11	71	D3
WHTF M45	10	B3
Philip St ECC M30	62	A4
Phillips Park Rd WHTF M45	11	D3
Phoebe St ORD M5	83	D1
Phoenix St CMANW * M2	4	A4
OLD OL1	22	B3
Phoenix Wy URM M41	79	D3
Phyllis St MDTN M24	18	B2
Piccadilly CMANE M1	4	B4
STKP SK1	130	A4
Piccadilly Plaza CMANE M1	4	B5
Piccadilly South CMANE M1	8	C1
Piccard Cl ANC M4	5	E1
Pickford's Brow STKP SK1	130	A4
Pickford St ANC M4	5	D3
Pickmere Av DID/WITH M20	115	C1
Pickmere Cl DROY M43	76	A4
Picton Cl CSLFD M3	2	A4
Picton Sq OLDE OL4	23	D3
Picton St CSLFD M3	68	A2
Picton Wk OLDTF/WHR M16	101	C2
Piercy Av BRO M7	68	A1
Piercy St ANC M4	71	C4
FAIL * M35	56	B2
Pigeon St CMANE M1	5	D4
Pike Av FAIL M35	58	B3
Pike Fold La BKLY M9	33	D2
Pilgrim Dr OP/CLY M11	72	A4
Pilkington Rd BKLY M9	35	D3
Pilling St NEWH/MOS M40	54	A4
Pimblett St CSLFD M3	69	C2
Pimlico Cl BRO * M7	50	B3
Pimlott Gv PWCH M25	28	B3
Pine Av WHTF M45	11	C2
Pine Gv ECC M30	62	B1
PWCH M25	11	D3
RUSH/FAL M14	103	D1
SWIN M27	44	A2
Pinehurst Rd NEWH/MOS M40	53	D4
Pine Rd DID/WITH M20	124	B1
Pine St CHAD OL9	20	B1
CMANE M1	4	A5
EDGY/DAV SK3	129	C4
MDTN M24	18	B2
Pinetop Cl CCHDY M21	113	C2
Pine Tree Rd OLDS OL8	40	A4
Pinetree St GTN M18	90	B3
Pinewood CHAD OL9	19	D2
Pinewood Ct SALE M33	110	A4
Pinewood Rd CCHDY * M21	111	D2
Pinfold Av BKLY M9	35	D3
Pinfold La WHTF M45	10	B1
Pingot Av NTHM/RTH M23	122	A3
Pink Bank La WGTN/LGST M12	104	B1
Pin Mill Brow WGTN/LGST M12	88	A1
Pinner Pl BNG/LEV M19	117	D3
Pintail Av EDGY/DAV SK3	132	A3
Pioneer Rd SWIN M27	28	A3
Pioneer St OP/CLY M11	73	C2
Piperhill Av WYTH/NTH M22	123	C4
Pipewell Av GTN M18	90	B3
Pipit Cl DTN/ASHW M34	76	B3
Pitman Cl OP/CLY M11	89	C1
Pitsford Rd NEWH/MOS M40	53	D4
Pit St CHAD OL9	39	C4
Pittbrook St WGTN/LGST M12	88	A2
Pitt St EDGY/DAV SK3	132	A1
OLDE OL4	23	D3
Plainsfield Cl OLDTF/WHR M16	100	C1
Plane Ct SLFD * M6	66	B3
Plane Rd FAIL M35	57	C4
Plantation St GTN M18	91	D4
Plant Cl SALE M33	108	B4
Plant Hill Rd BKLY M9	15	D4
Plant St CMANE * M1	4	C5
Plant Ter BKLY * M9	16	A4
Plate St OLD OL1	23	C2
Plato St CHAD OL9	22	A2
Plattbrook Cl RUSH/FAL M14	102	A4
Platt La RUSH/FAL M14	101	C4
Plattwood Wk HULME * M15	85	C3
Playfair St RUSH/FAL M14	102	A1
Pleachway HTNM SK4	127	C3
Pleasant Rd ECC M30	62	B4
Pleasant St BKLY M9	53	C2
Pleasington Dr NEWH/MOS M40	36	B3
Ploughbank Dr CCHDY M21	113	C2
Plowley Cl DID/WITH M20	125	C5
Plumbley Dr OLDTF/WHR M16	99	D2
Plumbley St OP/CLY * M11	91	D2
Plumley Cl EDGY/DAV SK3	133	C4
Plummer Av CCHDY M21	112	A3
Plumpton Wk BRUN/LGST * M13	104	A1
Plum Tree Ct SLFD M6	66	B5
Plum St OLDS OL8	40	A4
Pluto St SLFD * M6	67	D1
Plymouth Av BRUN/LGST M13	88	B4
Plymouth Gv BRUN/LGST M13	88	A4
Plymouth Gv West BRUN/LGST M13	88	A4
Plymouth Rd OLDS OL8	41	C1
Plymouth Vw BRUN/LGST M13	88	A4
Plymtree Cl CHH M8	31	D3
Pochin St NEWH/MOS M40	71	D2
Poland St ANC M4	5	E2
Polebrook Av WGTN/LGST M12	88	A3
Polefield Ap PWCH M25	12	A3
Polefield Cir PWCH M25	12	A3
Polefield Gdns PWCH M25	12	A3
Polefield Gra PWCH M25	12	A3
Polefield Gv PWCH M25	12	A3
Polefield Hall Rd PWCH M25	12	A3
Polefield Rd BKLY M9	34	A3
PWCH M25	12	A3
Pole La FAIL M35	57	C1
Polesworth Cl WGTN/LGST M12	89	D3
Police St CMANW M2	3	E4
ECC M30	61	D3
Pollard Ct OLD * OL1	22	B1
Pollard St ANC M4	5	F5
Pollard St East NEWH/MOS M40	71	C5
Polletts Av RDSH SK5	121	D3
Pollitt Cl WGTN/LGST * M12	89	C3
Pollitts Cl ECC M30	61	C3
Polonia Ct OLDS OL8	39	D2
Polruan Rd CCHDY M21	98	B3
Polworth Rd BKLY M9	34	B4
The Polygon BRO * M7	49	D3
ECC M30	61	D3
Polygon Av BRUN/LGST M13	87	D3
Polygon Rd CHH M8	32	A4
Polygon St BRUN/LGST M13	9	E4
Pomfret St SLFD * M6	46	B4
WGTN/LGST M12	89	D3
Pomona Crs ORD M5	84	A2
Pomona Strd HULME M15	83	D4
Ponds Cl CCHDY * M21	99	C4
Ponsford Av BKLY M9	35	D3
Ponsonby Rd STRET M32	97	C2
Pontefract Cl SWIN M27	46	A2
Pool Bank St MDTN M24	17	D4
Pool Fold FAIL M35	57	D3
Pool St OLDS OL8	41	C1
Poolton Rd BKLY M9	33	C1
Poorfield St OLDS OL8	22	B4
Poplar Av BNG/LEV M19	118	A2
OLDS OL8	40	A3
Poplar Ct EDGY/DAV * SK3	133	C4
Poplar Dr PWCH M25	29	D3
Poplar Gv GTN M18	106	A1
URM M41	94	B3
Poplar Rd BNG/LEV M19	126	A2

ECC M30 ....62 B1
SWIN M27 ....44 A2
Poplar St *FAIL* M35 ....56 A3
HTNM SK4 ....126 B3
OP/CLY M11 ....88 B1
Poplin Dr *CSLFD* M5 ....21 C1
Poppleton La *PWCH* M25 ....3 D1
Poppy Cl *MDTN* M24 ....19 C2
Poppythorn La *PWCH* M25 ....11 D4
Porchfield Sq *CSLFD* M5 ....7 D1
Porlock Av *DTN/ASHW* M34 ......93 D1
Porter Dr *NEWH/MOS* M40 ....53 C3
Porter St *OLD* M1 ....21 D4
Portland Crs *BRUN/LGST* M13 ...88 A4
Portland Gv *HTNM* SK4 ....128 A1
Portland Rd *BRUN/LGST* M13 ....104 A2
ECC M30 ....63 C2
STRET M32 ....97 D1
SWIN M27 ....45 D2
Portland St *CMANE* M1 ....8 A1
Portman Rd *OLDTF/WHR* M16 ...100 B2
Portrea Cl *EDGY/DAV* SK3 ....132 B4
Portree Cl *ANC* M4 ....61 C3
Portsmouth Cl *BRO* M7 ....50 A4
Portsmouth St *BRUN/LGST* M13 ..87 C3
Port Soderick Av *OLD* M5 ....6 B4
Portstone Cl *OLDTF/WHR* M16 ...100 B1
Portstone Cl *OLDTF/WHR* M16 ...100 B1
Port St *CMANE* M1 ....4 C4
OLDS OL8 ....41 C1
STKP SK1 ....129 D3
Portugal Rd *PWCH* M25 ....30 A3
Portugal St *ANC* M4 ....5 F1
Portugal St East *CMANE* M1 ....9 E1
Portville Rd *BNG/LEV* M19 ....104 B4
Portwood Pl *SWIN* M27 ....130 A3
Postal St *CMANE* * M1 ....4 C4
Postbridge Cl *BRUN/LGST* M13 ..87 D3
Potato Whf *CSLFD* M3 ....6 B2
Potters La *BKLY* M9 ....53 D2
Pottery La *OP/CLY* M11 ....89 D1
Pott St *SWIN* M27 ....26 A3
Poulton St *OP/CLY* M11 ....91 D2
Powell St *OLDTF/WHR* M16 ....99 D1
OP/CLY * M11 ....74 A3
Pownall Av *DID/WITH* M20 ....114 B3
Poynter St *NEWH/MOS* M40 ....36 B4
Poynton St *HULME* M15 ....86 A3
Praed Rd *TRPK* M17 ....81 D4
The Precinct *EDGY/DAV* * SK3 ...132 B2
Premier Rd *CHH* M8 ....69 C1
Premier St *OLDTF/WHR* M16 .....100 A1
Prenton St *OP/CLY* M11 ....91 D1
Prescot Rd *BKLY* M9 ....53 C2
Press St *OP/CLY* M11 ....91 C2
Presswood Ct *SLFD* * M6 ....46 B3
Prestage St *BNG/LEV* M13 ....105 C3
OLDTF/WHR M16 ....100 A1
Prestbury Av *RUSH/FAL* M14 ....101 C4
Prestfield Rd *WHTF* M45 ....11 D1
Preston Av *ECC* M30 ....63 D2
Preston Cl *ECC* * M30 ....63 D2
Preston Rd *BNG/LEV* M19 ....117 D1
Preston St *GTN* M18 ....90 B3
MDTN M24 ....17 D1
OLDE OL4 ....23 D3
Prestwich Hills *PWCH* M25 ....29 D3
Prestwich Park Rd South *PWCH* M25 ...29 D3
Prestwood Rd *SLFD* M6 ....64 B3
Pretoria Rd *OLDS* OL8 ....39 D1
Price St *ANC* * M4 ....71 C4
Prichard St *STRET* M32 ....97 C3
Pridmouth Rd *DID/WITH* M20 ...115 D3
Priestley Rd *WALK* M28 ....43 D1
Priestnall Rd *HTNM* SK4 ....127 C2
Priest St *STKP* SK1 ....133 C1
Primrose Av *URM* * M41 ....94 A3
Primrose Bank *OLDS* OL8 ....22 B4

Primrose Cl *ORD* M5 ....66 A3
Primrose Dr *DROY* M43 ....76 B2
Primrose St *ANC* M4 ....5 D2
OLDS OL8 ....22 B4
Primrose Wk *OLDS* * OL8 ....22 B4
Prince Albert Av *BNG/LEV* * M19 ...104 B3
Princedom St *BKLY* M9 ....53 D1
Prince's Av *DID/WITH* M20 ....125 D1
DID/WITH M20 ....123 C2
HULME M15 ....7 F5
PWCH * M25 ....30 B1
RUSH/FAL M14 ....114 A1
Princess Av *PWCH* M25 ....30 B3
Princess Dr *MDTN* M24 ....16 B1
Princess Pde *RUSH/FAL* M14 ...101 C4
Princess Pkwy *WYTH/NTH* M22 ...122 B4
Princess Rd *OLDS* OL9 ....37 D2
DID/WITH M20 ....123 C2
HULME M15 ....7 F5
PWCH * M25 ....30 B1
RUSH/FAL M14 ....114 A1
Princess St *CMANW* M2 ....3 F5
ECC M30 ....61 D3
FAIL M35 ....56 B2
HULME M15 ....6 A5
NEWH/MOS M40 ....53 D1
OP/CLY M11 ....72 B3
SLFD M6 ....64 B2
SWIN M27 ....45 D2
Prince's Vw *OLD* * OL1 ....23 D4
Prince's St *STKP* SK1 ....129 D4
Princeton Cl *SLFD* M6 ....64 B2
Printer St *OLD* OL1 ....23 C3
OP/CLY * M11 ....91 C1
Printon Av *BKLY* M9 ....33 C1
Printworks La *BNG/LEV* M19 .....105 D3
The Priory *BRO* M7 ....49 D3
Priory Av *BRO* M7 ....49 D3
CCHDY M21 ....112 A1
Priory Cl *OLDS* OL8 ....40 A2
SALE M33 ....110 A3
Priory Ct *RDSH* SK5 ....119 D1
Priory Gv *BRO* M7 ....49 D3
CHAD OL9 ....38 B1
Priory La *RDSH* SK5 ....119 D1
Priory Rd *SALE* M33 ....110 A4
SWIN M27 ....25 D4
Pritchard St *CMANE* * M1 ....8 B2
Propps Hall Dr *FAIL* M35 ....56 A3
Prospect Dr *FAIL* M35 ....57 C4
Prospect Rd *CHAD* OL9 ....21 D2
Prospect Vw *SWIN* M27 ....45 D2
Prout St *WGTN/LGST* M12 ....104 B2
Providence St *ANC* M4 ....71 C4
Provident Av *BNG/LEV* M19 ......105 D4
Provis Rd *CCHDY* M21 ....112 A2
Pryme St *HULME* M15 ....6 C3
Pulford Av *CCHDY* M21 ....123 D1
Pullman Cl *BNG/LEV* M19 ....118 A1
Pullman Dr *STRET* M32 ....95 C3
Purcell St *WGTN/LGST* M12 ......104 B2
Purley Av *NTHM/RTH* M23 ....122 A4
Purslow Cl *WGTN/LGST* M12 .....71 D4
Pym St *ECC* M30 ....62 A3
NEWH/MOS * M40 ....54 A1
Pyramid Cl *BRO* M7 ....50 A3
Pytha Fold Rd *DID/WITH* M20 ...116 A4

Q

The Quadrant *BKLY* M9 ....35 D2
DROY M43 ....75 C4
STKP SK1 ....131 C4
Quantock Cl *HTNM* SK4 ....129 D3
Quantock St *OLDTF/WHR* * M16 ...100 B1
Quarmby Rd *GTN* M18 ....107 C1
Quarry Wk *OP/CLY* * M11 ....72 A4
The Quays *SALQ* M50 ....83 C2

Quay St *CSLFD* M3 ....2 C5
Quay Vw *ORD* M5 ....83 D1
Quebec St *CHAD* OL9 ....21 D1
Queen Alexandra Cl *ORD* * M5 ....84 B1
Queenhill Rd *WYTH/NTH* M22 ....123 D4
Queensbury Pde *NEWH/MOS* * M40 ....71 D2
Queens Cl *HTNM* SK4 ....127 D3
Queens Ct *NEWH/MOS* M40 ....53 C4
Queens Dr *GTN* SK4 ....127 D3
  PWCH M25 ....30 B3
Queensferry St *NEWH/MOS* M40 ....55 D3
Queen's Gv *WGTN/LGST* M12 ....104 B1
Queensland Rd *URM* M18 ....90 A4
Queens Rd *CHAD* OL9 ....20 D3
  CHH M8 ....52 A4
  NEWH/MOS M40 ....53 C4
  OLDS OL8 ....23 D4
  URM M41 ....94 A4
Queenston Rd *DID/WITH* M20 ....124 A1
Queen St *CMANW* M2 ....3 E5
  CSLFD M3 ....3 D2
  ECC * M50 ....63 C4
  FAIL M35 ....56 B2
  MDTN M24 ....18 B1
  OLD OL1 ....23 C2
  SLFD M6 ....47 C4
  STKP SK1 ....130 B3
Queen St West *DID/WITH* M20 ....115 C2
Queensway *BNG/LEV* M19 ....126 A3
  SWIN M27 ....26 B3
  URM M41 ....94 B1
Queen Victoria St *ECC* M30 ....61 D3
Quenby St *HULME* M15 ....6 B5
Quendon Av *BRO* M7 ....68 B1
Quilter Gv *BKLY* M9 ....33 C3
Quinney Crs *OLDTF/WHR* M16 ....101 C2
Quinn St *OP/CLY* M11 ....72 B3
Quinton Wk *BRUN/LGST* M13 ....9 D1
Quixall St *OP/CLY* M11 ....72 B3

R

Raby St *OLDTF/WHR* M16 ....100 B1
Rachel St *WGTN/LGST* M12 ....9 F3
Rackhouse Rd *NTHM/RTH* M23 ....122 A4
Radbourne Cl *WGTN/LGST* M12 ....89 D3
Radcliffe Park Crs *SLFD* M6 ....46 A4
Radcliffe Park Rd *SLFD* M6 ....46 A4
Radcliffe St *OLD* OL1 ....22 B2
Radclyffe St *CHAD* OL9 ....21 C1
Radford Dr *BKLY* M9 ....53 D1
Radford St *BRO* M7 ....49 D1
Radium St *ANC* M4 ....5 D2
Radlett Wk *BRUN/LGST* * M13 ....87 D4
Radley St *DROY* M43 ....91 D1
  OLDTF/WHR M16 ....101 C3
Radnor St *CHAD* OL9 ....21 D4
  GTN M18 ....105 D3
  HULME M15 ....86 A4
  STRET M32 ....97 C3
Radstock Cl *RUSH/FAL* M14 ....102 A4
Radstock Rd *STRET* M32 ....96 C3
Raglan Av *SWIN* M27 ....27 C3
  WHTF M45 ....12 A1
Raglan Rd *STRET* M32 ....96 A2
Raglan Wk *HULME* * M15 ....86 A3
Rail Pl *HULME* * M15 ....86 B3
Railton Av *OLDTF/WHR* M16 ....100 B1
Railton Ter *BKLY* * M9 ....54 A2
Railway Rd *CHAD* OL9 ....22 A3
  CHAD OL9 ....38 B3
  EDGY/DAV SK3 ....132 B2
  STRET M32 ....83 C2
  URM M41 ....94 A3
Railway St *GTN* M18 ....90 B3
  HTNM SK4 ....129 C3
Rainbow Cl *CCHDY* M21 ....112 A1
Raincliff Av *BRUN/LGST* M13 ....104 A3
Rainford Av *DID/WITH* M20 ....114 B2
Rainforth St *BRUN/LGST* M13 ....104 A2
Rainham Dr *CHH* M8 ....51 D2
Rainham Wy *CHAD* OL9 ....21 C3
  RDSH SK5 ....121 C3
Rainow Av *DROY* M43 ....91 D1
Rainsough Av *PWCH* M25 ....29 C4
Rainsough Brow *PWCH* M25 ....29 C4
Rainsough Cl *PWCH* M25 ....29 D4
Rainwood *CHAD* OL9 ....19 D1
Raja Cl *CHH* M8 ....52 A2
Rake La *SWIN* M27 ....26 A2
Raleigh Cl *DID/WITH* M20 ....114 B4
  OLD OL1 ....23 C1
Raleigh St *RDSH* SK5 ....129 D1
  STRET M32 ....97 C3
Ralli Cts *CSLFD* M3 ....3 C5
Ralph Green St *CHAD* OL9 ....39 C2
Ralph St *OP/CLY* M11 ....74 A4
Ralston Cl *BRO* M7 ....51 C1
Ralstone Av *OLDS* OL8 ....41 C1
Ramage Wk *WGTN/LGST* M12 ....74 A1
Ramsbury Dr *NEWH/MOS* M40 ....37 C3
Ramsdale St *CHAD* OL9 ....20 B2
Ramsden Cl *OLD* OL1 ....22 B2
Ramsden Crs *OLD* OL1 ....22 B2
Ramsden St *OLD* OL1 ....22 B2
Ramsey Av *BNG/LEV* M19 ....106 A4
Ramsey Cl *CHAD* OL9 ....21 C4
  NEWH/MOS M40 ....73 D1
Ramsgate Rd *NEWH/MOS* M40 ....73 D1
  RDSH SK5 ....120 A2
Ramsgate St *BRO* M7 ....50 B4
Ranby Av *BKLY* M9 ....35 C1
Randerson St *WGTN/LGST* * M12 ....9 E3
Ransfield Rd *CCHDY* M21 ....98 B3
Ranulph Ct *SLFD* * M6 ....47 C4
Ranworth Av *HTNM* SK4 ....127 C3
Ratcliffe St *BNG/LEV* M19 ....105 C4
  STKP * SK1 ....133 C1
Rathbourne Av *BKLY* M9 ....34 A2
Rathen Rd *DID/WITH* M20 ....115 C4
Rathmore Av *NEWH/MOS* M40 ....53 D4
Rattenbury Ct *SLFD* M6 ....46 B4
Raveley Av *RUSH/FAL* M14 ....116 A1
Ravelston Dr *BKLY* M9 ....53 C3
Raven Av *CHAD* OL9 ....20 B4
Raven Cl *DROY* M43 ....76 B2
Ravenhead Cl *RUSH/FAL* M14 ....116 A1
Ravenoak Av *BNG/LEV* M19 ....118 A1
Ravenoak Dr *FAIL* M35 ....57 D1
Ravensbury St *OP/CLY* M11 ....73 C3
Ravens Cl *PWCH* M25 ....29 D3
Ravensdale Gdns *ECC* M30 ....62 B2
Ravensdale St *RUSH/FAL* M14 ....102 B2
Ravenside Pk *CHAD* OL9 ....20 B4
Ravenstone Dr *SALE* M33 ....110 B4
Raven St *WGTN/LGST* M12 ....9 F2
Ravensway *PWCH* M25 ....31 C3
Ravenswood Av *HTNM* SK4 ....127 D4
Ravenswood Dr *BKLY* M9 ....34 B2
Ravenswood Rd *STRET* M32 ....83 C4
Raven Wy *SLFD* M6 ....66 A2
Ravenwood *CHAD* OL9 ....19 C2
Ravine Av *BKLY* M9 ....53 D2
Rawcliffe St *RUSH/FAL* M14 ....102 A2

Rawdon Cl *BNG/LEV* M19	105	C4
Rawkin Cl *HULME* M15	85	D4
Rayburn Wy *CHH* M8	51	D4
Raycroft Av *BKLY* M9	35	D3
Raydon Av *NEWH/MOS* * M40	53	C4
Rayleigh Av *OP/CLY* M11	92	A2
Raymond Av *OLD9*	39	C1
Raymond Rd *NTHM/RTH* M23	122	A3
Raymond St *SWIN* N/27	46	A4
Rayner La *AULW* OL7	77	D3
Raynham Av *DID/WITH* M20	125	C2
Rayson Hill Dr *BKLY* * M9	33	D3
Rayson St *BKLY* M9	33	D3
Reabrook Av *WGTN/LGST* M12	89	C3
Reading Cl *OP/CLY* M11	90	B1
Reading St *SLFD* M6	49	C4
Readitt Wk *OP/CLY* M11	73	C3
Reaney Wk *WGTN/LGST* * M12	89	D3
Reather Wk *NEWH/MOS* M40	70	B2
Rebecca St *CHH* M8	51	D4
Recreation Rd *FAIL* M35	38	B4
Recreation St *PWCH* M25	30	B1
Rectory Av *CHH* M8	32	B4
Rectory Cl *CHH* M8	32	B4
PWCH M25	30	A1
Rectory Flds *STKP* SK1	130	B4
Rectory Gdns *PWCH* M25	30	A1
Rectory Gn *PWCH* M25	29	D1
STKP SK1	130	B4
Rectory Gv *PWCH* M25	30	A2
Rectory La *PWCH* M25	29	D1
Rectory Rd *CHH* M8	32	A4
Redacre Rd *GTN* M18	91	D4
Red Bank *ANC* M4	69	D2
Redbrook Av *NEWH/MOS* M40	53	D4
Redby St *OP/CLY* * M11	90	B2
Redcar Av *DID/WITH* M20	115	C3
Redcar Rd *SWIN* M27	46	B2
Redclyffe Av *RUSH/FAL* M14	102	B2
Redclyffe Rd *DID/WITH* M20	114	B4
URM M41	79	C1
Redcote St *NEWH/MOS* M40	54	B1
Redcourt Av *DID/WITH* M20	125	C1
Redcroft Gdns *BNG/LEV* M19	126	B1
Reddaway Cl *SLFD* M6	48	B4
Reddish La *GTN* M18	106	B2
Reddish Rd *RDSH* SK5	120	A3
Reddish Vale Rd *RDSH* SK5	120	B2
Redesmere Cl *DROY* M43	76	A4
Redfern St *ANC* M4	4	A2
Redfield Cl *OP/CLY* M11	72	A4
Redford Rd *CHH* M8	32	A1
Redgate La *WGTN/LGST* M12	89	D4
Redgates Wk *CCHDY* * M21	99	C4
Redhill St *ANC* M4	5	D4
Redland Av *RDSH* SK5	120	A4
Redland Crs *CCHDY* M21	112	A3
Red Lion St *ANC* * M4	4	B3
Redmere Gv *RUSH/FAL* M14	115	D1
Redmoor Sq *CMANE* * M1	9	C3
Red Pike Wk *OLD* OL1	23	D1
Red Rose Crs *BNG/LEV* M19	118	B2
Redruth St *RUSH/FAL* M14	102	A3
Redshaw Cl *RUSH/FAL* M14	103	C4
Redstone Rd *BNG/LEV* M19	126	A2
Redthorn Av *BNG/LEV* M19	117	C2
Redvale Rd *BRO* M7	50	B3
Redvers St *OLD* OL1	22	A1
OP/CLY M11	88	B1
Redwood *CHAD* OL9	19	C2
Redwood Dr *CHH* M8	52	A4
Redwood St *SLFD* M6	66	B1
Reed Ct *OLD* * OL1	22	B1
Reedham Wk *CHAD* * OL9	39	D1
NEWH/ M40	71	C1
Reedshaw Rd *BKLY* M9	52	B3
Reed St *GTN* M18	91	C3
Reeves Rd *CCHDY* M21	112	A2
Reform Wk *OP/CLY* M11	90	A1
Regal Cl *WHTF* M45	12	A1
Regan Av *CCHDY* M21	113	C2
Regatta Cl *CHAD* OL9	38	B2
Regatta St *SLFD* M6	48	A3
Regency Cl *NEWH/MOS* M40	53	C2
OLDS OL8	40	A1
Regency Ldg *PWCH* * M25	29	D2
Regent Av *RUSH/FAL* M14	101	C3
Regent Ct *HTNM* SK4	118	B4
Regent Crs *FAIL* M35	56	B3
Regent Pl *RUSH/FAL* M14	102	B3
Regent Rd *OFTN* SK2	133	D3
ORD M5	84	A1
Regents Pk *ORD* * M5	84	B1
Regent Sq *ORD* M5	84	A1
Regent St *ECC* M30	63	D3
NEWH/MOS M40	56	A4
OLD OL1	23	D2
Reginald St *OP/CLY* M11	92	A2
SWIN M27	25	C4
Reilly St *HULME* M15	7	E5
Reins Lee Av *OLDS* OL8	41	D3
Reliance St *NEWH/MOS* M40	55	D3
Rena Cl *HTNM* M32	129	C2
Rendel Cl *STRET* M32	97	C3
Rennie Cl *STRET* M32	97	C3
Renshaw Av *ECC* M30	62	A4
Renshaw St *ECC* M30	62	A4
Renton Rd *STRET* M32	97	D3
Repton Av *DROY* M43	74	A2
DTN/ASHW M34	107	D2
NEWH/MOS M40	37	D2
OLDS OL8	40	A2
Reservoir Rd *EDGY/DAV* SK3	132	A2
Reservoir St *CSLFD* M3	3	D1
SLFD M6	66	A3
Retiro St *OLD* OL1	23	C2
Reuben St *HTNM* SK4	129	D1
Reynard Rd *CCHDY* M21	112	A2
Reynell Rd *BRUN/LGST* M13	104	A3
Reyner St *CMANE* M1	8	A1
Reynolds Dr *GTN* M18	91	C3
Reynolds Rd *OLDTF/WHR* M16	99	D1
Rhine Dr *CHH* M8	50	B4
Rhodes Bank *OLD* OL1	23	C3
Rhodes St *NEWH/MOS* M40	71	D1
OLD OL1	23	D2
Rhos Av *MDTN* M24	17	D2
RUSH/FAL M14	116	B1
Rialto Gdns *BRO* * M7	50	B3
Ribble Dr *OLDS* OL8	39	D2
Ribblesdale Dr *NEWH/MOS* M40	52	B4
Ribchester Wk *HULME* M15	7	F5
Ribston St *HULME* M15	85	D5
Rice St *CSLFD* M3	6	C2
Richardson Rd *ECC* M30	62	B3
Richardson St *OP/CLY* M11	91	D2
STKP SK1	133	D2
Richard St *FAIL* M35	57	C2
STKP SK1	130	A3
Richborough Cl *BRO* M7	50	B4
Richmond Av *CHAD* OL9	38	B1
PWCH M25	30	B4
URM M41	94	B3
Richmond Cl *WHTF* M45	10	A2
Richmond Dr *WALK* M28	43	D1
Richmond Gv *BRUN/LGST* M13	103	C1
Richmond Gv East *WGTN/LGST* M12	88	B4
Richmond Rd *DTN/ASHW* * M34	107	D2
FAIL M35	57	D1
HTNM SK4	127	C3
RUSH/FAL M14	116	A1
TRPK M17	80	B2
Richmond St *CMANE* M1	8	B1
CSLFD M3	2	C1
DROY * M43	76	B3
Richmond Wk *CHAD* OL9	22	A3
Ridge Crs *WHTF* M45	12	A1

Ridgefield *CMANW* M2 ....3 E5
Ridgefield St *FAIL* M35 ....56 A2
Ridge Gv *WHTF* M45 ....12 A1
Ridgemont Av *HTNM* SK4 ....128 A3
Ridgeway *SWIN* M27 ....27 C4
Ridgeway St *NEWH/MOS* M40 ....71 C3
Ridgewood *CHAD* OL9 ....19 D1
Ridgewood Av *NEWH/MOS* M40 ....53 D4
Riding Fold *DROY* M43 ....77 C2
Riding Fold La *WALK* M28 ....42 B4
Ridings St *NEWH/MOS* M40 ....54 A4
   OP/CLY M11 ....90 A1
Riding St *CSLFD* M5 ....2 C4
Ridings Wy *CHAD* OL9 ....21 D3
Ridley Cl *OLDE* * OL4 ....23 D3
Ridley Wk *HULME* * M15 ....86 A4
Ridsdale Av *DID/WITH* M20 ....115 C3
Rifle Rd *SALE* M33 ....111 C4
Rifle St *OLD* OL1 ....23 C1
Riga Rd *RUSH/FAL* M14 ....102 B4
Riga St *ANC* M4 ....4 B2
Rigby St *BRO* M7 ....50 A1
Rigel Pl *BRO* M7 ....67 D2
Rigel St *ANC* M4 ....5 F1
Rigton Cl *WGTN/LGST* M12 ....89 D4
Rimmer Cl *OP/CLY* M11 ....88 B4
Rimmington Cl *BKLY* M9 ....35 D3
Rimworth Dr *NEWH/MOS* M40 ....70 B3
Ringcroft Gdns *NEWH/MOS* M40 ....36 A4
Ringley Cha *WHTF* M45 ....10 B1
Ringley Cl *WHTF* M45 ....10 A1
Ringley Dr *WHTF* M45 ....10 A1
Ringley Hey *WHTF* M45 ....10 A1
Ringley Pk *WHTF* M45 ....10 A1
Ringley St *BKLY* * M9 ....53 C1
Ringlow Av *SWIN* M27 ....43 D2
Ringlow Park Rd *SWIN* M27 ....43 D3
Ringmere Ct *OLD* * OL1 ....22 B4
Rings Cl *FAIL* M35 ....57 C3
Ringstead Dr *NEWH/MOS* M40 ....70 B2
Ringstone *PWCH* M25 ....29 D2
Ringwood Av *DTN/ASHW* M34 ....76 B4
   WGTN/LGST M12 ....105 C3
Ringwood Wy *CHAD* * OL9 ....21 D3
Rink St *RUSH/FAL* M14 ....116 A2
Ripley Cl *ANC* * M4 ....88 A1
Ripon Cl *CHAD* OL9 ....21 C3
   STKP * SK1 ....133 D3
Ripon Crs *STRET* M32 ....95 C2
Ripon Gv *SALE* M33 ....108 A3
Ripon Rd *STRET* M32 ....95 C2
Ripon St *OLD* OL1 ....22 A1
Rippenden Av *CCHDY* M21 ....98 B3
Rippingham Rd *DID/WITH* M20 ....115 C3
Rishworth Dr *NEWH/MOS* M40 ....56 B1
Rising La *OLDS* OL8 ....40 B3
Risley Av *BKLY* M9 ....53 C1
Risley St *OLD* OL1 ....23 C1
Rita Av *RUSH/FAL* * M14 ....102 A2
Ritson Ct *DTN* M18 ....90 A1
Riva Rd *BNG/LEV* M19 ....126 A3
Riverdale Rd *BKLY* M9 ....32 B2
Rivermead Wy *WHTF* M45 ....11 D1
Riverpark Rd *NEWH/MOS* M40 ....72 B2
River Pl *HULME* M15 ....7 D3
Riversdale Dr *OLDS* OL8 ....41 D4
Rivershill *SALE* M33 ....108 A3
Riverside *BRO* M7 ....67 D2
Riverside Gdns *SALE* M33 ....108 B3
Rivers La *URM* M41 ....78 B4
River St *HULME* M15 ....7 E4
   STKP SK1 ....131 C2
   WGTN/LGST M12 ....9 F2
River Vw *RDSH* SK5 ....120 B2
River View Cl *PWCH* M25 ....29 C3
Rivington Av *SWIN* M27 ....46 B2
Rivington Gv *DTN/ASHW* M34 ....93 D1

Rivington Rd *SLFD* M6 ....64 B1
Rivington Wk *WGTN/LGST* * M12 ....88 B4
Roachwood Cl *CHAD* OL9 ....19 D2
Robert Hall St *ORD* M5 ....84 A1
Robert Malcolm Cl *NEWH/MOS* M40 ...53 C4
Robertshaw Av *CCHDY* M21 ....112 A3
Roberts St *ECC* M30 ....62 A4
Robert St *CSLFD* M3 ....69 C2
   FAIL M35 ....38 B2
   NEWH/MOS M40 ....54 A4
   PWCH M25 ....30 B2
Robin Hood St *CHH* M8 ....51 C1
Robins Cl *DROY* M43 ....76 B2
Robinson St *CHAD* OL9 ....21 C3
   EDGY/DAV SK3 ....132 A2
   OLDS OL8 ....41 C2
Robin St *OLD* * OL1 ....22 B1
Robson Av *URM* M41 ....79 D2
Robson St *OLD* OL1 ....23 C3
Roby Rd *ECC* M30 ....78 B1
Roby St *CMANE* M1 ....9 F5
Rochdale Rd *ANC* M4 ....4 C5
   BKLY M9 ....34 A2
Rochester Av *CCHDY* M21 ....113 C3
   PWCH M25 ....30 B3
Rochester Rd *URM* M41 ....94 A1
Rochester Wy *CHAD* OL9 ....21 C3
Rochford Av *WHTF* M45 ....10 A2
Rockall Wk *OP/CLY* * M11 ....72 A4
Rock Bank *BRO* * M7 ....49 D3
Rockdove Av *HULME* M15 ....7 E4
Rocket St *CSLFD* M3 ....2 B4
Rockfield Dr *BKLY* * M9 ....53 D1
Rockhampton St *GTN* M18 ....91 D4
Rockhouse Cl *ECC* M30 ....79 C1
Rockingham Cl *WGTN/LGST* M12 ....88 A3
Rockley Gdns *SLFD* M6 ....67 C1
Rocklyn Av *NEWH/MOS* M40 ....36 B3
Rockmead Dr *BKLY* M9 ....34 B2
Rock Rd *URM* M41 ....95 C3
Rock St *BRO* M7 ....50 A3
   OLD OL1 ....23 C2
   OP/CLY M11 ....91 D2
Rocky La *ECC* M30 ....62 A1
Roda St *BKLY* M9 ....53 A2
Rodenhurst Dr *NEWH/MOS* M40 ....54 B3
Rodmell Av *NEWH/MOS* * M40 ....53 C4
Rodmill Ct *RUSH/FAL* M14 ....102 B3
Rodney Ct *ANC* M4 ....5 E1
Rodney St *ANC* M4 ....5 F2
   CSLFD M3 ....2 A4
Roe Gn *WALK* M28 ....42 B1
Roe Green Av *WALK* M28 ....42 B1
Roe St *ANC* M4 ....5 E1
Roger St *ANC* M4 ....69 D2
Rokeby Av *STRET* M32 ....97 C4
Roker Av *BRUN/LGST* M13 ....104 A3
Roland Rd *RDSH* SK5 ....120 A2
Rolla St *CSLFD* M3 ....3 D2
Rolleston Av *NEWH/MOS* M40 ....71 C3
Rolls Crs *HULME* M15 ....86 A3
Rollswood Dr *FAIL* M35 ....57 D1
Roman Rd *FAIL* M35 ....57 D1
   HTNM SK4 ....129 D1
   OLDS OL8 ....39 C4
   PWCH M25 ....29 C4
Romer Av *NEWH/MOS* * M40 ....37 C4
Rome Rd *NEWH/MOS* M40 ....5 E1
Romford Cl *OLDS* OL8 ....22 B4
Romiley St *SLFD* M6 ....47 C2
   STKP SK1 ....131 C3
Romley Rd *URM* M41 ....94 A1
Romney St *NEWH/MOS* M40 ....54 B1
   SLFD M6 ....48 B4
Romney Wk *CHAD* OL9 ....21 C3
Romney Wy *RDSH* SK5 ....121 C3
Romsley Cl *WGTN/LGST* M12 ....89 D3
Ronaldsay Gdns *ORD* M5 ....65 D4

Ronald St *OP/CLY* M11 ....74 A4
Rondin Cl *WGTN/LGST* M12 ....88 B2
Rondin Rd *WGTN/LGST* M12 ....88 B2
Rookery Av *GTN* M18 ....92 A3
Rookfield Av *SALE* M33 ....109 D4
Rookley Wk *RUSH/FAL * M14 ....102 B2
Rook St *HULME* M15 ....85 D4
Rookway *MDTN* M24 ....17 C2
Rooth St *HTNM* SK4 ....129 C3
Rope Wk *CSLFD* M3 ....3 D1
Rosa Gv *BRO* M7 ....50 A3
Rosamond Dr *CSLFD* M3 ....2 B1
Rosamond St *HULME* M15 ....8 A5
Rosamond St West *HULME* M15 ....8 A5
Rosary Cl *OLDS* OL8 ....41 C4
Rosary Rd *OLDS* OL8 ....41 D4
Roscoe St *EDGY/DAV* SK3 ....132 A1
      OLD OL1 ....23 D3
Rosebank Rd *NEWH/MOS* M40 ....73 C1
Roseberry St *OLDS* OL8 ....22 A3
Rosebery St *RUSH/FAL* M14 ....101 C2
Rose Cottage Rd *DID/WITH* M20 ....115 C3
Rosedale Rd *HTNM* SK4..........................119 C4
      RUSH/FAL M14 ....101 D3
Rosefield Cl *EDGY/DAV* SK3 ....132 B4
Rosegarth Rd *DID/WITH* M20 ....123 C3
Rose Hey La *FAIL* M35 ....74 B1
Rose Hill Av *NEWH/ * MOS * M40 ....73 C5
Rosehill Cl *SLFD* M6 ....66 A3
Rosehill Rd *SWIN* M27 ....26 A3
Roseland Av *DID/WITH* M20 ....125 C1
Roseland Dr *PWCH* M25 ....12 B3
Rosemary Gv *BRO* M7 ....49 D4
Rosemary La *STKP* SK1 ....130 B4
Rosemary Rd *CHAD* OL9 ....9 D4
Roseneath Av *BNG/LEV* M19 ....105 C4
Rosen Sq *CHAD * OL9 ....21 C2
Rose St *CHAD* OL9 ....38 B2
      MDTN M24 ....18 B1
      RDSH SK5 ....130 A2
Rosevale Av *BNG/LEV* M19 ....116 B3
Rosewell Cl *NEWH/MOS* M40 ....71 C1
Rosewood Av *DROY* M43 ....76 A3
      HTNM SK4 ....127 D4
Rosford Av *RUSH/FAL* M14 ....102 A3
Rosgill Cl *HTNM* SK4 ....126 B3
Rosina St *OP/CLY* M11 ....92 A2
Roslin St *OP/CLY* M11 ....74 A3
Roslyn Rd *EDGY/DAV* SK3 ....132 A3
Rossall Av *STRET* M32 ....96 B2
Rossall Wy *SLFD* M6 ....66 B2
Ross Av *CHAD* OL9 ....38 A2
      EDGY/DAV SK3 ....132 B4
      WHTF M45 ....11 C3
Ross Dr *SWIN* M27 ....25 D1
Rossendale Av *BKLY* M9 ....35 C4
Rosshill Wk *HULME* M15 ....6 B5
Rossington St *NEWH/MOS* M40................56 A4
Ross Lave La *DTN/ASHW* M34 ....121 D1
Rosslyn Rd *NEWH/MOS* M40 ....35 D4
      OLDTF/WHR M16 ....98 B3
Ross St *OLDS* OL8 ....22 A4
Rostherne Av *RUSH/FAL* M14..................101 C4
      EDGY/DAV SK3 ....132 B4
Rostherne St *SLFD* M6 ....66 B2
Roston Rd *BRO* M7 ....50 B1
Rostrevor Rd *EDGY/DAV* SK3 ....132 B4
Rostron Av *WGTN/LGST* M12 ....88 B3
Rostron St *BNG/LEV* M19 ....105 C4
Rothay Dr *RDSH* SK5 ....120 A1
Rothbury Av *AULW* OL7 ....59 D4
Rotherwood Av *STRET* M32 ....97 D2
Rothesay Rd *CHH* M8 ....31 D3
Rothman Cl *FAIL* M35 ....55 D3
Rothwell St *NEWH/MOS* M40 ....55 D3
Roughlea Av *SWIN* M27 ....44 B3
Round Thorn Rd *MDTN* M24 ....18 A2
Rousdon Cl *NEWH/MOS * M40 ....53 C4

Rowan Av *OLDTF/WHR* M16 ....100 A2
      URM M41 ....94 A2
Rowan Cl *FAIL* M35 ....57 C4
Rowanlea *PWCH * M25 ....30 B1
Rowan Pl *PWCH* M25 ....30 A2
Rowan Tree Rd *OLB* OL8 ....40 A4
Rowanwood *CHAD* OL9 ....19 D2
Rowany Cl *PWCH* M25 ....29 D3
Rowendale St *CMANE * M1 ....7 E2
Rowland Av *URM* M41 ....94 A3
Rowland St *ORD* M5 ....83 D1
Rowood Av *CHH* M8 ....52 A3
      RDSH SK5 ....107 C3
Rowsley Av *DID/WITH* M20 ....123 D1
Rowsley Gv *RDSH* SK5 ....119 D2
Rowsley Rd *ECC* M30 ....78 B1
      STRET M32 ....95 D2
Rowsley St *OP/CLY* M11 ....71 D3
      SLFD M6 ....49 C4
Roxburgh St *GTN* M18 ....91 C4
Roxton Rd *HTNM* SK4 ....118 B3
Royal Av *CCHDY* M21 ....111 D2
      DROY M43 ....76 A3
      URM M41 ....94 A3
Royal Ex *CMANW* M2 ....3 F4
Royal Exchange Ar *CMANW* M2 ....3 F4
Royal George St *EDGY/DAV* SK3 ....132 B1
Royal Oak Yd *STKP * SK1 ....130 A4
Royce Rd *HULME* M15 ....6 C5
Roydale St *NEWH/MOS* M40 ....71 D2
Royden Av *BKLY* M9 ....16 A4
Royds Cl *BRUN/LGST* M13 ....88 A4
Royd St *OLDS* OL8 ....39 D1
Royle Cl *OFTN* SK2 ....133 D4
      OLDS OL8 ....41 C2
Royle St *ORD * M5 ....66 A4
      RUSH/FAL M14 ....116 A2
      STKP SK1 ....133 C2
Royley Rd *OLDS* OL8 ....40 B1
Royston Av *DTN/ASHW* M34 ....107 C4
      OLDTF/WHR M16 ....100 A2
Royston Rd *OLDTF/WHR* M16 ....99 C2
      URM M41 ....94 B2
Rozel Sq *CSLFD* M3 ....7 D1
Ruabon Rd *DID/WITH* M20 ....125 D3
Ruby St *HULME* M15 ....86 B3
Rudcroft Cl *BRUN/LGST* M13 ....9 D5
Rudd St *NEWH/MOS* M40 ....54 B2
Rudston Av *NEWH/MOS* M40 ....36 A3
Rudheath Av *DID/WITH* M20 ....114 B2
Rudman Dr *ORD* M5 ....84 B1
Rudyard Gv *HTNM* SK4 ....119 C3
Rudyard Rd *SLFD* M6 ....66 A3
Rudyard St *BRO* M7 ....50 A3
Rufford Pl *GTN * M18 ....107 C1
Rufford Rd *OLDTF/WHR* M16 ....100 A1
Rufus St *RUSH/FAL* M14 ....116 B2
Rugby Rd *SLFD* M6 ....63 D2
Rugby St *BRO* M7 ....68 B1
Rugeley St *SLFD* M6 ....49 C4
Ruislip Av *NEWH/MOS* M40 ....53 D4
Runcorn St *HULME* M15 ....84 B1
Runhall Cl *WGTN/LGST* M12 ....89 D3
Runnymeade *SLFD* M6 ....45 D5
Rupert St *NEWH/MOS* M40 ....74 B1
      RDSH SK5 ....119 D2
Rushbrooke Av *OP/CLY* M11 ....73 D2
Rushden Rd *BNG/LEV* M19 ....104 B3
Rushen St *OP/CLY* M11 ....73 D4
Rushfield Dr *BRUN/LGST* M13 ....103 D2
Rushford Av *BNG/LEV* M19 ....104 B3
Rushford St *WGTN/LGST* M12 ....104 B1
Rushley Av *BRO* M7 ....49 C2
Rushmere Av *BNG/LEV* M19 ....105 C4
Rushmere Wk *OLDTF/WHR* M16 ....85 C4
Rusholme Gv *RUSH/FAL* M14 ....102 B2
Rusholme Pl *RUSH/FAL* M14 ....102 B1

Rushton Gv OP/CLY M11.....................91 D2
Rushton St DID/WITH M20.................125 C3
Rushwick Av NEWH/MOS M40..............53 D3
Rushworth St HTNM SK4..................118 B4
Ruskin Av CHAD OL9.........................38 A2
　DTN/ASHW M34............................93 D2
　RUSH/FAL M14.............................102 A1
Ruskin Crs PWCH M25.......................29 C2
Ruskingtion Dr BKLY M9.....................9 D3
Ruskin Rd DROY M43.........................75 D3
　OLDTF/WHR M16...........................99 D2
　PWCH M25....................................28 B2
　RDSH SK5.....................................106 B4
Ruskin St CHAD OL9.........................22 A1
Russell Av OLDTF/WHR M16...............100 A3
　SALE M33.....................................110 A4
Russell Gdns SK4............................128 A4
Russell Rd OLDTF/WHR M16...............100 A3
　SLFD M6.......................................46 A4
Russell St CHAD * OL9......................21 C3
　CHH M8...69 C1
　ECC M30.......................................62 B3
　OFTN SK2.....................................133 D3
　OLDTF/WHR M16...........................101 C2
　PWCH M25....................................30 B1
Russet Rd BKLY M9..........................34 A4
Ruth Av NEWH/MOS M40....................37 D4
Ruthen La OLDTF/WHR M16.................99 D1
Rutherford Av RUSH/FAL M14............102 A2
Rutherglade CI NEWH/MOS M40...........52 B3
Rutherglen Wk NEWH/MOS M40...........53 D4
Ruthin Av BKLY M9...........................15 D4
　MDTN M24....................................17 D3
Ruthin CI OLDS OL8..........................39 C3
Ruth St GTN M18.............................106 A2
　OLD OL1.......................................23 C1
Rutland Av DID/WITH M20.................114 B4
　OLDTF/WHR M16.............................98 B2
　SWIN M27.....................................26 A3
　URM M41.......................................94 B3
Rutland Dr BRO M7...........................49 D1
Rutland La SALE M33.......................111 C4
Rutland Rd DROY M43.......................74 B3
　ECC M30.......................................63 C2
Rutland St CHAD OL9.......................21 D4
　FAIL * M35...................................57 C1
　GTN M18.......................................91 D3
　SWIN M27.....................................25 D4
Ryall Av SWIN M27...........................45 C3
Ryall Av WHTF M45...........................11 C1
Rydal Rd STRET M32.........................97 C2
Ryde Av HTNM SK4..........................128 A3
Ryder Av DROY M43.........................74 B4
　ECC M30.......................................61 C1
　MDTN M24....................................17 C3
　SALE M33.....................................108 A4
Rydal Av DROY M43.........................74 B4
Ryder Brow GTN M18.......................106 A1
Ryderbrow Rd GTN M18....................106 A1
Ryder St NEWH/MOS M40...................71 C1
Ryebank Ms CCHDY * M21.................98 A4
Ryebank Rd CCHDY M21....................98 A4
Rye Bank Rd OLDTF/WHR M16............98 B3
Rye Croft SLFD M6...........................64 B2
Ryecroft CI OLD OL9.........................38 A2
Ryecroft La WALK M28.......................60 A1
Ryecroft Rd STRET M32.....................96 B4
Ryecroft Vw DTN/ASHW M34..............93 D1
Ryedale Av NEWH/MOS M40...............53 C4
Ryedale CI HTNM SK4......................128 A1
Rylance St OP/CLY M11.....................71 D4
Rylands St GTN * M18.......................91 D3
Rylane Wk NEWH/MOS M40................53 C4
Rylstone Av CCHDY M21...................123 D2
Ryther Gv BKLY M9...........................15 C4
Ryton Av GTN M18...........................105 D2

S

Sabden CI NEWH/MOS M40..................71 D2
Sabrina St CHH M8............................50 B4
Sackville St CMANE M1........................8 A1
　CSLFD M5..2 C3
Saddlecote WALK * M28.....................60 B1
Saddle Gv DROY M43.........................77 C2
Saddlewood Av BNG/LEV M19.............126 A3
Sadie Av STRET M32..........................95 D1
Sadler Ct HULME M15.........................85 C4
Sagar St CHH M8...............................69 C1
St Agnes Rd BRUN/LGST M13............104 A3
St Agnes St RDSH SK5.....................107 C2
St Aidan's Gv BRO M7........................49 C3
St Alban's Av HTNM SK4...................118 B4
　NEWH/MOS M40..............................55 C4
St Albans CI OLDS OL8......................41 C1
St Alban's Ter CHH M8........................51 C4
St Aldwyn's Rd DID/WITH M20...........115 C4
St Ambrose Gdns SLFD * M6..............66 A3
St Andrew's Av DROY M43..................74 B4
　ECC M30.......................................62 B4
St Andrews CI HTNM SK4..................128 A1
St Andrews Rd HTNM SK4.................128 A1
　STRET M32....................................96 A3
St Andrew's Sq CMANE M1....................9 F1
St Andrew's St CMANE M1.....................9 E1
St Anne's Av SLFD M6.......................65 D1
St Annes Ct SLFD * M6......................66 A1
St Annes Rd CCHDY M21...................112 A2
St Anne's St NEWH/MOS M40...............54 A3
St Anns CI PWCH M25........................29 D2
St Anns Pas CMANW M2.......................3 F4
St Ann's Rd PWCH M25.......................29 C2
St Ann's Sq CMANW M2........................3 F4
St Ann's St CMANW M2........................3 E4
　SWIN M27.......................................44 B1
St Augustine St NEWH/MOS M40...........53 C4
St Bartholomew's Dr ORD M5...............84 B1
St Bees CI RUSH/FAL M14..................101 C4
St Benedicts Av WGTN/LGST * M12......89 C3
St Benedict's Sq WGTN/LGST M12.......89 C3
St Bernard's Av SLFD M6....................66 A1
St Boniface Rd BRO M7.......................67 D1
St Brannock's Rd CCHDY M21..............99 D3
St Brelades Dr BRO M7.......................51 C1
St Brendan's Rd DID/WITH M20..........115 C2
St Brendan's Rd North
　DID/WITH M20...............................115 C2
St Brides Wy OLDTF/WHR M16.............85 C4
St Catherine's Rd DID/WITH M20.........115 C2
St Chads Crs OLDS OL8......................40 A4
St Chad's Rd DID/WITH M20...............116 A2
St Chad's St CHH * M8........................69 D1
St Christophers CI DID/WITH M20........114 A3
St Clements Ct OLDS * OL8.................22 B4
St Clement's Dr ORD M5.....................84 A2
St Clements Fold URM * M41...............94 B3
St Clement's Rd CCHDY M21..............111 D1
St Cuthberts Fold OLDS OL8...............41 C4
St Domingo PI OLD * OL1.....................22 B2
St Dominics Wy MDTN M24..................17 D2
St Edmund's Rd NEWH/MOS M40..........53 D3
St Elisabeth's Wy RDSH SK5..............119 D2
St Georges Av HULME M15....................6 B5
St Georges Ct STRET * M32.................96 B4
St George's Crs SLFD * M6..................63 D2
St George's Dr NEWH/MOS M40............55 C2
St George's Rd DROY M43....................75 C2
　RUSH/FAL M14..............................116 B2
　STRET M32....................................96 A3

St George's Sq *CHAD* OL9 ....**37** D2
St Georges Wy *SLFD* M6 ....**66** F3
St Helier's Dr *BRO* M7 ....**51** C1
St Hilda's Dr *OLD* OL1 ....**22** A1
St Hilda's Rd *OLDTF/WHR* M16 ....**84** A4
  WYTH/NTH M22 ....**123** C4
St Ignatius Wk *ORD* M5 ....**84** A1
St Ives Rd *RUSH/FAL* M14 ....**102** A3
St James' Ct *SLFD* M6 ....**64** A2
St James Rd *HTNM* SK4 ....**118** A4
St James's Rd *BRO* M7 ....**50** B3
St James's Sq *CMANE* M1 ....**3** F1
St James St *CMANE* M1 ....**62** B3
  ECC M30 ....**62** B3
St John's Av *WHTF* M45 ....**76** A3
St John's Cl *BRO* * M7 ....**50** B3
St Johns Ct *BRO* * M7 ....**50** A3
St John's Rd *BRUN/LGST* M13 ....**104** A1
  HTNM SK4 ....**126** B3
  OLDTF/WHR M16 ....**99** D1
St John's St *BRO* M7 ....**50** A3
  CHAD OL9 ....**21** D4
St John St *CSLFD* M3 ....**7** D1
  ECC M30 ....**62** A4
  SWIN M27 ....**47** C3
St John's Wk *CHAD* * OL9 ....**21** D3
St Josephs Av *WHTF* M45 ....**12** A2
St Joseph's Dr *ORD* M5 ....**84** A1
St Kildas Av *DROY* M43 ....**75** C2
St Lawrence Quay *SALQ* M50 ....**83** C2
St Leonard's Rd *HTNM* SK4 ....**119** C4
St Lukes Ct *CHAD* OL9 ....**20** D2
St Luke's Rd *SLFD* M6 ....**65** C3
St Margaret's Av *BNG/LEV* M19 ....**117** C3
St Margaret's Cl *PWCH* M25 ....**12** B3
St Margarets Gdns *OLDS* * OL8 ....**39** D2
St Margaret's Rd *NEWH/MOS* M40 ....**37** C2
  PWCH M25 ....**12** B4
St Mark's La *CHH* M8 ....**51** C2
St Mark's St *BNG/LEV* M19 ....**105** D4
St Martin's Av *HTNM* SK4 ....**128** B3
St Martins Cl *DROY* M43 ....**75** C2
St Martin's Dr *BRO* M7 ....**51** C1
St Martin's Rd *OLDS* OL8 ....**41** D3
St Marys Cl *PWCH* M25 ....**29** C1
  STKP SK1 ....**130** B4
St Marys Ct *NEWH/MOS* M40 ....**55** C3
  OLD * OL1 ....**22** B2
St Mary's Dr *RDSH* SK5 ....**120** A4
St Marys Est *OLD* OL1 ....**23** C2
St Mary's Ga *CMANE* M1 ....**3** F3
St Marys Gate *M2* **3** F3
St Mary's Hall Rd *CHH* M8 ....**32** A4
St Marys Parsonage *CSLFD* * M3 ....**3** E4
  CSLFD M3 ....**3** E4
St Mary's Rd *ECC* M30 ....**63** C3
  NEWH/MOS M40 ....**55** C3
  PWCH M25 ....**29** C1
  SALE M33 ....**108** A4
St Mary's St *CSLFD* M3 ....**3** E4
  HULME M15 ....**8** C5
  OLD OL1 ....**23** C1
  OLDTF/WHR M16 ....**101** C1
St Mary's Wy *OLD* OL1 ....**22** B2
  STKP SK1 ....**130** B4
St Matthews Ct *STRET* * M32 ....**96** B4
St Matthew's Rd *EDGY/DAV* SK3 ....**132** A1
St Matthews Ter *EDGY/DAV* * SK3 ....**132** A1
St Michael's Sq *ANC* * M4 ....**4** B1
St Modwen Rd *STRET* M32 ....**80** A4
St Oswald's Rd *BNG/LEV* M19 ....**105** C3
St Paul's Rd *BRO* M7 ....**30** D1
  DID/WITH M20 ....**115** D3
  HTNM SK4 ....**128** A1
St Paul's St *STKP* SK1 ....**130** B2
St Peters Ct *STRET* * M32 ....**97** D2
St Petersgate *STKP* SK1 ....**130** A4
St Peter's Rd *SWIN* M27 ....**44** B2

St Peters Sq *CMANW* * M2 ....**7** F1
  CMANW M2 ....**7** F1
  STKP * SK1 ....**129** D4
St Philip's Pl *CSLFD* * M3 ....**3** A3
St Philip's Rd *GTN* M18 ....**106** A1
St Simon St *CSLFD* M3 ....**68** A2
St Stephen's Cl *BRUN/LGST* M13 ....**88** A4
St Stephens Ct *BKLY* * M9 ....**53** C2
St Stephens St *OLD* * OL1 ....**23** D1
St Stephen St *CSLFD* M3 ....**2** C5
  OLD OL1 ....**23** D1
St Stephens Vw *DROY* M43 ....**75** D3
St Teresa's Rd *OLDTF/WHR* M16 ....**98** B2
St Thomas' Pl *CHH* * M8 ....**68** D1
St Thomas's Cir *OLDS* OL8 ....**22** A4
St Thomas's Pl *STKP* SK1 ....**133** C1
St Thomas St North *OLDS* * OL8 ....**22** A4
St Thomas St South *OLDS* OL8 ....**22** A4
St Vincent St *ANC* M4 ....**5** F3
St Werburgh's Rd *CCHDY* M21 ....**112** B1
St Wilfrids St *HULME* M15 ....**6** C5
Salcombe Rd *OP/CLY* M11 ....**91** C1
Salcot Wk *NEWH/MOS* * M40 ....**70** B2
Salford Ap *CSLFD* M3 ....**3** E2
Salisbury Dr *PWCH* M25 ....**30** B3
Salisbury Rd *CCHDY* M21 ....**99** C4
  ECC M30 ....**63** C1
  SWIN M27 ....**44** B2
  URM M41 ....**94** A1
  WHTF M45 ....**11** C1
Salisbury St *RDSH* SK5 ....**120** A1
  RUSH/FAL M14 ....**101** D1
Salmon St *ANC* M4 ....**4** B3
Salop St *SLFD* M6 ....**66** B1
Saltergate Ms *SLFD* * M6 ....**66** B3
Salteye Rd *ECC* M30 ....**60** B4
Saltford Av *ANC* M4 ....**5** F3
Saltford Ct *ANC* M4 ....**5** F3
Saltire Gdns *BRO* M7 ....**50** B1
Saltney Av *DID/WITH* M20 ....**114** A2
Salutation St *HULME* M15 ....**7** F5
Sam Cowan Cl *RUSH/FAL* M14 ....**101** D2
Samian Gdns *BRO* M7 ....**49** D4
Samlesbury Cl *DID/WITH* M20 ....**124** A2
Samouth Cl *NEWH/MOS* * M40 ....**71** C2
Sampson Sq *RUSH/FAL* M14 ....**101** D1
Sam Swire St *HULME* M15 ....**85** D4
Samuel Ogden St *CMANE* M1 ....**8** B4
Samuel St *BNG/LEV* M19 ....**118** A1
  FAIL M35 ....**57** C1
  HTNM SK4 ....**129** C2
Sanby Av *GTN* M18 ....**105** D1
Sanby Rd *GTN* M18 ....**105** D1
The Sanctuary *HULME* M15 ....**7** F5
Sanctuary Cl *BRUN/LGST* M13 ....**87** C4
Sandal St *NEWH/MOS* M40 ....**71** D2
Sandbach Av *RUSH/FAL* M14 ....**114** A1
Sandbach Rd *RDSH* * SK5 ....**106** B3
Sanderson Cl *WALK* M28 ....**43** C1
Sanderson St *NEWH/MOS* M40 ....**53** D4
Sanderstead Dr *BKLY* M9 ....**34** B2
Sandford Av *GTN* * M18 ....**91** C3
Sandford Station La *RDSH* SK5 ....**106** A3
Sandgate Av *OP/CLY* M11 ....**74** A3
Sandgate Rd *CHAD* OL9 ....**21** C3
  WHTF M45 ....**12** A2
Sandheys Gv *GTN* M18 ....**106** B1
Sandhurst Av *DID/WITH* M20 ....**114** A3
Sandhurst Rd *DID/WITH* M20 ....**125** C3
Sandhutton Rd *BKLY* M9 ....**34** A4
Sandileigh Av *DID/WITH* M20 ....**115** C4
  RDSH SK5 ....**121** C4
Sandiway Dr *DID/WITH* M20 ....**124** B2
Sandown Av *SLFD* M6 ....**65** D3
Sandown Crs *GTN* M18 ....**106** A2
Sandown St *GTN* M18 ....**91** D3
Sandpiper Dr *EDGY/DAV* SK3 ....**132** A3
Sandray Gv *ORD* M5 ....**65** D4

Sandridge Wk *WGTN/LGST* M12..............88 B3
Sandringham Av *DTN/ASHW* M34..........107 D2
Sandringham Dr *HTNM* SK4..................127 D4
Sandringham Gra *PWCH* M25...............31 D2
Sandringham Rd *MPL/ROM* SK6..........131 D2
Sandringham St *UR* M18.....................105 D1
Sands Av *CHAD* OL9............................19 C1
Sandsend Cl *CHH* M8...........................50 B4
Sandstone Wy *CCHDY* M21..................113 C3
Sand St *NEWH/MOS* M40......................70 B1
Sandwell Dr *SALE* M33........................109 C3
Sandwich Rd *ECC* M30...........................63 C2
Sandy Bank Rd *CHH* M8.........................51 C1
Sandy Brow *BKLY* M9............................34 A3
Sandygate Cl *SWIN* M27.........................44 B2
Sandy Gv *SLFD* M6...............................65 D2
    SWIN M27....................................45 C1
Sandyhill Rd *BKLY* M9...........................32 B2
Sandylands Dr *PWCH* M25.....................29 C4
Sandy La *CCHDY* M21..........................112 A1
    DROY M43....................................76 B2
    MDTN M24....................................18 A2
    OLDS * OL8..................................22 A3
    PWCH M25....................................29 D3
    RDSH SK5...................................129 D2
    SLFD M6.......................................65 D2
    STRET M32...................................96 A4
Sandy Meade *PWCH* M25......................29 D2
Sandyway *PWCH* * M25.........................29 D2
Sandywell Cl *OP/CLY* M11......................91 C2
Sandywell St *OP/CLY* M11......................91 C1
Sandy Wd *SLFD* M6..............................65 D2
Sanfold La *BNG/LEV* M19......................105 D3
Sangster Ct *ORD* M5.............................83 D1
Sankey Gv *BKLY* M9..............................33 C3
Santiago St *RUSH/FAL* M14..................102 A2
Santley St *WGTN/LGST* M12.................104 B2
Santon Av *RUSH/FAL* M14.....................116 B1
Sapling Rd *SWIN* M27............................44 A4
Sarah St *ECC* M30...............................61 C4
    MDTN M24.....................................17 C1
    OP/CLY M11...................................89 C1
Sargent Dr *OLDTF/WHR* M16.................100 B1
Sark Rd *CCHDY* M21............................98 B3
Saturn Gv *SLFD* M6..............................67 D3
Saunton Rd *OP/CLY* M11........................91 C1
Saville St *MDTN* M24.............................19 C2
Savio Wy *MDTN* M24.............................17 D2
Sawley Rd *NEWH/MOS* M40...................71 C1
Saxby St *SLFD* M6................................46 B4
Saxelby Dr *CHH* M8..............................52 A3
Saxon Av *CHH* M8.................................32 B3
Saxon Dr *CHAD* OL9.............................19 D1
    DROY M43....................................75 D2
Saxon St *DROY* M43.............................76 A3
    MDTN M24....................................18 A1
    NEWH/MOS M40.............................71 D2
Saxthorpe Wk *WGTN/LGST* M12...........88 B3
Saxwood Av *BKLY* M9............................34 A4
Scale St *ORD* M5.................................67 C4
Scarborough St *NEWH/MOS* M40............54 B1
Scarcroft Rd *WGTN/LGST* M12..............89 D3
Scargill Cl *RUSH/FAL* * M14..................115 D3
Scarisbrick Av *DID/WITH* M20...............126 A2
Scarisbrick Rd *BNG/LEV* M19...............117 C3
Scarsdale Rd *RUSH/FAL* M14................103 D1
Scarsdale St *SLFD* M6..........................67 C2
Schofield Rd *DROY* M43.........................76 A4
    ECC M30.....................................60 B4
Schofield St *FAIL* * M35.........................57 C1
    OLDS OL8...................................40 B2
    OP/CLY M11.................................73 D3

    SWIN M27.....................................45 D1
Scholes Wk *PWCH* M25.........................30 A2
Scholfield Av *URM* M41.........................95 C4
School Av *STRET* * M32.........................98 A2
School Brow *WALK* M28..........................42 A3
School Ct *ANC* M4..................................5 E3
    EDGY/DAV SK3..............................133 C3
School Gv *DID/WITH* M20......................115 D3
    PWCH M25...................................29 D3
School Gv West *DID/WITH* * M20............115 D3
School House Flats *OLDS* * OL8..............39 D3
School La *BKLY* M9................................33 C3
    DID/WITH M20..............................125 D2
    HTNM SK4...................................118 B4
School Rd *ECC* M30...............................78 B1
    FAIL M35.....................................57 C2
    OLDS OL8....................................39 C4
    SALE M33...................................108 A4
    STRET M32...................................96 B3
Schoolside Cl *CHH* M8..........................52 A3
Schoolside La *MDTN* M24......................15 C2
Schools Rd *GTN* M18.............................91 D4
School St *ANC* M4...................................4 B1
    BRO M7..68 B1
    ECC M30......................................61 C2
    OLDS OL8....................................22 A4
School Wk *OLDTF/WHR* M16...................85 C4
Schuster Rd *RUSH/FAL* M14..................103 C2
Schwabe St *MDTN* M24.........................15 D1
Scoltock Wy *OLD* OL1...........................23 C2
Score St *OP/CLY* M11.............................72 B4
Scotforth Cl *HULME* M15..........................6 C1
Scotland *ANC* M4....................................4 A1
Scotland Hall Rd *NEWH/MOS* M40...........55 C4
Scotland St *NEWH/MOS* M40...................55 C4
Scott Av *CCHDY* M21.............................99 C3
    ECC M30......................................61 D2
Scott Cl *RDSH* SK5.............................130 A1
Scottfield *OLDS* OL8.............................22 B4
Scottia Gv *ECC* M30.............................78 A1
Scott Rd *DROY* M43...............................75 D2
    PWCH M25...................................29 C2
Scott St *OLDS* OL8...............................23 C4
    SLFD M6......................................67 D1
Scovell St *BRO* M7................................50 A3
Scropton St *NEWH/MOS* M40...................53 C4
Seabright Wk *OP/CLY* * M11...................72 A4
Seabrook Crs *URM* M41.........................94 A1
Seabrook Rd *NEWH/MOS* M40.................55 C4
Seacombe Av *RUSH/FAL* M14................101 D4
Seaford Rd *SLFD* M6.............................49 C4
Seaford Wk *CHAD* * OL9.........................21 C3
Seaham Wk *RUSH/FAL* M14..................102 A2
Sealey Wk *NEWH/MOS* * M40..................71 D1
Searby Rd *GTN* M18.............................105 C1
Seascale Av *OP/CLY* M11.......................73 C1
Seaton Ms *AULW* OL7............................77 D1
Sebastopol Wk *ANC* M4............................5 E3
Second Av *OLDS* OL8.............................39 D3
    OP/CLY M11..................................74 A3
    SWIN M27....................................44 A4
    TRPK M17....................................82 A4
Sedan Cl *ORD* M5.................................66 B4
Seddon Av *GTN* M18.............................91 C3
Seddon St *BNG/LEV* M19........................... B3
Sedgeborough Rd *OLDTF/WHR* M16........100 B2
Sedge Cl *RDSH* SK5............................120 B1
Sedgefield Cl *ORD* M5...........................66 B3
Sedgeford Rd *NEWH/MOS* M40................53 C4
Sedgemoor Wy *OLD* * OL1.......................22 B2
Sedgley Av *PWCH* M25..........................30 B3
Sedgley Cl *MDTN* M24...........................18 B3
Sedgley Park Rd *PWCH* M25....................30 B3
Sedgley Rd *CHH* M8..............................51 D1
Sedgley St *MDTN* M24...........................18 B2
Seedley Park Rd *SLFD* M6.......................65 D3
Seedley Rd *SLFD* M6.............................65 D2
    SLFD M6......................................66 A2

Seedley St *RUSH/FAL* M14 .... 102 A2
Seedley Ter *SLFD* M6 .... 65 C2
Seedley View Rd *ORD* M5 .... 65 D2
Sefton Cl *BRUN/LGST* M13 .... 9 C5
  MDTN M24 .... 16 B1
Sefton Crs *SALE* M33 .... 109 C3
Sefton Dr *SWIN* M27 .... 44 A3
  WALK M28 .... 42 B5
Sefton Rd *CCHDY* M21 .... 112 A1
  MDTN M24 .... 16 B1
  SALE M33 .... 109 C4
  SWIN M27 .... 26 A4
Sefton St *CHAD* OL9 .... 38 B3
  CHH M8 .... 51 F1
  WHTF M45 .... 11 C2
Selborne Rd *CCHDY* M21 .... 99 C4
Selby Av *OLDS* OL8 .... 40 A1
Selby Dr *SLFD* M6 .... 64 C2
Selby St *STRET* M32 .... 95 C2
Selby St *STRET* M32 .... 95 C2
Selby St *HTNM* SK4 .... 129 C1
  OP/CLY M11 .... 89 D1
Selden St *OLDS* OL8 .... 22 A4
Selham Wk *BRUN/LGST* * M13 .... 9 E4
Selhurst Av *OP/CLY* M11 .... 73 C3
Selkirk Av *OLDS* OL8 .... 40 A1
Selkirk Cl *BKLY* M9 .... 35 C2
Selkirk Rd *CHAD* OL9 .... 38 A1
Sellars Sq *DROY* M43 .... 75 D3
Sellers Wy *CHAD* OL9 .... 38 B2
Selsby Av *ECC* M30 .... 61 C3
Selside Wk *RUSH/FAL* M14 .... 115 D1
Selston Rd *BKLY* M9 .... 33 C1
Selworthy Rd *OLDTF/WHR* M16 .... 100 B1
Selwyn Av *BKLY* M9 .... 53 C1
Selwyn Cl *OLDS* * OL8 .... 22 B4
Senior Av *RUSH/FAL* M14 .... 116 B2
Senior St *CSLFD* M3 .... 3 F1
Sepal Cl *RDSH* SK5 .... 107 D4
Sequoia St *BKLY* M9 .... 53 D1
Sevenoaks Av *HTNM* SK4 .... 117 C4
  URM M41 .... 94 B1
Sevenoaks Dr *SWIN* M27 .... 45 D3
Sevenoaks Wk *BRUN/LGST* * M13 .... 87 D3
Seventh Av *OLDS* OL8 .... 39 D4
Severn Rd *CHAD* OL9 .... 20 A1
  OLDS OL8 .... 39 C4
Severn Wy *RDSH* SK5 .... 120 D4
Sewerby Cl *OLDTF/WHR* M16 .... 101 C1
Sewerby St *OLDTF/WHR* M16 .... 100 B1
Sexa St *OP/CLY* M11 .... 91 C1
Seymour Av *OP/CLY* M11 .... 74 A3
Seymour Cl *OLDTF/WHR* M16 .... 84 B4
Seymour Gv *OLDTF/WHR* M16 .... 99 C1
Seymour Pl *OLDTF/WHR* * M16 .... 84 A4
Seymour Rd *CHH* M8 .... 32 A4
Seymour Rd South *OP/CLY* M11 .... 74 A3
Seymour St *GTN* M18 .... 91 C3
Shackleton St *ECC* M30 .... 61 C3
Shackliffe Rd *NEWH/MOS* M40 .... 36 A3
Shaftesbury Av *ECC* M30 .... 78 B1
Shaftesbury Av *CHH* M8 .... 51 D2
  SWIN M27 .... 45 C2
Shakespeare Crs *DROY* M43 .... 75 D3
  ECC M30 .... 62 A3
Shakespeare Rd *DROY* M43 .... 75 D3
  PWCH M25 .... 29 C2
  SWIN M27 .... 44 A1
Shakespeare Wk *BRUN/LGST* * M13 .. 87 D3
Shakleton Av *BKLY* M9 .... 35 D2
Shaldon Dr *NEWH/MOS* M40 .... 74 B1
Shambles Sq *ANC* M4 .... 3 F3
Shandon Av *WYTH/NTH* M22 .... 123 D4
Shanklin Cl *CCHDY* M21 .... 98 B4
Shanley Ct *CHAD* OL9 .... 21 C1
Sharcott Cl *OLDTF/WHR* M16 .... 101 C1
Shardlow Cl *NEWH/MOS* M40 .... 71 C1
Sharnford Sq *WGTN/LGST* * M12 ...... 89 D3
Sharon Cl *AULW* OL7 .... 77 D4

Sharples St *HTNM* SK4 .... 129 D2
Sharp St *ANC* M4 .... 4 C1
  MDTN M24 .... 17 C1
  PWCH * M25 .... 29 D1
Shawbrook Rd *BNG/LEV* M19 .... 117 D4
Shawbury St *MDTN* M24 .... 18 B2
Shawcross Fold *STKP* * SK1 .... 130 A3
Shawcross St *SLFD* M6 .... 66 A4
  STKP SK1 .... 133 C1
Shawfield Cl *RUSH/FAL* M14 .... 114 B1
Shawford Rd *NEWH/MOS* M40 .... 36 B3
Shawgreen Cl *HULME* M15 .... 6 B5
Shaw Head Dr *FAIL* M35 .... 57 C3
Shaw Heath *EDGY/DAV* SK3 .... 132 B1
Shawheath Cl *HULME* M15 .... 85 C3
Shawhill Wk *NEWH/MOS* M40 .... 71 C3
Shawlea Av *BNG/LEV* M19 .... 116 B3
Shaw Rd *HTNM* SK4 .... 118 A4
Shaw Rd South *EDGY/DAV* SK3 ...... 132 B3
Shaw St *CSLFD* M3 .... 3 F1
  OLD OL1 .... 23 D1
Shayfield Av *CHAD* OL9 .... 19 D1
Sheader Dr *ORD* M5 .... 64 B5
Shearer Wy *SWIN* M27 .... 47 C2
Shearsby Cl *HULME* M15 .... 85 D5
Sheepfoot La *PWCH* M25 .... 31 C2
Sheerness St *GTN* M18 .... 91 C4
Sheffield St *CMANE* M1 .... 9 D1
  HTNM SK4 .... 129 D2
Shefford Cl *OP/CLY* M11 .... 89 C1
Shelderton Cl *NEWH/MOS* M40 .... 54 B2
Sheldon St *OP/CLY* M11 .... 73 C3
Shelford Av *GTN* M18 .... 105 C1
Shelley Gv *DROY* M43 .... 75 D4
Shelley Rd *CHAD* OL9 .... 38 A2
  PWCH M25 .... 29 C2
  RDSH SK5 .... 106 A4
  SWIN M27 .... 44 A1
Shelley St *NEWH/MOS* M40 .... 55 D1
Shenfield Wk *NEWH/MOS* M40 .... 71 C2
Shepherd St *BKLY* * M9 .... 34 A4
  FAIL M35 .... 38 C1
Shepley St *CMANE* M1 .... 8 C1
  FAIL M35 .... 38 B4
Sheraton Rd *OLDS* OL8 .... 40 B1
Sherborne Rd *URM* M41 .... 94 A4
Sherborne St *CHH* M8 .... 51 D5
  CSLFD M3 .... 69 C1
Sherborne St West *CSLFD* M3 .... 68 B2
Sherbourne St *PWCH* * M25 .... 29 D1
Sherdley Ct *CHH* M8 .... 32 B4
Sherdley Rd *CHH* M8 .... 32 B4
Sheridan Wy *CHAD* * OL9 .... 19 D1
Sheringham Dr *SWIN* M27 .... 45 C3
Sheringham Rd *RUSH/FAL* M14 ...... 116 A2
Sherlock St *RUSH/FAL* M14 .... 116 A2
Sherratt St *ANC* M4 .... 5 D2
Sherrington St *WGTN/LGST* M12 .... 104 B2
Sherwell Rd *BKLY* M9 .... 33 C1
Sherwood Av *BRO* M7 .... 49 C2
  DROY M43 .... 76 B3
  HTNM SK4 .... 127 D4
  RUSH/FAL M14 .... 115 D1
  SALE M33 .... 109 D4
Sherwood St *ORD* M5 .... 65 D2
Sherwood Dr *SWIN* M27 .... 46 A2
Sherwood St *OLD* OL1 .... 22 A1
  RUSH/FAL M14 .... 115 D1
Shetland Rd *NEWH/MOS* M40 .... 71 C2
Shetland Wy *URM* M41 .... 79 C2
Shevington Gdns *NTHM/RTH* M23 .. 122 A1
Shieldborn Dr *BKLY* M9 .... 53 C2
Shevington Gdns *NTHM/RTH* M23 .. 122 A1
Shield Cl *OLDS* OL8 .... 22 B3
Shield Dr *WALK* M28 .... 24 B4
Shield St *EDGY/DAV* SK3 .... 132 B1
Shilford Dr *ANC* M4 .... 5 D1
Shipla Cl *CHAD* OL9 .... 22 B2
Shipley Av *SLFD* M6 .... 64 B2
Shippey St *RUSH/FAL* M14 .... 116 A2

Shiredale Dr BKLY M9	53	C2
Shiregreen Av NEWH/MOS M40	52	B4
Shirehills PWCH M25	29	D2
Shireoak Rd DID/WITH M20	116	A2
The Shires DROY M43	77	C2
Shirley Av BRO M7	48	B2
CHAD OL9	37	D3
DTN/ASHW M54	95	D1
ECC M30	78	B1
STRET M32	98	A2
SWIN M27	46	B2
Shirley Gv EDGY/DAV SK3	132	B4
Shirley Rd CHH M8	51	D2
Shoreditch Cl HTNM SK4	118	A4
Shoreham Cl CHAD * OL9	20	B3
Shore St OLD OL1	23	D3
Shorland St SWIN M27	43	D2
Short Av DROY M43	92	A1
Shortcroft St HULME M15	7	E5
Shortland Crs BNG/LEV M19	126	A3
Short St ANC M4	4	B4
BRO M7	68	B2
HTNM SK4	129	D2
Short St East HTNM SK4	129	D2
Shotton Wk RUSH/FAL * M14	102	A2
Shrewsbury Ct OLDTF/WHR * M16	85	C4
Shrewsbury Rd DROY M43	75	D3
PWCH M25	29	D2
Shrewsbury St RDSH SK5		
Shropshire Av RDSH SK5	121	D3
Shropshire Rd FAIL M35	57	D3
Shropshire Sq WGTN/LGST * M12	88	B3
Shrowbridge Wk WGTN/LGST M12	89	D3
Shudehill ANC M4	4	A3
Shuttle St ECC * M30	63	C3
Shuttleworth Cl OLDTF/WHR M16	113	D1
Siam St OP/CLY M11	89	C1
Sibley Rd HTNM SK4	128	A4
Sibley St GTN M18	91	C4
Sibson Rd CCHDY M21	98	B4
Sickle St CMANW M2	4	A4
OLDE OL4	23	D4
Sidbury Rd CCHDY M21	112	B1
Siddall St OLD OL1	22	C1
WGTN/LGST M12	104	B3
Siddington Av DID/WITH M20	114	B1
Sidebottom St DROY * M43	75	C4
Side Cl OLDS OL8	39	D3
OP/CLY M11	73	D3
The Sidings WALK M28	42	B4
Sidley Av BKLY M9	35	C1
Sidmouth Dr BKLY M9	34	A3
Sidmouth St CHAD OL9	21	D3
Sidney Rd BKLY M9	34	A4
Sidney St CMANE M1	8	B4
CSLFD * M3	2	B3
CSLFD * M3	3	E5
Sigwell Wk ANC * M4	71	C4
Signal Cl ECC M30	61	C3
Signal Dr NEWH/MOS M40	53	C3
Signet Wk CHH M8	52	A4
Silburn Wy MDTN M24	15	D2
Silchester Dr NEWH/MOS M40	53	C3
Silfield Cl OP/CLY M11	71	D4
Silkin Cl BRUN/LGST M13	7	G7
Silkstone St OP/CLY M11	90	B2
Silk St ANC M4	5	D2
CSLFD M3	2	A1
MDTN M24	17	C1
NEWH/MOS M40	55	D3
Sillavan Wy CSLFD M3	3	H3
Silsden Av BKLY M9	15	C4
Silton St BKLY M9	54	A2
Silver Birch Gv SWIN M27	46	A3
Silverbirch Wy FAIL M35	57	C2
Silvercroft St HULME M15	6	C3
Silverdale SWIN M27	26	B3
Silverdale Av CHAD OL9	20	B3

PWCH M25	31	D3
Silverdale St OP/CLY M11	99	D4
HTNM SK4	128	B1
Silverdale St OP/CLY M11	92	A2
Silverlea Dr BKLY M9	33	D3
Silverstone Dr NEWH/MOS M40	74	A1
Silver St CMANE M1	4	B5
OLD OL1	23	D2
Silverwell St NEWH/MOS M40	56	A4
Silverwood CHAD OL9	19	D2
Silverwood Av CCHDY M21	112	A3
Simeon St ANC * M4	4	C1
Simister Gn PWCH M25	13	C1
Simister La PWCH M25	13	C1
Simister Rd FAIL M35	57	C2
Simister St BKLY M9	53	D1
Simkin Wy OLDS OL8	41	D4
Simms Cl CSLFD M3	2	A3
Simon Freeman Cl BNG/LEV M19	118	B5
Simpson Av SWIN M27	27	D3
Simpson St ANC M4	4	B1
CHAD OL9	39	C1
EDGY/DAV SK3	132	B1
OP/CLY M11	72	B4
Sindsley Rd SWIN M27	25	C3
Singleton Cl BRO M7	30	B4
Singleton Rd BRO M7	30	B4
HTNM SK4	128	A1
Sirdar St OP/CLY * M11	92	A1
Sirius Pl BRO M7	68	A2
Sir Matt Busby Wy OLDTF/WHR M16	85	C4
Sir Richard Fairey Rd HTNM SK4	118	A1
Sir Robert Thomas Ct BKLY * M9	53	C1
Sisley Cl BRO M7	49	C1
Sisson St FAIL M35	56	B2
Sisters' Cl DROY M43	92	B1
Sixth Av OLDS OL8	8	A4
Sixth St TRPK M17	82	A4
Skarratt Cl WGTN/LGST M12	89	C3
Skelton Gv BRUN/LGST M13	104	A3
Skelton Rd STRET M32	97	C2
Skerry Cl BRUN/LGST M13	9	D4
Skerton Rd OLDTF/WHR M16	99	C1
Skip Pl CSLFD M3	69	D2
Skipton Av NEWH/MOS M40	37	D1
Skipton Cl RDSH SK5	119	D1
Skye Rd URM M41	79	C4
Slack La SWIN M27	26	B4
Slack Rd CHH M8	33	D4
Slade Gv BRUN/LGST M13	104	A2
Slade Hall Rd WGTN/LGST M12	104	B3
Slade La BNG/LEV M19	104	A4
Slade Mt BNG/LEV * M19	117	C1
Slaithwaite Dr OP/CLY M11	73	D3
Slate Av ANC M4	5	F4
Slate La AULW OL7	77	D4
Slater St CHAD * OL9	22	B3
DTN/ASHW M54	93	D1
ECC M30	61	C3
FAIL M35	38	A4
Slate Whf HULME * M15	6	B2
Sleaford Cl NEWH/MOS M40	71	C2
Sledmere Cl OP/CLY M11	72	C2
Sloane St OP/CLY * M11	72	B3
Smallridge Cl NEWH/MOS M40	71	C2
Smallfield Dr BKLY M9	53	C1
Smallridge Cl NEWH/MOS M40	71	C2
Smallwood St NEWH/MOS M40	55	D3
Smart St WGTN/LGST M12	104	B2
Smeaton Cl STRET M32	97	C2
Smeaton St CHH M8	52	A3
Smedley La CHH M8	52	A3
Smedley Rd CHH M8	52	B3
Smedley St CHH M8	51	D3
Smethurst St BKLY M9	34	A4
MDTN M24	19	C2
Smith St OLDTF/WHR M16	84	B3

Smithy La *CSLFD* * M3 ....3 E4
Smyrna St *ORD* M5 ....65 D4
Snell St *ANC* M4 ....71 M4
Snipe Wy *DTN/ASHW* M34 ....77 C4
Snowden St *OLDS* OL8 ....41 C1
Snowdon Rd *ECC* M30 ....63 D2
Soap St *ANC* M4 ....4 B3
Solent Av *CHH* M8 ....32 B3
Solway Cl *OLDS* OL8 ....22 B4
   SWIN M27 ....25 D1
Somerfield Rd *BKLY* M9 ....34 A4
Somerford Av *DID/WITH* M20 ......114 B1
Somerford Bank *RDSH* SK5 ....107 D3
Somerset Cl *RDSH* SK5 ....131 D1
Somerset Pl *SALE* M33 ....109 C3
Somerset Rd *DROY* M43 ....75 D2
   ECC M30 ....63 D1
   FAIL M35 ....56 B3
Somers Rd *RDSH* SK5 ....107 C4
Somerwood Wk *WGTN/LGST* * M12 ...89 C3
Sopwith Dr *RUSH/FAL* M14 ....101 D4
Sorbus Cl *SLFD* M6 ....67 C3
Sorrel Bank *SLFD* M6 ....66 A1
Sorrell Bank *RDSH* SK5 ....107 C4
Sorrell St *HULME* M15 ....6 C5
Sorrel St *HULME* M15 ....6 C5
Sorton St *CMANE* * M1 ....8 B3
Soudan Rd *OFTN* SK2 ....133 D3
Southall St *CSLFD* M3 ....69 C2
Southampton Cl *BRO* M7 ....50 A4
Southam St *BRO* M7 ....51 C2
South Av *BNG/LEV* M19 ....117 C2
   SWIN M27 ....44 A4
Southbank Rd *BNG/LEV* M19 ....116 A4
Southbourne Av *URM* M41 ....95 C3
Southbourne St *SLFD* M6 ....65 D3
Southbrook Av *CHH* M8 ....32 A2
Southcliffe Rd *RDSH* SK5 ....120 A3
South Cliffe St *OP/CLY* M11 ....92 A3
South Crs *NEWH/MOS* M40 ....37 C2
   OP/CLY M11 ....74 A3
Southcross Rd *GTN* M18 ....106 A2
South Croston St *BRUN/LGST* M13 ...104 A1
Southdene Av *DID/WITH* M20 ....123 D1
Southdown Cl *HTNM* SK4 ....129 C3
Southdown Crs *BKLY* M9 ....35 D3
South Dr *CCHDY* M21 ....112 A3
Southend Av *HULME* M15 ....6 A5
Southern Ap *SWIN* M27 ....27 D2
Southernby St *CSLFD/LGST* * M13 ...104 A1
Southern Rd *SALE* M33 ....108 B3
Southern St *CSLFD* M3 ....7 D1
   SLFD M6 ....65 D2
Southgarth Rd *SLFD* M6 ....65 D2
Southgate *CCHDY* M21 ....112 A4
   HTNM SK4 ....118 B4
Southgate Av *NEWH/MOS* * M40 .....72 B1
Southgate College Land *CSLFD* M3 ...3 E4
Southgate Rd *CHAD* OL9 ....37 D2
Southgate St *OLD* OL1 ....23 C3
South Gv *BRUN/LGST* M13 ....88 A4
South Hall St *ORD* * M5 ....84 B1
South Hill St *OLDE* OL4 ....23 D1
South King St *CMANW* M2 ....3 E4
   ECC M30 ....61 C1
South Langworthy Rd *ORD* M5 ....66 A4
Southlea Rd *DID/WITH* M20 ....116 A4
Southlink *OLDE* * OL4 ....23 D3
South Lonsdale St *STRET* M32 ....97 D2
South Meade *CCHDY* M21 ....112 A4
   PWCH M25 ....31 C3
   SWIN M27 ....44 B3
Southmere Cl *BKLY* M9 ....36 B3
South Mesnefield Rd *BRO* M7 ....48 B3
Southmill St *CMANW* M2 ....7 E1
South Pump St *CMANE* * M1 ....8 C1
South Radford St *BRO* M7 ....48 B2
South Rd *DID/WITH* M20 ....125 C3

STRET M32 ....95 D1
   SWIN M27 ....28 A3
South Rw *PWCH* M25 ....29 C4
Southsea St *OP/CLY* M11 ....91 C2
South St *OLDS* OL8 ....39 C3
   OP/CLY M11 ....90 A1
   WGTN/LGST M12 ....88 B4
South Vw *RDSH* SK5 ....107 C2
Southway *DROY* M43 ....92 B1
   NEWH/MOS M40 ....38 A3
South Wy *OLDS* OL8 ....40 B3
Southwell Cl *STRET* * M32 ....96 B4
Southwell St *BKLY* M9 ....53 D2
Southwood Dr *BKLY* M9 ....14 B4
Southyard St *BNG/LEV* * M19 ....118 A1
Sovereign St *SLFD* M6 ....66 B1
Spa Cl *RDSH* SK5 ....119 D1
Sparkle St *CMANE* M1 ....5 D5
Sparrow Cl *RDSH* SK5 ....106 B3
Sparta Wk *OP/CLY* M11 ....89 D1
Sparthfield Rd *HTNM* SK4 ....129 C2
Sparth La *HTNM* SK4 ....129 C2
Sparth Rd *NEWH/MOS* M40 ....56 A4
Spa St *HULME* M15 ....87 C4
Sparth Rd *DID/WITH* M20 ....124 B2
Spaw St *CSLFD* M3 ....2 C2
Spear St *CMANE* M1 ....4 C4
Spectator St *ANC* M4 ....71 C3
Spencer Av *OLDTF/WHR* M16 ....99 D3
Spencer St *CHAD* OL9 ....39 C1
   ECC M30 ....61 D4
   OLD OL1 ....23 D2
   RDSH SK5 ....120 A1
Spender Av *CHH* M8 ....51 D3
Speyside Cl *WHTF* * M45 ....11 D1
The Spinney *SWIN* * M27 ....43 D3
Spinning Jenny Wk *ANC* M4 ....5 F3
Spire Wk *WGTN/LGST* * M12 ....88 A1
Sportsmans Dr *OLDS* OL8 ....41 D2
Spreadbury St *NEWH/MOS* M40 ......54 B2
Springbank *CHAD* * OL9 ....20 B2
Spring Bank Pl *EDGY/DAV* * SK3 ....132 B2
Spring Bank St *CHAD* OL9 ....39 D1
Spring Bridge Rd *OLDTF/WHR* M16 ...101 C3
Spring Clough *SWIN* M27 ....43 C4
Springdale Gdns *DID/WITH* M20 ....124 B2
Springfield Av *HTNM* SK4 ....119 D2
Springfield Cl *FAIL* M35 ....56 B1
Springfield La *CSLFD* M3 ....3 D1
Springfield Rd *DROY* M43 ....75 C2
Spring Gdns *CMANW* M2 ....4 A2
   STKP SK1 ....130 B4
Springhead Av *DID/WITH* M20 ....114 B2
Springside *HTNM* SK4 ....119 C2
Springside Wk *HULME* * M15 ....85 C3
Springs Rd *MDTN* M24 ....19 D3
Spring St *WGTN/LGST* M12 ....104 B3
Spring Ter *CHAD* OL9 ....20 B2
Spring V *MDTN* M24 ....17 D1
   PWCH M25 ....29 D1
Springville Av *BKLY* M9 ....54 A2
Springwell Cl *SLFD* * M6 ....65 D3
Springwood Av *SWIN* M27 ....46 A3
Springwood Hall Rd *OLDS* OL8 ....41 D3
Spruce Ct *SLFD* M6 ....67 C3
Spruce St *HULME* M15 ....85 D3
Sprucewood *CHAD* OL9 ....19 C1
The Spur *OLDS* OL8 ....41 D3
The Square *HTNM* SK4 ....128 B3
   SWIN M27 ....44 B4
   WHTF * M45 ....10 B1
Squire Rd *CHH* M8 ....51 C2
Stableford Av *ECC* M30 ....61 D1
Stableford Av *ECC* M30 ....61 D1
The Stables *DROY* M43 ....77 C2
Stable St *CHAD* OL9 ....38 B3

Stafford Rd *ECC* M30......................62 B2
  FAIL M35.................................57 D4
  SWIN M27.................................45 C1
Stafford St *CHAD* OL9.....................39 D1
Stag Pasture Rd *OLDS* OL8..............40 A4
Stainburn Rd *OP/CLY* M11................90 A1
Stainer St *WGTN/LGST* M12............104 B2
Stainforth St *OP/CLY* M11................89 D1
Stainton Av *GTN* M18....................106 B1
Stakeford Dr *CHH* M8......................52 B1
Stalham Cl *NEWH/MOS* M40..............71 C2
Stamford Dr *FAIL* M35.....................58 A4
Stamford Rd *BRO* M7.......................49 C3
  BRUN/LGST M13.....................104 A2
Stamford St *OLDTF/WHR* M16.........100 A1
  SALE M33................................108 B3
  SWIN M27.................................26 B4
Stanage Av *BKLY * M9......................35 C1
Stanbank St *HTNM* SK4.................129 D1
Stanbrook St *BNG/LEV* M19...........105 D4
Stanbury Wk *NEWH/MOS * M40.........71 C2
Standish Rd *RUSH/FAL* M14...........116 A1
Standmoor Av *WHTF * M45................10 A1
Standmoor Rd *WHTF* M45.................10 A2
Stanhope Av *PWCH* M25..................11 D4
Stanhope Ct *PWCH* M25...................11 D3
Stanhope Rd *SLFD* M6......................47 D1
Stanhope St *BNG/LEV* M19.............105 C4
  *RDSH * SK5...............................119 D2
Stanhope Wy *FAIL* M35....................56 B1
Stanhorne Av *CHH* M8.....................32 B3
Stanier Av *ECC* M30........................62 A2
Stanier St *BKLY* M9.........................53 D1
Stan Jolly Wk *OP/CLY* M11...............90 B1
Stanley Av *RUSH/FAL* M14.............102 B2
Stanley Av North *PWCH* M25............11 D3
Stanley Av South *PWCH* M25............11 D3
Stanley Ct *OLDTF/WHR* M16.............84 B4
Stanley Dr *WHTF* M45......................11 C3
Stanley Gv *HTNM* SK4...................128 A1
  URM M41...................................94 A3
  WGTN/LGST M12....................104 B2
Stanley Rd *BRO* M7.........................50 B1
  CHAD OL9................................39 C2
  ECC M30..................................61 D4
  HTNM SK4..............................128 A1
  OLDTF/WHR M16......................84 B1
  OLDTF/WHR M16....................100 B1
  SWIN M27.................................45 D1
Stanley St *BKLY * M9........................53 D1
  CHAD OL9................................21 C2
  CHH M8...................................69 D1
  NEWH/MOS M40.......................54 A4
  OP/CLY M11..............................91 D2
  ORD M5.....................................2 D1
  PWCH M25................................30 B1
  *STKP * SK1...............................130 B3
Stanmore Av *STRET* M32..................96 A3
Stannard Rd *ECC* M30......................60 A4
Stannybrook Rd *FAIL* M35................59 C3
Stansby Gdns *WGTN/LGST* M12........88 B3
Stansfield Rd *FAIL* M35....................38 B4
Stansfield St *CHAD* OL9....................21 C4
  NEWH/MOS M40.......................74 A1
  OLD OL1..................................22 B3
  OP/CLY M11..............................91 C1
Stanthorne Av *DID/WITH* M20.........114 B2
Stanton Av *BRO* M7.........................49 C3
  *DID/WITH * M20.......................123 D1
Stanton Gdns *HTNM* SK4...............128 A4
Stanton St *CHAD* OL9......................39 C2
  OP/CLY M11..............................73 C3
  STRET M32...............................97 C1
Stanway Cl *MDTN* M24.....................18 A3
Stanway Rd *WHTF* M45....................12 A1
Stanway St *BKLY* M9.......................53 D1
  STRET M32...............................97 C2
Stanwell Rd *NEWH/MOS* M40...........36 B4

SWIN M27...................................44 B2
Stanwick Av *BKLY* M9......................32 B1
Stanworth Cl *OLDTF/WHR* M16.......100 B2
Stanyard Ct *ORD* M5........................83 D1
Stapleford Cl *SALE* M33.................110 D4
Staplehurst Rd *NEWH/MOS* M40.......72 B1
Stapleton St *SLFD* M6.......................46 B4
Star Gv *BRO* M7...............................50 B3
Starkie St *WALK* M28........................42 B1
Starling Cl *DROY* M43......................77 C2
Starmoor Dr *CHH* M8........................51 D3
Statford Av *ECC* M30.......................78 B3
Statham St *SLFD* M6.........................67 C3
Station Ap *CMANE* M1.......................4 C5
  CMANE M1................................8 A3
Station Rd *CHH* M8..........................32 B4
  ECC M30..................................61 D4
  EDGY/DAV SK3.......................129 D4
  EDGY/DAV SK3.......................132 B1
  HTNM SK4..............................126 B4
  RDSH SK5..............................106 B3
  STRET M32...............................97 C3
  SWIN M27.................................26 A4
  URM M41...................................94 A4
Station Vw *BNG/LEV* M19..............104 B4
Staton St *OP/CLY* M11......................90 B1
Staverton Cl *BRUN/LGST* M13...........9 E5
Staycott Cl *OLDTF/WHR* M16..........101 C1
Staycott St *OLDTF/WHR* M16.........101 C1
Stedman Cl *OP/CLY* M11...................71 D4
Steeple Cl *CHH* M8..........................51 D4
Steeple Dr *ORD* M5.........................83 D1
Stelfox Av *RUSH/FAL* M14..............101 C1
Stelfox St *ECC* M30..........................78 A1
Stella St *BKLY* M9............................33 C1
Stelling St *GTN* M18.........................91 C4
Stenbury Cl *RUSH/FAL* M14...........102 B2
Stenner La *DID/WITH* M20..............124 B3
Stephenson Av *DROY* M43................75 D3
Stephenson Rd *STRET* M32..............97 C4
Stephenson St *FAIL* M35...................38 B4
Stephens Rd *DID/WITH* M20...........115 D4
Stephen St *CSLFD* M3......................69 C1
  URM M41...................................94 B3
Stern Av *ORD * M5............................83 D1
Sterndale Rd *EDGY/DAV* SK3.........132 B4
Stevenson Pl *CMANE * M1...................4 C4
Stevenson Rd *SWIN* M27..................44 B1
Stevenson Sq *CMANE* M1..................4 C4
Stevenson St *CSLFD * M3....................2 A4
Stilton Dr *OP/CLY * M11....................89 D1
Stirling Av *DID/WITH* M20..............114 A1
Stirling Gv *WHTF* M45......................11 C3
Stirling Rd *CHAD* OL9.......................59 A1
Stirling St *CHAD* OL9.......................21 D2
Stirrup Ga *WALK* M28.......................42 B4
Stitch La *HTNM* SK4.......................129 C2
Stobart Av *PWCH* M25......................30 B3
Stockburn Dr *FAIL* M35....................58 A2
Stockdale Av *EDGY/DAV* SK3.........133 D3
Stockdale Rd *BKLY* M9.....................34 B1
Stockfield Mt *CHAD* OL9...................21 C3
Stockfield Rd *CHAD* OL9...................21 C2
Stockholm Rd *EDGY/DAV* SK3........132 A3
Stockholm St *OP/CLY* M11................73 C3
Stockland Cl *BRUN/LGST* M13...........8 C4
Stock La *CHAD* OL9..........................21 C2
Stockley Wk *HULME * M15..................85 C3
Stockport Rd *WGTN/LGST* M12..........9 F5
Stockport Rd West *MPL/ROM* SK6...131 D2
Stockport Village *STKP * SK1...........129 D4
Stocksfield Dr *BKLY* M9.....................34 B3
Stocks St *CHH* M8............................69 D1
Stocks St East *CHH* M8....................69 D1
Stockton Rd *CCHDY* M21.................111 D1
Stockton St *SWIN* M27......................44 B2
Stokes St *OP/CLY* M11......................74 A4
Stonall Av *HULME * M15......................6 B5

Stoneacre Ct SWIN M27 .... 45 C2
Stonechat Cl DROY * M43 .... 76 B2
Stonefield Dr CHH M8 .... 50 B4
Stonehead St BKLY * M9 .... 54 A2
Stonehurst Cl WGTN/LGST M12 ...... 89 D3
Stonelow Cl HULME M15 .... 7 F5
Stone Pale WHTF M45 .... 11 C2
Stone Pl RUSH/FAL M14 .... 102 B2
Stonesby Cl OLDTF/WHR * M16 ... 100 A1
Stone St CSLFD M5 .... 7 D2
Stoneyfield Cl OLDTF/WHR M16 .... 101 C3
Stoneygate Wk OP/CLY M11 .... 91 C2
Stoneyhurst Cl HULME M15 .... 86 A3
Stopford St EDGY/DAV SK3 .... 132 A1
    OP/CLY M11 .... 91 D2
Stores St PWCH M25 .... 30 B1
Store St CMANE M1 .... 5 E5
    OP/CLY * M11 .... 90 A2
Stortford Rd NTHM/RTH M23 .... 122 A3
Stothard Rd STRET M32 .... 96 A4
Stott La SLFD M6 .... 64 A2
Stott Milne St CHAD OL9 .... 21 C4
Stott Rd CHAD OL9 .... 37 D2
    SWIN M27 .... 44 A3
Stott's La NEWH/MOS M40 .... 56 A3
Stott St NEWH/MOS M40 .... 56 A3
Stovell Av WGTN/LGST M12 .... 104 B3
Stovell Rd NEWH/MOS M40 .... 56 B1
Stowell St ORD M5 .... 65 D4
Stowfield Cl BKLY M9 .... 33 C1
Stow Gdns DID/WITH M20 .... 114 B3
Stracey St NEWH/MOS * M40 .... 71 D2
Stradbroke Cl GTN M18 .... 90 A4
Strain Av BKLY M9 .... 34 A1
Strand Ct STRET M32 .... 109 D1
Stranton Dr WALK M28 .... 43 D1
Stratford Av DID/WITH M20 .... 114 A4
    OLDS OL8 .... 40 B2
Stratford Rd MDTN M24 .... 18 A4
Strathblane Cl DID/WITH * M20 ... 115 C2
Strathfield Dr OP/CLY M11 .... 73 C3
Strathmere Av STRET M32 .... 97 C2
Strathmore Av CCHDY M21 .... 99 C3
Stratton Rd OLDTF/WHR M16 .... 99 C3
    SWIN M27 .... 26 A4
Strawberry Bank SLFD * M6 .... 67 C2
Strawberry Hl SLFD M6 .... 67 C2
Strawberry Rd SLFD M6 .... 66 B2
Stray St OP/CLY M11 .... 91 D1
Stream Ter STKP SK1 .... 131 C4
Stretford Rd HULME M15 .... 7 E5
    URM M41 .... 94 A4
Stretton Av DID/WITH M20 .... 125 D2
    STRET M32 .... 95 D2
Stretton Cl NEWH/MOS M40 .... 53 C4
Stringer St STKP SK1 .... 130 B3
Stroma Gdns URM M41 .... 94 B1
Strong St BRO M7 .... 68 B1
Stroud Av ECC M30 .... 61 C2
Stroud Cl MDTN M24 .... 17 D4
Stuart Rd STRET M32 .... 97 C2
Stuart St MDTN M24 .... 18 B1
    OLDS OL8 .... 22 B4
    OP/CLY M11 .... 72 B3
Stuart St East OP/CLY M11 .... 72 B3
Stuart Wk MDTN M24 .... 17 D4
Stubbs Cl BRO M7 .... 49 C1
Studforth Wk HULME * M15 .... 86 A4
Styal Av RDSH SK5 .... 120 A4
    STRET M32 .... 95 D2
Style St ANC M4 .... 4 B1
Sudell St ANC M4 .... 5 D1
Suffield St MDTN M24 .... 17 C1
Suffolk Av DROY M43 .... 75 D2
Suffolk Dr RDSH SK5 .... 121 D3
Suffolk St CHAD OL9 .... 39 C1
    SLFD M6 .... 48 B4
Sulby Av STRET M32 .... 97 D3

Sulby St NEWH/MOS M40 .... 54 B1
Sullivan St WGTN/LGST M12 ...... 104 B2
Sulway Cl SWIN * M27 .... 45 D2
Sumac St OP/CLY M11 .... 74 A3
Summer Av URM M41 .... 94 B3
Summercroft CHAD OL9 .... 39 C2
Summerfield Av DROY M43 .... 74 B2
Summerfield Rd WALK M28 .... 42 B2
Summer Pl RUSH/FAL M14 .... 102 B3
Summerseat Cl ORD * M5 .... 83 D1
Summers St CHAD OL9 .... 21 D2
Summerville Av BKLY M9 .... 54 A2
Summerville Rd SLFD M6 .... 47 D4
Sumner Rd SLFD M6 .... 47 C4
Sunbury Dr NEWH/MOS M40 .... 74 A1
Sundew Pl MDTN M24 .... 19 C2
Sunfield Rd OLD OL1 .... 22 B1
Sunk La MDTN M24 .... 17 D2
Sunningdale Av OP/CLY M11 .... 73 C3
Sunningdale Dr PWCH M25 .... 11 D3
    SLFD M6 .... 45 D4
Sunny Bank Av DROY M43 .... 75 D4
Sunnybank Av ECC M30 .... 63 C2
    HTNM SK4 .... 127 C1
Sunny Bank Rd BRUN/LGST M13 . 103 D2
Sunnybank Rd DROY M43 .... 75 C4
Sunny Brow Rd GTN M18 .... 90 B4
Sunny Dr PWCH M25 .... 16 B1
Sunnyfield Rd HTNM SK4 .... 127 C2
    PWCH M25 .... 12 B2
Sunnylea Av BNG/LEV M19 .... 116 B4
Sunnyside Av DROY M43 .... 75 C3
Sunnyside Cl DROY * M43 .... 75 C1
Sunnyside Ct DROY * M43 .... 75 C2
Sunnyside Rd DROY M43 .... 75 C3
Sunset Av WYTH/NTH M22 .... 123 C3
Surbiton Rd NEWH/MOS M40 .... 55 C4
Surma Cl CHAD OL9 .... 22 A2
Surrey Av DROY M43 .... 75 D2
Surrey Rd BKLY M9 .... 34 A3
Surrey St BKLY * M9 .... 33 D3
    CHAD OL9 .... 21 D4
Surrey Wy RDSH SK5 .... 121 D4
Sussex Av DID/WITH M20 .... 125 C1
Sussex Cl CHAD OL9 .... 21 C3
    SWIN M27 .... 26 B3
Sussex Dr DROY M43 .... 75 D2
Sussex St BRO M7 .... 68 A2
    CMANW M2 .... 3 F4
Sutcliffe Av WGTN/LGST M12 ..... 104 B3
Sutcliffe St MDTN M24 .... 18 B1
    OLDS OL8 .... 22 B4
Sutherland Cl OLDS OL8 .... 41 C4
Sutherland Rd OLDTF/WHR M16 .. 98 B2
Sutherland St ECC M30 .... 61 C2
    SWIN M27 .... 25 D4
Suthers St CHAD OL9 .... 21 D3
Sutton Dr DROY M43 .... 74 B2
Sutton Dwellings SLFD M6 .... 66 A2
Sutton Rd GTN M18 .... 105 D2
    HTNM SK4 .... 128 B2
Swaine St EDGY/DAV SK3 .... 129 D4
Swainsthorpe Dr BKLY M9 .... 53 D1
Swallow St OLDS OL8 .... 40 A3
    OP/CLY M11 .... 72 A4
    STKP SK1 .... 133 C2
    WGTN/LGST * M12 .... 104 B3
Swanage Rd ECC M30 .... 61 C2
Swanhill Cl GTN M18 .... 92 A3
Swanley Av NEWH/MOS M40 .... 53 D4
Swan St ANC M4 .... 4 B2
Swarbrick Dr PWCH M25 .... 29 C3
Sweetnam Dr OP/CLY M11 .... 73 C3
Swayfield Av BRUN/LGST M13 ... 104 A2
Swinbourne Gv DID/WITH M20 ... 115 D2
Swinburne Av DROY M43 .... 75 D2
Swinburne Gn RDSH SK5 .... 106 A4

Swinburn St *BKLY* M9 .... 35 C4
Swindell's St *OP/CLY* * M11 .... 91 D2
Swindon Cl *GTN* M18 .... 91 C4
Swinfield Av *CCHDY* M21 .... 111 C1
Swinstead Av *WHTF/FAL* * M40 .... 53 D4
Swinton Gv *BRUN/LGST* M13 .... 87 D4
Swinton Hall Rd *SWIN* M27 .... 45 D1
Swinton Park Rd *SLFD* M6 .... 46 A4
Sycamore Av *CHAD* OL9 .... 38 A2
Sycamore Cl *DID/WITH* * M20 .... 115 D2
Sycamore Ct *SLFD* M6 .... 66 B2
Sycamore Gv *FAIL* M35 .... 58 A2
Sycamore Pl *WHTF* M45 .... 11 C3
Sycamore Rd *ECC* M30 .... 60 B1
Sydney Av *ECC* M30 .... 62 A3
Sydney Jones Ct *NEWH/MOS* M40 .... 36 B4
Sydney St *FAIL* M35 .... 56 B2
  SLFD M6 .... 65 D3
  STRET M32 .... 97 C3
  SWIN M27 .... 44 A1
Sykes Cl *RDSH* SK5 .... 120 A1
Sylvan Av *FAIL* M35 .... 56 B4
  URM M41 .... 94 A2
Sylvandale Av *BNG/LEV* M19 .... 104 B4
Sylvan St *CHAD* OL9 .... 21 D2
Sylvia Gv *RDSH* SK5 .... 119 D2
Symms St *SLFD* M6 .... 67 C1
Symond Av *BKLY* M9 .... 16 B4
Symons Rd *SALE* M33 .... 109 C4
Symons St *BRO* M7 .... 50 B2
Syndall Av *WGTN/LGST* M12 .... 88 A3
Syndall St *WGTN/LGST* M12 .... 88 A3

Tabley Av *RUSH/FAL* M14 .... 102 A3
Tabley Gv *BRUN/LGST* M13 .... 104 A3
  RDSH SK5 .... 119 D2
Tabley St *SLFD* M6 .... 49 C4
Tackler Cl *SWIN* M27 .... 45 C2
Tagore Cl *BRUN/LGST* M13 .... 103 D1
Tahir Cl *CHH* M8 .... 52 A2
Talavera St *BRO* M7 .... 50 A4
Talbot Pl *OLDTF/WHR* M16 .... 84 A4
Talbot Rd *RUSH/FAL* M14 .... 116 B2
  STRET M32 .... 98 A1
Talbot St *ECC* M30 .... 62 B4
Talford Gv *DID/WITH* M20 .... 114 B4
Talgarth Rd *NEWH/MOS* M40 .... 70 B1
Talland Wk *BRUN/LGST* M13 .... 88 A4
Tallarn Cl *DID/WITH* M20 .... 115 D2
Tallis St *WGTN/LGST* M12 .... 104 B2
Tallyman Wy *SWIN* M27 .... 47 D2
Talmine Av *NEWH/MOS* M40 .... 53 D4
Tamar Ct *HULME* M15 .... 85 D4
Tamarin Cl *SWIN* M27 .... 47 D2
Tamerton Dr *CHH* M8 .... 51 D3
Tame St *ANC* M4 .... 71 C4
Tamworth Av West *ORD* * M5 .... 85 D1
  WHTF M45 .... 12 A2
Tamworth Cl *HULME* M15 .... 85 D4
Tamworth Gn *STKP* SK1 .... 131 C3
Tamworth St *CHAD* OL9 .... 21 D3
  STKP SK1 .... 131 C3
Tamworth Wk *ORD* M5 .... 83 D1
Tandis Cl *SLFD* * M6 .... 63 D2
Tandlewood Ms *NEWH/MOS* M40 ..... 55 D4
Tangmere Cl *NEWH/MOS* * M40 .... 36 B2
Tanhill La *OLDS* OL8 .... 41 D3
Tanners Fold *OLDS* OL8 .... 41 D3
Tanners Gn *SLFD* M6 .... 66 A2
Tansey Gv *BRO* M7 .... 51 C2
Tansley Rd *CHH* M8 .... 32 B3
Tan Yard Brow *GTN* M18 .... 106 B1
Tanyard Gn *RDSH* SK5 .... 120 A4

Taplin Dr *GTN* M18 .... 90 B4
Taplow Wk *RUSH/FAL* M14 .... 103 D2
Tariff St *CMANE* M1 .... 5 D4
Tarleton Wk *BRUN/LGST* * M13 .... 87 D3
Tarnbrook Cl *WHTF* M45 .... 12 B1
Tarnbrook Wk *HULME* * M15 .... 86 A4
Tarporley Av *RUSH/FAL* M14 .... 114 B1
Tarrington Cl *WGTN/LGST* M12 .... 89 D3
Tartan St *OP/CLY* M11 .... 73 C3
Tarvin Av *DID/WITH* M20 .... 114 B2
  HTNM SK4 .... 119 C2
Tarvington Cl *NEWH/MOS* * M40 ...... 52 B3
Tasle Aly *CMANW* M2 .... 3 F5
Tatchbury Rd *FAIL* M35 .... 57 C2
Tatham St *CHAD* OL9 .... 22 A3
Tatton Cl *BRUN/LGST* M13 .... 104 A2
Tatton Gv *DID/WITH* M20 .... 115 C3
Tatton Pl *SALE* M33 .... 109 C4
Tatton Rd *SALE* M33 .... 109 C4
Tatton Rd North *HTNM* SK4 .... 118 B4
Tatton Rd South *HTNM* SK4 .... 128 B1
Tatton St *HULME* M15 .... 6 A5
  ORD M5 .... 84 A1
  STKP * SK1 .... 130 A4
Taunton Av *ECC* M30 .... 61 C2
  RDSH SK5 .... 121 D1
Taunton Gv *WHTF* M45 .... 11 D3
Taunton St *ANC* M4 .... 71 C4
Tavern Court Av *FAIL* M35 .... 57 D2
Tavery Cl *ANC* * M4 .... 5 F3
Tay Cl *OLDS* OL8 .... 22 B4
Taylor Rd *URM* M41 .... 79 D2
Taylorson St *ORD* M5 .... 84 A2
Taylorson St South *ORD* M5 .... 83 D3
Taylor's Rd *STRET* M32 .... 97 D1
Taylor St *CHAD* OL9 .... 20 B2
  DROY M43 .... 75 D4
  GTN M18 .... 90 B3
  MDTN M24 .... 17 D1
  PWCH M25 .... 30 B1
  RUSH/FAL M14 .... 102 B2
Teak Dr *FWTH* BL4 .... 25 C1
Tealby Av *OLDTF/WHR* M16 .... 99 D1
Tealby Rd *GTN* M18 .... 105 C1
Teasdale Cl *CHAD* OL9 .... 37 D2
Tebbutt St *ANC* M4 .... 5 D1
Teddington Rd *NEWH/MOS* M40 .... 36 B4
Ted Jackson Wk *OP/CLY* * M11 .... 89 C1
Teer St *NEWH/MOS* M40 .... 71 C3
Teignmouth Av *NEWH/MOS* * M40 ... 70 B1
Teignmouth St *NEWH/MOS* M40 ...... 70 B1
Telfer Av *BRUN/LGST* M13 .... 103 D3
Telfer Rd *BRUN/LGST* M13 .... 105 D3
Telford St *CHH* M8 .... 52 B4
Telford Wk *OLDTF/WHR* M16 .... 100 A1
Tellson Cl *SLFD* M6 .... 47 C3
Tellson Crs *SLFD* M6 .... 47 C3
Temperance St *WGTN/LGST* M12 .... 9 E2
Temple Dr *SWIN* M27 .... 46 A2
Ten Acre Ct *WHTF* * M45 .... 10 A2
Ten Acre Dr *WHTF* M45 .... 10 A2
Ten Acres La *NEWH/MOS* M40 .... 54 B4
Tenax Rd *TRPK* M17 .... 81 C2
Tenbury Cl *SLFD* * M6 .... 66 A2
Tenbury Dr *MDTN* M24 .... 17 D2
Tenby Av *DID/WITH* M20 .... 115 C3
  STRET M32 .... 97 D1
Tenby St *HULME* * M15 .... 84 B3
Tenby Dr *SLFD* M6 .... 47 C4
Tenby Rd *OLDS* OL8 .... 39 C3
Teneriffe St *BRO* M7 .... 50 A4
Tennis St *OLDTF/WHR* M16 .... 127 D4
Tennyson Cl *HTNM* SK4 .... 29 C2
Tennyson Gdns *PWCH* M25 .... 29 C2
Tennyson Rd *DROY* M43 .... 75 D3
  RDSH SK5 .... 106 A2
  SWIN M27 .... 44 A1

Tennyson St *BRUN/LGST* M13 ....87 D4
   SLFD M6 ....67 D1
Tenth St *TRPK* M17 ....82 A3
Terence St *NEWH/MOS* M40 ....56 A4
The Terrace *PWCH* M25 ....30 A2
Terrington Cl *CCHDY* M21 ....113 D2
Tetlow Gv *ECC* M30 ....61 D4
Tetlow La *BRO* M7 ....50 B1
Tetlow St *MDTN* M24 ....17 D1
   NEWH/MOS M40 ....55 D4
Teviot St *BRUN/LGST* M13 ....103 D1
Teviot Wy *STKP* SK1 ....130 A2
Tewkesbury Av *DROY* M43 ....75 D2
   URM M41 ....94 A1
Tewkesbury Dr *PWCH* M25 ....30 B3
Tewkesbury Rd *NEWH/MOS* M40 ......71 C2
Textile St *WGTN/LGST* M12 ....89 D2
Textilose Rd *TRPK* M17 ....81 C4
Thackeray Cl *CHH* M8 ....51 D3
Thackeray Gv *DROY* M43 ....75 D3
Thames Cl *OP/CLY* M11 ....90 A1
Thames Dr *HULME* M15 ....85 C3
Thames St *OLD* O1 ....23 D1
Thanet Cl *BRO* M7 ....50 B4
Thankerton Av *DTN/ASHW* M34 ....77 D3
Thatcher St *OLDS* OL8 ....41 D2
Thatch Leach *CHAD* OL9 ....20 A4
Thatch Leach La *WHTF* M45 ....11 D2
Thaxmead Dr *NEWH/MOS* M40 ....74 A1
Theatre St *OL1* 23 C2
Thekla St *CHAD* OL9 ....22 A1
Thelwall Av *RUSH/FAL* M14 ....114 A1
Theta Cl *OP/CLY* M11 ....73 C3
Thetford Dr *CHH* M8 ....52 A2
Third Av *OLDS* OL8 ....39 D5
   OP/CLY M11 ....73 D5
   SWIN M27 ....44 B4
   TRPK M17 ....82 A4
Thirlmere Av *STRET* M32 ....96 B2
   SWIN M27 ....45 D2
Thirsfield Dr *OP/CLY* M11 ....73 D5
Thirsk St *WGTN/LGST* M12 ....9 E3
Thistledown Cl *ECC* M30 ....78 B1
Thomas Gibbon Cl *STRET* * M32 ....96 B4
Thomas Johnson Cl *ECC* * M30 ....61 D4
Thomas St *ANC* M4 ....4 B3
   CHH M8 ....51 C1
   STKP SK1 ....133 C2
   STRET M32 ....97 C2
Thomas St West *OFTN* SK2 ....133 C2
Thomas Telford Basin *CMANE* M1........5 D5
Thompson Av *WHTF* M45 ....11 D2
Thompson La *CHAD* OL9 ....38 B1
Thompson Rd *TRPK* M17 ....79 D1
Thompson St *ANC* M4 ....4 C2
   CHAD OL9 ....22 A2
   CSLFD M3 ....69 C2
   NEWH/MOS M40 ....54 A4
Thomson Rd *GTN* M18 ....105 D1
Thomson St *BRUN/LGST* M13 ....87 D3
   EDGY/DAV SK3 ....132 B3
Thoralby Cl *WGTN/LGST* M12 ....89 D2
Thoresway Rd *BRUN/LGST* M13 ....103 D2
Thor Gv *ORD* M5 ....84 B1
Thorley Cl *CHAD* OL9 ....37 D3
Thorley Dr *URM* M41 ....94 A3
Thorley St *FAIL* M35 ....57 C1
Thornage Dr *NEWH/MOS* M40 ....70 B1
Thorn Av *FAIL* M35 ....57 C3
Thorn Bank *DROY* * M43 ....75 C2
Thornbridge Av *CCHDY* M21 ....112 A1
Thornbury Rd *STRET* M32 ....95 D4
Thornbury Wy *GTN* M18 ....90 B4
Thorncliff Av *OLDS* OL8 ....40 B2
Thorncliffe Gv *BNG/LEV* M19 ....105 D4
Thorncombe Rd *OLDTF/WHR* M16 .....100 B2
Thorn Ct *SLFD* M6 ....67 D3
Thorncross Cl *HULME* M15 ....84 B2

Thorneycroft Av *CCHDY* M21 ....112 A4
Thorney Hill Cl *OLDE* OL4 ....23 D3
Thornfield Dr *SWIN* M27 ....44 B2
Thornfield Rd *BNG/LEV* M19 ....116 B4
   HTNM SK4 ....127 D2
Thornfield St *ORD* M5 ....65 C4
Thorngate Rd *CHH* M8 ....51 D4
Thorn Gv *RUSH/FAL* M14 ....116 A4
Thornhill Cl *DTN/ASHW* M34 ....107 D3
Thornhill Rd *DROY* M43 ....76 A3
Thornholme Cl *GTN* M18 ....105 C2
Thornley Brow *ANC* M4 ....4 A3
Thornlea *DROY* M43 ....74 B4
Thornlea Av *OLDS* OL8 ....39 C4
   SWIN M27 ....44 A3
Thornleigh Rd *RUSH/FAL* M14 ....102 A4
Thornley La North *RDSH* SK5 ....107 C2
Thornley La South *RDSH* SK5 ....107 C4
Thornley Rd *WHTF* M45 ....12 B2
Thornmere Cl *SWIN* M27 ....24 B3
Thorn Rd *SWIN* M27 ....44 B3
The Thorns *CCHDY* M21 ....112 A2
Thornsett Cl *BKLY* * M9 ....53 D1
Thornton Av *DTN/ASHW* M34 ....93 D1
Thornton Crs *PWCH* M25 ....11 C4
Thornton Pl *HTNM* SK4 ....128 A1
Thornton Rd *RUSH/FAL* M14 ....101 D3
Thornton St *NEWH/MOS* M40 ....70 B1
   OLDE * OL4 ....23 C4
Thornton St North *NEWH/MOS* M40 ...52 B4
Thorntree Cl *BKLY* M9 ....53 D2
Thornwood Av *GTN* M18 ....106 B1
Thorpe Av *SWIN* M27 ....25 D4
Thorpebrook Rd *NEWH/MOS* M40 ......54 B3
Thorpe Gv *HTNM* SK4 ....119 C3
Thorpeness Sq *GTN* M18 ....91 C3
Thorpe St *MDTN* M24 ....15 D2
   OLDTF/WHR M16 ....99 D1
Thorp Rd *NEWH/MOS* M40 ....54 B3
Thorp St *ECC* M30 ....78 A1
Thrapston Av *DTN/ASHW* M34 ....77 C4
Throstles Cl *DROY* M43 ....76 B2
Thruxton Cl *OLDTF/WHR* M16 ....100 B2
Tharland St *CHAD* OL9 ....22 A2
Thurlby Av *BKLY* M9 ....19 D1
Thurlby St *BRUN/LGST* M13 ....105 C1
Thurleigh Rd *DID/WITH* M20 ....125 C1
Thurloe St *RUSH/FAL* M14 ....102 B2
Thurlow St *SALQ* M50 ....66 A4
Thurlston Crs *CHH* M8 ....52 A2
Thurlwood Av *DID/WITH* M20 ....114 B2
Thursfield Rd *SLFD* M6 ....49 C4
Tiber Av *OLDS* OL8 ....39 D4
Tib La *CMANW* M2 ....3 F5
Tib St *ANC* M4 ....4 B4
Tidesville Av *NEWH/MOS* M40 ....71 C4
Tideswell Rd *DROY* M43 ....74 B2
Tideway Cl *SWIN* M27 ....48 A1
Tidworth Av *ANC* M4 ....5 F3
Tilbury St *OLD* OL1 ....23 D1
Tilney Av *STRET* M32 ....97 D4
Tilshead Wk *BRUN/LGST* * M13 ....87 D3
Times St *MDTN* M24 ....18 A1
Timothy Cl *SLFD* M6 ....64 A2
Timperley Cl *OLDS* OL8 ....41 D3
Timperley St *CHAD* OL9 ....22 A2
   OP/CLY * M11 ....90 B1
Timson St *FAIL* M35 ....57 C2
Tindall St *ECC* M30 ....78 A1
   RDSH SK5 ....107 C2
Tinningham Cl *OP/CLY* M11 ....91 D2
Tinshill Cl *WGTN/LGST* M12 ....89 D4
Tinsley Cl *NEWH/MOS* M40 ....57 D1
Tintern Av *DID/WITH* M20 ....114 A4
Tintern Gv *STKP* SK1 ....131 C4
Tintern St *RUSH/FAL* M14 ....102 A3
Tirza Av *BNG/LEV* M19 ....117 C2
Tithe Barn Rd *HTNM* SK4 ....127 C1

Titherington Cl RDSH * SK5 ....106 A4
Titterington Av CCHDY M21 ....99 C3
Tiverton Rd URM M41 ....94 B1
Tiviot Dl STKP SK1 ....130 A3
Tiviot Wy RDSH SK5 ....130 A3
Tivoli St CSLFD M3 ....3 D5
Tobermory Cl OP/CLY M11 ....74 A4
Todd St BRO M7 ....50 A3
  CSLFD M3 ....4 A2
Toft Rd GTN M18 ....105 D1
Toledo St OP/CLY M11 ....74 A4
Tollard Av NEWH/MOS M40 ....53 C4
Toll Bar St WGTN/LGST M12 ....88 B3
Tollesbury Cl NEWH/MOS M40 ....71 C1
Toll Gate Cl BRUN/LGST M13 ....103 D1
Tolworth Dr CHH M8 ....52 A2
Tomlinson Cl OLDS OL8 ....22 B4
Tomlinson St HULME M15 ....85 D5
  NEWH/MOS M40 ....54 B2
Tommy Browell Cl RUSH/FAL M14 .....101 D2
Tommy Johnson Wk RUSH/FAL M14 ...101 D2
Tommy Taylor Cl NEWH/MOS * M40 .....55 D4
Tonbridge Rd BNG/LEV M19 ....118 A1
  RDSH SK5 ....120 A1
Tonge Hall Cl MDTN M24 ....18 A1
Tonge Roughs MDTN M24 ....19 C1
Tonge St WGTN/LGST * M12 ....88 A2
Tonman St CSLFD M3 ....7 D1
Tootal Dr SLFD M6 ....64 B2
Tootal Gv SLFD M6 ....64 B3
Tootal Rd ORD M5 ....64 B3
Topley St BKLY M9 ....52 B3
Top O' Th' Gn CHAD OL9 ....39 D1
Top Schwabe St MDTN M24 ....15 D1
Torah St CHH M8 ....69 D1
Torbay Rd CCHDY M21 ....112 B1
  URM M41 ....94 B4
Torcross Rd BKLY M9 ....15 C4
Torkington Av SWIN M27 ....26 A4
Torkington St EDGY/DAV SK3 ....132 A2
Torness Wk OP/CLY M11 ....75 C4
Toronto Rd OFTN SK2 ....133 D3
Torquay Cl BRUN/LGST M13 ....87 D4
Torrax Cl SLFD M6 ....46 A3
Torrens St EDGY/DAV SK3 ....47 C4
Torrin Cl EDGY/DAV SK3 ....132 A1
Torrington Av BKLY M9 ....35 D3
Torrington Rd SWIN M27 ....46 A3
Torside Wy SWIN M27 ....26 A3
Totland Cl WGTN/LGST M12 ....104 B2
Totnes Rd CCHDY M21 ....112 B1
Tottington La PWCH M25 ....10 B4
Tottington St OP/CLY M11 ....73 D1
Totton Rd FAIL M35 ....57 C2
Towcester Cl ANC M4 ....71 C4
Tower Sq BRUN/LGST M13 ....3 E5
Towey Cl GTN M18 ....91 C3
Towncliffe Wk HULME * M15 ....85 C3
Townfield Wk HULME M15 ....6 B5
Town Hall La CMANW * M2 ....3 F5
Townley St CHH M8 ....51 C4
  OP/CLY * M11 ....89 C1
Townsend Rd SWIN M27 ....26 A4
Towton St BKLY M9 ....53 D1
Towyn Av ORD M5 ....65 D3
Toxteth St OP/CLY M11 ....91 D2
Tracey St CHH M8 ....32 B4
Traders Av URM M41 ....79 D5
Trafalgar Av DTN/ASHW M34 ....93 D2
Trafalgar Gv BRO * M7 ....50 A3
Trafalgar Pl DID/WITH M20 ....124 B1
Trafalgar Rd SALE M33 ....109 D3
  SLFD M6 ....63 D2
Trafalgar St BRO M7 ....50 B4
  OLD OL1 ....22 B1
Trafford Av URM M41 ....94 B2
Trafford Bank Rd OLDTF/WHR * M16 ...84 B4
Trafford Bvd URM M41 ....78 B3

Trafford Gv STRET M32 ....97 C4
Trafford Park Rd TRPK M17 ....81 C1
Trafford Pl HULME M15 ....85 C3
Trafford Rd ECC M30 ....79 C1
  ORD M5 ....83 D3
Trafford St CSLFD M3 ....7 D2
  OLDS OL8 ....22 B4
Trafford Wharf Rd TRPK M17 ....81 D2
  TRPK M17 ....83 D2
Trail St SLFD M6 ....65 D3
Tram St OP/CLY M11 ....90 B2
Tranmere Cl GTN M18 ....90 A4
Transvaal St OP/CLY M11 ....74 A4
Travis Brow HTNM SK4 ....129 C4
Travis St CMANE M1 ....9 E1
Tree Av DROY M43 ....93 D2
Treelands Wk ORD M5 ....84 A3
Tregaer Fold MDTN M24 ....18 B1
Trenam Pl ORD M5 ....67 C3
Trenant Rd SLFD M6 ....47 C4
Trencherbone CLO 19 D1
Trent Bridge Wk OLDTF/WHR M16 ......98 B2
Trent Cl RDSH SK5 ....121 D4
Trent Ct HULME * M15 ....85 C3
Trentham Av HTNM SK4 ....127 C2
Trentham Gv NEWH/MOS M40 ....35 C2
Trentham Lawns SLFD M6 ....66 B1
Trentham Rd OLDTF/WHR M16 ....98 B2
Trentham St HULME M15 ....84 B2
  SWIN * M27 ....25 D3
Trent Wk DROY M43 ....93 C1
Tresco Av STRET M32 ....97 C3
Trevelyan St ECC M30 ....63 D3
Trevor Dr NEWH/MOS M40 ....37 D3
Trevor Rd ECC M30 ....61 C2
  SWIN M27 ....44 B3
Trevor St OP/CLY M11 ....91 D2
Trimdon Cl OP/CLY M11 ....73 C3
Trimley Av NEWH/MOS M40 ....53 C4
Trinity Av MDTN * M24 ....17 C1
  OLD OL1 ....22 B1
Trinity Wy CSLFD M3 ....2 C4
Tripps Ms DID/WITH M20 ....124 A1
Triscombe Wy OLDTF/WHR M16 ....100 B3
Tristam Cl BRUN/LGST M13 ....9 E5
Trojan Gdns BRO M7 ....49 D4
Trough Ga OLDS OL8 ....40 A3
Troutbeck Av ANC M4 ....5 F3
Trowbridge Dr NEWH/MOS M40 ....36 B3
Trowtree Av WGTN/LGST M12 ....88 B3
Troydale Dr NEWH/MOS M40 ....54 B3
Troy Wk ORD * M5 ....84 A2
Trumpet St CMANE M1 ....7 E2
Truro Av RDSH SK5 ....121 D4
  STRET M32 ....97 D3
Trust Rd GTN M18 ....105 D2
Tudbury Wy CSLFD M3 ....2 B1
Tudor Av BKLY M9 ....34 B4
  CHAD OL9 ....37 C2
Tudor Cl RDSH SK5 ....119 D2
Tudor Ct PWCH M25 ....30 B2
Tudor St MDTN M24 ....18 A1
  OLDS OL8 ....22 B4
Tuer St BRUN/LGST M13 ....86 B3
Tugford Cl OLDTF/WHR M16 ....100 B2
Tuley St OP/CLY M11 ....89 C2
Tulip Cl CHAD OL9 ....19 D2
  EDGY/DAV SK3 ....132 A4
Tulip St CHH M8 ....32 B4
Tully Pl BRO M7 ....68 B1
Tully St BRO M7 ....50 B2
Tully St South BRO M7 ....50 B2
Tulpen Sq CHAD OL9 ....21 C2
Tunbridge Sq ORD M5 ....66 B3
Tunstall St HTNM * SK4 ....129 D3
  OP/CLY * M11 ....91 D2
Tunstead Av DID/WITH M20 ....114 A3
Turf La CHAD OL9 ....38 B2
Turley St CHH M8 ....52 A3

Turnbull Av PWCH M25 .... 12 B2
Turnbull Rd BRUN/LGST M13 .... 104 A3
   GTN M18 .... 107 C2
Turnbury Cl SALE M33 .... 109 C3
Turncroft La STKP SK1 .... 130 B4
Turnell Wy WALK M28 .... 42 B4
Turner Av FAIL M35 .... 56 B3
Turner Dr URM M41 .... 95 C3
Turner St ANC M4 .... 4 B3
   BRO M7 .... 50 B2
   GTN M18 .... 91 C4
   OLDTF/WHR M16 .... 84 B3
   OP/CLY M11 .... 73 D4
Turn Moss Rd STRET M32 .... 111 C1
Turnpike Gn SLFD * M6 .... 66 A2
Turnpike Wy OP/CLY M11 .... 72 A4
Turton La PWCH M25 .... 11 C4
Turton St OP/CLY M11 .... 91 C2
Tuscany Vw BRO M7 .... 49 C1
Tutbury St ANC M4 .... 71 C4
Tuxford Wy NEWH/MOS M40 .... 53 C4
Tweedale Av BKLY M9 .... 15 D4
Tweedale Dr OLD OL9 .... 38 A3
Tweed Cl OLDS OL8 .... 22 B3
Tweedle Hill Rd BKLY M9 .... 33 C1
Twillbrook Dr CSLFD * M3 .... 3 D1
Twining Rd TRPK M17 .... 79 D1
Twyford Cl DID/WITH M20 .... 124 A2
Tydden St OLDS OL8 .... 41 C2
Tyldesley St RUSH/FAL M14 .... 101 D2
Tymm St NEWH/MOS M40 .... 55 D1
Tyndall Av NEWH/MOS M40 .... 35 D4
Tynedale La RDSH SK5 .... 119 D4
Tyrol Wk OP/CLY M11 .... 89 C3
Tyro St OL8 .... 41 C2
Tyrrel Rd RDSH SK5 .... 107 C4
Tysoe Gdns CSLFD M3 .... 2 B2
Tyson St CHH M8 .... 51 C1
Tytherington Dr RDSH SK5 .... 106 A4

U

Ukraine Rd BRO M7 .... 48 B3
Ulverston Av CHAD OL9 .... 20 D3
   DID/WITH M20 .... 114 A2
Underhill Wk NEWH/MOS M40 .... 73 C1
Under La CHAD OL9 .... 39 C2
Underwood Cl GTN M18 .... 92 A3
Unicorn St ECC M30 .... 78 A1
Union St ANC M4 .... 4 B3
   CHAD OL9 .... 39 C1
   GTN M18 .... 91 D3
   OLD OL1 .... 23 C3
   RUSH/FAL * M14 .... 102 A2
   SLFD M6 .... 66 B1
   STKP SK1 .... 133 C1
   SWIN M27 .... 44 B1
   WGTN/LGST M12 .... 9 F3
Union St West CHAD OL9 .... 22 B3
Union Ter CHH * M8 .... 51 C1
United Rd OLDTF/WHR M16 .... 82 B3
Unity Dr BRO M7 .... 50 B3
Unity Wy STKP SK1 .... 133 C2
University Rd SLFD M6 .... 67 C2
University Rd West ORD * M5 .... 67 C3
Unsworth Wy OLD * OL1 .... 22 B1
Unwin Av GTN M18 .... 106 A1
Upland Rd OLDS OL8 .... 40 B1
Uplands MDTN M24 .... 17 D3
Upper Brook St BRUN/LGST M13 .... 8 C5
   STKP SK1 .... 130 B4
Upper Camp St BRO M7 .... 50 A4
Upper Chorlton Rd OLDTF/WHR M16 .... 99 D3
Upper Cleminson St CSLFD M3 .... 2 A3
Upper Conran St BKLY M9 .... 53 D3
Upper Cyrus St NEWH/MOS M40 .... 71 D3

Upper Dover St OP/CLY M11 .... 72 B4
Upper Gloucester St SLFD M6 .... 66 B3
Upper Helena St NEWH/MOS M40 .... 71 D3
Upper Kent Rd RUSH/FAL M14 .... 103 C2
Upper Kirby St ANC M4 .... 5 F4
Upper Lloyd St RUSH/FAL M14 .... 101 D2
Upper Medlock St HULME M15 .... 7 F5
Uppermill Dr BNG/LEV M19 .... 126 A2
Upper Monsall St NEWH/MOS M40 .... 53 D3
Upper Moss La HULME M15 .... 85 D3
Upper Park Rd BRO M7 .... 31 C4
   RUSH/FAL M14 .... 102 B1
Upper West Gv BRUN/LGST M13 .... 88 A4
Upper Wharf St ORD M5 .... 67 D4
Upper Wilton St PWCH M25 .... 30 B1
Upton Av HTNM SK4 .... 126 B1
Upton Cl MDTN M24 .... 17 D4
Upton St CMANE M1 .... 8 C1
Urmston La STRET M32 .... 97 D4
Urmston Pk URM M41 .... 94 B3
Usk Cl WHTF M45 .... 12 B2

V

Vaal St OLDS OL8 .... 39 D2
Valance Cl WGTN/LGST M12 .... 89 D3
Vale Av SALE M33 .... 110 B4
   SWIN M27 .... 26 B4
Vale Cl HTNM SK4 .... 127 C3
Vale Dr OLD OL9 .... 22 A3
   PWCH M25 .... 29 D3
Vale La FAIL M35 .... 57 D4
Valencia Rd BRO M7 .... 49 C3
Valentia Rd BKLY M9 .... 34 A1
Valentine St FAIL M35 .... 56 B2
Valerie Wk HULME M15 .... 7 F4
Vale Rd DROY M43 .... 76 A2
   HTNM SK4 .... 127 C4
Vale St MDTN M24 .... 18 A1
   OP/CLY M11 .... 73 D3
Vale Top Av BKLY M9 .... 53 D2
Valetta Cl RUSH/FAL M14 .... 102 A4
Valewood Av HTNM SK4 .... 127 D4
Valley Wy OP/CLY M11 .... 72 A4
Vancouver Quay SALQ M50 .... 83 C2
Vandyke Av SLFD M6 .... 64 A2
Vane St ECC M30 .... 61 D3
Varden Gv EDGY/DAV SK3 .... 132 A4
Varey St GTN M18 .... 91 C4
Varley St NEWH/MOS M40 .... 71 C1
Varna St OP/CLY M11 .... 91 C2
Vauban Dr SLFD M6 .... 64 A2
Vaughan Av NEWH/MOS M40 .... 54 B1
Vaughan Rd CCHDY M21 .... 113 C1
   HTNM SK4 .... 129 C2
Vaughan St ECC M30 .... 61 C2
   WGTN/LGST M12 .... 89 C2
Vauxhall St NEWH/MOS M40 .... 70 A1
Vega St CHH M8 .... 68 B1
Velmere Av BKLY M9 .... 14 B4
Velour Cl BRO M7 .... 50 B1
   CSLFD M3 .... 2 A1
Vendale Av SWIN M27 .... 44 A3
Venetia St NEWH/MOS * M40 .... 55 D4
Venice St CMANE * M1 .... 8 C2
Ventnor Av BNG/LEV M19 .... 118 B1
   SALE M33 .... 109 C3
Ventnor Rd DID/WITH M20 .... 125 D2
   HTNM SK4 .... 127 D3
Ventnor St BKLY M9 .... 53 C1
   SLFD M6 .... 49 C4
Ventura Cl RUSH/FAL M14 .... 101 D4
Venture Scout Wy BRO M7 .... 51 C3
Venwood Ct PWCH * M25 .... 29 C3
Venwood Rd PWCH M25 .... 29 C3

Verdon St *ANC* M4 ....4 A1
Verdun Av *SLFD* M6 ....64 A2
Verdun Rd *ECC* M30 ....61 C1
Verdure Cl *FAIL* M35 ....58 A1
Vere St *SALO* M50 ....66 A4
Verity Cl *DID/WITH* M20 ....115 C3
Verne Av *SWIN* M27 ....44 B4
Vernon Av *ECC* * M30 ....63 C3
   STKP SK1 ....131 C5
   STRET M32 ....97 C4
Vernon Dr *PWCH* M25 ....29 D3
Vernon Rd *BRO* M7 ....30 B1
   DROY M43 ....74 B3
Vernon St *BKLY* M9 ....53 D2
   BRO M7 ....50 A4
Verona Dr *NEWH/MOS* M40 ....73 D1
Veronica Rd *DID/WITH* M20 ....125 C2
Verrill Av *NTHM/RTH* M23 ....122 B4
Vesper St *FAIL* M35 ....57 D1
Vesta St *ANC* M4 ....5 F4
Vestris Dr *SLFD* M6 ....64 A2
Viaduct St *CSLFD* M3 ....3 D2
   EDGY/DAV SK3 ....129 D4
   WGTN/LGST M12 ....88 B1
Vicarage Cl *DID/WITH* M20 ....64 A2
Vicarage Gdns *EDGY/DAV* * SK3 ....132 B1
Vicarage Gv *ECC* M30 ....63 C3
Vicarage La *MDTN* M24 ....19 C2
Vicarage Rd *EDGY/DAV* SK3 ....132 B1
   SWIN M27 ....44 B1
Vicarage St *OLDS* OL8 ....39 D3
Vicars Rd *CCHDY* M21 ....111 C1
Vicars St *ECC* M30 ....63 C3
Vicker Cl *SWIN* M27 ....26 A3
Vicker Gv *DID/WITH* M20 ....114 A4
Vickers St *NEWH/MOS* M40 ....71 D2
Victoria Av *BKLY* M9 ....15 D4
   BNG/LEV M19 ....117 D1
   DID/WITH M20 ....124 A3
   ECC M30 ....63 C2
   SWIN M27 ....45 D1
   WHTF M45 ....11 D3
Victoria Av East *BKLY* M9 ....35 C3
Victoria Bridge St *CSLFD* M3 ....3 E2
Victoria Cl *EDGY/DAV* * SK3 ....132 A1
Victoria Crs *ECC* M30 ....63 C2
Victoria Gv *HTNM* SK4 ....118 B4
   RUSH/FAL M14 ....115 D2
Victoria La *SWIN* M27 ....44 A1
   WHTF M45 ....11 C2
Victoria Ldg *BRO* * M7 ....49 D4
Victoria Pl *TRPK* M17 ....83 C4
Victoria Rd *ECC* M30 ....62 B2
   OLDTF/WHR M16 ....100 A3
   RUSH/FAL M14 ....115 D3
   STKP SK1 ....131 C4
   STRET M32 ....97 C4
Victoria Sq *ANC* * M4 ....5 D2
Victoria Station Ap *CSLFD* M3 ....5 D1
Victoria St *CHAD* OL9 ....21 C2
   CSLFD M3 ....3 E2
   FAIL M35 ....56 A3
   MDTN M24 ....17 D1
   OLDE * OL4 ....23 D3
   OP/CLY M11 ....90 B1
Victoria Ter *WGTN/LGST* M12 ....104 B1
Victor Mann St *OP/CLY* M11 ....92 B2
Victor St *CSLFD* M3 ....2 B1
   NEWH/MOS M40 ....70 B1
   OLDS OL8 ....39 C4
Victory Gv *DTN/ASHW* M34 ....93 D2
Victory St *RUSH/FAL* M14 ....102 B2
Vienna Rd *EDGY/DAV* SK3 ....132 A3
Vienna Rd East *EDGY/DAV* SK3 ....132 A3
Viking Cl *OP/CLY* M11 ....72 A4
Village Ct *TRPK* M17 ....81 D3
Village St *BRO* M7 ....49 D4

Village Wy (Ashburton Rd East) *TRPK* M17 81
   C3
Villa Rd *OLDS* OL8 ....41 C1
Villiers Ct *WHTF* M45 ....11 D3
Villiers Dr *OLDS* OL8 ....22 B4
Vinca Gv *BRO* M7 ....50 A3
Vincent Av *CCHDY* M21 ....98 B3
Vincent St *BRO* M7 ....50 A2
   OP/CLY M11 ....92 B3
Vine Av *SWIN* M27 ....46 A1
Vine Ct *STRET* M32 ....97 C4
Vine Fold *NEWH/MOS* M40 ....38 A4
Vine St *BRO* M7 ....49 C1
   CHAD OL9 ....39 C2
   ECC M30 ....61 D4
   OP/CLY M11 ....91 D2
Viola St *OP/CLY* M11 ....74 A3
Violet St *GTN* M18 ....92 A3
   OFTN SK2 ....133 C3
Violet Wy *MDTN* M24 ....19 C2
Virgil St *HULME* M15 ....84 B3
Viscount St *RUSH/FAL* M14 ....102 B2
Vixen Cl *CCHDY* M21 ....113 C2
Voltaire Av *SLFD* M6 ....64 A2
Vorlich Dr *CHAD* OL9 ....20 A1
Vyner Gv *SALE* M33 ....108 A3

W

Waddington St *CHAD* OL9 ....21 D1
Wadeford Cl *ANC* M4 ....5 F2
Wadesmill Wk *BRUN/LGST* * M13 ....8 C1
Wadeson Rd *BRUN/LGST* M13 ....9 D4
Wade St *MDTN* M24 ....19 C3
Wade Wk *OP/CLY* M11 ....89 D1
Wadhurst Wk *BRUN/LGST* * M13 ....87 D1
Wadlow Cl *CSLFD* * M3 ....2 C1
Wadsworth Ms *DROY* M43 ....75 C4
Waggoners Ct *SWIN* M27 ....45 C2
Wagstaffe Dr *FAIL* M35 ....57 C2
Waincliffe Av *CCHDY* M21 ....123 C1
Wainman St *SLFD* M6 ....49 C4
Wainwright Av *DTN/ASHW* M34 ....107 C2
Wainwright Cl *OFTN* SK2 ....133 C2
Wainwright St *OLDS* OL8 ....22 B4
Wakefield Dr *SWIN* M27 ....25 C1
Wakefield St *CMANE* * M1 ....8 A3
Walcott Cl *BRUN/LGST* M13 ....88 A1
Wald Av *RUSH/FAL* M14 ....116 A3
Walden Cl *RUSH/FAL* M14 ....114 B1
Walderton Av *NEWH/MOS* M40 ....54 B3
Walker Av *FAIL* * M35 ....58 A3
   WHTF M45 ....11 D3
Walker Rd *BKLY* M9 ....34 B1
   CHAD OL9 ....38 B1
   ECC M30 ....60 B1
Walker's Cft *CSLFD* M3 ....3 F2
Walker's Rd *OLDS* OL8 ....39 D3
Walker St *MDTN* M24 ....15 D2
   OLDS * OL8 ....22 A3
   STKP * SK1 ....129 D4
Wallace Av *RUSH/FAL* M14 ....103 C2
Wallace St *OLDS* OL8 ....41 C1
Wallasey Av *RUSH/FAL* M14 ....101 D1
The Walled Gdn *SWIN* M27 ....44 B3
Waller Av *RUSH/FAL* M14 ....115 D1
Wallingford Rd *URM* M41 ....94 B2
Wallis St *CHAD* OL9 ....38 B1
   NEWH/MOS * M40 ....55 D4
Wallness La *SLFD* M6 ....67 C3
Wallshaw Pl *OLD* OL1 ....23 D2
Wallshaw St *OLD* OL1 ....23 D2
Wall St *OLDS* OL8 ....23 C4
   SLFD M6 ....66 A3
Wall Wy *GTN* M18 ....106 B1
Wallwork St *OP/CLY* M11 ....91 D1

RDSH * SK5	107	C3
Wallworth Av *GTN* M18	91	C1
Wally Sq *BRO* M7	50	B3
Walmersley Rd *NEWH/MOS* M40	37	D3
Walmer St *GTN* M18	91	C1
RUSH/FAL M14	102	A2
Walmer St East *RUSH/FAL* M14	102	B2
Walmsley Gv *URM* * M41	94	A3
Walmsley St *RDSH* SK5	130	A2
Walnut Cl *SWIN* M27	25	C1
Walnut Rd *ECC* M30	60	B1
Walnut St *GTN* M18	91	C5
Walnut Wk *STRET* M32	109	D1
Walsall St *SLFD* M6	48	B4
Walsden St *OP/CLY* M11	73	D3
Walsh Av *BKLY* M9	33	D3
Walshaw Dr *SWIN* M27	45	C2
Walsh St *CHAD* OL9	21	D1
Walsingham Av *DID/WITH* M20	124	A1
MDTN M24	17	D4
Walters Dr *OLDS* OL8	41	D2
Walter St *BKLY* M9	53	C1
GTN M18	91	D3
OLDTF/WHR M16	99	D1
PWCH M25	29	C1
Waltham Rd *OLDTF/WHR* M16	100	B4
Walton Hall Dr *RDSH* SK5	106	A4
Walton Houses *FAIL* * M35	57	C1
Walton Rd *BKLY* M9	16	A4
Walton St *STKP* SK1	133	C2
Walwyn Cl *STRET* M32	97	D4
Wandsworth Av *OP/CLY* M11	74	A3
Wansbeck Cl *STRET* M32	97	C3
Wansfell Wk *ANC* M4	71	C3
Wansford St *RUSH/FAL* M14	101	D2
Wanstead Av *BKLY* M9	35	D2
Warbeck Cl *RDSH* SK5	107	D3
Warbeck Rd *NEWH/MOS* M40	37	C3
Warburton St *DID/WITH* M20	125	C3
ECC M30	62	B4
ORD M5	84	A3
Warden St *NEWH/MOS* M40	55	C3
Warde St *HULME* M15	85	D3
Wardle Cl *STRET* M32	97	D3
Wardle St *NEWH/MOS* M40	71	D2
Wardley Av *CCHDY* M21	113	D1
Wardley Hall La *WALK* M28	42	B3
Wardley Hall Rd *WALK* M28	24	A4
Wardley St *SWIN* M27	45	C2
Ward Rd *DID/WITH* M20	125	C2
DROY M43	76	A4
Wardsend Wk *HULME* * M15	85	C3
Ward St *BKLY* M9	33	D5
CHAD OL9	21	D2
FAIL M35	56	B1
NEWH/MOS M40	54	A1
STKP SK1	133	C2
Wareham Gv *ECC* M30	61	D2
Wareham St *CHH* * M8	53	C4
Wareford St *ANC* M4	70	A1
The Warke *WALK* M28	42	B4
Warley Rd *OLDTF/WHR* M16	98	B2
Warmbly Gdns *OLDS* OL8	40	A4
Warmington Dr *WGTN/LGST* M12	88	B3
Warne Av *DROY* M43	76	B3
Warnford Cl *NEWH/MOS* M40	74	A1
Warren Bank *BKLY* M9	33	D2
Warren Bruce Rd *TRPK* M17	82	A3
Warren Dr *SWIN* M27	44	A4
Warren Rd *EDGY/DAV* SK3	132	B3
TRPK M17	81	C3
Warren St *BKLY* M9	33	D3
BRO M7	51	C1
STKP SK1	130	A3
Warrington Rd *BKLY* M9	33	D1
Warstead Wk *BRUN/LGST* * M13	87	D2
Warwick Av *DID/WITH* M20	124	A1
SWIN M27	25	C3

WHTF M45	12	A2
Warwick Cl *HTNM* SK4	128	D1
MDTN M24	17	D4
WHTF M45	11	D2
Warwick Ct *MDTN* * M24	17	D1
OLDTF/WHR M16	98	B2
Warwick Gv *DTN/ASHW* M34	93	D1
Warwick Rd *CCHDY* M21	99	C4
FAIL M35	57	C4
HTNM SK4	128	B2
MDTN M24	18	A4
OLDTF/WHR M16	83	C4
Warwick Rd South *OLDTF/WHR* M16	98	B2
Warwick St *ANC* M4	4	C3
CHAD OL9	21	D4
HULME M15	85	D3
PWCH M25	29	C4
SWIN M27	26	A4
Wasdale Wk *OLD* OL1	23	C1
Wash Brook *CHAD* OL9	39	C1
Washbrook Dr *STRET* M32	96	A4
Washington St *CHAD* OL9	21	D2
Wasnidge Wk *HULME* * M15	86	A4
Waterbridge *WALK* M28	42	B4
Waterdale Dr *WHTF* M45	11	D1
Waterfield Wy *FAIL* M35	57	D3
Waterford Av *DID/WITH* M20	123	C2
Waterfront Quay *SALQ* M50	83	C2
Watergate *DTN/ASHW* M34	93	D1
Waterhouse Rd *GTN* M18	106	B1
Water La *DROY* M43	74	B4
Waterloo Pl *STKP* * SK1	130	A4
Waterloo Rd *BKLY* M9	33	D4
CHH M8	68	B1
STKP SK1	130	A4
Waterloo St *CHH* M8	52	B1
CMANE M1	8	A1
OLD OL1	23	C2
OLDE OL4	23	D4
Watermans Cl *BKLY* M9	54	A1
Waterpark Rd *BRO* M7	50	B3
Waterside *TRPK* M17	83	C3
Waterside Cl *CCHDY* M21	123	C1
Waterslea *ECC* M30	61	D3
Watermeet *STRET* M32	96	B1
Waterson Av *NEWH/MOS* M40	54	B2
Water's Reach *TRPK* M17	83	C3
Water St *BKLY* M9	33	D3
CSLFD M3	6	B1
MDTN M24	17	C1
STKP SK1	130	B2
Watford Av *RUSH/FAL* M14	102	A3
Watkin Cl *BRUN/LGST* M13	87	C3
Watkins Dr *PWCH* M25	31	D2
Watkin St *CSLFD* * M3	68	A2
Watson Sq *STKP* SK1	130	A4
Watson St *CMANW* M2	7	E2
ECC M30	61	D3
SWIN M27	26	A4
Watton Cl *SWIN* * M27	26	A3
Watts St *BNG/LEV* M19	118	A1
CHAD OL9	21	C2
OLDS OL8	40	A3
Waugh Av *FAIL* M35	57	C3
Waverley Av *STRET* M32	97	D2
Waverley Crs *DROY* M43	75	D2
Waverley Rd *BKLY* M9	54	A2
SALE M33	109	D3
SWIN M27	26	A3
Waverley Rd West *NEWH/MOS* M40	54	A3
Waverton Av *HTNM* SK4	119	C2
Waverton Rd *RUSH/FAL* M14	101	D4
Wavertree Rd *BKLY* M9	33	D1
Wayfarers Wy *SWIN* M27	44	B2
Wayland Rd *GTN* M18	106	A2
Wayland Rd South *RDSH* SK5	106	A2
Wayne Cl *DROY* M43	76	B1
Wayne St *OP/CLY* M11	91	D1

Weald Cl BRUN/LGST M13 ....9 E5
Weardale Rd BKLY M9 ....15 C4
Weaste Dr SLFD M6 ....65 C2
Weaste La ORD M5 ....65 C2
Weaste Rd ORD M5 ....65 C4
Weatherall St North BRO M7 ....51 C2
Weatherley Cl OLDS OL8 ....41 C4
Weaver Cl HULME * M15 ....85 C3
Weaverham St BRUN/LGST M13 ....104 A2
Webb La STKP SK1 ....133 D1
Webdale Dr NEWH/MOS M40 ....54 B2
Webster Gv PWCH M25 ....29 C3
Webster St OLDS OL8 ....23 C4
Wedgewood St NEWH/MOS M40 ....72 A1
Wedgwood Rd SWIN M27 ....29 C3
Weedall Av ORD M5 ....83 D3
Weir St FAIL M35 ....56 B2
Welbeck Av CHAD OL9 ....37 C3
  URM M41 ....94 B2
Welbeck Gv BRO M7 ....50 B2
Welbeck Rd ECC M30 ....62 B1
  RDSH SK5 ....120 A1
  WALK M28 ....43 C3
Welbeck St GTN M18 ....91 C3
Welby St BRUN/LGST M13 ....103 C1
Welcomb St OP/CLY M11 ....90 A2
Welcroft St STKP SK1 ....133 C1
Weldon Dr BKLY M9 ....16 A4
Weld Rd DID/WITH M20 ....116 A2
Welford Rd CHH M8 ....32 A1
Welford St SLFD M6 ....67 C1
Welkin Rd MPL/ROM SK6 ....131 D2
Welland Cl HULME * M15 ....85 C3
Welland Ct HULME M15 ....85 C3
Welland St OP/CLY M11 ....91 C1
  RDSH SK5 ....107 C4
Wellbank PWCH * M25 ....29 C2
Wellbank Cl OLDS OL8 ....41 D1
Wellens Wy MDTN M24 ....15 D2
Weller Av CCHDY M21 ....113 C2
Wellesley Av GTN M18 ....91 C3
Wellfield Rd CHH M8 ....51 D1
Wellgate Av BNG/LEV M19 ....118 A1
Wellhead Cl HULME M15 ....86 A1
Wellhouse Dr BKLY M9 ....36 B2
Welling Rd NEWH/MOS M40 ....56 B1
Wellington Av OLDTF/WHR M16 ....100 A3
Wellington Cl SALE M33 ....109 D3
Wellington St OLDS * OL8 ....40 A1
Wellington Crs OLDTF/WHR M16 ....99 D2
Wellington Gv HULME M15 ....85 C3
  OFTN SK2 ....133 C1
Wellington Rd CHH M8 ....52 A1
  ECC M30 ....62 B3
  OLDS OL8 ....39 D1
  OLDTF/WHR M16 ....100 B3
  RUSH/FAL M14 ....115 D2
  SWIN M27 ....45 C1
Wellington Rd North HTNM SK4 ....118 A2
Wellington Rd South HTNM SK4 ....129 D4
Wellington St CHAD OL9 ....21 C1
  CSLFD M3 2
  FAIL * M35 ....38 B4
  GTN M18 ....91 C4
  OLDE OL4 ....23 C3
  STKP SK1 ....130 A4
  STRET M32 ....96 B4
Wellington St East BRO M7 ....50 A2
Wellington St West BRO M7 ....50 A3
Wellington Ter ORD M5 ....65 C3
Wellmead Cl CHH M8 ....51 C4
Wellock St NEWH/MOS M40 ....54 A1
Wells Av PWCH M25 ....30 B3
Wells Cl MDTN M24 ....15 D2
  OP/CLY M11 ....92 A1
Wells Dr HTNM * SK4 ....126 B3
Wellwood Dr NEWH/MOS M40 ....54 B2

Welney Rd OLDTF/WHR M16 ....99 C2
Welshpool Cl NTHM/RTH M23 ....122 A3
Welton Av DID/WITH M20 ....125 D3
Welwyn Cl URM M41 ....78 B4
Welwyn Dr SLFD M6 ....45 D4
Welwyn Wk NEWH/MOS M40 ....71 C3
Wembley Gv RUSH/FAL M14 ....115 D1
Wembley Rd GTN M18 ....105 D1
Wembury St BKLY * M9 ....53 D2
Wembury St North BKLY M9 ....53 D2
Wem St CHAD OL9 ....38 B1
Wemyss Av RDSH SK5 ....107 C4
Wenfield Dr BKLY M9 ....35 D2
Wenlock Cl SWIN M27 ....44 A1
Wenlock Wy WGTN/LGST M12 ....89 D3
Wensley Dr DID/WITH M20 ....115 C4
Wensley Rd BRO M7 ....29 D4
  RDSH SK5 ....130 A1
Wentworth Av GTN M18 ....91 D4
  SLFD M6 ....64 B2
  WHTF M45 ....10 A2
Wentworth Cl MDTN M24 ....16 B1
Wentworth Dr SALE M33 ....108 A4
Wentworth Rd ECC M30 ....63 C1
  RDSH SK5 ....107 C4
  SWIN M27 ....44 A3
Werneth Av RUSH/FAL M14 ....102 A3
Werneth Crs OLDS OL8 ....39 D1
Werneth Hall Rd OLDS OL8 ....22 A4
Werneth St STKP SK1 ....131 C2
Wesley Dr WALK M28 ....42 A1
Wesley Gn ORD M5 ....84 A1
Wesley St ECC M30 ....61 D3
  FAIL M35 ....38 B4
  OP/CLY M11 ....89 D1
  STKP SK1 ....130 A4
  STRET M32 ....97 C3
  SWIN M27 ....45 C1
West Ashton St SALQ M50 ....83 C1
West Av BNG/LEV M19 ....117 C2
  GTN * M18 ....91 C4
  NEWH/MOS M40 ....37 C4
West Bank OP/CLY M11 ....92 B2
Westbank Rd DID/WITH M20 ....116 A4
West Bank St ORD M5 ....84 B1
Westbourne Gv BKLY M9 ....53 C1
  DID/WITH M20 ....114 B3
  RDSH SK5 ....120 A1
Westbourne Pk URM M41 ....94 A2
Westbourne Range GTN M18 ....107 C2
Westbourne Rd ECC M30 ....61 C1
  RUSH/FAL M14 ....116 A1
  URM M41 ....94 A3
Westbourne St CHAD OL9 ....22 A2
Westbrook Rd SWIN M27 ....44 B2
  TRPK M17 ....81 D2
Westbrook Sq WGTN/LGST M12 ....89 D3
Westbury Rd CHH M8 ....32 B4
West Canteen Rd TRPK M17 ....96 B1
West Central Dr SWIN M27 ....46 A2
West Charles St ORD M5 ....67 C4
Westcott Av DID/WITH M20 ....114 B3
Westcourt Rd SALE M33 ....108 B4
Westcraig Av NEWH/MOS M40 ....36 B4
West Craven St ORD M5 ....84 A2
Westcroft Rd DID/WITH M20 ....126 A1
West Crown Av ORD M5 ....84 A1
Westdale Gdns BNG/LEV M19 ....117 D4
Westdean Crs BNG/LEV M19 ....117 C4
West Dean St ORD M5 ....67 C4
West Dr DROY M43 ....75 C4
  SLFD M6 ....47 D3
  SWIN M27 ....46 A2
West Duke St ORD M5 ....2 A5
West Egerton St ORD M5 ....67 C4
West End St CHAD OL9 ....22 A2
Westerham Av ORD M5 ....66 B4
Wester Hill Rd OLDS OL8 ....41 D4

Westerling Wy *OLDTF/WHR* M16 .... **100** B2
Western Access *TRPK* * M17 .... **80** A1
Western Av *SWIN* M27 .... **28** A3
Western Cir *BNG/LEV* M19 .... **117** C3
Western St *GTN* M18 .... **91** D3
   SLFD M6 .... **65** D2
Westfield *SLFD* M6 .... **65** D1
Westfield Av *MDTN* M24 .... **17** D2
Westfield Rd *CCHDY* M21 .... **99** C4
   DROY M43 .... **74** B5
Westfield St *BRO* M7 .... **51** C4
   CHAD OL9 .... **21** D1
Westgate Av *BKLY* * M9 .... **33** D3
Westgate Dr *SWIN* M27 .... **45** C3
Westgate Rd *SLFD* M6 .... **64** A1
West Gn *MDTN* M24 .... **15** C2
West Gv *BRUN/LGST* M13 .... **88** A4
West High St *ORD* M5 .... **66** B3
Westholm Av *HTNM* SK4 .... **118** A2
Westholme Rd *DID/WITH* M20 .... **115** C4
   WHTF M45 .... **12** B2
West Hope St *ORD* M5 .... **67** C4
Westinghouse Rd *TRPK* M17 .... **81** C3
West King St *CSLFD* M3 .... **2** C2
Westland Av *STKP* * SK1 .... **131** C4
Westland Dr *BKLY* M9 .... **34** A1
The Westlands *SWIN* M27 .... **46** A3
Westlands *WHTF* M45 .... **11** C3
Westlea Dr *GTN* M18 .... **106** A2
Westleigh Dr *PWCH* M25 .... **31** C3
Westleigh St *BKLY* M9 .... **34** A4
West Marwood St *BRO* M7 .... **50** B2
Westmead Dr *CHH* M8 .... **50** B4
West Meade *CCHDY* M21 .... **111** D2
   PWCH * M25 .... **31** C3
   SWIN M27 .... **44** B3
West Meadow *RDSH* SK5 .... **107** D4
Westmere Dr *BKLY* M9 .... **52** B3
Westminster Av *HTNM* SK4 .... **119** C4
   OLDTF/WHR M16 .... **99** D3
   WHTF M45 .... **11** C1
Westminster Rd *ECC* M30 .... **62** B2
   FAIL M35 .... **58** A1
   URM M41 .... **94** A1
Westminster St *BNG/LEV* * M19 .... **105** C4
   HULME * M15 .... **84** B2
   SWIN M27 .... **25** C4
Westmorland Cl *RDSH* * SK5 .... **121** C3
Westmorland Dr *RDSH* SK5 .... **121** C3
Westmorland Rd *DID/WITH* M20 .... **124** B3
   ECC M30 .... **45** D4
West Mosley St *CMANW* M2 .... **4** A5
Westmount Cl *NEWH/MOS* M40 .... **52** B3
Weston Av *NEWH/MOS* M40 .... **37** D4
   SWIN M27 .... **26** A1
Weston Gv *HTNM* SK4 .... **118** B3
Weston St *NEWH/MOS* * M40 .... **71** C4
   RDSH * SK5 .... **129** D1
Westover St *SWIN* M27 .... **25** D4
West Park Rd *STKP* SK1 .... **131** C4
West Park St *ORD* M5 .... **84** A2
West Pl *BNG/LEV* M19 .... **117** C3
Westray Crs *SLFD* * M6 .... **65** D4
Westray Rd *BRUN/LGST* M13 .... **103** D3
West Rd *PWCH* M25 .... **11** C4
   STRET M32 .... **95** D1
West Rw *PWCH* M25 .... **29** C4
West St *CHAD* OL9 .... **22** A2
   EDGY/DAV SK3 .... **129** C4
   FAIL M35 .... **56** B2
   OP/CLY M11 .... **73** C3
West Towers St *SLFD* M6 .... **66** A4
Westville Gdns *BNG/LEV* M19 .... **116** B4
Westway *BKLY* M9 .... **14** B3
   DROY M43 .... **92** B2
Westwood Av *BRO* M7 .... **50** B1
   NEWH/MOS * M40 .... **37** D4
   URM M41 .... **95** C4

Westwood Crs *ECC* M30 .... **61** C1
Westwood Dr *CHAD* OL9 .... **22** A2
   SWIN M27 .... **46** B3
Westwood Rd *STRET* M32 .... **96** A3
West Works Rd *TRPK* M17 .... **96** B1
Wetherall St *BNG/LEV* M19 .... **105** C4
Wetherby St *OP/CLY* M11 .... **91** D2
Weybourne Av *BKLY* M9 .... **35** D3
Weybridge Rd *ANC* M4 .... **5** F3
Weybrook Rd *HTNM* SK4 .... **118** A2
Weylands Gv *SLFD* M6 .... **46** A4
Weymouth Rd *ECC* M30 .... **61** C2
Whalley Av *BNG/LEV* M19 .... **105** C3
   CCHDY M21 .... **112** B2
   OLDTF/WHR M16 .... **100** A2
   SALE M33 .... **109** D4
   URM M41 .... **94** B2
Whalley Gv *OLDTF/WHR* M16 .... **100** A3
Whalley Rd *OLDTF/WHR* M16 .... **100** A3
Whalley St *NEWH/MOS* M40 .... **71** C3
Wharf Cl *CMANE* M1 .... **5** D5
Wharfedale Av *NEWH/MOS* M40 .... **35** D4
Wharfedale Rd *RDSH* SK5 .... **119** D1
Wharf End *TRPK* M17 .... **83** D3
Wharf Rd *SALE* M33 .... **109** C4
Wharfside Av *ECC* M30 .... **79** C1
Wharfside Wy
   (Trafford Park Rd) *TRPK* M17 .... **82** B3
Wharf St *CHAD* OL9 .... **39** C2
   HTNM SK4 .... **129** D2
Wharton Av *CCHDY* M21 .... **113** C2
Wharton Ldg *ECC* M30 .... **62** B2
Wheat Cl *BRUN/LGST* M13 .... **87** D4
Wheat Cft *EDGY/DAV* SK3 .... **133** C4
Wheater's Crs *BRO* M7 .... **67** D1
Wheater's St *BRO* M7 .... **68** A1
Wheater's Ter *BRO* M7 .... **68** A1
Wheatley Rd *SWIN* M27 .... **25** C3
Wheatley Wk *WGTN/LGST* M12 .... **89** C3
Wheler St *OP/CLY* M11 .... **91** C1
Whernside Av *NEWH/MOS* M40 .... **35** D4
Whernside Cl *HTNM* SK4 .... **129** D3
Whickham Cl *RUSH/FAL* M14 .... **102** A2
Whiley St *BRUN/LGST* M13 .... **104** A1
Whimberry Cl *ORD* M5 .... **84** A2
Whirley Cl *HTNM* SK4 .... **119** C4
Whiston Rd *CHH* M8 .... **52** A1
Whitaker St *MDTN* M24 .... **17** C1
Whitburn Av *BRUN/LGST* M13 .... **103** D3
Whitby Av *OLDTF/WHR* M16 .... **100** A2
   RUSH/FAL M14 .... **116** B1
   SLFD M6 .... **64** B1
   URM M41 .... **94** B3
Whitby Rd *RUSH/FAL* M14 .... **116** A1
Whitchurch Dr *OLDTF/WHR* M16 .... **85** C4
Whitchurch Rd *DID/WITH* M20 .... **114** A2
Whitchurch St *BRO* M7 .... **68** B2
Whitacres *SWIN* M27 .... **43** D2
White Bank Av *RDSH* SK5 .... **131** D1
White Bank Rd *OLDS* OL8 .... **40** A4
Whitebeam Cl *SLFD* M6 .... **66** B2
Whitebeam Ct *SLFD* * M6 .... **66** B2
Whitebrook Rd *RUSH/FAL* M14 .... **102** A4
Whitecar Av *NEWH/MOS* M40 .... **37** C4
Whitechapel St *DID/WITH* M20 .... **125** C2
White City Wy *OLDTF/WHR* M16 .... **83** D4
Whitecliff Cl *RUSH/FAL* M14 .... **102** A4
Whitecroft Gdns *BNG/LEV* M19 .... **126** B1
Whitefield *HTNM* SK4 .... **129** C2
Whitefield Rd *SALE* M33 .... **108** A4
Whitegate Av *CHAD* OL9 .... **38** A1
Whitegate Cl *NEWH/MOS* M40 .... **37** D4
Whitegate Dr *ORD* M5 .... **65** C2
   SWIN M27 .... **27** C3
Whitegate La *CHAD* OL9 .... **38** B1
Whitegate Rd *CHAD* OL9 .... **37** C2
Whitehall Rd *DID/WITH* M20 .... **125** D2

Whitehall St *OLD* OL1 ....23 C1
Whitehaven Gdns *DID/WITH* M20 ....124 B3
Whitehead Rd *CCHDY* M21 ....111 C1
  SWIN M27 ....27 C3
Whitehill Dr *NEWH/MOS* M40 ....54 B2
Whitehill St *HTNM* SK4 ....129 D1
  RDSH SK5 ....120 A4
Whitehill St West *HTNM* SK4 ....129 C1
Whiteholme Av *CCHDY* M21 ....123 C3
White Horse Gdns *SWIN* * M27 ....43 D3
Whitehurst Rd *HTNM* SK4 ....127 C1
Whitekirk Cl *BRUN/LGST* M13 ....9 D5
Whitelea Dr *EDGY/DAV* SK3 ....132 A4
Whiteley Dr *MDTN* M24 ....18 B2
Whiteley St *CHAD* OL9 ....39 C1
  OP/CLY M11 ....73 C3
Whitelow Rd *CCHDY* M21 ....111 D1
  HTNM SK4 ....127 D2
White Moss Av *CCHDY* M21 ....112 B1
White Moss Rd *BKLY* M9 ....34 B2
Whitemoss Rd East *BKLY* M9 ....35 C1
Whiteoak Rd *RUSH/FAL* M14 ....115 D1
Whites Cft *SWIN* M27 ....45 C1
Whiteside Cl *ORD* M5 ....65 C3
Whitestone Wk *BRUN/LGST* * M13 ......88 A4
White St *HULME* M15 ....85 C3
  SLFD M6 ....65 D4
White Swallows Rd *SWIN* M27 ....45 D3
Whitethorn Av *BNG/LEV* M19 ....117 D2
  OLDTF/WHR M16 ....100 A2
Whitewater Dr *BRO* M7 ....48 A2
Whiteway St *BKLY* M9 ....53 D2
Whitewillow Cl *FAIL* M35 ....57 D3
Whitfield St *CSLFD* M3 ....69 D2
Whitford Wk *NEWH/MOS* M40 ....71 C2
Whitland Dr *OLDS* OL8 ....39 C3
Whit La *SLFD* M6 ....48 A3
Whitley Rd *HTNM* SK4 ....128 A2
  NEWH/MOS M40 ....70 B1
Whitman St *BKLY* M9 ....54 A1
Whitmore Rd *RUSH/FAL* M14 ....102 A4
Whitnall Cl *OLDTF/WHR* M16 ....100 B2
Whitsbury Av *GTN* M18 ....106 A2
Whitstable Cl *CHAD* OL9 ....21 C3
Whitstable Rd *NEWH/MOS* * M40 ....36 B4
Whittaker La *PWCH* M25 ....30 B1
Whittaker St *CHAD* OL9 ....21 C2
  NEWH/MOS M40 ....54 B1
  WGTN/LGST M12 ....88 A1
Whittingham Gv *OLD* OL1 ....22 A1
Whittle's Cft *CMANE* * M1 ....5 D5
Whittle St *ANC* * M4 ....6 A1
  SWIN M27 ....44 B2
Whitwell Wy *GTN* M18 ....90 B4
Whitworth La *RUSH/FAL* M14 ....103 C4
Whitworth St *CMANE* M1 ....8 B2
  OP/CLY M11 ....90 A2
Whitworth St East *OP/CLY* M11 ....90 B2
Whitworth St West *CMANE* M1 ....7 F2
Whixhall Av *WGTN/LGST* M12 ....88 B3
Wickentree La *FAIL* M35 ....38 B4
Wicket Gv *SWIN* M27 ....25 D1
Wicklow Gv *OLDS* OL8 ....40 B2
Widdop St *CHAD* OL9 ....22 A2
Widgeon Cl *RUSH/FAL* M14 ....115 C1
Widnes St *OP/CLY* * M11 ....90 B2
Wiggins Wk *RUSH/FAL* * M14 ....102 B2
Wigley St *WGTN/LGST* M12 ....88 B2
Wigmore Rd *CHH* M8 ....52 A2
Wigsby Av *NEWH/MOS* M40 ....36 B4
Wilbraham Rd *CCHDY* M21 ....112 A1
  OLDTF/WHR M16 ....100 B4
Wilburn St *ORD* M5 ....6 A1
Wilby St *CHH* M8 ....52 A3
Wilcock Cl *OLDTF/WHR* M16 ....100 B1
Wildbrook Crs *OLDS* OL8 ....41 D3
Wildbrook Ter *OLDS* * OL8 ....41 D2

Wildcroft Av *NEWH/MOS* M40 ....35 D4
Wilderswood Cl *DID/WITH* M20 ....115 D4
Wild St *OLD* OL1 ....23 D2
Wilfred St *NEWH/MOS* M40 ....54 B1
Wilfrid St *SWIN* M27 ....45 C1
Wilkinson Rd *HTNM* SK4 ....129 D3
Wilkinson St *HTNM* * SK4 ....129 D3
  MDTN M24 ....17 C1
Willan Rd *BKLY* M9 ....33 D1
  ECC M30 ....62 B3
Willaston Cl *CCHDY* M21 ....111 D2
Willdale Cl *OP/CLY* M11 ....72 B3
Willenhall Rd *NTHM/RTH* M23 ....122 B3
Willerby Rd *BRO* M7 ....50 B4
Willesden Av *BRUN/LGST* M13 ....103 C3
Will Griffith Wk *OP/CLY* M11 ....88 B1
William Chadwick Cl *NEWH/MOS* M40 ...70 B2
William Jessop Ct *CMANE* M1 ....5 E5
William Kay Cl *HULME* M15 ....100 A1
William Lister Cl *NEWH/MOS* * M40 .....74 A1
Williams Crs *CHAD* OL9 ....38 A2
Williamson La *DROY* M43 ....93 C1
Williamson St *ANC* M4 ....20 A5
  RDSH SK5 ....119 D2
Williams Rd *GTN* M18 ....90 B4
  NEWH/MOS M40 ....55 C2
Williams St *GTN* M18 ....105 D1
William St *CSLFD* M3 ....2 C3
  DID/WITH M20 ....125 C2
  FAIL M35 ....38 B4
  MDTN M24 ....18 A1
  WGTN/LGST M12 ....88 A1
Willingdon Dr *PWCH* M25 ....12 A4
Willis Rd *EDGY/DAV* SK3 ....132 B3
Willock St *BRO* M7 ....50 B3
Willoughby Av *DID/WITH* M20 ....125 D1
Willoughby Cl *SALE* M33 ....108 B4
Willow Av *MDTN* M24 ....18 B2
  RDSH SK5 ....130 A1
  URM M41 ....94 B3
Willow Bank *RUSH/FAL* M14 ....115 D1
Willowbrook Av *NEWH/MOS* M40 ....54 B2
Willow Ct *SALE* M33 ....110 B4
Willowdene Cl *NEWH/MOS* M40 ....52 B4
Willow Fold *DROY* M43 ....93 C1
Willow Gv *CHAD* * OL9 ....21 C1
  GTN * M18 ....106 B1
Willow Hill Rd *CHH* M8 ....32 B3
Willow Rd *ECC* M30 ....60 B1
  PWCH M25 ....31 C1
The Willows *CCHDY* M21 ....111 D2
Willows Dr *FAIL* M35 ....75 C1
Willows Rd *ORD* * M5 ....65 C3
Willow St *CHH* M8 ....68 B1
  OP/CLY M11 ....72 B1
  SWIN M27 ....44 A1
  WALK M28 ....43 D2
Willow Wy *DID/WITH* M20 ....125 D2
Wilma Av *BKLY* M9 ....33 D1
Wilmcote Rd *NEWH/MOS* M40 ....70 B1
Wilmington Rd *STRET* * M32 ....96 A3
Wilmott St *HULME* M15 ....7 F4
Wilmslow Rd *DID/WITH* M20 ....115 D3
  RUSH/FAL M14 ....102 B1
Wilmur Av *BRO* M7 ....50 B3
  WHTF M45 ....11 D2
Wilpshire Av *WGTN/LGST* M12 ....105 C2
Wilson Av *SWIN* M27 ....27 C3
Wilson Rd *BKLY* M9 ....34 A4
  HTNM SK4 ....128 A1
Wilsons Pk *NEWH/MOS* * M40 ....53 D4
Wilson St *BRUN/LGST* M13 ....87 D3
  OLDS OL8 ....40 B3
  OP/CLY M11 ....89 D1
  STRET M32 ....97 C1
Wilson Wy *OLD* OL1 ....23 C2
Wilsthorpe Cl *BNG/LEV* M19 ....118 B3
Wilton Av *OLDTF/WHR* M16 ....98 B2

PWCH M25	31	C3
SWIN M27	46	B2
Wilton Ct DTN/ASHW M34	107	D1
Wilton Gv DTN/ASHW M34	107	D1
Wilton Paddock DTN/ASHW M34	107	D1
Wilton Pl CSLFD M3	2	A3
Wilton Rd CCHDY M21	112	A1
CHH M8	32	B5
SLFD M6	64	A1
Wilton St BRO M7	39	C2
MDTN M24	15	C2
PWCH M25	30	B1
RDSH SK5	107	C5
WHTF M45	11	C2
Wiltshire Av RDSH SK5	131	D1
Wiltshire Rd CHAD OL9	21	C4
FAIL M35	57	C3
Wiltshire St BRO M7	50	B3
Wimbledon Rd FAIL M35	58	A1
Wimborne Av URM M41	94	A1
Wimpole St OLD OL1	23	D1
Wimpory St OP/CLY M11	91	C2
Wince Cl MDTN M24	18	B3
Wincham Cl HULME M15	85	C5
Winchester Av PWCH M25	30	B3
Winchester Dr HTNM SK4	128	A3
Winchester Pk DID/WITH M20	124	A2
Winchester Rd ECC M30	63	D1
URM M41	94	A2
Wincombe St RUSH/FAL M14	102	A3
Windcroft Cl OP/CLY M11	89	C1
Winder Dr ANC M4	5	F4
Windermere Av DTN/ASHW M34	107	D3
SWIN M27	45	D2
Windermere Cl OP/CLY M11	89	D1
PWCH M25	10	B4
STRET M32	96	B2
Winders Wy SLFD M6	67	C1
Windle Av CHH M8	32	A2
Windmill Av ORD M5	84	A3
Windmill La RDSH SK5	107	C4
Windmill St CMANW M2	7	E1
Windrush Dr BKLY M9	53	C2
Windsor Cl CHAD OL9	38	B3
FAIL M35	58	A1
HTNM SK4	127	D4
SALE M33	109	C3
SWIN M27	26	B3
WHTF M45	11	D2
Windsor Dr DTN/ASHW M34	77	C4
Windsor Rd BKLY M9	53	D2
BNG/LEV M19	104	A4
DROY M43	74	A3
DTN/ASHW M34	107	D2
MPL/ROM SK6	131	D2
NEWH/MOS M40	74	B1
OLDS OL8	22	A4
PWCH M25	31	D2
Windsor St FAIL M35	57	D1
GTN M18	105	D1
NEWH/MOS M40	74	B1
OFTN SK2	133	D3
ORD M5	67	C4
Windybank BKLY M9	15	D4
Winfell Dr NEWH/MOS M40	71	D4
Winfield Av DID/WITH M20	116	A4
Winfield Dr GTN M18	91	D3
Winford St BKLY M9	53	D1
Wingate Dr DID/WITH M20	125	D3
Wingate Rd HTNM SK4	128	B1
Wingfield Dr SWIN M27	45	D3
Wingfield St STRET M32	97	C1
Winifred Rd DID/WITH M20	125	C2
NEWH/MOS M40	55	C2
OFTN SK2	133	C4
Winifred St ECC M30	61	C4
Winnie St NEWH/MOS M40	54	B1
Winning Hill Cl GTN M18	106	A1
Winnipeg Quay SALQ M50	83	C2
Winscombe Dr NEWH/MOS M40	70	B1
Winser St CMANE M1	8	A2
Winsford St RUSH/FAL M14	101	D4
Winslow Pl BNG/LEV M19	117	C3
Winslow St OP/CLY M11	89	D1
Winstanley Rd NEWH/MOS M40	71	C2
SALE M33	109	D4
Winster Av BRO M7	49	C5
DID/WITH M20	123	D1
STRET M32	95	D2
Winster Cl WHTF M45	12	A1
Winster Gv OFTN SK2	133	D3
Winster Rd ECC M30	78	A1
Winston Rd BKLY M9	35	C4
SALE M33	108	A4
Winswell Cl OP/CLY M11	73	C5
Winterbottom St CHAD * OL9	22	A2
Winterburn Av CCHDY M21	122	B1
Winterdyne St BKLY M9	53	D2
Winterford Av BRUN/LGST M13	88	A4
Winterford Rd CHH M8	51	C2
Wintermans Rd CCHDY M21	113	C5
Winterton Rd RDSH SK5	107	D4
Winthrop Av NEWH/MOS M40	53	C4
Winton Av NEWH/MOS M40	37	C4
Winton Rd SLFD M6	47	C3
Wirral Cl SWIN * M27	26	B3
Wiseley St OP/CLY M11	88	B1
Wiseman Ter PWCH M25	30	B1
Wishaw Sq CCHDY M21	113	D3
Wisley Cl RDSH SK5	120	A1
Wistaria Rd GTN M18	91	C4
Withington Rd CCHDY M21	113	C1
OLDTF/WHR M16	100	A2
Withington St SLFD M6	67	C3
Withins Rd OLDS OL8	39	C3
Withnell Rd DID/WITH M20	126	A2
Withycombe Pl SLFD M6	48	B4
Withy Gv ANC M4	4	A3
Wittenbury Rd HTNM SK4	128	A3
Witterage Cl WGTN/LGST * M12	89	C3
Woburn Rd OLDTF/WHR M16	98	B3
Woburn St OLDTF/WHR M16	101	C2
Woden's Av ORD M5	84	B2
Woden St ORD M5	84	B2
Wolfreton Crs SWIN M27	26	B2
Wolseley Pl DID/WITH M20	115	C3
Wolseley Rd SALE M33	109	C3
Wolverton Av OLDS OL8	40	A2
Woodacre OLDTF/WHR M16	100	B4
Woodbine Crs OFTN SK2	133	C2
Woodbourne Rd HTNM SK4	118	B3
Woodbray Av BNG/LEV M19	116	B4
Woodchurch Wk CHAD * OL9	21	C3
Woodcock Cl DROY M43	76	B2
Woodcroft Av BNG/LEV M19	126	B1
Woodfield Cl OLDS OL8	39	D1
Woodfield Gv ECC M30	61	D4
SALE M33	108	B3
Woodfield Rd CHH M8	32	B4
MDTN M24	16	B3
SLFD M6	65	C1
Woodfold Av BNG/LEV M19	104	B3
Woodfold Rd FAIL M35	57	D1
Woodford Av ECC M30	61	D3
Woodford Dr SWIN M27	25	D3
Woodford Gdns DID/WITH M20	124	B3
Woodgarth Av NEWH/MOS M40	56	A4
Woodgarth Dr SWIN M27	44	B3
Woodgarth La WALK M28	42	A4
Woodgate Dr PWCH M25	12	B3
Woodgate Rd OLDTF/WHR M16	100	B4
Woodgrange Cl SLFD M6	65	D3
Woodhall Av DID/WITH M20	114	B2
WHTF M45	10	A3
Woodhall Crs RDSH SK5	130	B1
Woodhall Rd RDSH SK5	130	B1

Woodhall St FAIL M35	57	C1
Woodhall Rd CHH M8	51	D1
Woodhead St OLDTF/WHR M16	100	B1
Woodheys HTNM SK4	127	C2
Woodhill Cl WGTN/LGST M12	105	C1
Woodhill Dr PWCH M25	30	A3
Woodhill Gv PWCH M25	30	A2
Woodhouse St GTN M18	91	C4
NEWH/MOS M40	54	A4
Woodlake Av CCHDY M21	122	B1
Woodland Av GTN M18	106	B1
Woodland Crs PWCH M25	30	A3
Woodland Rd BNG/LEV M19	117	D1
GTN M18	106	B1
The Woodlands DROY * M43	74	B2
Woodlands FAIL M35	74	B1
Woodlands Av STRET M32	97	C3
SWIN M27	43	D3
Woodlands Rd CHH M8	51	D1
HTNM SK4	126	A3
OLDTF/WHR M16	100	B4
SALE M33	109	D4
Woodlands St CHH M8	51	C1
Woodland St WGTN/LGST M12	90	A4
Woodland Wy MDTN M24	17	C3
Wood La MDTN M24	18	A2
Woodlark Cl CSLFD * M3	2	B4
Woodlawn Ct OLDTF/WHR M16	99	D2
Woodlea CHAD OL9	19	C2
Woodlea Av BNG/LEV M19	116	B3
Woodleigh Dr DROY M43	76	B1
Woodleigh St BKLY M9	53	C4
Woodman St STKP SK1	129	D3
Woodmere Dr BKLY M9	53	C4
Woodnewton Cl GTN M18	105	D1
Woodpark Cl OLDS OL8	41	D2
Wood Rd OLDTF/WHR M16	99	D2
Wood Rd North OLDTF/WHR M16	99	D2
Woodrow Wk WGTN/LGST M12	89	C3
Woodside Av BNG/LEV M19	117	C4
Woodside Dr SLFD M6	64	B2
Woodside Rd OLDTF/WHR M16	99	C3
Woodsmoor Rd SWIN M27	44	A2
Wood Sq DROY M43	92	B1
Woodstock Av RDSH SK5	120	A4
Woodstock Dr SWIN M27	45	D3
WALK M28	42	B3
Woodstock Gn RDSH SK5	120	B4
Woodstock Rd NEWH/MOS M40	36	B4
OLDTF/WHR M16	99	C2
Woodstock St OLDS OL8	23	C4
Wood St CSLFD M3	3	D5
EDGY/DAV SK3	129	D4
OP/CLY M11	90	A2
Woodthorpe Ct PWCH M25	31	C3
Woodthorpe Gra PWCH M25	31	C3
Woodvale Wk OP/CLY * M11	72	A4
Wood Vw WYTH/NTH M22	123	C4
Woodview Av BNG/LEV M19	117	C4
Woodville Dr SALE M33	108	B4
Woodville Gv RDSH SK5	120	A3
Woodville Rd SALE M33	108	B4
Woodville Ter NEWH/MOS M40	35	C4
Woodward Ct ANC M4	5	F5
Woodward Pl ANC M4	5	F5
Woodward Rd PWCH M25	29	C3
Woodward St ANC M4	5	F5
Woolden St ECC M30	61	C2
Woollacot St OLD OL1	23	C2
Woollam Pl CSLFD M3	6	B1
Woolley Cl CHH M8	69	C1
Woolpack Gn SLFD * M6	66	A2
Worcester Av RDSH SK5	121	D4
Worcester Rd MDTN M24	17	C4
SLFD M6	64	B1
SWIN M27	25	C3
Worcester St BRO M7	50	B3
CHAD OL9	21	C4

Wordsworth Av CHH M8	51	D3
DROY M43	75	C3
Wordsworth Crs AULW OL7	59	D4
Wordsworth Gdns PWCH M25	29	C2
Wordsworth Rd OLDTF/WHR M16	99	D2
RDSH SK5	106	A4
SWIN M27	25	C4
Wordsworth St SLFD M6	67	D1
Workesleigh St NEWH/MOS M40	55	D4
Worrall St EDGY/DAV SK3	132	B2
NEWH/MOS M40	54	B3
ORD M5	84	B2
Worsefold St NEWH/MOS * M40	54	B1
Worsley Av NEWH/MOS M40	35	C4
Worsley Gv BNG/LEV M19	104	B4
Worsley Rd ECC M30	61	C3
WALK M28	42	B4
Worsley St CSLFD M3	3	D4
CSLFD * M3	7	D2
HULME M15	6	A3
SWIN M27	45	D3
SWIN M27	26	A3
Worthenbury Wk RUSH/FAL M14	103	D2
Worthing St RUSH/FAL M14	102	A3
Worthington Dr BRO M7	31	C4
Worthington St NEWH/MOS M40	55	D1
Wortley Av SLFD M6	64	B2
Wortley Gv NEWH/MOS M40	36	A3
Wren Av SWIN M27	27	C2
Wrenbury Dr DID/WITH M20	114	A2
Wren Cl DTN/ASHW M34	76	B3
Wrexham Cl OLDS OL8	39	C3
Wright Robinson Cl OP/CLY M11	88	B1
Wright St CHAD OL9	21	C4
FAIL M35	57	C1
OLD * OL1	23	D2
OLDTF/WHR M16	84	B4
Wrigley Crs FAIL M35	57	C2
Wrigley Head FAIL M35	57	C1
Wrigley Head Crs FAIL * M35	57	C1
Wroe St CSLFD M3	2	A4
SWIN M27	26	A2
Wroe Ter SWIN * M27	26	A2
Wrotham Cl ORD M5	66	B4
Wroxham Av DTN/ASHW M34	107	D2
Wroxham Rd BKLY M9	33	C2
Wyatt Av ORD * M5	84	B2
Wyatt St HTNM SK4	129	D3
Wychbury St SLFD M6	65	D3
Wychwood Cl MDTN M24	18	A2
Wycliffe St ECC M30	61	D3
HTNM SK4	129	C1
Wycombe Av GTN M18	91	D3
Wycombe Cl URM M41	78	B4
Wye Av FAIL * M35	57	C2
Wye St OLDS OL8	22	A4
Wykeham St RUSH/FAL M14	101	D2
Wylam Wk WGTN/LGST M12	105	C2
Wyndale Dr FAIL M35	57	C4
Wyndale Rd OLDS OL8	41	C3
Wyndham Av SWIN M27	26	A3
Wynford Sq SALO M50	66	A4
Wynne Av SWIN M27	26	A2
Wynne Cl OP/CLY M11	89	C1
Wynne St SLFD M6	67	C1
Wynnstay Gv RUSH/FAL M14	115	D1
Wynnstay Rd SALE M33	109	C4
Wyre St CMANE M1	9	D2
Wythburn Av CHH M8	52	B3
Wythburn St SLFD M6	65	D1
Wythenshawe Rd NTHM/RTH M23	122	B4
Wythop Gdns ORD M5	66	B4
Wyvern Av HTNM SK4	128	A3
Wyverne Rd CCHDY M21	113	C1
Wyville Dr BKLY M9	15	C3
SLFD M6	66	A2
SWIN M27	44	B3

Y

Yarburgh St *OLDTF/WHR* M16 ....100 B2
Yardley Av *STRET* M32 ....95 D3
Yardley Cl *STRET* M32 ....95 D3
Yarmouth Dr *NTHM/RTH* M23 ....122 A4
Yarn Wk *ANC* M4 ....5 C4
Yasmin Gdns *OLD* OL1 ....22 A1
Yates St *MDTN* M24 ....15 D2
OLD OL1 ....23 D1
STKP SK1 ....131 C2
Yealand Av *HTNM* SK4 ....129 C1
Yeb Fold *NEWH/MOS ** M40 ....36 A4
Yeoman Wk *OP/CLY* M11 ....72 A4
Yeovil St *OLDTF/WHR* M16 ....101 C2
Yewbarrow Rd *OLD* OL1 ....23 D1
Yewdale *SWIN* M27 ....27 C3
Yewdale Dr *FAIL* M35 ....58 A4
Yewlands Av *BKLY* M9 ....16 A4
Yew St *BRO* M7 ....49 D3
HTNM SK4 ....128 B4
HULME M15 ....85 D4
Yew Tree Av *BNG/LEV* M19 ....104 B4
RUSH/FAL M14 ....101 D2
WYTH/NTH M22 ....123 C4
Yew Tree Crs *RUSH/FAL* M14 ....102 A3
Yew Tree Dr *MDTN* M24 ....19 C2
PWCH M25 ....30 A1
WYTH/NTH M22 ....123 C4
Yewtree La *WYTH/NTH* M22 ....123 C4
Yew Tree Rd *RUSH/FAL* M14 ....102 A3

York Av *OLDS* OL8 ....40 A1
OLDTF/WHR M16 ....99 D3
PWCH M25 ....31 C3
SALE M33 ....109 C4
SWIN M27 ....25 C3
York Rd *CCHDY* M21 ....112 A1
CHAD OL9 ....20 C2
DROY M43 ....75 C2
HTNM SK4 ....118 A4
SALE M33 ....108 B4
Yorkshire St *CSLFD* M3 ....3 D1
OLD OL1 ....23 D2
York St *BKLY* M9 ....53 D1
BNG/LEV M19 ....117 D1
CHAD OL9 ....22 B3
CMANE M1 ....8 A2
CMANW M2 ....4 A4
DID/WITH M20 ....125 C2
EDGY/DAV SK3 ....132 A1
WHTF M45 ....11 C1
York Ter *SALE ** M33 ....108 B3
Young St *CSLFD* M3 ....3 D5
Yule St *EDGY/DAV* SK3 ....132 A1

Z

Zebra St *BRO* M7 ....51 C2
Zeta St *BKLY* M9 ....54 A2
Zetland Rd *CCHDY* M21 ....112 A1
Zion Crs *HULME* M15 ....85 D3
Zyburn Ct *SLFD ** M6 ....63 D2

Index - featured places

Abbey Hey Primary School *GTN* M18 ....91 D4
Abbey Tutorial College *CMANW* M2 ....3 F5
Abbott Primary School *NEWH/MOS* M40 ....70 B2
Abingdon Primary School *RDSH* SK5 ....120 A1
Abraham Moss Centre
  City College Manchester *CHH* M8 ....52 A1
Abraham Moss High School *CHH* M8 ....52 A1
Acacias CP School *BNG/LEV* M19 ....117 C2
Acorn Business Park *EDGY/DAV* SK3 ....129 C4
Adswood Clinic *EDGY/DAV* SK3 ....132 B4
Adswood Industrial Estate
  EDGY/DAV SK3 ....132 A4
Adswood Primary School *EDGY/DAV* SK3 ....132 A4
Adult Learning Centre *RUSH/FAL* M14 ....101 D1
Agecroft Crematorium *SWIN* M27 ....48 A1
Air & Space Museum *CSLFD* M3 ....7 D1
Albany Trading Estate *CCHDY* M21 ....99 C4
Albert Close Trading Estate *HTNM* SK4 ....11 D1
Albert Square *CMANW* M2 ....3 E5
Albion Drive Clinic *DROY* M43 ....75 D2
The Albion High School *BRO* M7 ....50 A4
Albion Trading Estate *SLFD* M6 ....66 B1
Alder Park CP School *ECC* M30 ....61 C1
Aldwyn CP School *DTN/ASHW* M34 ....76 B4
Alexandra Park Junior School *OLDS* OL8 ....41 D1
Alexandra Retail Park *OLDE* OL4 ....23 C3
Alkrington Clinic Centre *MDTN* M24 ....17 D4
Alkrington Moss Primary School
  MDTN M24 ....18 A4
All Hallows RC High School *SLFD* M6 ....65 C2
Alliston House Medical Centre *URM* M41 ....94 A3
All Saints CE Primary School *HTNM* SK4 ....129 D4
  NEWH/MOS M40 ....55 D1
All Saints Primary School *GTN* M18 ....90 A3
Alma Lodge Hotel *OFTN* SK2 ....133 D3
Alma Park Primary School *BNG/LEV* M19 ....117 D1
Ancoats Hospital *ANC* M4 ....5 C3
Angel Trading Estate *ANC* M4 ....4 B1
Anson Medical Centre *RUSH/FAL* M14 ....103 C1
Apollo Theatre *WGTN/LGST* M12 ....9 F5
Arcadia Sports Centre *BNG/LEV* M19 ....104 B3
Armitage CE Primary School
  WGTN/LGST M12 ....88 B3
Arndale Shopping Centre *ANC* M4 ....4 A3
  STRET M32 ....96 B4
Ashbury Primary School *OP/CLY* M11 ....89 C1

Ash Lea School *ECC* M30 ....62 B2
Aspinal Primary School *GTN* M18 ....106 B2
Astra Business Park *TRPK* M17 ....80 A1
Atlas Trading *RDSH* SK5 ....119 D2
Audenshaw Primary School
  DTN/ASHW M34 ....93 D2
Avenue Medical Centre *BKLY* M9 ....16 B4
Avicenna Grammar School
  DID/WITH M20 ....124 A1
Bamford Business Park *RDSH* SK5 ....119 D4
Band on the Wall *ANC* M4 ....4 B2
Bankfield Trading Estate *RDSH* SK5 ....129 D1
Bank Meadow Primary School
  WGTN/LGST M12 ....88 A1
Bare Trees J & I School *CHAD* OL9 ....21 C1
Baring Street Industrial Estate *CMANE* M1 ....9 F2
Barlow Hall Primary School *CCHDY* M21 ....112 A1
Barlow Medical Centre *DID/WITH* M20 ....124 B2
The Barlow RC High School
  DID/WITH M20 ....113 D4
Barton Business Park *ECC* M30 ....61 D4
Barton Clough Primary School *STRET* M32 ....95 C1
Barton Moss Primary School *ECC* M30 ....60 A4
BBC North *CMANE* M1 ....8 B3
Beaver Road Primary School
  DID/WITH M20 ....125 D3
Beever Primary School *OLD* OL1 ....23 D1
Beis Rochel Girls School *CHH* M8 ....32 A4
Belle Vue Regional Hockey Centre
  WGTN/LGST M12 ....104 B1
Bentinck Street Industrial Estate
  HULME M15 ....6 A1
Birches Health Centre *PWCH* M25 ....12 B3
The Birches School *DID/WITH* M20 ....114 A4
Birchfields Primary School *RUSH/FAL* M14 ....103 D4
Bishop Bilsborrow RC Primary School
  OLDTF/WHR M16 ....101 C3
Blackbrook Trading Estate *BNG/LEV* M19 ....118 A1
Blackley Cemetery *BKLY* M9 ....32 B1
Blackley Crematorium *BKLY* M9 ....32 B1
Blue Coat CE School *OLD* OL1 ....23 C2
Bnos Yisroel Schools *BRO* M7 ....50 B2
Boarshaw Industrial Estate *MDTN* M24 ....18 A1
Boggart Hole Clough Track *BKLY* M9 ....33 C3
Bond Street Industrial Estate
  WGTN/LGST M12 ....9 E2

Booth Hall Childrens Hospital *BKLY* M9 .... 35 C2
The Borchardt Medical Centre
    DID/WITH M20 .... 114 A3
Bower Hotel *CHAD* OL9 .... 38 A3
Bowker Bank Industrial Park *CHH* M8 .... 33 C3
Bowker Vale Primary School *BKLY* M9 .... 32 A1
Bowling Alley *OLDTF/WHR* M16 .... 83 D3
Bradshaw Trading Estate *MDTN* M24 .... 19 C4
Branwood Preparatory School *ECC* M50 .... 62 B2
Bretnall Primary School *BRO* M7 .... 50 A2
Bridge Hall Primary School
    EDGY/DAV SK3 .... 132 A3
Bridge Mills Business Park *SLFD* M6 .... 48 A4
Bridgewater Concert Hall *CMANW* M2 .... 7 F2
Bridgewater School *WALK* M28 .... 42 B3
Brighton Road Industrial Estate
    HTNM SK4 .... 128 A4
Brindale Primary School *RDSH* SK5 .... 131 D1
Brindle Heath Industrial Estate *SLFD* M6 ...... 66 A1
Brinnington Health Centre *RDSH* SK5 .... 121 D4
Briscoe Lane J & I School *NEWH/MOS* M40 .. 55 C4
Broadfield Primary School *OLDS* OL8 .... 41 C1
Broadhurst Primary School
    NEWH/MOS M40 .... 55 D2
Broadoak Business Park *TRPK* M17 .... 80 A2
Broadoak Primary School *SWIN* M27 .... 43 D3
Broadstone Hall Primary School
    HTNM SK4 .... 119 C3
Broadwalk Primary School *SLFD* M6 .... 66 B2
Broadway Business Park *CHAD* OL9 .... 21 C1
    CHAD OL9 .... 37 C1
Broadway Industrial Estate *ORD* M5 .... 83 D1
Brookburn Primary School *CCHDY* M21 ...... 111 D2
Brookdale Golf Club *FAIL* M35 .... 58 A4
Brooks Bar Medical Centre
    OLDTF/WHR M16 .... 100 A1
Brookside Business Park *MDTN* M24 .... 19 C3
Broughton Baths *BRO* M7 .... 50 A3
Broughton Cricket Club *BRO* M7 .... 49 D3
Broughton Jewish Cassel-Fox
    Primary School *BRO* M7 .... 50 A1
Brunswick Health Centre *BRUN/LGST* M13 ...... 9 E5
Bulle Hill High School *SLFD* M6 .... 65 C1
Burgess Primary School *BKLY* M9 .... 53 D2
Burnage High School For Boys
    BNG/LEV M19 .... 117 C4
Burnage RFC *HTNM* SK4 .... 126 B4
Business & Arts Centre *HTNM* SK4 .... 119 C2
Business & Technology Centre *ECC* M50 ...... 61 D3
Butterstile Primary School *PWCH* M25 .... 29 D3
Cale Green Primary School
    EDGY/DAV SK3 .... 132 B3
Camberwell Park School *BKLY* M9 .... 33 D1
Cambridge Industrial Estate *BRO* M7 .... 68 B1
Cambridge Street Industrial Area *BRO* M7 .... 68 B2
Campanile Hotel *ORD* M5 .... 85 C2
Canon Williamson CE High School
    ECC M30 .... 60 A4
Canterbury Road J & I School *URM* M41 ...... 94 A2
Carioca Business Park *NEWH/MOS* M40 ...... 71 D2
    WGTN/LGST M12 .... 88 A3
Castlefield Gallery *CSLFD* M3 .... 7 D2
Castle Hill School *RDSH* SK5 .... 121 D3
Cathedral Visitor Centre *CSLFD* M3 .... 3 F5
Cavendish Road Primary School
    DID/WITH M20 .... 114 A4
Central Industrial Estate *MDTN* M24 .... 17 D1
Central Retail Park *ANC* M4 .... 5 G4
Chadderton AFC *CHAD* OL9 .... 21 C1
Chadderton Cemetery *CHAD* OL9 .... 20 B1
Chadderton Industrial Estate *MDTN* M24 ...... 18 B4
Chadderton Shopping Precinct *CHAD* OL9 .... 21 C1
Chadderton Sports Centre & Public Baths
    CHAD OL9 .... 21 C2
Chadderton Town Health Centre
    CHAD OL9 .... 21 C2
Chapel Street Primary School
    BNG/LEV M19 .... 105 C4
Charlestown Health Centre *BKLY* M9 .... 35 D3
Charlestown Primary School *BKLY* M9 .... 36 A2
    SLFD M6 .... 67 C1
Cheetham CE Community School *BRO* M7 .... 51 C2
Cheetham Hill Cricket Club *CHH* M8 .... 51 D4
Cheetwood Community & Sports Centre
    CHH M8 .... 51 C3
Cheetwood Primary School *CHH* M8 .... 68 B1
Chester Court Hotel *STRET* M32 .... 98 A1
Chethams School of Music *CSLFD* M3 .... 3 F2
Chinese Medical Centre *CSLFD* M3 .... 7 D1
Choriton-cum-Hardy CE Primary School
    CCHDY M21 .... 111 D1
Choriton-cum-Hardy Cricket Club
    CCHDY M21 .... 112 A3
Choriton-cum-Hardy Golf Club
    CCHDY M21 .... 112 B4

Choriton Leisure Centre *CCHDY* M21 .... 99 C4
Choriton Park Primary School
    CCHDY M21 .... 112 B2
Choriton Shopping Centre *CCHDY* M21 .... 98 B4
Choriton Water Park *CCHDY* M21 .... 122 B1
Christ Church CE Primary School
    CHAD OL9 .... 20 B3
Christie Hospital & Holt Radium Institute
    DID/WITH M20 .... 115 C3
Christie Street Industrial Estate
    STKP SK1 .... 133 D2
City Centre Campus *CSLFD* M3 .... 2 C4
City College Manchester *DID/WITH* M20 ...... 124 A1
    NTHM/RTH M23 .... 122 B4
City Course Trading Estate *OP/CLY* M11 ...... 89 D2
City Court Trading Estate *ANC* M4 .... 5 E2
City Park Business Village
    OLDTF/WHR M16 .... 84 A4
Claremont Primary School
    RUSH/FAL M14 .... 101 D2
Clarendon Cottage School *ECC* M30 .... 63 C2
Clarendon Road Primary School *ECC* M30 .... 63 C2
Clarke Industrial Estate *STRET* M32 .... 80 B4
Clayton Health Centre *OP/CLY* M11 .... 73 C5
Clayton Industrial Estate *OP/CLY* M11 .... 91 C2
Cleavley Athletics Track *ECC* M30 .... 60 B2
Clifton Country Park *SWIN* M27 .... 27 D2
Clifton Primary School *SWIN* M27 .... 44 B1
Cloughside School *PWCH* M25 .... 11 C3
Coldhurst Community School *OLD* OL1 .... 22 B1
Coldhurst Industrial Estate *OLD* OL1 .... 22 B1
Collegiate Medical Centre *CHH* M8 .... 51 D2
Comfort Inn *WGTN/LGST* M12 .... 89 D5
Comfort Inn Hotel *WGTN/LGST* M12 .... 88 B4
Coppice Industrial Estate *OLDS* OL8 .... 22 A4
Coppice J & I School *OLDS* OL8 .... 40 B1
Copthorne Hotel *SALQ* M50 .... 83 D5
Cornbrook Estate *HULME* M15 .... 6 A3
Cornerhouse Cinema *CMANE* M1 .... 7 F4
Cornwall Street Industrial Estate
    OP/CLY M11 .... 91 C2
Corpus Christi RC Primary School
    CHAD OL9 .... 39 C1
Corpus Christi with St Anne
    RC Primary School *ANC* M4 .... 71 C4
Crab Lane Primary School *BKLY* M9 .... 35 C1
Craft Centre *ANC* M4 .... 4 B3
Cravenwood Primary School *CHH* M8 .... 51 C2
Cromwell House Community
    Mental Health Centre *ECC* M30 .... 62 A3
Cromwell Special School *DTN/ASHW* M34 .... 107 C3
Crowcroft Park Primary School
    WGTN/LGST M12 .... 104 B2
Crown Business Centre *FAIL* M35 .... 57 C1
Crowne Plaza *CMANW* M2 .... 7 F1
Crown Industrial Estate *ANC* M4 .... 5 G3
Crown Royal Industrial Park *STKP* SK1 .... 133 C1
Crumpsall Lane Primary School *CHH* M8 ...... 52 B4
Dagenham Road Industrial Estate
    RUSH/FAL M14 .... 102 B2
Daisy Nook Country Park *OLDS* OL8 .... 59 D2
Dancehouse Theatre &
    Northern Ballet School *CMANE* M1 .... 8 A3
Dane Bank Primary School
    DTN/ASHW M34 .... 107 D3
Dane Road Industrial Estate *M33* M33 .... 109 D4
David Cuthbert Business Centre
    OP/CLY M11 .... 90 B2
David Medical Centre *CCHDY* M21 .... 112 B3
The Deans CP School *SWIN* M27 .... 44 B1
Deans Road Industrial Estate *SWIN* M27 ...... 44 A1
De la Salle Centre & Pendleton College
    SLFD M6 .... 64 B2
Derwent Street Trading Estate *ORD* M5 ...... 84 B2
The Designer Outlet *SALQ* M50 .... 83 C2
Devonshire Street Industrial Estate
    WGTN/LGST M12 .... 88 A3
Didsbury CE Primary School
    DID/WITH M20 .... 125 C2
Didsbury Cricket Club *DID/WITH* M20 .... 125 D4
Didsbury Golf Club *WYTH/NTH* M22 .... 124 B1
Didsbury Medical Centre *DID/WITH* M20 .... 124 B1
Didsbury Road Primary School
    HTNM SK4 .... 127 C3
Downing Street Industrial Estate
    CMANE M1 .... 9 G3
Droylsden AFC *DROY* M43 .... 75 C4
Droylsden High School For Girls
    DROY M43 .... 74 A3
Droylsden Sports Centre *DROY* M43 .... 74 B3
Droylsden Swimming Pool *DROY* M43 .... 92 B1
Ducie Athletics Ground Running Track
    GTN M18 .... 105 C1
Ducie High School *RUSH/FAL* M14 .... 101 D1
Ducie High School For Boys
    RUSH/FAL M14 .... 102 A1

Ducie Sports Centre *RUSH/FAL* M14 .... 102 A1
Eccles College *ECC* M30 .... 63 C1
Eccles Health Centre *ECC* M30 .... 63 C3
Eccles Recreation Centre *ECC* M30 .... 63 C4
Eccleston Avenue *RUSH/FAL* M14 .... 101 D4
Eccles Town Hall *ECC* M30 .... 63 C3
Elladene Park *CCHDY* M21 .... 112 B1
Elm Wood Primary School *MDTN* M24 .... 18 B1
Elsinore Business Centre *OLDTF/WHR* M16 ... 98 B1
Empress Business Centre
    OLDTF/WHR M16 .... 84 B3
Enterprise Trading Estate *GTN* M18 .... 91 D3
    TRPK M17 .... 80 B1
ETZ Chaim School *CHH* M8 .... 31 D3
Express by Holiday Inn *GTN* M18 .... 114 B4
    SALQ M50 .... 85 C2
The Eye Clinic *CMANW* M2 .... 3 F5
Fahay Industrial Estate *NEWH/MOS* M40 ..... 71 D3
Failsworth Health Centre *FAIL* M35 .... 58 A1
Failsworth Industrial Estate *FAIL* M35 .... 55 D3
Failsworth School (Upper) *FAIL* M35 .... 57 D2
Failsworth Shopping Centre *FAIL* M35 .... 57 C2
Fairfield Golf & Sailing Club
    DTN/ASHW M34 .... 93 C2
Fairfield High School for Girls *DROY* M43 ..... 92 A1
Fairfield Road Primary School *DROY* M43 ..... 92 A1
Falcon Business Centre *OL9* 21 D1
Fallowfield Medical Centre
    RUSH/FAL M14 .... 116 A1
Fallowfield Shopping Centre
    RUSH/FAL M14 .... 103 D3
Farjo Medical Centre *CMANE* M1 .... 8 B1
Fir Tree Primary School *RDSH* M35 .... 106 B3
Fitton Hill Shopping Precinct *OLDS* OL8 ...... 59 C1
Five Fold Industrial Park *CHAD* OL9 .... 22 A3
Fourways Trading Estate *TRPK* M17 .... 80 B5
Freehold Community Primary School
    CHAD OL9 .... 21 D3
The Friars Primary School *CSLFD* M3 .... 2 B1
Gallery of Costume *RUSH/FAL* M14 .... 102 B3
Garrick Theatre *EDGY/DAV* SK3 .... 129 D4
Gateway Industrial Estate *CMANE* M1 .... 5 C5
George H Carnall Leisure Centre *URM* M41 ... 94 B1
Gloucester House Medical Centre
    URM M41 .... 94 A3
GMB National College *OLDTF/WHR* M16 ...... 99 A3
GMEX Centre *CMANW* M2 .... 7 D3
Golden Tulip Hotel *TRPK* M17 .... 85 C3
Gorse Hill Health Centre *STRET* M32 .... 97 D2
Gorse Hill Primary School *STRET* M32 .... 97 D1
Gorton Brook First School
    WGTN/LGST M12 .... 89 D3
Gorton Industrial Estate *GTN* M18 .... 90 B3
Gorton Medical Centre *GTN* M18 .... 91 C4
Gorton Mount Primary School *GTN* M18 .... 105 D2
Gorton Retail Market *GTN* M18 .... 91 C4
Granada Studios *CSLFD* M3 .... 2 C5
Grand Central Pools *EDGY/DAV* SK3 .... 129 D4
Grange School *CHAD* OL9 .... 22 A2
    RUSH/FAL M14 .... 102 B5
Green End Junior School *BNG/LEV* M19 ...... 116 B4
Greengate Industrial Estate *MDTN* M24 .... 18 B4
Greenheys Business Centre *HULME* M15 ...... 86 B4
Greenhill Primary School *OLDE* OL4 .... 23 C4
Green Lane Industrial Estate *HTNM* SK4 ..... 128 B4
Green Room Theatre *CMANE* M1 .... 7 F3
Greenside Primary School *DROY* M43 .... 75 D4
Greenside Trading Centre *DROY* M43 .... 75 D4
Greenwood Business Centre *ORD* M5 .... 66 B4
Greenwood Primary School *ECC* M30 .... 62 B1
Greyhound & Speedway Stadium
    ORD M5 .... 90 A4
Greyland Medical Centre *PWCH* M25 .... 12 A5
Griffin Business Centre *SLFD* M6 .... 49 C4
Grosvenor Road Primary School
    SWIN M27 .... 46 A5
Guinness Road Trading Estate *TRPK* M17 .... 80 A1
Hampson Street Trading Estate *ORD* M5 ...... 2 A5
Hardman Fold Special School *FAIL* M35 .... 56 A2
Harphurey Business Centre *BKLY* M9 .... 34 A4
Harp Trading Estate *TRPK* M17 .... 80 B5
Harpurhey Health Centre *BKLY* M9 .... 53 C1
Harpur Mount Primary School *BKLY* M9 .... 53 C1
Hartford Industrial Estate *CHAD* OL9 .... 21 D3
Hathershaw Technology College
    OLDS OL8 .... 41 C3
Hat Museum *EDGY/DAV* SK3 .... 129 D4
Hawksley Industrial Estate *OLDS* OL8 .... 39 D2
Hazeldene Medical Centre
    NEWH/MOS M40 .... 37 D4
Heald Place Primary School
    RUSH/FAL M14 .... 102 A3
Heaton Hall *PWCH* M25 .... 13 D4
Heaton Moor Golf Club *HTNM* SK4 .... 117 D4

Heaton Moor Medical Centre *HTNM* SK4 ..... 118 B4
Heaton Moor RUFC *HTNM* SK4 .... 128 A2
Heaton Norris Health Centre *HTNM* SK4 ...... 129 C2
Heaton Park Golf Centre *PWCH* M25 .... 13 D5
Heaton Special School *HTNM* SK4 .... 118 A4
Henshaw Society for the Blind
    OLDTF/WHR M16 .... 98 B1
Higginshaw Sports Club *OLD* OL1 .... 23 D1
Highbank Trading Estate *OP/CLY* M11 .... 91 C1
Higher Broughton Health Centre *BRO* M7 ...... 50 B3
Higher Lane Primary School *WHTF* M45 .... 10 B1
Highfield Primary School *URM* M41 .... 95 C3
High Lea Tuition Service *DID/WITH* M20 .... 115 D2
High Point Hotel *OLDS* OL8 .... 22 A3
Hillcrest Grammar School *EDGY/DAV* SK3 ... 133 C3
Hillgate Business Centre *STKP* SK1 .... 130 A4
HM Prison *CHH* M8 .... 69 C1
Hollinwood Business Centre *FAIL* M35 .... 58 A1
Hollinwood Cemetery *OLDS* OL8 .... 59 D4
Hollinwood Cricket Club *OL8* 58 B1
Hollywood Bowl *NEWH/MOS* M40 .... 71 D3
Holt Town Industrial Estate
    NEWH/MOS M40 .... 71 D3
Holy Cross & All Saints RC Primary School
    ECC M30 .... 79 C1
Holy Family RC Primary School *OLDS* OL8 ... 59 C1
Holy Name RC Primary School
    HULME M15 .... 86 B4
Holy Rosary RC Primary School *OLD* OL1 ..... 41 C3
Holy Trinity CE Primary School *BKLY* M9 ...... 53 D1
Hope Hospital *SLFD* M6 .... 64 A3
Horton Mill Primary School *OLDE* OL4 .... 23 D1
Hotel Ibis *CMANE* M1 .... 8 A1
    CMANE M1 .... 8 B3
Houldsworth Golf Club *RDSH* SK5 .... 119 D1
Houldsworth Medical Centre *RDSH* SK5 ...... 120 A2
Hubert House Jewish Boys School
    BRO M7 .... 50 A1
Hubert Jewish High School for Girls
    BRO M7 .... 49 D1
Hulme Adult Education Centre
    HULME M15 .... 85 D3
Hulme Arch *HULME* M15 .... 7 F5
The Hulme Grammar School for Girls & Boys
    OLDS OL8 .... 40 A1
Hurstfield Industrial Estate *HTNM* SK4 .... 119 D3
IMAX Cinema *ANC* M4 .... 4 A3
IMEX Business Park *BRUN/LGST* M13 .... 104 A2
Imperial War Museum North *TRPK* M17 .... 82 B2
Indoor Tennis Centre *OP/CLY* M11 .... 72 A3
Inland Revenue Office *CSLFD* M3 .... 3 D4
The Instructor College *STKP* SK1 .... 129 D4
International Convention Centre
    CMANW M2 .... 7 E1
Jewish Museum *CHH* M8 .... 69 D1
Jewish Senior Boys School *BRO* M7 .... 50 A1
John Rylands Library *CSLFD* M3 .... 3 E5
Jury's Inn *CMANE* M1 .... 7 E2
Kaskenmoor Comprehensive School
    OLDS OL8 .... 39 C4
King David Junior & High School *CHH* M8 ..... 32 A4
Kingfisher Community Special School
    CHAD OL9 .... 20 A4
Kings Road Primary School
    OLDTF/WHR M16 .... 98 B2
Kingsway CP School *URM* M41 .... 94 B1
Knoll Street Industrial Park *BRO* M7 .... 50 A2
Kratos Industrial Estate *URM* M41 .... 80 A4
Ladybarn Primary School *DID/WITH* M20 ..... 116 A3
Ladywell Hospital Lodge *SALQ* M50 .... 63 D3
Lancashire CCC (Old Trafford)
    OLDTF/WHR M16 .... 98 A1
Lancasterian School *DID/WITH* M20 .... 113 D3
Lance Burn Health Centre *SLFD* M6 .... 66 B3
Langdon College *BRO* M7 .... 31 D1
Langford Clinic *STRET* M32 .... 98 A1
Langworthy Clinic *SLFD* M6 .... 66 A3
Langworthy Road Primary School
    SLFD M6 .... 66 A3
Lavenham Business Centre *CHAD* OL9 .... 21 D3
Le Méridien Victoria & Albert Hotel
    ORD M5 .... 2 B5
Levenshulme Baths *BNG/LEV* M19 .... 105 C4
Levenshulme Health Centre
    BNG/LEV M19 .... 105 C4
Levenshulme High School For Girls
    BNG/LEV M19 .... 117 D2
Levenshulme Trading Estate
    BNG/LEV M19 .... 105 D3
Light Oaks Primary School *SLFD* M6 .... 64 A1
Lily Lane J & I School *NEWH/MOS* M40 .... 54 B1
Limehurst Primary School *OLDS* OL8 .... 59 C1
Limeside Primary School *OLDS* OL8 .... 39 D4

Littlemoss Business Park *DROY* M43 76   B2
Littlemoss High School *DROY* M43 76   B1
Longfield Shopping Centre *PWCH* M25 11   C4
Longford Park Special School *STRET* M32 ... 98   A3
Longford Trading Estate *STRET* M32 97   C2
Longsight Cricket Club *WGTN/LGST* M12 ... 104   B2
Longsight Health Centre
 BRUN/LGST M13 104   A1
Longsight Industrial Estate
 WGTN/LGST M12 104   A1
Longsight Shopping Centre
 WGTN/LGST M12 104   A1
Lostock College *STRET* M32 95   D2
Lower Broughton Health Centre *BRO* M7 8   A4
Lower Kersal Primary School *BRO* M7 49   C3
The Lowry Hotel *CSLFD* M3 3   D3
The Lowry *SALQ* M50 82   B2
Lyndhurst Primary School *OLDS* OL8 40   A2
Lyntown Trading Estate *ECC* M30 61   C4
The Mall Shopping Centre *ECC* M30 63   C3
Mancentral Trading Estate *ORD* M5 2   B4
Manchester Aquatics Centre
 BRUN/LGST M13 8   C3
Manchester Business School *HULME* M15 ... 86   B3
Manchester Cathedral *CSLFD* M3 3   F2
Manchester Central Library *CMANW* M2 7   F1
Manchester Centre for Vision
 BRUN/LGST M13 87   C4
Manchester City Art Galleries *CMANE* M1 4   A5
Manchester City FC (City of
 Manchester Stadium) *OP/CLY* M11 72   A4
Manchester College of Arts & Technology
 CMANE M1 4   C4
 OP/CLY M11 90   A1
Manchester Conference Centre & Hotel
 CMANE M1 8   C2
Manchester Crematorium *CCHDY* M21 112   B3
Manchester Golf Club *BKLY* M9 36   A1
Manchester Grammar School
 RUSH/FAL M14 103   C3
Manchester High School for Girls
 RUSH/FAL M14 102   B4
Manchester Industrial Centre *CSLFD* M3 6   B1
Manchester Islamic High School
 CCHDY M21 111   D1
Manchester Jewish Grammar School
 PWCH M25 30   A2
Manchester Junior Girls School
 BRO M7 31   C4
Manchester Metropolitan University
 CMANE M1 8   A3
 CMANE M1 8   C1
 DID/WITH M20 124   A2
 DID/WITH M20 125   C3
 OLDTF/WHR M16 101   C4
 RUSH/FAL M14 102   D1
 RUSH/FAL M14 103   C3
Manchester Metropolitan University
 Institute of Education (Didsbury)
 DID/WITH M20 124   B3
Manchester Museum *BRUN/LGST* M13 8   C5
Manchester Preparatory School
 DID/WITH M20 125   C1
Manchester Road CP School *DROY* M43 74   B3
Manchester Royal Infirmary
 BRUN/LGST M13 87   D4
Manchester School of Management
 BRUN/LGST M13 8   B5
Manchester Southern Cemetery
 CCHDY M21 113   C3
Manchester United FC (Old Trafford)
 OLDTF/WHR M16 83   C4
Manchester United Museum & Tour Centre
 OLDTF/WHR M16 82   B4
Manchester University *BRUN/LGST* M13 87   C4
Manchester Youth Theatre *HULME* M15 86   A4
Manley Park Infant School
 OLDTF/WHR M16 99   D3
Manley Park Primary School
 OLDTF/WHR M16 99   D3
Manor Golf Club *FWTH* BL4 24   A4
Marland Fold Special School *OLDS* OL8 41   D4
Mauldeth Medical Centre *DID/WITH* M20 ... 116   A2
Mauldeth Road Primary School
 DID/WITH M20 116   B2
Meade Hill School *BKLY* M9 32   A1
Meadow Industrial Estate *FAIL* M35 56   A3
 RDSH SK5 130   A2
The Meadows School *BKLY* M9 35   C1
Medlock Court *BRUN/LGST* M13 9   H6
Medlock Leisure Centre *DROY* M43 76   A2
Medlock Valley Community School
 OLDS OL8 41   D2
Melland High School *RDSH* SK5 106   A3
MEN Arena *CSLFD* M3 3   F1

Menzies Avant Hotel *CHAD* OL9 22   A3
Mersey Road Industrial Estate *FAIL* M35 39   C4
Mersey Trading Estate *HTNM* SK4 127   C4
Mersey Vale Primary School *HTNM* SK4 127   D4
Merseyway Centre *STKP* SK1 130   A4
Middleton Public Baths *MDTN* M24 17   D1
Middleton Shopping Centre *MDTN* M24 17   C1
Middleton Technology School *MDTN* M24 ... 18   A1
Miles Platting Pool *NEWH/MOS* M40 71   C2
Mill 5 Belgrave Industrial Estate *OLDS* OL8 ... 41   D2
Mills Hill Primary School *CHAD* OL9 19   D1
Milo Industrial Park *DROY* M43 76   A3
Moat House School *HTNM* SK4 129   D2
Monde Trading Estate *TRPK* M17 80   B1
Montague Business Park *OLDTF/WHR* M16... 98   B1
Monton Bowling Club *ECC* M30 62   B2
Monton Cricket Club *ECC* M30 62   B1
Monton Medical Centre *ECC* M30 61   D1
Moor Allerton School *DID/WITH* M20 124   A1
Moorlands Junior School *SALE* M33 110   B4
Moorside High School *SWIN* M27 44   A2
Moorside Leisure Centre *SWIN* M27 44   A2
Moorside Primary School *SWIN* M27 44   A2
Moravian College *DROY* M43 92   B1
Mossfield County Primary School
 SWIN M27 26   A4
Moss Park Junior School *STRET* M32 96   A3
Moss Side Health Centre *RUSH/FAL* M14 .. 101   D1
Moss Side Leisure Centre *HULME* M15 101   D1
Moston Fields Primary School
 NEWH/MOS M40 35   D4
Moston Indoor Market *NEWH/MOS* M40 54   A1
Moston Lane Primary School *BKLY* M9 53   D1
Mount Carmel RC Junior School *BKLY* M9 .. 34   A4
Mount Carmel RC Primary School
 BKLY M9 34   A4
Mountheath Industrial Park *PWCH* M25 30   A4
The Museum of Science &
 Industry in Manchester *CSLFD* M3 6   B1
Museum of Trade Union History
 CMANE M1 8   A1
Nasmyth Business Park *ECC* M30 61   D3
National Cycling Centre (Velodrome)
 OP/CLY M11 72   B3
National Squash Centre *OP/CLY* M11 72   A3
Natural History Museum *OLDS* OL8 21   D4
Navigation Trading Estate
 NEWH/MOS M40 54   B4
Neville Street Industrial Estate *CHAD* OL9 ... 21   D2
New Ardwick Sports Centre
 BRUN/LGST M13 88   A3
New Croft High School *SLFD* M6 66   A2
Newhaven Business Park *ECC* M30 62   B4
New Kingsway Health Centre
 DID/WITH M20 126   A1
New Moston Primary School
 NEWH/MOS M40 37   D3
New Museum *OLD* OL1 22   B3
New North Manchester Golf Club
 MDTN M24 16   A1
Newton Street Police Museum *CMANE* M1... 4   C4
Nicholas Varley Community School
 NEWH/MOS M40 71   D1
Nicholls Sixth Form Centre
 WGTN/LGST M12 88   A2
Norris Bank Medical Centre *HTNM* SK4 128   B4
Norris Bank Primary School *HTNM* SK4 128   B4
North Area Sixth Form College
 HTNM SK4 118   B3
Northenden Golf Club *WYTH/NTH* M22 123   D3
Northenden Primary School
 WYTH/NTH M22 123   C4
Northern Cemetery *SWIN* M27 48   A3
North Grecian Street Primary School
 BRO M7 49   D3
North Heaton Primary School *HTNM* SK4 .. 118   B3
North Manchester
 Community School for Girls *BKLY* M9 35   D3
North Manchester General Hospital
 CHH M8 33   D4
North Manchester High School for Boys
 BKLY M9 36   A1
North Reddish Health Centre *RDSH* SK5 ... 106   B4
North Reddish Infant School *RDSH* SK5 107   C4
Novotel Hotel *CMANE* M1 7   F1
Oakleigh Medical Centre *CHH* M8 33   C4
Odeon Cinema *CCHDY* M21 112   A4
 SLFD M6 46   B4
Odeon Cinema *CMANE* M1 7   F4
Old Hall Drive Primary School *GTN* M18 106   A1
Oldham Broadway Business Park
 CHAD OL9 19   D1
Oldham Business Centre *OLD* OL1 23   C3
Oldham Central Clinic *CHAD* OL9 22   B3

Oldham College *CHAD* OL9 .... 22 B2
Oldham County Court *OLD* OL1 .... 22 B2
Oldham Crematorium *OLDS* OL8 .... 39 D4
Oldham Sports Centre *OLD* OL1 .... 22 C3
Oldham 6th Form College *OLDS* OL8 .... 22 B3
Oldham West Business Centre *CHAD* OL9 .... 21 C2
Old Moat J & I School *DID/WITH* M20 .... 114 B2
Old Trafford Community School
  OLDTF/WHR M16 .... 84 B4
Olympia Trading Estate *HULME* M15 .... 7 D5
The Open University *CCHDY* M21 .... 99 C4
Opera House *CSLFD* M3 .... 3 D5
The Operating Theatre *STRET* M32 .... 97 D2
Orchard Industrial Estate *SLFD* M6 .... 66 B1
Orchard Trading Estate *SLFD* M6 .... 48 A4
Ordsall Hall Museum *ORD* M5 .... 84 A3
Ordsall Health Centre *ORD* M5 .... 84 A1
Ordsall Recreation Centre *ORD* M5 .... 83 D2
Oriel Bank High School *EDGY/DAV* SK3 .... 133 C4
Oriental Arch *CMANE* M1 .... 4 A5
Orion Trading Estate *TRPK* M17 .... 80 B1
Osborne Trading Estate *CHAD* OL9 .... 21 D1
Oswald Road Primary School *CCHDY* M21 .... 98 B4
Our Lady of Grace RC Primary School
  PWCH M25 .... 11 D3
Our Ladys RC Primary School
  OLDTF/WHR M16 .... 100 A2
Our Ladys RC School *BKLY* M9 .... 16 A3
Palace Hotel *CMANE* M1 .... 8 A2
Palace Theatre *CMANE* M1 .... 8 A2
Palm Business Centre *CHAD* OL9 .... 21 C2
Parish Church CE Junior School *OLD* OL1 .... 22 B2
Parkfield Industrial Estate *MDTN* M24 .... 16 B1
Park Road CP School *SALE* M33 .... 108 B5
Parkview Centre *OLDS* OL8 .... 23 C4
Park View Primary School *PWCH* M25 .... 30 A2
Parkway Business Centre
  OLDTF/WHR M16 .... 101 C4
Parkway Four Industrial Estate *TRPK* M17 .... 80 B4
Parkway Trading Estate *STRET* M32 .... 80 B4
Parrenthorn High School *PWCH* M25 .... 13 C1
Patricroft CE School *ECC* M30 .... 61 D5
Peacock County Primary School *GTN* M18 .... 90 B3
Peacock Primary School *HULME* M15 .... 6 C4
Pear New Mill Industrial Estate
  MPL/ROM SK6 .... 131 D5
The Peel Centre *STKP* SK1 .... 130 A3
Peel Moat Recreation Centre *HTNM* SK4 .... 118 A4
Pendleton College *SLFD* M6 .... 65 C1
Pendleton Health Centre *SLFD* M6 .... 66 B3
Peterloo Medical Centre *MDTN* M24 .... 16 B1
Philips High School *WHTF* M45 .... 10 B1
Phoenix Industrial Estate *FAIL* M35 .... 59 C1
Phoenix Medical Centre *STKP* SK1 .... 133 C1
Piccadilly Trading Estate *ANC* M4 .... 9 F1
  CMANE M1 .... 4 C5
Pike Fold Primary School *BKLY* M9 .... 33 C2
Pinnacle Business Centre *HTNM* SK4 .... 129 D2
Piper Hill School *NTHM/RTH* M23 .... 122 A3
Plant Hill High School *BKLY* M9 .... 33 C1
Plasman Industrial Centre
  BNG/LEV M19 .... 104 B4
  BNG/LEV M19 .... 106 A4
Playhouse Theatre *ORD* M5 .... 66 B3
Plymouth Court Business Centre
  BRUN/LGST M13 .... 87 C4
Plymouth Grove Primary School
  BRUN/LGST M13 .... 88 B4
Poland Industrial Estate *ANC* M4 .... 5 E2
Portwood Trading Estate *STKP* SK1 .... 130 B3
Precinct Centre *BRUN/LGST* M13 .... 8 B5
Premier Lodge *CMANW* M2 .... 3 F1
  CSLFD M5 .... 3 F5
  MDTN M24 .... 15 C2
  STKP SK1 .... 130 A4
  SWIN M27 .... 44 B2
  SWIN M27 .... 46 B2
Premier Lodge (City South) *HULME* M15 .... 7 E4
Prestwich Community School
  PWCH M25 .... 12 A4
Prestwich Golf Club *PWCH* M25 .... 29 D4
Prestwich Health Centre *PWCH* M25 .... 11 D4
Prestwich Hospital *PWCH* M25 .... 11 C4
Prestwich Preparatory School *PWCH* M25 .... 12 B3
Priestnall School *HTNM* SK4 .... 127 C2
The Printworks Leisure Complex *ANC* M4 .... 4 B3
Props Hall Primary School *FAIL* M35 .... 56 B3
Pump House People's History Museum
  CSLFD M3 .... 2 C1
Radclyffe Athletics Centre *CHAD* OL9 .... 20 A2
Radclyffe Primary School *ORD* M5 .... 83 D2
The Radclyffe School (Upper) *CHAD* OL9 .... 20 A2
Railway Street Industrial Estate *GTN* M18 .... 90 B3
Ravensdale Community School
  OP/CLY M11 .... 72 B3

Reddish Vale Golf Club *RDSH* SK5 .... 120 B3
Reddish Vale School *RDSH* SK5 .... 120 A2
Red Rose Retail Centre *ORD* M5 .... 67 C4
Regal Industrial Estate *WGTN/LGST* M12 .... 89 C2
Regent Trading Estate *CSLFD* M3 .... 2 A4
Reliance Trading Estate *NEWH/MOS* M40 .... 55 D2
Richmond J & I School *CHAD* OL9 .... 22 A3
Richmond Park Athletics Stadium
  AULW OL7 .... 77 D1
Richmond Park School *WGTN/LGST* M12 .... 88 B4
Rolls Crescent Primary School
  HULME M15 .... 85 D4
Roman Fort *CSLFD* M3 .... 6 C2
Rosedale Shopping Centre
  NEWH/MOS M40 .... 55 C4
Roxy Cinema *OLDS* OL8 .... 38 B4
Royal Exchange Clinic *CMANW* M2 .... 3 F4
Royal Exchange Shopping Centre *ANC* M4 .... 3 F5
Royal Exchange Theatre Co *CMANW* M2 .... 3 F4
Royal Manchester Childrens Hospital
  SWIN M27 .... 46 A2
Royal Northern College of Music
  M1 .... 8 B5
Royal Oak Industrial Estate *STKP* SK1 .... 133 C1
Royce Trading Estate *TRPK* M17 .... 80 A2
Sacred Heart RC Infant School *GTN* M18 .... 105 D1
St Agnes CE Primary School
  BRUN/LGST M13 .... 104 A2
St Aidans Catholic Primary School
  NTHM/RTH M23 .... 122 A4
St Alphonsus RC Primary School
  OLDTF/WHR M16 .... 85 C4
St Ambrose Barlow RC High School
  SWIN M27 .... 45 C2
St Ambrose RC Primary School
  CCHDY M21 .... 123 C1
  EDGY/DAV SK3 .... 132 A4
St Andrews CE Primary School
  BNG/LEV M19 .... 118 A1
St Andrews CE Primary School *ECC* M50 .... 62 B4
St Andrews Medical Centre *ECC* M30 .... 62 B3
St Annes RC High School *HTNM* SK4 .... 129 C1
St Annes RC Primary School *CHH* M8 .... 51 D1
  DTN/ASHW M34 .... 92 B2
St Anns J & I School *STRET* M32 .... 97 C3
St Antonys RC High School *URM* M41 .... 95 C3
St Augustine of Canterbury RC School
  OLDS OL8 .... 40 A2
St Augustines CE Primary School
  NEWH/MOS M40 .... 53 D4
  SWIN M27 .... 46 A1
St Barnabas Primary *OP/CLY* M11 .... 90 A1
St Bedes College *OLDTF/WHR* M16 .... 100 B1
St Bernadettes RC Primary School
  RDSH SK5 .... 131 C1
St Bernards RC Primary School
  BNG/LEV M19 .... 117 C3
St Boniface RC Primary School *BRO* M7 .... 49 D5
St Brigids RC Primary School *OP/CLY* M11 ...... 72 B4
St Catherines RC Primary School
  DID/WITH M20 .... 125 D2
St Chads RC Primary School *CHH* M8 .... 51 D4
St Charles RC Primary School *SWIN* M27 .... 44 B4
St Chrysostoms CE Primary School
  BRUN/LGST M13 .... 87 C4
St Clares RC Primary School *BKLY* M9 .... 15 C4
St Clement (Egerton) CE Primary School
  ORD M5 .... 84 A2
St Clements CE Primary School
  OP/CLY M11 .... 91 D2
St Cuthberts RC Primary School
  DID/WITH M20 .... 115 D4
St Dunstans RC Primary School
  NEWH/MOS M40 .... 54 B1
St Edmunds RC Primary School
  NEWH/MOS M40 .... 53 D3
St Edwards RC Primary School
  RUSH/FAL M14 .... 102 A3
St Elisabeths CE Primary School
  RDSH SK5 .... 119 C1
St Gabriels CE Primary School *MDTN* M24 ...... 18 B2
St Gabriels Medical Centre *RUSH* M14 .... 31 C3
St Georges CE Primary School *OFTN* SK2 ..... 133 C5
St Gilberts RC Primary School *ECC* M50 .... 60 B3
St Herberts RC Primary School *CHAD* OL9 ...... 20 B2
St Hildas CE Primary School *OLD* OL1 .... 22 A1
  OLDTF/WHR M16 .... 99 C2
  PWCH M25 .... 30 B1
St Hugh of Lincoln Primary School
  STRET M32 .... 95 C2
St James J & I School *GTN* M18 .... 104 A2
St James's CE School *SLFD* M6 .... 66 C4
St John Bosco RC Primary School
  BKLY M9 .... 35 D1

St Johns Cathedral *CSLFD* M3 .... 2 A3
St Johns CE Infant School *FAIL* M35 .... 57 C1
St Johns CE Junior School *FAIL* M35 .... 57 D2
St Johns CE Primary School *HTNM* SK4 .... 126 B3
   SLFD M6 .... 46 B3
St Johns RC Primary School *CCHDY* M21 .... 98 B4
St John Vianney School *HTNM* SK4 .... 128 A3
St John Vianney Upper School
   OLDTF/WHR M16 .... 99 C3
St Josephs RC Primary & Nursery School
   RDSH SK5 .... 119 D1
St Josephs RC Primary School
   BRUN/LGST M13 .... 103 D1
   ORD M5 .... 84 A1
   STKP SK1 .... 130 A4
St Judes CE Primary School *ANC* M4 .... 5 E3
St Kentigerns Catholic School
   FAIL M14 .... 101 D4
St Lukes CE Primary School *CHAD* OL9 .... 20 B2
   ORD M5 .... 65 C4
   WGTN/LGST M12 .... 88 B4
St Lukes CE Primary School *SLFD* M6 .... 46 B4
St Malachys RC Primary School
   NEWH/MOS M40 .... 52 B4
St Margaret Marys RC School
   NEWH/MOS M40 .... 37 C2
St Margarets CE Primary School
   OLDS OL8 .... 39 D3
   OLDTF/WHR M16 .... 100 A3
   PWCH M25 .... 12 B1
St Marks CE Primary School
   NEWH/MOS M40 .... 71 C2
   WALK M28 .... 42 A3
St Marks CE Primary School *SWIN* M27 .... 26 B3
St Marys Catholic Cemetery *WALK* M28 .... 43 C1
St Marys CE Primary School *DROY* M43 .... 76 A4
   NEWH/MOS M40 .... 36 B3
   OLDTF/WHR M16 .... 100 B3
St Mary's CE Primary School *PWCH* M25 .... 29 D1
St Marys CE Primary School *RDSH* SK5 .... 120 B3
St Mary's Primary School *BRUN/LGST* M13 .. 102 B1
St Marys Medical Centre *OLD* OL1 .... 23 C2
St Marys RC Primary School
   BNG/LEV M19 .... 117 D1
St Mary's RC Primary School *ECC* M30 .... 62 B4
St Marys RC Primary School *FAIL* M35 .... 56 B5
   HTNM SK4 .... 129 D3
   SWIN M27 .... 45 C1
St Matthews CE Primary School
   EDGY/DAV SK3 .... 132 A1
St Matthews RC High School
   NEWH/MOS M40 .... 36 B3
St Michaels CE Primary School *MDTN* M24 ... 17 D4
St Michaels RC Primary School *WHTF* M45 ... 12 A1
St Monicas RC High School *PWCH* M25 .... 30 B2
St Patrick's High School *ECC* M30 .... 61 C3
St Patricks RC Primary School *ANC* M4 .... 7 E2
   NEWH/MOS M40 .... 70 B2
   OLDS OL8 .... 22 B3
St Pauls CE Primary School *BRO* M7 .... 49 C1
   DID/WITH M20 .... 125 C1
   SLFD M6 .... 131 C1
St Pauls New Windsor CE Primary School
   ORD M5 .... 67 C4
St Peter & St John Primary School
   CSLFD M3 .... 6 B5
St Peters CE Primary School *SWIN* M27 .... 44 B1
St Peters RC High School & Lower School
   GTN M18 .... 106 A3
St Peter's RC High School Upper School
   GTN M18 .... 91 D1
St Peters RC Primary School *MDTN* M24 .... 17 D2
St Philips CE Primary School *BRO* M7 .... 30 B4
St Philips School *CSLFD* M3 .... 2 A4
St Phillips CE Primary School *HULME* M15 ..... 7 F5
St Richard's RC Primary School
   WGTN/LGST M12 .... 105 C2
St Sebastians RC Primary School *SLFD* M6 ... 48 B4
St Stephens & All Martyrs Infant School
   OLD OL1 .... 23 C1
St Stephens CE School *DROY* M43 .... 75 D3
St Teresas RC Primary School *STRET* M32 ..... 98 B2
St Thomas Aquinas RC High School
   CCHDY M21 .... 112 B2
St Thomas CE Primary School *HTNM* SK4 .... 118 D3
   OLDS OL8 .... 22 B4
   STKP SK1 .... 133 C1
St Thomas Hospital *EDGY/DAV* SK3 .... 132 B1
St Thomas More RC Primary School
   MDTN M24 .... 17 D4
St Thomas CE Primary School *CHH* M8 .... 17 D4
St Thomas RC Primary School *BRO* M7 .... 50 B3
St Wilfrids CE Primary School
   NEWH/MOS M40 .... 56 A4
St Wilfrids RC Primary School *HULME* M15 ..... 7 D5

St Willibrords RC Primary School
   OP/CLY M11 .... 73 D2
St Winifreds RC Primary School
   NEWH/MOS M40 .... 127 D3
Sale Cricket Club *SALE* M33 .... 111 D3
Sale Golf Club *SALE* M33 .... 110 A4
Sale Leisure Centre *SALE* M33 .... 109 D4
Salford City Reds RLFC (The Willows)
   ORD M5 .... 65 C3
Salford College *ECC* M30 .... 60 B3
   ORD M5 .... 83 D2
   SLFD M6 .... 67 C1
Salford County Court *ORD* M5 .... 66 B4
Salford Medical Centre *SLFD* M6 .... 65 D2
Salford Museum & Art Gallery *ORD* M5 .... 67 D1
Salford Shopping City *SLFD* M6 .... 66 B2
Salford University Business Park *SLFD* M6 ..... 67 C1
Saviour CE Primary School
   NEWH/MOS M40 .... 52 B4
Savoy Cinema *HTNM* SK4 .... 127 B4
Saxon Holme Hotel *SLFD* M6 .... 67 C1
Seaford Industrial Estate *SLFD* M6 .... 67 C1
Sedgley Park Primary School *PWCH* M25 ...... 31 A3
Sedgley Park RUFC *WHTF* M45 .... 30 A4
Sedgley Park Trading Estate *PWCH* M25 .... 30 A4
Seedley Primary School *SLFD* M6 .... 65 D3
Seminar Centre *CMANW* M2 .... 7 E1
Severnside Trading Estate *TRPK* M17 .... 81 C4
Seymour Park Primary School
   OLDTF/WHR M16 .... 99 C1
Seymour Road Primary School
   OP/CLY M11 .... 74 A4
Shandon Clinic (Europe) *HULME* M15 .... 86 B4
Shawgrove School *DID/WITH* M20 .... 114 A3
Shaw Heath Health Centre
   EDGY/DAV SK3 .... 132 B2
Sherborne Trading Estate *CHH* M8 .... 51 C4
Shiv Lodge Medical Centre
   BRUN/LGST M13 .... 104 A2
Showcase Cinemas Belle Vue
   WGTN/LGST M12 .... 90 A1
Slough Industrial Estate *ORD* M5 .... 84 B1
Smedley Junior School *CHH* M8 .... 52 A3
South Chadderton School *CHAD* OL9 .... 43 D4
Southern Cross School *CCHDY* M21 .... 112 B4
South Failsworth Primary School
   FAIL M35 .... 56 B4
Southfield Industrial Estate *TRPK* M17 .... 81 C4
South Oldham Business Park *CHAD* OL9 .... 21 D1
South Reddish Medical Centre *RDSH* SK5 ... 130 A1
South West Manchester Cricket Club
   CCHDY M21 .... 99 D4
The Spindles Shopping Centre *OLD* OL1 .... 22 B3
Sport City *OP/CLY* M11 .... 72 A3
Sports Injury Centre *MDTN* M24 .... 17 D2
Spring Brook Special School *CHAD* OL9 .... 20 A4
Springfield Business Centre *CSLFD* M3 .... 3 E1
Springfield Industrial Estate *FAIL* M35 .... 56 B1
Springwood School *SWIN* M27 .... 45 B3
Spurley Hey High School *GTN* M18 .... 105 C3
Stanley Grove Primary School
   WGTN/LGST M12 .... 104 A1
Stanley Road Primary School *CHAD* OL9 ...... 39 C1
Stansfield Road J & I School *FAIL* M35 .... 57 C1
Star Industrial Estate *OLDS* OL8 .... 22 B4
Stella Maris School *HTNM* SK4 .... 126 B3
Stockport Art Gallery *EDGY/DAV* SK3 .... 132 B1
Stockport College of FE & HE
   EDGY/DAV SK3 .... 132 B1
Stockport County Court *STKP* SK1 .... 130 A4
Stockport County FC & Sale Sharks RUFC
   (Edgeley Park) *EDGY/DAV* SK3 .... 132 A3
Stockport Crematorium *OFTN* SK2 .... 133 D2
Stockport Cricket Club *EDGY/DAV* SK3 .... 133 C3
Stockport Grammar School *OFTN* SK2 .... 133 C4
Stockport Mega Bowl *EDGY/DAV* SK3 .... 132 B1
Stretford Grammar School *STRET* M32 .... 97 D4
Stretford High School *STRET* M32 .... 98 A1
Stretford Leisure Centre *STRET* M32 .... 98 A1
Stretford Memorial Hospital
   OLDTF/WHR M16 .... 99 C2
Students Union Building *CMANE* M1 .... 8 B4
Sudell Street Trading Estate *ANC* M4 .... 7 H2
Sugden Sports Centre *CMANE* M1 .... 8 B4
Summerville Primary School *CHAD* OL9 .... 22 B4
Summerville Primary School *SLFD* M6 .... 47 C4
Swinton Cemetery *SWIN* M27 .... 25 D3
The Swinton Country High School
   SWIN M27 .... 25 D4
Swinton Cricket Club *SWIN* M27 .... 45 D2
Swinton Industrial Estate *SWIN* M27 .... 45 D4
Swinton Leisure Centre *SWIN* M27 .... 45 C1
Swinton Park Golf Club *SWIN* M27 .... 45 A1
Tame Valley Primary School
   MPL/ROM SK6 .... 121 D2

Tashbar School *BRO* M7 .... 31 D4
Tavistock Industrial Estate *OP/CLY* M11 .... 91 C3
Taylors Sports Club *ECC* M50 .... 62 B4
Temple Primary School *CHH* M8 .... 52 A3
Ten Acres Sports Complex
 NEWH/MOS M40 .... 54 B4
Thames Industrial Estate *WGTN/LGST* M12 ... 88 A2
Tithe Barn Primary School *HTNM* SK4 .... 127 D2
Tootal Drive County Primary School
 SLFD M6 .... 64 B3
Towers Business Park *DID/WITH* M20 .... 123 D1
 DID/WITH M20 .... 125 C4
Town Square Shopping Centre *OLD* OL1 ...... 3 C3
Trafalgar Business Park *BRO* M7 .... 68 B1
Trafford Athletics Track *STRET* M52 .... 98 A4
Trafford Centre *TRPK* M17 .... 79 C3
Trafford Centre Leisure Complex
 TRPK M17 .... 78 A3
Trafford Retail Park *URM* M41 .... 78 A3
Trafford Water Sports Centre *SALE* M33 .... 110 B3
Travel Inn *CHAD* OL9 .... 37 D3
 CMANE M1 .... 8 A1
 OFTN SK2 .... 133 D3
 PWCH M25 .... 11 D4
 TRPK M17 .... 79 C3
Travel Inn Hotel *SALQ* M50 .... 79 C3
Travelodge *CHAD* OL9 .... 37 D1
 CSLFD M5 .... 3 E3
The Triangle *ANC* M4 .... 3 F5
Trinity CE High School *HULME* M15 .... 86 B3
Tulketh Street Industrial Estate
 NEWH/MOS M40 .... 54 A1
UCI Cinema *TRPK* M17 .... 79 C3
UGC Cinema *DID/WITH* M20 .... 126 A1
 EDGY/DAV SK3 .... 132 B1
UMIST *CMANE* M1 .... 8 C2
United Trading Estate *OLDTF/WHR* M16 .... 83 C4
University College Salford *CSLFD* M5 .... 2 B3
University Dental Hospital of Manchester
 HULME M15 .... 86 B3
University of Manchester *BRUN/LGST* M13 ... 8 C5
 RUSH/FAL M14 .... 103 C3
University of Manchester Institute of
 Science & Technology *BRUN/LGST* M13 .... 8 C4
University of Salford *SLFD* M6 .... 67 D2
Urbis *ANC* M4 .... 3 F2
Vaishall Medical Centre *CCHDY* M21 .... 99 C4
Vale Park Industrial Estate *CHH* M8 .... 52 B2
Varley Street Clinic *NEWH/MOS* M40 .... 71 C1
Varna Street Primary School
 OP/CLY M11 .... 91 C3
Vaughan Street Industrial Estate
 WGTN/LGST M12 .... 89 C2
Vauxhall Industrial Estate *RDSH* SK5 .... 119 D3
 RDSH SK5 .... 130 A1
Vernon Industrial Estate *STKP* SK1 .... 130 B5
Vernon Park Museum *STKP* SK1 .... 131 D3
Vernon Park Primary School *STKP* SK1 .... 130 B4
Victoria Avenue Primary School *BKLY* M9 ... 16 A4
Victoria Industrial Estate *ANC* M4 .... 71 C4
Victoria Medical Centre *URM* M41 .... 94 A3
Victoria Park Infant School *STRET* M52 .... 97 C3
Victoria Park Junior School *STRET* M52 .... 97 C3
Victoria Trading Estate *CHAD* OL9 .... 39 C2
Wadeson Junior School *BRUN/LGST* M13 .... 9 A4
Wardley Industrial Estate *WALK* M28 .... 94 B4
Warner Village *SALQ* M50 .... 83 C2
Waters Edge Business Park *ORD* M5 .... 84 A3
Watersports Centre *SALQ* M50 .... 83 C2
Waybridge Industrial Estate *ORD* M5 .... 82 A1
Weaste Trading Estate *ORD* M5 .... 65 C3

Webster Primary School *RUSH/FAL* M14 ... 101 D1
Welkin Road Industrial Estate *STKP* SK1 .. 131 C2
Wellfield Junior School *SALE* M33 .... 108 A5
Wellfield Medical Centre *CHH* M8 .... 51 C1
Wentworth High School *ECC* M30 .... 63 C1
Werneth Cricket Bowling & Tennis Club
 OLDS OL8 .... 22 B4
Werneth Golf Club *OLDS* OL8 .... 40 B4
Werneth J & I School *OLDS* OL8 .... 40 B4
Werneth Private Preparatory School
 OLDS OL8 .... 22 A4
Westbrook Trading Estate *TRPK* M17 .... 82 A2
West Croft Industrial Estate *MDTN* M24 ...... 15 D2
West End Primary School
 DTN/ASHW M34 .... 107 D2
West End Trading Estate *SWIN* M27 .... 26 A4
West Gorton Medical Centre
 WGTN/LGST M12 .... 89 C3
Westinghouse Industrial Estate *TRPK* M17 ... 82 A4
West Liverpool Street Primary School
 SLFD M6 .... 66 A3
Westmorland Primary School *RDSH* SK5 .... 121 D3
West One Retail Park *SALQ* M50 .... 63 D4
Westpoint Medical Centre *BNG/LEV* M19 ... 104 A4
Westwood Business Centre *CHAD* OL9 .... 22 A3
Westwood Industrial Estate *CHAD* OL9 .... 21 C2
Westwood Park Primary School *ECC* M30 ... 61 C2
Westwood Primary School *CHAD* OL9 .... 22 A2
Whalley Range FC *CCHDY* M21 .... 100 A1
Whalley Range High School
 OLDTF/WHR M16 .... 114 A1
Wharfside Business Centre *TRPK* M17 .... 85 C3
Wheatsheaf Industrial Estate *SWIN* M27 ...... 27 C4
White City Retail Park *OLDTF/WHR* M16 .... 83 D4
Whitefield Community Primary School
 WHTF M45 .... 11 D1
Whitefield Golf Club *WHTF* M45 .... 10 B2
Whitefield Medical Centre *WHTF* M45 .... 10 B1
Whitegate End Primary School *CHAD* OL9 ... 37 D2
Whitehill Primary School *HTNM* SK4 .... 119 D4
Whitehill Primary School *HTNM* SK4 .... 129 D1
Whitley Road Medical Centre
 NEWH/MOS M40 .... 70 B1
The Whitworth Art Gallery
 BRUN/LGST M13 .... 102 A1
Whitworth Park School *RUSH/FAL* M14 ..... 101 D1
Wilbraham Primary School
 RUSH/FAL M14 .... 101 D4
Willan Industrial Estate *ORD* M5 .... 66 A4
William Hulmes Grammar School
 OLDTF/WHR M16 .... 101 C4
Willow Bank Hotel *RUSH/FAL* M14 .... 115 D1
Willow Grove Cemetery *RDSH* SK5 .... 120 B4
Wilmslow Road Medical Centre
 RUSH/FAL M14 .... 102 B2
Withington Bowling Club *RUSH/FAL* M14 ... 115 D2
Withington Girls School *RUSH/FAL* M14 .... 115 C1
Withington Golf Club *DID/WITH* M20 .... 124 A3
Withington Hospital *DID/WITH* M20 .... 114 A3
Withington Swimming Baths
 DID/WITH M20 .... 115 C3
Woodbank Park Athletics Track *STKP* SK1 . 131 D4
Woodhouses Voluntary Primary School
 FAIL M35 .... 58 B3
Worsley Golf Club *ECC* M30 .... 61 D1
Wright Robinson Sports College *CTN* M18 ... 92 A3
Xaverian Sixth Form College
 RUSH/FAL M14 .... 102 B2
Yew Tree J & I School *CHAD* OL9 .... 38 A1
Y Sport & Leisure Centre *CSLFD* M3 .... 6 C1

Acknowledgements

The Post Office is a registered trademark of Post Office Ltd. in the UK and other countries.

Schools address data provided by Education Direct.

Petrol station information supplied by Johnsons

One-way street data provided by © Tele Atlas N.V. Tele Atlas

Garden centre information provided by:

Garden Centre Association  Britains best garden centres

Wyevale Garden Centres

Notes

QUESTIONNAIRE

Dear Atlas User

Your comments, opinions and recommendations are very important to us. So please help us to improve our street atlases by taking a few minutes to complete this simple questionnaire.

You do NOT need a stamp (unless posted outside the UK). If you do not want to remove this page from your street atlas, then photocopy it or write your answers on a plain sheet of paper.

Send to: The Editor, AA Street by Street, FREEPOST SCE 4598, Basingstoke RG21 4GY

ABOUT THE ATLAS...

Which city/town/county did you buy?

_____

Are there any features of the atlas or mapping that you find particularly useful?

_____
_____
_____

Is there anything we could have done better?

_____
_____
_____

Why did you choose an AA Street by Street atlas?

_____
_____
_____

Did it meet your expectations?

Exceeded ☐   **Met all** ☐   **Met most** ☐   **Fell below** ☐

Please give your reasons

_____
_____
_____
_____

MN042z

continued overleaf

Where did you buy it?

For what purpose? (please tick all applicable)

To use in your own local area ☐   To use on business or at work ☐

Visiting a strange place ☐   In the car ☐   On foot ☐

Other (please state)

LOCAL KNOWLEDGE...

Local knowledge is invaluable. Whilst every attempt has been made to make the information contained in this atlas as accurate as possible, should you notice any inaccuracies, please detail them below (if necessary, use a blank piece of paper) or e-mail us at *streetbystreet@theAA.com*

ABOUT YOU...

Name (Mr/Mrs/Ms)

Address

Postcode

Daytime tel no

E-mail address

Which age group are you in?

Under 25 ☐   25-34 ☐   35-44 ☐   45-54 ☐   55-64 ☐   65+ ☐

Are you an AA member?   YES ☐   NO ☐

Do you have Internet access?   YES ☐   NO ☐

Thank you for taking the time to complete this questionnaire. Please send it to us as soon as possible, and remember, you do not need a stamp (unless posted outside the UK).